SEVEN PILLARS OF CHRISTIANITY

An Introduction to the
Essential Christian Doctrines

Dr. William Ekane

Order this book online at www.trafford.com
or email orders@trafford.com

Most Trafford titles are also available at major online book retailers.

Printed in the United States of America.

ISBN: 978-1-4269-7482-3 (sc)
ISBN: 978-1-4269-7483-0 (hc)
ISBN: 978-1-4269-7621-6 (e)

Library of Congress Control Number: 2011912389

Trafford rev. 10/10/2011

 www.trafford.com

North America & international
toll-free: 1 888 232 4444 (USA & Canada)
phone: 250 383 6864 ♦ fax: 812 355 4082

STEP 1: GENERAL INFORMATION

About the Author:

Dr. William Ekane has been lead pastor of New Life Fellowship Global Ministries (NLFGM) in Atlanta, Georgia since 1999. Prior to establishing NLFGM, he served as Associate Professor of Instructional Technology at Grambling State University, Grambling, Louisiana. He published several articles there. William and his wife, Grace, have seven children.

About the Book:

Seven Pillars of Christianity is a clarion call for believers to return to the basics of authentic Christianity. This book offers rock-solid biblical content that will assist new converts to better understand their faith and the mature believer to grow deeper in God.

As reported by the Barna Research Group in a 2010 survey of American churches, more Christians are becoming less theologically literate, less outreach-oriented, and more ingrown. In this survey, Christians are less interested in spiritual disciplines but more desirous of secular, pragmatic techniques to solve life's problems. The results show that there is hardly any difference in the way Christians conduct themselves from non-Christians.

With this portrait of moral and spiritual degeneracy in the Christian Church, it is imperative that believers are equipped with essential truths. These are found in Hebrews 6:1-2. Chapter titles include:

- Deity of Jesus Christ
- Repentance from Dead Works
- Faith in God
- Instruction on Baptisms

- Laying on of Hands
- Resurrection of the Dead
- Eternal Judgment

Having taught these essential doctrines for over 12 years in Africa, Europe, and the United States, Dr. Ekane believes that *Seven Pillars* will help Christians to become rooted in the faith.

Key Words:

Ekane, Deity, Jesus Christ, Baptism, Repentance,

Faith, Resurrection, Laying of Hands, Judgment

Keynote/Teaser/Tagline:

A clarion call for Christians to get back to authentic Christianity. Introduction to the essentials of the Christian Faith. Life-Transforming.

Step 2: Interior Layout

Having served the body of Christ in Africa, Europe, and the United States, Dr. Ekane has observed a steady decline in biblical literacy as well as the moral and spiritual degeneracy of the Christian Church. To underscore and validate the author's cursory observation, a survey by the Barna Research Group of American churches throughout 2010 reported the spiritual commitment of believers is rapidly eroding. These findings indicate that at least six patterns have emerged.

First, a vast majority of believers have become less theologically literate. For example, most people regard Easter as a religious holiday, but only a minority of those surveyed associated Easter with the resurrection of Jesus Christ. Also, a growing majority of Christians believe that the Holy Spirit is a symbol of God's presence or power rather than the third person in the Godhead.

A second trend showed that Christians have become more ingrown and less outreach-oriented in focus. Furthermore, teens are far less likely to discuss Christianity with their peers than in past years.

A third trend indicated that a growing number of congregants are less interested in spiritual disciplines and truths but more desirous of learning secular, pragmatic solutions. Many Christ-followers today want someone to tell them how to be comfortable and successful using secular theories and techniques rather than acquiring biblically-based principles that would direct them to be obedient and kingdom-minded.

Fourth, an expanded focus on justice and service struck a chord with many believers. Ironically, while many have become more inwardly focused on a personal level, involvement and interest in community action is at an all-time high. However, when the social side of the Gospel is pursued at the expense of one's commitment to spiritual disciplines – reading, meditating on God's Word, and prayer – then the Gospel becomes an empty religion.

A fifth finding revealed that a mindset of tolerance has begun to take over the church. Aberrant values to the Christian faith such as abortion, homosexuality, and gay marriage are viewed with compromise and encouraged by mainstream denominations. This not only lends support to extant biblical illiteracy, but compounds the problem for many American Christians who lack spiritual confidence to make strong moral and theological decisions.

Finally, the secular culture has significantly influenced the community of faith to the point that the church thinks and acts like the world. In other words, the impact and influence of Christian values on the secular culture and in individual lives are largely invisible. While it is a historical fact that Christianity traditionally has added much of its value to culture, religion, philosophy, ideology, democracy, science, and the arts, contemporary Americans are hard pressed to identify any specific value added. This is partly due to the secularization of prestigious universities such as Harvard, Yale, and Princeton that were established on biblical values. Furthermore, the negative portrayal of Christianity and church leaders by the media has also accentuated the problem. A case in point is the important contribution the faith community made during the hurricane disaster in New Orleans, Louisiana, which went under-reported.

The challenge faced by today's church and Christian leadership is striking a delicate balance between representing truth and acting in love. For individual believers in the United States, the challenge is to be thoroughly grounded in the Word of God, to know how to share the Gospel with the unsaved, and to encourage fellow believers in their faith walk. When Christ-followers are in the public arena, they should be well- equipped (biblically) to know which battles are worth fighting and which are non-negotiable. Christian people must know that there is room for tolerance, but there must also be a point to draw the line in the sand. The Christian church must strive to portray a genuine image of its faith since life-changing decisions are made on the basis of such images.

As a result of the declining moral and spiritual conditions of Christianity worldwide and America in particular, it is the author's goal to share some practical, strategic insights gleaned from Scripture. These can possibly mitigate or eradicate the malice affecting the churches. In *Seven Pillars of Christianity,* a clear and systematic presentation of the Christian's core beliefs is made based on the text from Hebrew 6:1-2. Brief chapter highlights will follow.

In the introduction, a cogent and compelling case is made on why the Bible is sacred and reliable, as well as divine in origin, error-free, eternal, and authoritative in revelation. It is also based on historical, archaeological, and scientific facts that are verifiable.

Chapter One is based on the central figure of Scripture – the Lord Jesus Christ. The Holy Scriptures and the person of the Lord Jesus Christ are inseparably bound together. Time and again, Christ Himself declared that the teachings of the Old Testament actually speak about Him. Since Christ claimed that all of Scripture pointed to Him, an attempt has been made to portray the pre-incarnate Christ in every book of the Old Testament as well as the incarnate Christ in the New Testament. In addition, through an in-depth study of Old and New Testament Scriptures, conclusive evidence shows that Jesus Christ came in the flesh, being fully God and fully man.

In Chapter Two, the doctrine of repentance from dead works is explained.

Chapter Three discusses the truth about faith in God. Faith in God is simply absolute trust in the living God and in His written word.

The instructions about baptism are dealt with in Chapter Four. In this chapter, an explanation of the four types of baptisms is presented.

Chapter Five highlights the four benefits to be derived from the laying on of hands in both, the Old and New Testaments.

In Chapter Six, the teaching on the resurrection from the dead is presented and defended.

Finally, in Chapter Seven a description of the five major judgments in the Bible is presented. In the Appendix, three additional and equally important teachings are included: The Characteristics of The Model Church, God's Compound Names, and His Attributes. Appendix 4 lists the scriptures referenced in each chapter except for those printed in the chapter text.

References

Dedication:

This book is humbly dedicated to my Lord and Savior Jesus Christ, the One who showed me mercy when I deserved condemnation, the One who died in my place so that I may have eternal life, the One who is faithful in all things and has given me a purpose for living, and the One I look forward to seeing face to face. This book is also dedicated to my wife, Grace: my friend, lover, and confidante, who through our many years, has stood with me faithfully, prayerfully, and lovingly.

Acknowledgements:

With deepest thanks to:

Samuel and Zipporah Ekane whose tireless secretarial efforts have made this project possible.

Emmanuel and Ruth Foyere, Janet Bouy, Joshua Ekane, and Linda Watson for their proofing and editorial input.

Caleb Ekane, Hannah Matike-Tita, Melanie Cooper, and Kerry Starr for their prayers, encouragement, and financial support throughout this project.

A special thanks to the dynamic members of New Life Fellowship Global Ministries.

And lastly, to you, the reader. I am honored that you have taken the time to read this book. The purpose of this book is both to know Jesus in full majesty, power, and glory, and to make Him known.

The Ever-Growing Need
(Back to the Basics)

Hebrews 6 is a pivotal passage in the New Testament for instructing the believer in the Christian faith. It contains seven essentials for laying the foundation of our Christian beliefs. These include the author and perfecter of our faith – the Lord Jesus Christ, repentance from dead works, faith in God, the doctrine of baptisms, the laying on of hands, the resurrection of the dead, and eternal judgment. The rock foundation represents the Lord Jesus Christ Himself. To survive the storms of life, we must be anchored in the Rock of Ages.

Approximately 80% of church attendees do not have an adequate knowledge of the Bible according to a 2002 survey by the Barna Research Group. Another Barna survey reveals that Christians say they do best at relationships, worst in Bible knowledge. Also, in a 2010 survey by Barna of U.S. churches, Christians have become less theologically literate, less outreach-oriented, and more ingrown. In this survey, Christians are less interested in spiritual disciplines but more desirous of secular, pragmatic techniques to solve life's problems. The result is there is hardly any difference in the way Christians conduct themselves from non- Christians[1]. Let us, therefore, *study* the Bible to be wise, *believe* it to be safe, and *practice* it to be holy (Bill Crowder – *Word Hunger, Daily Bread*: November 17, 2006).

Problem

The 21st century is plagued with crises – from broken homes to nations that are at war with each other. The *only* book that reveals the true nature of God and man's sin/rebellion against God is the Bible. God alone has the right to set the standard for righteousness because He alone is holy.

There is also a growing attitude of neglect in the church, and believers have a tendency to ignore the application of biblical principles to their daily lives.

Purpose

The Purpose of *Seven Pillars of Christianity* is to firmly establish believers in the fundamental doctrines of the faith, provide new believers with a rock-solid, theological foundation, and assist more mature believers in sharpening their understanding of key biblical concepts and equip them for discipleship and evangelism.

What you have in your hand is a useful resource that has undergone years of refining, preparation, instruction, revision, and application. Having been taught and tested in classes in Africa, Europe, and the United States, these concepts have been proven effective through the lives they have impacted.

Of course, the power behind this book is not in its format or layout, but in the Word of God through the Spirit of God that will illuminate the hearts and minds of its readers. Whenever the Holy Spirit uses His Word on people's hearts, transformation of lives takes place. We welcome any suggestions as you explore the pages of this book. It is our hope that the teachings laid out in this book will help you build a strong spiritual foundation for your growth and assist you during this time of adventure.

Abundant blessings from the Father!

---

[1] Barna Group, "Six Megathemes Emerge from Barna Group Research in 2010". December 13, 2010, *http://www.barna.org/cultue-articles/462-six-megathemes-emerge-from-2010?q=2010+trends*

TABLE OF CONTENTS

INTRODUCTION

Essentials of Our Christian Faith

The *Seven Pillars of Christianity* has become foundational to the life of New Life Fellowship Global Ministries. It is used for our believers' classes, for evangelism, outreach, and as an introduction to what our church believes and stands for. Quite often, people who come to our fellowship for the first time get saved and begin a wonderful relationship with God through Jesus Christ during the classes. We believe that through learning the essential truths of our Christian faith, Jesus Christ and the Holy Spirit, the truth about man's sin and God's plan for salvation, and the truth about God's revealed will and promises, the body of Christ as well as our individual lives remain nurtured and sustained. What we are taught matters because wrong beliefs about God lead people astray (Matthew 7:22-23). But correct beliefs about God will lead them through faith to heaven. Christianity is a faith anchored on the truths of the Bible, which is God's *only* inspired written revelation and is profitable to us in all things that pertain to life and godliness (2 Peter 1:3).

Hebrews 6 is a pivotal text in the New Testament for building a spiritual foundation for the believer in the Christian faith. Paul's letter to the Corinthians states, "For no other foundation can anyone lay than that which is laid, which is Jesus Christ" (1 Corinthians 3:11). The author of Hebrews goes one step further to break down the components of this foundation who is Jesus Christ. These seven components are: the author and perfecter of our faith - the Lord Jesus Christ, repentance from dead works, faith in God, the doctrine of baptisms, the laying on of hands, the resurrection of the dead, and eternal judgment.

Christians agree that the Bible is the most important book to know and to live by. Therefore, a brief presentation of the Scriptures is in order before writing on the seven essentials of the Christian faith. My experience with the congregations I served as elder and now pastor shows a dismal lack of biblical knowledge. Surveys conducted by the Barna Group observed approximately 80% of church attendees do not have an adequate knowledge of the Bible. In order, therefore, to mitigate the extant biblical illiteracy in our congregation, we require new members to take this foundational class.

It is my prayer that this book will ground young believers in the faith and refresh the maturing Christian. There are two other benefits to be derived from reading and meditating on the scriptural principles contained in this book. First, the believer will be equipped with the essentials of the faith so that when the storms of adversity come, he or she will stand (Ephesians 6:11, 13). Second, the Christian will be able to contend for the faith whenever and wherever falsehood is presented.

The Bible – A Panoramic View

It is estimated that over 150,000 books are published every year in the United States. People who read and trust the Bible claim it to be the Word of God because in it, unlike any other book, God has revealed Himself to man. The Bible itself says that God is its divine author (2 Timothy 3:16). The divine record of God's self-revelation has His very thoughts, will, and ways. Therefore, the Bible is divine in authorship, human in personality, infallible in authority, and eternal in duration.

Through a careful study of the biblical doctrine regarding the nature of revelation, inspiration, inerrancy, and illumination, we discover a wealth of genuine and trustworthy knowledge of God and how mankind can develop a personal and lasting relationship with the Creator. Let's examine these teachings.

Revelation

Bible scholars have put forth three categories of the revealing knowledge of God—general, special, and personal. First and foremost, God has decided to make Himself known to man through His creation. The psalmist declares: "The heavens declare the glory of God; the skies proclaim the work of his hands. Day after day they pour forth speech; night after night they display knowledge. There is no speech or language where their voice is not heard. Their voice goes out into all the earth, their words to the ends of the world. In the heavens he has pitched a tent for the sun, which is like a bridegroom coming forth from his pavilion, like a champion rejoicing to run his course. It rises at one end of the heavens and makes its circuit to the other; nothing is hidden from its heat" (Psalm 19:1-6 NIV). Also, Paul writing to the Romans said, "For since the creation of the world His invisible attributes are clearly seen, being understood by the things that are made, even His eternal power and Godhead, so that they are without excuse" (Romans 1:20). Furthermore, the Father has revealed Himself through the written Word. In the Old Testament, the written Word is expressed with these synonyms: laws, testimonies, statutes, commandments, judgment, precepts, and ordinances. Thus, the psalmist writes, "The law of the Lord is perfect, converting the soul; the testimony of the Lord is sure, making wise the simple; the statutes of the Lord are right, rejoicing the heart; the commandment of the Lord is pure, enlightening the eyes; the fear of the Lord is clean, enduring forever; the judgments of the Lord are true and righteous altogether. More to be desired are they than gold, yea, than much fine gold; sweeter also than honey and the honeycomb. Moreover, by them Your servant is warned, and in keeping them there is great reward" (Psalm 19:7-11).

In the New Testament, the written Word becomes the Living Word that came and dwelt among humanity. John writes, "In the beginning was the Word, and the Word was with God, and the Word was God [notice who God is]....And the Word became flesh and dwelt among us, and we beheld His glory, the glory of the only begotten of the Father, full of grace and truth" (John 1:1, 14).

Finally, the Bible is the divine record of God's self-revelation in the person of the Lord Jesus Christ. Apostle Paul affirms that "God was in Christ reconciling the world to Himself" (2 Corinthians 5:19). And Jesus Himself declared to Philip, "He who has seen Me has seen the Father....Believe Me that I am in the Father and the Father in Me" (John 14:9,11). Earlier in John's gospel Jesus said, "I and My Father are one" (John 10:30). Through Jesus Christ, mankind can have a personal and eternal relationship with God. Jesus said, "I am the way, the truth, and the life. No one comes to the Father except through Me" (John 14:6). Because of the Bible's revelational knowledge, it serves as a supreme guide by which all human conduct, creeds, and religious opinion must be measured.

Inspiration

Another great truth of the Scripture is its claim of inspiration. Second Timothy 3:16 states, "All Scripture is given by inspiration of God and is profitable for doctrine, for reproof, for instruction, for training in righteousness." The Greek word for inspiration in this verse is *Theopneustos*. This word is made up of two words: *theo* means "God," and the word *opneustos* means "to breathe out" or "to exhale." Hence, all Scripture is the exhaling of God's breath. God Himself oversaw the composition of Scripture so that His message was accurately recorded by human penmanship. It is, however, interesting to note that God's inspirational words did not alter the human writer's personality nor influence his style of writing.

A second significant passage that expresses the Bible's claim to be absolutely true is that of Apostle Peter. Peter says, "Knowing this first, that no prophecy of Scripture is of any private interpretation. For prophecy never came by the will of man, but holy men of God spoke as they were moved by the Holy Spirit" (2 Peter 1: 20-21). In other words, Peter claims that even though the Bible was written by human authors, the Holy Spirit initiated, directed, and controlled the minds Himself as the Holy Word was written. These verses make an important claim. The Bible prophets did not originate what they wrote; rather, they recorded what was given to them by God through the Holy Spirit. This kept them from expressing their own ideas and introducing error that would creep into what they wrote.

A further scripture to buttress the two foregoing passages tells us again of another spiritual truth about the inspiration – the holy text. Paul said, "These things we also speak, not in words which man's wisdom teaches but which the Holy Spirit teaches..." (1 Corinthians 2:13). Clearly, the Bible's claim to be inspired is indisputable, and it remains the *only* message of God to mankind for all times, unadulterated.

Inerrancy

Not only is the Bible revealed and inspired, it is also without fault, mistakes, or contradictions. David declares, "The words of the Lord are pure words, like silver tried in a furnace of earth, purified seven times" (Psalm 12:6). This verse makes a compelling case that the words of Scripture are altogether trustworthy. The eternal God stands steadfast behind His words. The word "seven" in the Bible stands for perfection and completion. Since only God is perfect and complete in Himself, so too is His divine Word.

Another testimony of the purity of Scripture was recorded by Agur, the son of Jakeh, in Proverbs. He boldly declared, "Every word of God is pure" (Proverbs 30:5). Clearly, both the Old and New Testaments are without error.

Illumination

The divine record asserts that the minds of unbelievers are blinded by the god of this world so that the light of the glorious gospel of Christ should not shine on them (2 Corinthians 4:3-4). Hence, they move, eat, and work, but live in total spiritual darkness and cannot perceive the things of God. Only the illuminating power of the Holy Spirit can give them understanding of God's Word. Even the disciples of Jesus Christ had the minds of their understanding opened that they might comprehend the Scriptures (Luke 24:45). The disciples' comprehension involved seeing how God's plan of salvation was outlined in the Scriptures. The Bible clearly teaches that "no one knows the things of God except the Spirit of God... these things we also speak, not in words which man's wisdom teaches but which the Holy Spirit teaches" (1 Corinthians 2:11,13). It is the Holy Spirit of God who also grants the spirit of wisdom and revelation in the knowledge of Him and brings enlightenment to man's understanding of Scripture (Ephesians 1:10-18).

In sum, we have briefly examined the great teachings of the nature of revelation, inspiration, inerrancy, and illumination. These doctrines attest to the reliability of the Scriptures in both the Old and New Testaments as the message of God to mankind for all ages.

Apart from the *four* great doctrines taught by the Holy Scriptures, a presentation of the *four* reasons that demonstrate the Bible is the Word of God is also necessary.

1. Historical Accuracy

Some historians and scientists have sought to disprove the Bible. They claim, for instance, that the Hittites mentioned in the Bible never existed. In 1906, the Hittite capital was uncovered about 90 miles east of Ankara, the capital of Turkey, by archaeologists. Around the same time, archaeologists discovered tablets in the ancient city of Ebla in northern Syria to support the biblical record.

A linguist and paleontologist named Dr. Driver set out to disprove the authorship of Moses, who wrote the Pentateuch (Genesis, Exodus, Leviticus, Numbers, and Deuteronomy). Dr. Driver pointed out that it was impossible for Moses to write the Pentateuch. Why? Because he claimed that people did not know how to write during Moses' time. A couple of years later in northern Egypt, Dr. Petrie and his team discovered some clay tablets (referred to now as the Tel-el-Amarna tablets). These were letters written centuries before Moses was born. They contained business transactions between the Egyptian and Palestinian people. These tablets demonstrate that not only did this civilization know how to write, but they also were writing letters back and forth with a postal stamp.

The New Testament record also is supported by research and discovery. For example, the gospel of Luke and the book of Acts (written by Dr. Luke) have gained the respect of scholars who have investigated the numerous references to people and places in the Jewish and Roman world.

John Warwick Montgomery writes, "What then does a historian know about Jesus Christ? He knows first and foremost that the New Testament document can be relied upon to give an accurate portrait of Him. And he knows that this portrait cannot be rationalized away by wishful thinking."[2]

---

[2]   Quoted in Jonathan Hill, History of Christianity (Grand Rapids: Zondervan, 2006), 453

All in all, the Bible's assertion to present an accurate record of the true history of man is irrefutable. The Old as well as the New Testament speaks eloquently about specific people, places, and events. And the events cited in the Bible took place in our world with people like you and me.

2. Prophetic Fulfillment

Numerous prophetic utterances are recorded in the Bible. More than half of them are fulfilled, proof positive that the Bible is reliable and accurate. Isaiah states, "I have declared the former things from the beginning; they went forth from My mouth, and I caused them to hear it. Suddenly I did them, and they came to pass" (Isaiah 48:3). In Deuteronomy, it says that the prophet's authority is measured against the accuracy of his predictions. Allow me to cite a few examples of the fulfilled prophecies about Jesus Christ in the Bible:

- The Bible predicts that Jesus will be born by a virgin (Isaiah 7:14). This was fulfilled in Luke 1:26-35.
- The Scriptures foretell that Jesus will be born in Bethlehem (Micah 5:2), and this prediction was fulfilled in Matthew 2:1.
- His name was called Immanuel (Isaiah 7:14), and this declaration was fulfilled in Matthew 1:23.
- His ministry was to operate in Galilee (Isaiah 9:1-2), and its fulfillment was in Matthew 4:12-16.
- His triumphant entry was predicted in (Zechariah 9:9), and its fulfillment was realized in Matthew 21:1-11.

Another example of fulfilled prophecy was the destruction of the city of Tyre. Ezekiel predicted that the city would be destroyed, the ruins dumped into the sea, and that it will never be rebuilt (Ezekiel 26). To date, there is no trace of this city.

Still another prophecy about the successions of the great world powers of yesteryear is documented in the book of Daniel. Daniel predicted that Babylon the Great would be conquered by Medo-Persia, Medo-Persia would be crushed by Greece, and then the Roman Empire would dominate the world until a renewed Roman Empire is established (Daniel 2, 7).

More predictions of God's judgment on some countries came to pass. For example, God's judgment against Nineveh (Nahum 1-3), Moab and Ammon (Jeremiah 48-49), Babylon (Isaiah 13-14; Jeremiah 51), and Edom (Isaiah 34; Jeremiah 49; Ezekiel 25, 35) were all fulfilled as prophesied.

Therefore, it is clear that whenever the Bible speaks prophetically it comes to pass. Because hundreds of prophecies have been fulfilled, we can trust the Bible for accurate predictions.

3. Scientific Accuracy

A common question is, do the Bible and science conflict? No, because there is no legitimate justification. For example, in Galileo's era, some religious leaders foolishly believed that the earth was the center of the solar system. At the heart of today's debate is the question whether life is a result of an evolutionary process or the result of divine creation. Opponents of the biblical account deny the idea that a supreme being created the universe and all of the miracles contained in the Bible. In the final analysis, the Bible and science are in perfect agreement because the same God who inspired the Bible equally created the universe.

Theology is the science of studying God and how He relates to His creation. Some opponents to the Creation model feel that calling theology "science" is an oxymoron; however, they are unaware that modern science is a child of theologians since science began as an endeavor to discover God in His creation. Galileo, the father of modern science, called God the "...divine geometer of the universe, the mathematizing source and goal of all relationships." Galileo developed the theory of relativity. In his theory of relativity, Galileo said that one must have a fixed point of reference to establish trust. That point of reference for all truth is God.

Science is a wonderful thing. In studying science, one gets a glimpse of the very finger of God as He established universal laws governing the physical universe, and spiritual laws controlling the spiritual realm. In the study of science we can see the wonderful, complex mechanisms of creation. Theology used to be one of the sciences, but even as the second law of thermodynamics states, "everything goes from order to disorder," so science has gone from embracing the truth to believing a lie. True science, as opposed to pseudoscience, is the study of established laws and provable facts. It is also seeking new laws and facts that can help mankind progress. Absolute truth is a trademark of science because at its core is God. God created all things and holds them together by the mighty power of His Word (Genesis 1:1; Hebrews 1:3). God spoke everything visible and invisible into existence (Genesis 1:1) and is upholding *all* things by the word of His power (Hebrews 1:3). Biblical critics have abandoned Truth (God) and embraced secular and foolish ideas (Romans 1:18-25; 1 Corinthians 2:14).

4. The Bible's Life-Transforming Impact

The Bible also has proven itself trustworthy in its impact on cultures and individuals. Verifiable proof exists to demonstrate that lives have been transformed from the inside out when a clear presentation of the gospel is done in the power of the Holy Spirit. It is no wonder that the Bible is called by its adherents the "word of life" (Philippians 2:16). Its message is the Good News, which it calls "the power of God to salvation" (Romans 1:16). And it refers to itself as the "living and powerful" Word of God (Hebrews 4:12). Indeed, Hebrews 4:12 states, "For the word of God is living and powerful, and sharper than any two-edged sword, piercing even to the division of soul and spirit, and of joints and marrow, and is a discerner of the thoughts and intents of the heart."

Impact on Society

Wherever an honest investigation of the Bible's influence in any culture is done, it becomes evident that a higher morality, social change, improved living conditions, and a better life take place. For example, in lands where slavery was practiced, the power of the Word of God brought conviction (John 16:8) of the wrong and those held in bondage were set free. Also, in places where women were mistreated and considered second-class citizens, the presentation of the gospel brought freedom and respect from their taskmasters. Still, in other areas where there was severe oppression and cruelty to subgroups in culture (children, the handicapped, the aged), the conditions greatly improved when the Bible's truth was accepted. Generally speaking, whenever the scriptural message is received in the heart of a people, their aspirations soar, their morals are heightened, and their spirits are lifted.

Consider with me for a moment what would happen if the Bible were taken from society. What would happen to our laws, our police, and our judges? What would be the standard for determining morality? What would happen to the weak, the defenseless, the marginalized, the lonely, and the despairing? Society's moral code has its origin in the Bible. Therefore, the impact of the Bible on society is undeniable.

Life-Changing Impact on Individuals

Not only has the Bible had a tremendous impact on society, it has radically changed individual lives for the better. The reason is that God's Word is like a seed. It is like a sword. It is like a hammer that breaks the rock in pieces. Therefore, the entrance of the Word of God in the heart of man brings life and health (Proverbs 4:22). First Peter 1:23 says, "Having been born again, not of corruptible seed, but incorruptible, through the word of God which lives and abides forever." *Only* the Gospel of Christ saves sinners!

Think of God's servants of yesteryear – Augustine, Charles Spurgeon, Martin Luther, and Bill Bright – and those who are still with us Billy Graham and Charles Colson, to mention these who were transformed by the power of the Word of God.

Augustine, for example, was a foremost scholar in the fourth and fifth centuries who earlier lived a reckless and wicked life. Because he found no peace in his life, he began a long search for genuine peace, and he read these words in the Bible, "Let us walk properly, as in the day, not in revelry and drunkenness, not in lewdness and lust, not in strife and envy. But put on the Lord Jesus Christ, and make no provision for the flesh, to fulfill its lusts" (Romans 13:13-14). Later, Augustine wrote about the impact of this text: "No further would I read, nor needed I. For instantly at the end of the sentence, by a light as it were of serenity infused into my heart, all the darkness of doubt vanished away." This former alcoholic became the bishop of Hippo in northern Africa, founded the first monastery in that region, and influenced much of Christianity through his testimony and powerful penmanship.

Charles Haddon Spurgeon also sought for peace in all the wrong places until he heard a country preacher quote this verse: "Look to Me, and be saved, all you ends of the earth! For I am God, and there is no other" (Isaiah 45:22). He too was a popular pastor of the 18th century. He jealously proclaimed the Good News, and his writing had a great impact then and now.

Martin Luther, a Catholic monk, was very frustrated and unable to live a holy life. Despite many attempts to live righteously, he was beset by sins. After years of self-torture, fear, and constant striving to gain access to heaven by good works, he finally found peace by studying God's Word. He read these words: "The just shall live by his faith" (Habakkuk 2:4). He championed the Protestant Reformation Movement.

Bill Bright founded Campus Crusade for Christ which has won many to the Lord. In fact, some Christians believe that his organization has won more souls for the Kingdom than Billy Graham Ministries.

Billy Graham sought God about the authenticity of the Bible as God's Word. He accepted the Scripture as the divine Word by faith. As a result, he has distinguished himself as one of the great evangelists of our time.

Chuck Colson, a convicted Watergate conspirator, came to faith through a convicting witness of the Gospel message by his friends. He founded Prison Fellowship, a movement that has grown worldwide and reaches out to prisoners, ex-prisoners, and their families, both as an act of service to Jesus Christ and as a contribution to restoring peace to cities and communities endangered by crime. His book, *Born Again*, has influenced many bound in sin and led thousands to a personal saving faith in Jesus Christ.

Someone said, concerning the Bible, that it is so majestically deep that scholars could swim and never touch bottom. Yet, so wonderfully shallow, that a little child could come and get a drink of water without fear of drowning.

Jesus Authenticates the Bible's Reliability

Jesus, the Hero of Scripture, affirms that the Bible was the Word of God. Let's examine the following:

a) He used titles for the Bible to show that it was word perfect.

- "The Word of God" (Mark 7:13; John 10:35)
- "Scripture" (Luke 4:21; John 5:39; 10:35)
- "The Commandment of God" (Mark 7:8)

b) He affirms the historical person and events mentioned in the Old Testament.

- Adam and Eve (Matthew 19:4-5)
- Noah and the flood (Matthew 24:37-39)
- Lot, Lot's wife, and Sodom (Luke 17:28-32)
- Jonah (Matthew 12:38-41)

c) He acknowledged His own words as Scripture and, therefore, to be believed (John 12:48-49).

d) He held people responsible for what was written in Scripture (Matthew 12:3).

e) He answered His critics by quoting Scripture from the Old Testament as conclusive evidence.

- John 10:34, quoting Psalm 82:6
- Matthew 22:32, quoting Exodus 3:6,15
- Matthew 22:42-44, quoting Psalm 110:1

f) He declared the authority of Scripture to defeat Satan in the wilderness (Matthew 4:4,7,10).

It is evident that Jesus accepted the Scriptures and its claims as true. While on earth, the Living Word affirmed the written Word.

The Bible Writers' Claims for the Bible

The Bible writers affirmed the Bible's claims for itself by accepting the other parts of the Bible as God's Word. They also acknowledged it by the way they saw themselves as part of God's plan for making Himself known to man.

First, theologians (orthodox as opposed to liberal) agree that God has revealed Himself to man in the following ways:

- General revelation - deals with the created universe.
- Specific revelation - speaks about God's revelation through the Word of God.
- Personal revelation - explains an individual's encounter with the Lord Jesus Christ and having a personal relationship with God through His indescribable gift – the Lord Jesus Christ.

Second, through an examination of how the Bible authors viewed the Scriptures:

- When Daniel read Jeremiah's prophecy that the Jews would be held as captives for 70 years, he admitted it as true and began to pray and plan accordingly (Daniel 9:2).
- Peter accepted the supernatural origin of the writings of the Old Testament prophets (2 Peter 1:20-21).
- Again, Peter believed the writings of Paul were supernatural, even though he found them hard to understand (2 Peter 3:16).

Third, the Bible writers claimed that the Word of God came directly from God Himself:

- "Now the Lord called to Moses, and spoke to him from the tabernacle of meeting" (Leviticus 1:1).
- Isaiah began his book by announcing, "For the Lord has spoken" (Isaiah 1:2).
- Jeremiah opened his prophecy by declaring, "Then the word of the Lord came to me" (Jeremiah 1:4).
- Ezekiel, commissioned by God, proclaimed, "Thus says the Lord God" (Ezekiel 3:11).
- Paul claimed that the words he spoke were directly from God (Galatians 1:11-12; 1 Thessalonians 2:13).
- John the revelator said, "The Revelation of Jesus Christ, which God gave Him to show His servants—things which must shortly take place" (Revelation 1:1).

In closing, the Bible itself asserts to be God's book. Christ affirms this assertion, and the Bible writers themselves also affirm the Scriptures as the authentic Word of God.

The Bible's Protected Text

The miraculous protection of the text of the Bible is yet another potent argument to authenticate it. The supernatural protection occurred in two forms: 1) its unity and great diversity; and 2) the miraculous preservation of the text itself.

Let's examine the two ways that God has protected the text of His Word:

Unity in Diversity

Man's writings are filled with disunity and contradictions, especially those written by more than one author. They often contain glowing discrepancies in philosophy, facts, style, or ideas. Even those authored by a single individual may contain conflicting facts or logic. But Bible scholars have not ceased to be amazed by its unity and consistency of doctrine. From Genesis to Revelation, the Bible has a single narration theme: the redemption of mankind from sin through the death, burial, and resurrection of Jesus Christ.

In the Old Testament, Jesus is presented incognito (Genesis 3:15) as the hope for mankind, while in the New Testament He is revealed as incarnate hope. Consider the diversity in its origin:

- It was written by 40 different authors, over a period of 1,600 years in three languages: Hebrew, Aramaic, and Greek, in three continents (Africa, Asia, and Europe).
- Its writers came from different backgrounds: prophet (Jeremiah), priest (Zechariah), shepherd (Amos), king (David), servant (Nehemiah), doctor (Luke), tax collector (Matthew), and Pharisee (Paul), just to mention these.

Although a gap of more than 400 years separated the writings of the Old Testament from the New (see chart on page xxxi), the Bible remains unified and coherent in its content. In spite of the wide diversity, there is agreement in doctrine, details about prophecy, and what it says about Jesus Christ and His mission to save mankind from sin, Satan, and hell. Jesus' death on the cross as the perfect sacrifice, instituting the new covenant referred to by Jeremiah and quoted in Luke 22:20, shows the remarkable unity of the Old and New Testaments. It is a great book to be trusted. Read it, believe it. It is true.

Textual Preservation

The Bible can also be trusted because its text has been miraculously preserved. None of the original manuscripts written and canonized, accepted as inspired writing, has errors. Although none of the original manuscripts written by biblical authors is in existence, we are confident that the Scriptures we hold are translated from the original texts.

The Bible consists of the Old and New Testaments. Written primarily in Hebrew, the Old Testament is comprised of 39 books. Throughout the years, the Old Testament has been accurately preserved, and we can read it as the trustworthy Word of God. A distinct difference separates the Old Testament and the New Testament, but a fundamental unity joins both Testaments. The New Testament is the fulfillment of the Old. Theological themes that began with the Old Testament are often carried to completion in the New. For instance, the practice of sacrifice, which began as early as Genesis 4:4 (apparently without any divine institution), became an officially commanded practice of the Old Testament under the law given through Moses and was carried through to the climatic once-for-all sacrifice of Jesus Christ as the unique Lamb of God, *slain* from the foundation of the world.

One central theme runs through the Bible from the first to the last chapter of the Scripture. God is the central character of the Bible. His chief purpose is to bring redemption to humans. The Bible's teaching begins with the creation of humans and the world in which they live. The first man and woman sinned in deliberate rebellion against a holy and loving God, breaking their fellowship with Him. Their sin spread from them to all of their descendants, making sinful men alienated from God. So man's problem has always been the sin problem. God, in His wisdom, proceeds to develop the grand redemption plan, tracing various stages of God's revelation of Himself: the call of Abraham, the establishment of the covenant with the Israelites, the institution of the sacrificial system, teaching the people the proper way to approach God for forgiveness and regeneration for those dead in sin, the church as the new covenant community, the redeemed people of God on mission for Him in the world, and finally, the life to come, in heaven for the redeemed, and in hell for the unrepentant.

Also crucially important to the unity of the Bible is God's plan of redemption, bringing people into a right relationship with Him. This relationship begins with the call of Abraham and the establishment of a covenant with him. Subsequently, this covenant was reaffirmed with his son, Isaac; with Isaac's son, Jacob, whose name was changed to Israel; and finally, the covenant was reaffirmed with the whole nation of Israel. It was unconditional on God's part, but a conditional covenant from the human side. God's people were to live up to their covenant responsibilities. Most major portions of the Old Testament are stories of repeated failure to live up to their covenant responsibilities.

Jeremiah the prophet looked forward to a new day when God would write His covenant on the hearts of His people so that it could not be broken (Jeremiah 31:31-34), a prophecy of the new birth referred to by Jesus in John 3:1-8. Jesus termed His death on the cross as the sacrifice instituting the new covenant referred to by Jeremiah (Luke 22:20). This shows the remarkable unity of the Old and New Testaments in anticipation and fulfillment.

How We Got the Bible

The word "canon" means "a measuring device" or a standard. Out of the many religious writings that have been published, only 66 books were accepted as inspired by God. Throughout the process, the canon Scripture was being determined by God, not by man. In this process, the writings of Moses and the book of Joshua were immediately accepted as Scripture. Two verses that attest to their authorship are found in Exodus 24:3 and Joshua 24:26. In Exodus 24:3, Moses wrote, "So Moses came and told the people all the words of the Lord and all the judgments. And all the people answered with one voice and said, 'All the words which the Lord has said we will do.'" Joshua wrote, "Then Joshua wrote these words in the Book of the Law of God" (Joshua 24:26). In all, there are 39 sacred books.

For the books of the New Testament, their acceptance was based on the test of apostleship. They were received if they were written by an apostle, such as Peter, John, or Paul, or by someone close to an apostle, such as Luke or Mark, who also had apostolic authority. Early church fathers accepted the inspiration of the New Testament canon after carefully identifying and eliminating questionable works. The Council of Hippo (AD 393) and Carthage (AD 397) accepted the 27 books that now appear in the New Testament.

THE BIBLE AT A GLANCE

OLD TESTAMENT (39 books)				NEW TESTAMENT (27 books)		
HISTORY (17 books)	POETRY/WISDOM (5 books)	PROPHECY (17 books)		History (5 books)	Letters (21 books)	Prophecy (1 book)
a.) The Law		a.) Major Prophets		a.) Gospels	Paul's	
1. Genesis	1. Job	1. Isaiah		1. Matthew	1. Romans	1. Revelation
2. Exodus	2. Psalms	2. Jeremiah		2. Mark	2. 1 Corinthians 3. 2 Corinthians	
3. Leviticus	3. Proverbs	3. Lamentations		3. Luke	4. Galatians 5. Ephesians	
4. Numbers	4. Ecclesiastes	4. Ezekiel		4. John	6. Philippians	
5. Deuteronomy	5. The Song of Solomon	5. Daniel			7. Colossians 8. 1 Thessalonians	
b.) History of Governments		b.) Minor Prophets		b.) History of Early Church	9. 2 Thessalonians 10. 1 Timothy	
1. Joshua		1. Hosea			11. 2 Timothy	
2. Judges		2. Joel			12. Titus	
3. Ruth		3. Amos		5. Acts	13. Philemon	
4. 1 Samuel		4. Obadiah			General	
5. 2 Samuel		5. Jonah			1. Hebrews	
6. 1 Kings		6. Micah			2. James	
7. 2 Kings		7. Nahum			3. 1 Peter	
8. 1 Chronicles		8. Habakkuk			4. 2 Peter	
9. 2 Chronicles		9. Zephaniah			5. 1 John	
10. Ezra		10. Haggai			6. 2 John	
11. Nehemiah		11. Zechariah			7. 3 John	
12. Esther		12. Malachi			8. Jude	

(Between the two Testaments: 400 Years of silence between the Testaments)

Old Testament at a Glance

The Old Testament consists of 39 books classified as History, Poetry, and Prophets.

History

The Law

Consists of Genesis, Exodus, Leviticus, Numbers, and Deuteronomy, otherwise known as the Pentateuch. These books contain stories about the creation of the world, the flood, Abraham, Isaac, Jacob, the children of Israel in Egypt, the Exodus, and the wilderness experience before entering the Promised Land. The books of the law also recorded the law God gave to the Hebrew people on Mount Sinai, which laid down the regulations for sacrifice, worship, and daily living.

History of Government

Another subgroup is the history of governmental writings, such as Joshua, Judges, Ruth, 1 Samuel, 2 Samuel, 1 Kings, 2 Kings, 1 Chronicles, 2 Chronicles, Ezra, Nehemiah, and Esther. These 12 books continue the story of the Jewish people and their conquest of the Promised Land, especially the book of Joshua; but their unbroken cycle of stubbornness in the books of Judges and 1 Kings ushered in the united kingdom, a divided kingdom by the Assyrian invasion, the Babylonian invasion, the painful years of exile, and the slaves from captivity during the Persian rule.

Poetry and Wisdom

The five poetry and wisdom books include Job, Psalms, Proverbs, Ecclesiastes, and Song of Solomon. They demonstrate the creative ways the Hebrew people expressed themselves to God and related to each other. Furthermore, these portions of the old sacred writings contain devotional and wisdom literations of Israel, as well as some historical and prophetic material.

Prophets

The prophetic works are divided into two categories: Major and Minor Prophets.

Major

The term "prophets" stands over an entire portion of the sacred text even if every part of the section might not be predicted in nature. The five major prophetic books are Isaiah, Jeremiah, Lamentations, Ezekiel, and Daniel. They are not called "major" because these authors were greater in stature or more highly favored by God than the Minor Prophets. We call them major because their messages were lengthier. Major as well as Minor Prophets had the God-given mandate to convey the words of God to His covenant people regarding His promises to them and their duty to obey and abide by His laws given through Moses. Their messages also included warnings of judgment, hope, foretelling and forthtelling of future events and the hope of the coming Messiah.

Minor

In the last portion of the sacred writings of the Hebrew text are 12 Minor Prophets: Hosea, Joel, Amos, Obadiah, Jonah, Micah, Nahum, Habakkuk, Zephaniah, Haggai, Zechariah, and Malachi. These works are called "The Book of the Twelve" in the Hebrew Bible. They are just as important as the Major Prophets. They are called "minor" because of the shorter lengths of their texts. Their messages also contained prophetic declarations, warnings of judgment, and hope.

A period of about 400 years, dubbed "the silent years," separates the Old and New Testament writings. However, the Testaments are harmoniously woven together as one book. The New Testament is in the Old concealed, while the Old is in the New revealed! All of the authors of the Old Testament point to the person and work of the Lord Jesus Christ. The gospel writers reveal the Lord Jesus Christ and His works, while the book of Acts proclaims the Gospel of the Lord Jesus Christ and believers performed miraculous signs and wonders in His name. The epistles explain the entire Gospel, and the Revelation describes Jesus exalted in His glorified state. It is my strong belief that any time the Gospel is preached Jesus Christ must be the central focus.

The New Testament

Like the Old Testament, the New Testament has divisions as well. These are the Gospels, Acts, Paul's Letters (Epistles), General Letters, and Prophecy (Revelation).

What is the Gospel?

The four gospels - Matthew, Mark, Luke, and John are *not* a collection of His famous sayings and biographies, seeking to explain Jesus' lifestyle, friendships, or His mental and emotional dimensions. They are *not* histories of heroic accomplishments; rather, the Gospel is the Good news from God that is presented by eyewitness accounts of the life, works, and words of Jesus. This Good news from God also describes the death, burial, resurrection, ascension, and return of Jesus Christ in His Second Coming. In thumbnail, it is the perfect redemptive work of God in Jesus Christ.

Acts - The History of the First-Century Church

Acts is part two of Luke's gospel. Luke continues to recount the investigation of the life and works of Jesus to his friend, Theophilus, which he started in his gospel narrative. Acts basically sets out to summarize the work of the apostles of Christ through the power of the Holy Spirit sent from Him. This book can be broken into six divisions (see chart below).

Brief Outline of Acts

Division	Passage	Content	Key Verse
1	Acts 1:1 - 6:7	Early events in Jerusalem (day of Pentecost; Peter's sermon; ministry of Peter and John; early persecutions and controversies in the church; Ananias and Sapphira; neglect of widows)	Acts 6:7
2	Acts 6:8 - 9:31	Church spreads throughout Palestine; martyrdom of Stephen; struggle with Jews	Acts 9:31
3	Acts 9:32 - 12:24	Spread of church to Antioch; conversion of Cornelius; further struggles with the Jews	Acts 12:24
4	Acts 12:25 - 16:5	Church spreads to Asia Minor; Paul's first missionary journey	Acts 16:5
5	Acts 16:6 - 19:20	Extension of church to Europe; Paul's second and third missionary journeys	Acts 19:20
6	Acts 19:21 - 28:31	Paul goes to Rome; his arrest and hearings in Jerusalem and Caesarea; his voyage and stay in Rome	Acts 28:30-31

Paul's Letters (Epistles)

The nature and style of Paul's writings are different from the letters most people nowadays will write. Writing materials were scarce, so authors conserved space when writing. Moreover, the greetings and benedictions in the New Testament letters are different from the sort of correspondence we would see today, although in some respects they are similar to the introductions and conclusions found in other first century letters. The major goals of these letters were to address problems that arose in the churches that were established as well as communicate the Good news of Jesus Christ to the seekers. Paul's letters include Romans, 1 Corinthians, 2 Corinthians, Galatians, Ephesians, Philippians, Colossians, 1 Thessalonians, 2 Thessalonians, 1 Timothy, 2 Timothy, Titus, and Philemon.

General Letters (Epistles)

The eight epistles are Hebrews, James, 1 Peter, 2 Peter, 1 John, 2 John, 3 John, and Jude, these were written by the apostles bearing their names. Hebrews is the only epistle where the author is uncertain. There is much debate among Bible scholars as to whom the actual author is. Suffice it to say that it is part of the canon. The book of Hebrews was written to believers in the diaspora to provide guidance, encouragement through persecution, warnings of false prophets, and to show the supremacy and sufficiency of Jesus Christ over angels, Moses, and the sacrificial system of the old covenant.

Prophecy (Revelation)

Reflecting a genre (writing style) of literature only familiar to the Jews called "apocalyptic," the book of Revelation is unique among the New Testament books. It sets out to establish, in vivid and emotional terms, the triumph of Christ and His church over all His enemies. This triumph is in accordance with Jesus' discussion in Matthew 24, 25, and Mark 13 regarding His second advent (coming). Earlier, the book of Revelation addresses a message to the seven churches in Asia Minor (modern day Turkey). Its message was to encourage believers experiencing persecution. Revelation also illustrates that God is in control and we, who are alive, better take seriously the warnings delivered to the churches. In the final analysis, Jesus

Christ and His church will reign triumphantly over Satan and his followers.

CHAPTER 1

Deity of Jesus Christ
(Elementary Principles of Christ)

"...Without Him, nothing was made that was made."
(John 1:3)

Throughout the Old and New Testaments, Jesus Christ is the central figure of Scripture. He is concealed in the Old Testament, but revealed in the New Testament. Speaking to the Jewish religious leaders of His day, Jesus said, "You search the Scriptures, for in them you think you have eternal life; and these are they [the Scriptures] which testify of Me" (John 5:39; also see Luke 24:27). Noted Bible scholar and teacher, Elmer Towns, succinctly captures the essence of this verse by stating that "Christ is the 'warp and woof' of all Scripture. He is found throughout the Old Testament by type, prophecy, and implication, and His shadow is always evident."[1] In the New Testament, Christ is revealed as God, Servant, Son of God, Son of Man, our High Priest, and King of Kings.

The Lord Jesus Christ in the Old Testament

The goal here is to portray the Lord Jesus Christ in each of the 39 books of the Old Testament with corresponding New Testament text for confirmation. This is also to affirm Jesus' statement in John 5. "You search the Scriptures, for in them you think you have eternal life, and these are they which testify of Me." (John 5:39)

---

[1]   Elmer L. Towns, Theology for Today (Ohio: Cengage Learning, 2008), 194

Christ in Genesis

In Genesis, the Lord Jesus Christ is described as both creator and redeemer. First, as creator, Genesis 1:1 states, "In the beginning God created the heavens and the earth." The word "God" in this verse is derived from *Elohim* in Hebrew. *Elohim*, usually translated "God," means three or more, in its plural form. Jesus the Son is depicted here as co-creator with the Father and Holy Spirit. Verse 26 demonstrates the use of the word Elohim as co-creators. It says, "Then God said, 'Let Us make man in Our image, according to Our likeness...'" (Genesis 1:26 NIV). The Lord Jesus Christ is creator of humanity. He created us to love, for His glory and pleasure. Thus, in the Genesis account, Christ is the agent of all creation. "For by Him all things were created" (Colossians 1:16). Elsewhere, the Old Testament uses plural personal pronouns when speaking of God. It pertains to God deciding to confuse human language at the tower of Babel: "Let Us go down..." (Genesis 11:6-9). The last reference is the call to mission: "Who will go for Us?" (Isaiah 6:1-8).

Second, not only is Christ portrayed as creator, He is also depicted as redeemer of mankind. Just as God commanded Abraham to offer Isaac as a sacrifice, so too has He promised in Genesis 3:15 that Christ will be man's substitute and sacrificial lamb to restore humanity back to Himself. Through Abraham's seed, the Lord Jesus Christ, all families of the earth will be blessed.

Christ in Exodus

Exodus pictures the Lord Jesus Christ as redeemer. God freed His people from Egyptian slavery, portraying Christ's deliverance of sinners from their sin and its attendant consequences. Christ was with Israel as the rock that followed them through their sojourn from slavery to Canaan (Exodus 17:6; see also 1 Corinthians 10:4). Also, the Lord Jesus Christ is pictured as the Passover Lamb who came to take away the sins of the world (Exodus 12:11; John 1:36; 19:36) and serve as the bridge to God.

Christ in Leviticus

Leviticus offers multiple aspects of Christ's atoning sacrifice. Specific sacrifices, found in chapter 16, suggest several aspects of the Lord Jesus Christ's atoning work. Chapters 21-22 foreshadow Christ's perfect priesthood as our ultimate High Priest. "So also Christ did not glorify

Himself to become High Priest, but it was He who said to Him 'You are My Son, Today I have begotten You'" (Hebrews 5:5).

Christ in Numbers

Numbers metaphorically portrays Christ both as the water-giving Rock (1 Corinthians 10:4) and as the serpent that gives life to all those who looked up to Him (John 3:14-15). The author of Numbers foresees Christ as a star that will come out of Jacob and a scepter out of Israel. Both prophecies were fulfilled when David brought down the wicked nation of Moab and when Jesus Christ (David's descendant) subdued all of God's enemies at the cross of Calvary.

Christ in Deuteronomy

In Deuteronomy, Moses tells of a prophet such as himself who God will raise up among the Jews (Deuteronomy 18:15-22). Later, in the New Testament, Christ is seen as the fulfillment of that prophecy (Acts 3:22; 7:37). Another prediction about Christ states that His body shall not remain overnight on the tree (Deuteronomy 21:23). Christ became a curse for all mankind to redeem us from the curse of the law (Galatians 3:13).

Christ in Joshua

The very name Joshua is a variation of Jesus. Joshua, as leader, took the Israelites to possess the Promised Land, foreshadowing Christ leading redeemed mankind to everlasting life. Joshua's encounter with the "Commander of the Lord's army" (Joshua 5:15) is undoubtedly the pre-incarnate Christ.

Christ in Judges

Judges reviews God's agents for delivering His people from their enemies. In a similar vein, Christ is foreshadowed as the One who will confront and defeat Satan and his co-hosts, thereby liberating God's people from their enemies. This theme runs through the gospels of Matthew, Mark, and Luke, and in Paul's letter to the Ephesians, as well as in Revelation.

Christ in Ruth

In Ruth, Boaz effectively performed the role of kinsman–redeemer. Christ is fulfilled in this role both as our brother and redeemer. Ruth prominently figures in the genealogy of Christ as the great-grandmother of Israel's messiah, King David.

Christ in 1 Samuel

First Samuel records Israel's first two kings, Saul and David. These kings of the Jewish nation prefigure Israel's real king, Jesus Christ. Christ is in the lineage of David, called "son of David," a term that is similar to Messiah. The author, Samuel, who was a prophet, priest, and political leader, prefigures Jesus' role as prophet, priest, and king. Also, included in First Samuel is the first mention of a person called the anointed of Yahweh. This is significant because the word Messiah means "anointed one."

Christ in 2 Samuel

In 2 Samuel, David models Christ's kingship as founder of the dynasty, where Jesus, son of David, is the eternal King. One of the ways David illustrates Christ's kingship is in his compassion and loyalty to Mephibosheth – the grandson of King Saul. Jesus epitomizes love by dying for undeserving humanity.

Christ in 1 Kings

First Kings is the continuation of the Davidic dynasty in Israel, where Solomon, David's son and Israel's third king, is prominent. The wisdom, fame, and splendor of Solomon are known beyond the borders of Israel. This splendid era in Israel's history points to the wisdom, majesty, and glory of Christ. In Luke's gospel, Jesus told His audiences that the Queen of Sheba made a long journey to hear Solomon. He also spoke of One greater than Solomon who was currently among them (Luke 11:31).

Christ in 2 Kings

Second Kings describes the ministries of Elijah and Elisha, prophets through whom God demonstrates His mighty power. Apostle Luke notes that Jesus was "a Prophet mighty in deed and word before God and all the people" (Luke 24:19). The Davidic dynasty was preserved in Israel as long as it was because of God's unfailing promise to David (2 Kings 8:19). Israel can count on God to keep a lamp for David forever (Revelation 21:23).

Christ in 1 Chronicles

First Chronicles focuses on the messianic promise of a son of David to rule over Israel (chapter 17). It traces the family lineage of Israel's kings (chapter 3), showing how God has been faithful to maintain a son of David to rule Israel even in the face of exile. This son of David points to the eternally beloved Son of God (1 Chronicles 17:13; Luke 1:32-33; Hebrews 1:5). Equally significant is the establishment of David's dynasty describing David's achievements both religiously and militarily. Finally, David's prayer of praise (1 Chronicles 29:10-13) applies to Jesus (Revelation 5:12-13).

Christ in 2 Chronicles

In 2 Chronicles, Solomon's glorious reign foreshadows Christ's eternal and glorious reign in the New Jerusalem (Revelation 21-22).

Christ in Ezra

Ezra was the leading character whom God used to lead the Jewish captives in Babylon back to Judea. Jesus, in His sermon to the Jewish synagogue of Nazareth, declared that one of His goals was "to proclaim liberty to the [human] captives" held by Satan (Luke 4:18).

Christ in Nehemiah

God used Nehemiah as another leading character in the restoration of God's people from Babylon to Jerusalem. Nehemiah appealed to the post-exiled people of Israel to serve God with undivided loyalty in rebuilding the city wall. Jesus, in the same vein, said, "He who is not with Me is against Me, and he who does not gather with Me scatters" (Luke 11:23).

Christ in Esther

Nowhere in Scripture is the case of God for the Israelites more evident than in the book of Esther even though the name of God is not mentioned. Prior to His arrest, Jesus prayed, "While I was with them in the world, I kept them in Your name. Those whom You gave Me I have kept; and none of them is lost except the son of perdition, that the Scripture might be fulfilled" (John 17:12). Esther saved the Jewish nation by overturning the king's decree as Christ overturned God's wrath for humanity.

Christ in Job

Job, a blameless and upright servant of God, lost family, health, and possessions, yet he never cursed God. "And he said, 'Naked I came from my mother's womb, and naked shall I return there. The Lord gave, and the Lord has taken away; blessed be the name of the Lord.' In all this, Job did not sin nor charge God with wrong" (Job 1:21-22). Although Job cried out for a mediator to stand between him and God, he found none. Christ later became the answer to Job's request. "For there is one God and one Mediator between God and men, the Man Christ Jesus" (1 Timothy 2:5).

Christ in the Psalms

In the Psalms, two major predictions about Christ's first and second comings are recorded. Psalm 22 forebodes His crucifixion while Psalm 2 looks forward to the time that He will establish His kingdom (Matthew 13, 16, 24).

Christ in the Proverbs

One of God's attributes is His infinite wisdom. Wisdom, as an attribute of God, is depicted as a person in Proverbs. However, God revealed as Christ is described in the New Testament as the Wisdom of God, by whom the worlds were created and sustained (Luke 11:49; Hebrews 1:2-3).

Christ in Ecclesiastes

In Ecclesiastes, we discover that apart from God, life is empty and meaningless. Analogous to this graphic picture is one described by Jesus when He used the imagery of a vine with its branches to underscore this truth. "I am the vine, you are the branches. He who abides in Me, and I in him, bears much fruit; for without Me you can do nothing" (John 15:5).

Christ in Song of Solomon

At the heart of Song of Solomon is a book of romantic love poetry. A bride and groom (or wife and husband) celebrate with exhilarating passion God's wonderful gift of the love that is shared between the two. This love between a husband and wife is portrayed by Paul as a picture of the love of Christ and His bride, the church (Ephesians 5:32).

Christ in Isaiah

Both the stunning and precise prophecy of the virgin birth of Christ (Isaiah 7:14), and the Christ as the suffering servant is foretold by Isaiah (52:13 - 53:12; compare Matthew 1:23; 16:21).

Christ in Jeremiah

Jeremiah contains numerous parallels between the author's suffering and that of Jesus as Israel's Messiah. Both wept over Jerusalem (Jeremiah 9:1; Luke 19:41) and both prophesied about the imminent destruction of the temple in Jerusalem (Jeremiah 7:11-15).

Christ in Lamentations

Lamentations describes the devastation of God's wrath poured out on the city of Jerusalem just as wrath was poured out on His beloved Son, the Lord Jesus Christ on the cross. Foreshadowing the cruel punishment that Jesus bore on the cross, the author states, "Is it nothing to you, all you who pass by? Behold and see if there is any sorrow like my sorrow, which has been brought on me, which the Lord has inflicted in the day of His fierce anger" (Lamentations 1:12).

Christ in Ezekiel

God used the term "Son of Man" more than 90 times in Ezekiel. This expression "Son of Man" is used by Jesus most frequently to refer to Himself. It is interesting to note that this designation has two different meanings. First, it refers to His humanity. Second, it is designated to a divine being. When Christ calls Himself "Son of Man," it carries both of these meanings.

Christ in Daniel

Of all the Old Testament books, Daniel defined kingdom perspectives more than any other. Jesus came preaching about the kingdom that had been predicted by Daniel. Another significant aspect connecting this book with Christ is the vision of the author, in which the author states, "One like the Son of Man, coming with the clouds of heaven" (Daniel 7:13). This was the prophecy of Christ's Second Coming, when He will rule with power and great glory over the nations.

Christ in Hosea

Hosea, the eighth century prophet to the Northern Kingdom of Israel, was married to an adulterous wife. The children she bore drew a parallel to God's "marriage" to His spiritually adulterous people, Israel. Christ came to His own – the Jewish people – and they rejected Him. Another parallel recorded in Matthew 2:15 is quoted from Hosea 11:1, where God is calling Israel as He called Jesus, "out of Egypt I called My Son" (Matthew 2:15). Following Herod's threat to kill all male children, Joseph and Mary took baby Jesus to Egypt to escape Herod's wrath. When Herod died, Jesus' family returned to Nazareth.

Christ in Joel

Joel predicted the coming of God's Spirit on all flesh: "Your sons and your daughters shall prophesy, your old men shall dream dreams, your young men shall see visions" (Joel 2:28). Peter and Paul, in the New Testament, explained that the prophecies about the "day of the Lord" applied to the Second Coming of Jesus (1 Thessalonians 5:2; 2 Peter 3:10). However, according to Peter, this prediction began to be fulfilled on the day of Pentecost, when the Holy Spirit filled Jesus' disciples in the upper room (Acts 2:16-21).

Christ in Amos

Amos' main message to the nations surrounding Israel (including Judah) was focused on repentance from injustice and idolatry in order to restore God's favor. In short, Amos proclaimed the righteousness of God. Jesus, too, preached about the high standards of God's righteousness to His followers, indicating that He did not come to abolish the law but to fulfill God's righteous requirements.

Christ in Obadiah

Obadiah prophesied that God would judge Edom, descendants of Esau, for its pride against God and for looking down on Judah's misfortune. Herod the Great, who ruled Judea during the time of Jesus' birth, was from Edomite ancestry. The wickedness of Edom against Israel is portrayed in Herod's attempt to kill baby Jesus.

Christ in Jonah

Jesus referred to Jonah when the crowds who heard Him clamored for a sign. Jesus said that the only sign they would be given is the sign of Jonah. As Jonah was in the belly of the fish for three days, so was Jesus going to be in the belly of the earth for three days and afterward resurrect (Luke 11:29-32).

Christ in Micah

Micah makes two outstanding predictions: Israel's messianic promise centering in the exaltation of God's temple as a worship place for all nations, and the end of all wars. This will be possible because God will once again visit Bethlehem, bringing forth an everlasting king. "But you, Bethlehem Ephrathah, though you are little among the thousands of Judah, yet out of you shall come forth to Me, the One to be Ruler in Israel, whose goings forth are from of old, from everlasting" (Micah 5:2; compare Matthew 2:6).

Christ in Nahum

A clear parallel exists between Nahum's prophecy to Judah and Christ. This prophecy tells us of a messenger who would bring the Good news of Assyria's downfall, thus proclaiming peace for the entire world (Nahum 1:15). Similarly in the New Testament, Jesus is seen as God's favorite messenger. He will preach peace to the world (Acts 10:36). Even as God rebukes the seas and dries up rivers (Nahum 1:4), so too Jesus rebuked the sea and calmed the storm (Matthew 8:26).

Christ in Habakkuk

Perplexed by the nature of evil and its punishment, Habakkuk asked why God would allow evil to exist. In response, God answered by revealing His righteousness and sovereignty. The prophet then responded with worship and faith (Habakkuk 3:17-18). Like Habakkuk, the apostle John stood in awe of God's holiness and power when the risen Christ appeared to him on the isle of Patmos (Revelation 1:17).

Christ in Zephaniah

Zephaniah's prophesy had a two-pronged message. He predicted the coming judgment against the nations. His main message was against Judah, whose sins were so grave that they would go into exile on "the

9

day of the Lord," but would later be restored. Second, he proclaimed that the King of Israel was already in their midst (Zephaniah 3:15). Jesus was crucified as King of the Jews (Mark 15:26). Yet, many Jewish leaders (Judah included) did not recognize the presence of God in Jesus Christ working in their circumstances.

Christ in Haggai

Haggai was God's primary spokesman proclaiming God's command in rebuilding the temple. The glory of the second temple will be greater than the first. The nation will come to worship at the new temple that God will fill with glory (Haggai 2:6-7). Simon saw in the baby Jesus a light that would both bring the Gentile nations and Israel together to worship the King of Kings (Luke 2:32).

Christ in Zechariah

Zechariah predicted the welfare of Jerusalem as God's beloved holy city through night visions and prophetic oracles. This is the same city which King Jesus would enter riding on a donkey. A cursory look at the gospels reveals the incorporation of more passage references from Zechariah than from any other prophetic writing. For example, in Zechariah chapter 12, we see a foreshadowing of the piercing of Jesus' body on the cross (Zechariah 12:10; compare John 19:34,37; Revelation 1:7).

Christ in Malachi

Malachi, God's spokesman, rebuked God's people for breaking God's covenant laws concerning sacrifices, divorce, and tithes. He also prophesied the coming of Christ as the Son of righteousness who brings healing to His people. Malachi further predicted that Christ will come as a refined fire to purify the sons of Levi so they could serve God in righteousness.

The Lord Jesus Christ in the New Testament

The Lord Jesus Christ is revealed in the New Testament as the following: the True God, our High Priest, the Perfect Man, the Only Savior, the Servant, the Son of God, the Lord of Lords, and the King of Kings. We now turn our focus to identify the Lord Jesus as He is revealed in each of the New Testament books.

Christ in Matthew

Matthew's gospel demonstrates more emphatically Jesus' fulfillment as the promised Messiah. To make his case, Matthew quotes from the Old Testament more than any other gospel writer. To affirm Matthew's declaration of Jesus as Messiah, there was placed the inscription above Jesus' head at the cross. It read, *"THIS IS JESUS THE KING OF THE JEWS"* (Matthew 27:37).

Christ in Mark

Mark describes Christ as the suffering servant who performed mighty miracles and met the needs of the people. As a suffering servant, He died for the sins of mankind, becoming a "ransom for many" (Mark 10:45). Christ urged all His followers to carry their cross daily and follow Him.

Christ in Luke

Luke's gospel portrays Jesus as Savior of all sinners. He lived and ministered as the perfect man, but equally arose to affirm His perfect divinity. Jesus not only offered salvation to Jews and Gentiles alike, but also showed great compassion toward the marginalized and downtrodden of His day.

Christ in John

Jesus is depicted in John's gospel as the Word of God which was both with God and was God. Jesus is proclaimed by John as God in the flesh. Jesus Himself affirms John's declaration by saying that He is the Bread of Life, the Light of the World, the Door of the sheep, the Good Shepherd, the Resurrection and the Life, the Way, the Truth, and the Life, the True Vine. Based on His death and resurrection, Jesus proved again that He was the Son of God, the One who gives eternal life.

Christ in Acts

It is said that Acts is best referred to as the acts of the Holy Spirit. The deeds Jesus' apostles did in the 30 or so years following His return to heaven were empowered by the Holy Spirit. After spending 40 days with His disciples, Jesus ascends to the Father. Ten days later He sends the Holy Spirit to empower His believers to continue to do the work of ministry. This would build on His church wisdom, miracles, signs, and wonders in the Holy Spirit.

Christ in Romans

Paul the apostle, author of Romans, presents the Christ as a descendant of David who according to the flesh was established as the powerful Son of God by the resurrection from the dead (Romans 1:3-4). The righteousness of God and forgiveness of sins is given freely to all those who have faith in Jesus Christ. Salvation was made possible through the death, burial, and resurrection of Jesus Christ.

Christ in 1 Corinthians

Paul, in his letter to the Corinthians, points to Jesus Christ as both the power (1 Corinthians 1:18, 24) and the wisdom (1 Corinthians 1:21, 24, 30) of God. The problems any congregation may have, whether doctrinal or practical, will be resolved as that body of believers submits to the lordship of Christ and practices the art of *agape* (love) toward one another, authentically.

Christ in 2 Corinthians

In Paul's second epistle to the Corinthians, Jesus Christ is portrayed as God's Son. God's goal for the Christian life is to conform us to the image of His Son. This is brought about as Christ works through the Holy Spirit, who dwells in every child of God.

Christ in Galatians

In this letter to the Galatians, Paul emphasizes that no human work can contribute to a person's right standing with God. Salvation comes by faith alone through Christ alone. Why Christ alone? Because He became a curse for us so we can be redeemed from the curses of the law (Galatians 3:13). Christ Himself is our very life (Galatians 2:19-20). No wonder Christians are crucified with Him, yet live.

Christ in Ephesians

Ephesians is another New Testament epistle authored by Paul the apostle. It focuses on the unity between Christ (the head of the church) and the church (the expression of the body of Christ). Ephesians also deals with the unity between Jews and Gentiles in God's greatest masterpiece. Only through His death did Christ bring peace between man and God, as well as between Jews and Gentiles.

Christ in Philippians

In the epistle to the Philippians, Paul presents Jesus as One who existed in the form of God, but did not consider Himself as equal to God because He emptied Himself of all privileges of God by becoming a human being and the servant of all. After Christ's perfect obedience by His sacrificial death on the cross, God highly exalted Him and gave Him the name that is above every name. So that, at the name of Jesus every knee will bow and every tongue confess that He is Lord to the glory of God the Father.

Christ in Colossians

The major theme in Paul's letter to the Colossians is the preeminence of Christ in all things, whether creation or redemption. Christ is not only creator of all things (visible and invisible), but He is also both supreme Lord of the universe and head of the church. Therefore, He is the only One through whom forgiveness is possible, making legal matters or philosophical treaties irrelevant in matters of salvation. The fullness of the Godhead bodily dwells in Christ through Jesus' atoning death, reconciling all things to Himself.

Christ in 1 Thessalonians

First Thessalonians addresses Paul's intent for the believer to know of the imminent return of Christ to earth. "For the Lord Himself will descend from heaven with a shout, with the voice of an archangel, and with the trumpet of God. And the dead in Christ will rise first. Then we who are alive and remain shall be caught up together with them in the clouds to meet the Lord in the air. And thus we shall always be with the Lord" (1 Thessalonians 4:16-17). This text brings hope and comfort to all believers. We will soon join those who have died and be together with the Lord Jesus Christ.

Christ in 2 Thessalonians

In the second epistle to the Thessalonians, Paul outlines divine principles to counter false teachings of end times. The believers are encouraged to stand firm in their faith. At Christ's Second Coming, He will punish both God's enemies and all those who rejected peace made possible by the death of Christ.

Christ in 1 Timothy

Paul masterfully and forcefully presents himself as the worst of sinners. If Christ, whose purpose in coming into the world is to save sinners, saved him, then any sinner can find salvation in Christ. Paul shows himself as the perfect showcase of God's mercy. Paul also summarizes his understanding of "the mystery of godliness" to Timothy, as recited by early Christians: "God was manifested in the flesh, justified in the Spirit, seen by angels, preached among the Gentiles, believed on in the world, received up in glory" (1 Timothy 3:16).

Christ in 2 Timothy

Paul admonishes Timothy, his son in the Lord, in this second epistle to commit the treasure of the gospel to others who would faithfully transmit it to the next generation. Timothy was to follow Paul, just as he (Paul) had committed his eternal destiny to the One who would help him until that Day (2 Timothy 1:12). The rationale for this urging was based on the fact that Christ has abolished death, bringing eternal life through His death, burial, and resurrection.

Christ in Titus

Sound doctrine is the major emphasis of this book. This doctrine is the doctrine of Christ, which is God come in the flesh to redeem human beings from lawlessness. This is in order to create a special people, eager to do good works now and to look forward to Christ's second appearing. In His first coming, Jesus died to "redeem us from every lawless deed and purify for Himself His own special people...." (Titus 2:14). These redeemed people long for the day of full salvation at His return, the "blessed hope" (Titus 2:13) of His appearing.

Christ in Philemon

This is Paul's letter to Philemon. Paul instructs that everyone who has repented of sin (master or slave) is a brother or sister in the Lord. Christ's forgiveness is offered to the rich and poor, slave and free, Jew and Gentile, master and servant alike. In Christ, all become one.

Christ in Hebrews

The author of Hebrews makes a compelling case that Christianity (and Christ) is better than or superior to all other forms of religion (and their founders). Jesus Christ, who is superior to angels, Moses, Joshua, and the Hebrew high priests, made a better sacrifice and established a better covenant, ensuring that the old way is outdated and faith in God is the better way to live. Christ is also God's agent of creation, upholding all things by the power of His Word. He is the source of our faith. He never changes. As the author says, "Jesus Christ is the same yesterday, today, and forever" (Hebrews 13:8).

Christ in James

This epistle is authored by James, probably the half-brother of Jesus. James focuses on the importance of good works as the evidence of genuine faith in Christ Jesus. As such, it perfectly complements Galatians. Jesus' resurrection made James a believer in the salvation He offered. In all the trials and hardships in life, James encourages the believer to exercise patience as he looks forward to the return of Christ.

Christ in 1 Peter

In 1 Peter, Peter emphasizes hope for suffering believers as he reminds them of the sufferings of Christ and the glory that followed His sufferings. Jesus is pictured as the Lamb without blemish. His sinless blood cleanses all who have believed. Nevertheless, believers can expect to suffer as Christ suffered, looking forward with joy to the future of their soon coming Messiah in glory.

Christ in 2 Peter

Peter, in his second epistle, demonstrates the significance of holding firmly to the truth to counter any counterfeit teachings, particularly the truth that Jesus will visibly, bodily, and gloriously return, bringing about the end of the world as it now exists. Peter testifies that he was an eyewitness to the life, death, and resurrection of Jesus in space and time. He further testifies that he, James, and John witnessed Christ's glory on the mount of transfiguration, after hearing the Father uttering these words, "This is My beloved Son, in whom I am well pleased" (2 Peter 1:17).

Christ in 1 John

John, in his first epistle, proclaims that Jesus is the Word of life. He came from heaven to earth and was seen, heard, and touched. He further declares that Jesus came to reveal God to mankind so that man will have fellowship with both God the Father (1 John 1:3) and also with other believers (1 John 1:7). This is made possible because of the blood that cleanses us from all sins, sins that separate us from God.

Christ in 2 John

John, in his second epistle, affirms that Christ has come in the flesh. He warns his readers not to accept any other teachings and not to have fellowship with people who deny or modify this doctrine.

Christ in 3 John

In his third letter, John urges Christians to be committed to "the truth" and to show hospitality, citing Christ as the supreme example. He exhorts his readers not to imitate evil but to imitate the goodness of Christ.

Christ in Jude

Jude, another half-brother of Jesus, is the author of this letter. This letter is a reminder to Christians that we are soldiers of Christ, involved in spiritual warfare. He strongly urges believers to "contend" or continue in the good fight of faith. Soon, the day will come when Jesus will reward His followers. He also encourages believers to know that eternal life is based on the finished work of Jesus (Jude 21).

Christ in Revelation

John, the apostle of Jesus Christ, is author of this book. John declares that Jesus, the Lord of history and glory, will return to earth to destroy all evil opposition to Him and the kingdom of God. John further declares that Christ is the Alpha and Omega, the First and the Last, the One who is coming again. John was instructed by Jesus to write down all the things He would show him, the things that would take place later.

Deity of the Christ

Jesus, the God-man, is a fundamental teaching of the Scriptures. In the Bible, Christ is revealed as divine and human. The principles of the "doctrine of Christ" are mentioned in Hebrews 6:1, as well as in 2 John 9. This doctrine refers to the belief that Jesus is God come "in the flesh" (2

John 7). Thus, the clear teaching about Christ is that He is 100% divine. The Word of God warns believers that "if anyone comes to you and does not bring this doctrine, do not receive him into your house nor greet him; for he who greets him shares in his evil deeds" (2 John 10-11). What a severe admonition!

To authenticate that Jesus Christ was perfectly God and perfectly man while being the promised Messiah, Matthew records nine miracles (Matthew 8:1-9:34; also see John 10:36; Acts 2:22). Specifically, he describes Christ's authority over demonic powers (Matthew 8:16-17,28-34), people (Matthew 8:18-22; 9:9), nature (Matthew 8:23-27), and diseases (Matthew 8:1-15). His humanity is also portrayed in His tiredness (verse 24). Even the disciples marveled when the storms and sea obeyed Him (verses 26-27). Overall, Jesus' miracles display His power and authority over all creation. Other passages in Scripture that affirm Jesus is God are:

- "'Behold, the virgin shall be with child, and bear a Son, and they shall call His name Immanuel,' which is translated, 'God with us'" (Matthew 1:23).
- "Jesus said to them, 'Most assuredly, I say to you, before Abraham was, I AM'" (John 8:58).
- "Jesus said to him [Philip], 'Have I been with you so long, and yet you have not known Me, Philip? He who has seen Me has seen the Father; so how can you say, "Show us the Father?"'" (John 14:9).
- Thomas, after putting his finger into Jesus' hands and side, said "My Lord and my God" (John 20:28).
- "Of whom are the fathers and from whom, according to the flesh, Christ came, who is over all, the eternally blessed God. Amen" (Romans 9:5).
- "Which none of the rulers of this age knew; for had they known, they would not have crucified the Lord of glory" (1 Corinthians 2:8).
- "The first man was of the earth, made of dust; the second Man is the Lord from heaven" (1 Corinthians 15:47).
- "And without controversy great is the mystery of godliness: God was manifested in the flesh, justified in the Spirit, seen by angels, preached among the Gentiles, believed on in the world, [and] received up in glory" (1 Timothy 3:16).

- "Looking for the blessed hope and glorious appearing of our great God and Savior Jesus Christ" (Titus 2:13).
- "But to the Son He [God] says: 'Your throne, O God, is forever and ever; a scepter of righteousness is the scepter of Your kingdom'" (Hebrews 1:8).
- "And we know that the Son of God has come and has given us an understanding, that we may know Him who is true; and we are in Him who is true, in His Son Jesus Christ. This is the true God and eternal life" (1 John 5:20).
- One of the foremost attributes of God is that He is holy. "Be holy, for I am holy" (1 Peter 1:16). Jesus shares the same sinless nature with the Father God. Below are some supportive verses from the Bible that demonstrate Jesus' holiness:
- "For He made Him who knew no sin to be sin for us, that we might become the righteousness of God in Him" (2 Corinthians 5:21).
- "For we do not have a High Priest who cannot sympathize with our weaknesses, but was in all points tempted as we are, yet without sin" (Hebrews 4:15).
- Christ, "who committed no sin, nor was deceit found in His mouth" (1 Peter 2:22).
- "And you know that He was manifested to take away our sins, and in Him there is no sin" (1 John 3:5).

Origins of the Christ

The Scriptures teach that Jesus Christ is eternal. He pre-existed, meaning that He has no beginning or end. Let's examine the following scriptures that affirm this truth. Speaking about the pre-incarnate Christ, the psalmist declares:

- "Before the mountains were brought forth, or ever You had formed the earth and the world, even from everlasting to everlasting, You are God" (Psalm 90:2).
- "Your years are throughout all generations" (Psalm 102:24b).
- "But You are the same, and Your years will have no end" (Psalm 102:27).

Micah predicted: "But you, Bethlehem Ephrathah, though you are little among the thousands of Judah, yet out of you shall come forth to Me the One to be Ruler in Israel, whose goings forth are from old, from everlasting" (Micah 5:2).

Daniel, in his night visions, said, "I was watching in the night visions, and behold, One like the Son of Man, coming with the clouds of heaven! He came to the Ancient of Days, and they brought Him near before Him" (Daniel 7:13).

The New Testament also affirms that Christ has no origin. John the apostle said: "In the beginning was the Word, and the Word was with God, and the Word was God....And the Word became flesh and dwelt among us, and we beheld His glory, the glory as of the only begotten of the Father, full of grace and truth" (John 1:1,14). The term "Word" refers to Jesus, who was God become flesh. The purpose that the Word has become flesh (John 1:14) is so that qualified witnesses can see, touch, and hear the revelation of God (1 John 1:1-4). The author of Hebrews declares, "Jesus Christ is the same yesterday, today, and forever" (Hebrews 13:8).

Birth of Jesus Christ

Before the birth of baby Jesus, God had predetermined that the redemption of the world would be accomplished through Jesus Christ, the Lord of glory. Jesus' birth was carried out by the Holy Spirit. So the seed that was deposited in the womb of Mary by the Holy Spirit was the holy seed of God. When God became human in the person of Jesus Christ, He had a body. "Therefore, when He came into the world, He said, 'Sacrifice and offering You did not desire, but a body You have prepared for Me'" (Hebrews 10:5); a soul, "Now my soul is troubled, and what shall I say? 'Father, save Me from this hour?' But for this purpose I came to this hour" (John 12:27); and a spirit, "But immediately, when Jesus perceived in His spirit that they reasoned thus within themselves" (Mark 2:8; see also Luke 23:46).

Even though Jesus took on a human body, He was still one with the Father and Holy Spirit in essence, power, and glory. "I and My Father are one" (John 10:30; see also John 12:44-45; 17:11- 12; 16:5-15). Before Jesus was born, His birth was prophesied. Isaiah announced, "Therefore the Lord Himself will give you a sign: Behold, the virgin shall conceive and bear a

Son, and shall call His name Immanuel" (Isaiah 7:14). Isaiah further said, "For unto us a Child is born, unto us a Son is given; and the government will be upon His shoulder. And His name will be called Wonderful, Counselor, Mighty God, Everlasting Father, Prince of Peace" (Isaiah 9:6).

Matthew comes on the scene 700 years later to announce the fulfillment of Isaiah's prediction. "'Behold, the virgin shall be with child, and bear a Son, and they shall call His name Immanuel,' which is translated, 'God with us'" (Matthew 1:23; also see Luke 1:31,34-35). Jesus fulfilled hundreds of Old Testament prophecies. In the table below, some of such fulfilled predictions are listed. Notice the remarkable similarities between the Old Testament prophecies and their New Testament fulfillment in the chart below.

Prophecy	Old Testament Prediction	New Testament Fulfillment
The Messiah would be the seed of a woman	Genesis 3:15	Galatians 4:4
The Messiah would be a descendant of Abraham	Genesis 12:3	Matthew 1:1
The Messiah would be a descendant of Israel	Genesis 17:19	Luke 3:34
The Messiah would be a descendant of Jacob	Numbers 24:17	Matthew 1:2; 2:2
The Messiah would be from the tribe of Judah	Genesis 49:10	Luke 3:33
The Messiah would be an heir of the throne of David	Isaiah 9:7	Luke 1:32-33
The Messiah would be born in Bethlehem	Micah 5:2	Luke 2:4-5,7
The Messiah would be born of a virgin	Isaiah 7:14	Luke 1:26-27,30-31

Prophecy	Old Testament Prediction	New Testament Fulfillment
The Messiah's birth would trigger a slaughter of children	Jeremiah 31:15	Matthew 2:16-18
The Messiah would also come from Egypt	Hosea 11:1	Matthew 2:14-15
The Messiah would be sold for 30 pieces of silver	Zechariah 11:12-13	Matthew 27:5,7-8
The Messiah's triumphant entry into Jerusalem	Psalm 118:26	Matthew 21:1-10
The Messiah would be buried in a rich man's tomb	Isaiah 53:9	John 19:38-42
The Messiah's bones were not to be broken	Exodus 12:46	John 19:31-36
The Messiah would justify many from their sins	Isaiah 53:12	Romans 5:15-19
The Messiah would die with transgressors	Isaiah 53:12	Mark 15:27-28; Luke 22:37
The Messiah would resurrect from the dead	Psalm 16:10	Matthew 27:53
The Messiah's body would not see corruption (decay)	Psalm 16:10	Acts 2:24-31; 13:35-37
The Messiah would be forsaken by the Father	Psalm 22:1	Matthew 27:38-46
The Messiah would be exalted	Isaiah 52:13	Philippians 2:9
The Messiah is now at God's right hand	Psalm 110:1	Mark 16:19; Luke 20:42

Jesus' Life and Ministry

One thing that distinguished Jesus' humanity from the rest of the other human beings is His sinless life. He was conceived by the Virgin Mary without sin. Luke records Mary's encounter with an angel. "Then Mary said to the angel, 'How can this be, since I do not know a man?' And the angel answered and said to her, 'The Holy Spirit will come upon you, and the power of the Highest will overshadow you; therefore, also, that Holy One who is to be born will be called the Son of God'" (Luke 1:34-35; see also 1 John 3:5).

Because of His sinless life, Jesus had the power to forgive sins. John the apostle records what Jesus' forerunner, John the Baptist, said, "Behold! The Lamb of God who takes away the sin of the world!" (John 1:29). Later in his epistle, John declared, "And you know that He was manifested to take away our sins, and in Him there is no sin" (1 John 3:5; see also Isaiah 53:9; Matthew 9:1-8).

Dr. Luke attests to the fact that even Pilate was able to testify that Jesus was without sin. "Then Pilate, when he had called together the chief priests, the rulers, and the people, said to them, 'You have brought this Man to me, as one who misleads the people. And indeed, having examined Him in your presence, I have found no fault in this man concerning those things of which you accuse Him'" (Luke 23:13-14).

It must be emphasized that since Jesus' conception was initiated by the Holy Spirit through a young virgin, Jesus did not inherit our sinful Adamic nature; hence, His early life was void of sin as well. Only God the Father and the Holy Spirit are without sin. Jesus voluntarily exchanged His glory for flesh because only a human could experience sin. Although Jesus never sinned nor broke God's law, He allowed His purity to be violated by our wickedness. Indeed, God made Jesus "who knew no sin to be sin for us, that we might become the righteousness of God in Him" (2 Corinthians 5:21).

Jesus not only has power to forgive sins, but He also has authority over created things because He is co-creator with God the Father and Holy Spirit. "Then God said, 'Let *Us* make man in *Our* image, according to *Our* likeness...'" (Genesis 1:26, emphasis added; also see Colossians 1:16). He exercised His awesome power over nature. Mark documents

Jesus' authority over the wind and the waves: "Now when they had left the multitude, they took Him along in the boat as He was. And other little boats were also with Him. And a great windstorm arose, and the waves beat into the boat, so that it was already filling. But He was in the stern, asleep on a pillow. And they awoke Him and said to Him, 'Teacher, do You not care that we are perishing?' Then He arose and rebuked the wind, and said to the sea, 'Peace, be still!' And the wind ceased and there was a great calm" (Mark 4:36-39).

Jesus also commanded an unclean spirit out of a man in the synagogue. Jesus rebuked the spirit, saying "Be quiet, and come out of him" (Mark 1:25). The people of Capernaum were amazed and asked, "What new doctrine is this?" Another miracle that Jesus performed was the healing of Peter's mother-in-law from a fever. Jesus "took her by the hand and lifted her up, and immediately the fever left her. And she served them" (Mark 1:30-31). Still another miracle Jesus wrought was raising back to life the ruler of the synagogue's daughter. Jesus "took the [dead] child by the hand, and said to her, 'Talitha, cumi' which is translated, 'Little girl, I say to you, arise'" (Mark 5:41; see also Matthew 20:28; John 17:2-3; 1 John 5:11).

Besides the wonderful miracles Jesus performed, He accepted worship as God and claimed to deserve the same honor as the Father. When the disciples saw Jesus walking on the sea, they exclaimed, "It is a ghost!" But Jesus comforted them saying, "Be of good cheer! It is I; do not be afraid." When Jesus entered the boat, the disciples in the boat came and worshipped Him, saying, "Truly you are the Son of God" (Matthew 14:26-27,33; see also 28:17-18; John 5:22-23; 9:38; 17:5). Jesus claimed to be the divine Son of God, a title the Jews *rightly* understand to be a claim of equality with God.

Jesus healed a paralyzed man on the Sabbath. According to the Jewish religious leaders, this act was seen as a violation deserving of the death penalty. The Jews, therefore, sought to kill Jesus, not only because He healed on the Sabbath, but also because He said that God was His Father, making Himself equal with God. He demanded honor just as they honored the Father (John 5:16-23; see also 10:30; 19:7).

Below is a chart that compares some characteristics between God the Father and God the Son:

A Comparison of Some Attributes Between God the Father and God the Son

Attributes Unique to God	Attributes of Jesus
Creation is the work of His hands alone (Genesis 1:1; Psalm 102:25; Isaiah 44:24)	Creation is the work of His hands – all things created in and through Him (John 1:3; Colossians 1:16; Hebrews 1:2,10)
The first and the last (Isaiah 44:6)	"The first and the last" (Revelation 1:17; 22:13)
"Lord of lords" (Deuteronomy 10:17; Psalm 136:3)	"Lord of lords" (1 Timothy 6:15; Revelation 17:14; 19:16)
Unchanging and eternal (Psalm 90:2; 102:26-27; Malachi 3:6)	Unchanging and eternal (John 8:58; Colossians 1:17; Hebrews 1:11-12; 13:8)
Only Savior; no other God can save (Isaiah 43:11; 45:21-22; Hosea 13:4)	Savior of the world; no salvation apart from Him (John 4:42; Acts 4:12; Titus 2:13; 1 John 4:4)
Redeems from their sins a people for His own possession (Exodus 19:5; Psalm 130:7-8; Ezekiel 37:23)	Redeems from their sins a people for His own possession (Titus 2:14)
Hears and answers prayers of those who call on Him (Psalm 86:5-7; Isaiah 55:6-7; Jeremiah 33:3; Joel 2:32; Isaiah 65:24)	Hears and answers prayers of those who call on Him (John 14:14; Romans 10:12-13; 2 Corinthians 12:8-9; 1 Peter 3:12)
Only God has divine glory (Isaiah 42:8; 48:11) and was worshipped by angels (Psalm 97:7)	Jesus has divine glory (John 17:5) and was worshipped by angels (Hebrews 1:6)

Jesus is Fully Man and Fully God

Furthermore, the Scriptures teach that Jesus Christ the Lord was fully man. As a child, He grew physically, intellectually, socially, and spiritually (Luke 2:40,52). Later, in His adult years, He experienced some sinless limitation of human life. He was hungry (Matthew 4:2), weary, grew tired (John 4:6), thirsty (John 19:28), slept (Matthew 8:24), and sweated (Luke 22:44).

However, the Bible also clearly shows that Jesus was fully God. While on earth, Jesus did what only God could do. He commanded the forces of nature to submission (Matthew 8:23-27; 14:22,33), forgave sins (Mark 2:1-12), *rightly* claimed to be superior to the Sabbath (John 5:17-18), and gave life to whomever He pleased (John 5:19-23). Paul declared that God purchased the church with His own blood (Acts 20:28). Finally, all the fullness of God's deity, power, glory, and being resides in Jesus' risen body (Colossians 2:9).

Jesus' Mission

Jesus Christ, the Lord, came to earth for the purpose of preaching the Kingdom of God. His message is called the Good news. He said to His disciples, "Let us go into the next towns, that I may preach there also, because for this purpose I have come forth" (Mark 1:38). Why? Because His ultimate goal was that "the kingdoms of this world have become the kingdoms of our Lord and of His Christ, and He shall reign forever and ever" (Revelation 11:15). To this end, He gave His disciples power and authority to cast out demons, preach the kingdom of God, cure diseases, and heal the sick (Luke 9:1-2). Like His disciples, He came to seek and save that which was lost (Luke 19:10), destroy the works of the enemy (1 John 3:8), give His life as a ransom (Mark 10:45), and enter once and for all into the Holy Place with His own blood (Hebrews 9:24-25), thus obtaining eternal redemption (Hebrews 9:12), and thereby reconciling the world to God (2 Corinthians 5:19).

Some Common Attributes of the Father, the Son, and the Holy Spirit

Divine Attributes	FATHER	SON	HOLY SPIRIT
Eternal	Romans 16:26-27	Revelation 1:17	Hebrews 9:14
Creator of all things	Psalm 100:3	Colossians 1:16	Psalm 104:30
Gives life	Genesis 1:11-31; John 5:21	John 1:4; 5:21	Romans 8:10-11; John 3:8
Wills and acts supernaturally	Ephesians 1:5	Matthew 8:31	1 Corinthians 12:11
Strengthens believers	Psalm 138:3	Philippians 4:13	Ephesians 3:16
Omnipresent (capable of being all places at once)	Jeremiah 23:24	Ephesians 1:23	Psalm 139:7
Omniscient (knows all things)	1 John 3:20	John 21:17	1 Corinthians 2:10
God	1 Corinthians 15:24	John 5:16-23	Acts 5:3-4

Therefore, we know:

- Jesus Christ is Omniscient (John 16:30).
- Jesus Christ is Omnipresent (Matthew 28:20).
- Jesus Christ is Omnipotent (Matthew 28:18).
- Jesus Christ is Immutable (Hebrews 13:8).
- Jesus Christ is Eternal (Revelation 1:17).

Jesus' Death and Resurrection

Jesus Christ, the Lord of glory, came to earth in human form to die. He bled and died on Calvary's cross. "So when Jesus had received the sour wine, He said, 'It is finished!' And bowing His head, He gave up His spirit...but one of the soldiers pierced His side with a spear, and immediately blood and water came out" (John 19:30,34). He was buried in Joseph's tomb. "Now in the place where He was crucified there was a garden, and in the garden a new tomb in which no one had yet been laid. So there they laid Jesus, because of the Jews' Preparation Day, for the tomb was nearby" (John 19:41-42; compare Matthew 27:57-61; Mark 15:42-47; Luke 23:50-56).

Jesus Christ, the Lord of glory, rose triumphantly from the dead! Matthew testifies, "He is not here; for He is risen, as He said. Come, see the place where the Lord lay. And go quickly and tell His disciples that He is risen from the dead, and indeed He is going before you into Galilee; there you will see Him. Behold, I have told you" (Matthew 28:6-7). After His resurrection from the dead, He ate and drank with people and let them see His scars and touch His body (Luke 24:39-43; John 20:27-29; Acts 10:41). Jesus later made appearances to Mary to prove that He had conquered death and the grave. Central to the Christian faith is the bodily resurrection of Jesus; and by recording, the resurrection appearance in the four gospels provides positive proof of this monumental and historic event. His appearances took places in or around Jerusalem:

- To Mary Magdalene (Mark 16:9; John 20:11-18)
- To other women (Matthew 28:8-10)
- To Peter (Luke 24:34)
- To ten disciples (Luke 24:36-43; John 20:19-25)
- To the eleven disciples including Thomas (Mark 16:14; John 20:26-29)

- To the disciples on the Emmaus road (Mark 16:12-13; Luke 24:13-35)
- In Galilee (Matthew 28:16-20; John 21:1-24)
- To five hundred people (1 Corinthians 15:6)
- To James and the apostles (1 Corinthians 15:7)
- At the Ascension (Mark 16:19-20; Luke 24:50-53; Acts 1:9-11)
- To Paul on the road to Damascus (Acts 9:1-6; 22:1-10; 26:12-18; 1 Corinthians 15:8)

After 40 days on earth, Jesus ascended to heaven. "Now when He had spoken these things, while they watched, He was taken up, and a cloud received Him out of their sight. And while they looked steadfastly toward heaven as He went up, behold, two men stood by them in white apparel, who also said, 'Men of Galilee, why do you stand gazing up into heaven? This same Jesus, who was taken up from you into heaven, will so come in like manner as you saw Him go into heaven'" (Acts 1:9-11; see also Mark 16:19-20; Luke 24:50-53).

In closing, Jesus Christ, the Lord of glory, spoke everything into existence (Genesis 1:1), holds the universe by the word of His power (Hebrews 1:3), and through Him all things exist and without Him nothing exists (John 1:3).

CHAPTER 2

Repentance from Dead Works

"Repent therefore and be converted, that your sins may be blotted out,
so that times of refreshing may come from the presence of the Lord."
(Acts 3:19)

This chapter sets forth to define and discuss the concepts of "repentance and dead works" (Hebrews 6:1), as well as other concepts associated with the fundamental teachings on salvation and reconciliation. Precisely and biblically, just what do these words mean?

Definitions

Repentance

Repentance is translated from the Greek word *metanoia*. *Metanoia* is a compound word which becomes two words when broken up - *meta* which stands for a change and *noia* which means mind. Thus, the word *metanoia* means a change of mind and focus. But what does this mean biblically? Scripturally speaking, a sinner recognizes his sinful state and immediately admits to offending a holy God. In other words, repentance implies not only sorrow about sin but a complete turnaround to change one's mind about sin, Satan, and the world, and receive God's provision of salvation and a wholehearted return to Him. The biblical concept of *sin* is to "miss the mark" or fall short of God's holy standard. "For all have sinned and fall short of the glory of God" (Romans 3:23).

Dead Works

God's standard for salvation is perfection. God is holy and perfect. "But as He who called you is holy, you also be holy in all your conduct, because it is written, 'Be holy, for I am holy'" (1 Peter 1:15-16). Because God is holy, He cannot have fellowship or a relationship with sinful man. Therefore, all of man's efforts, works, religion, and morals cannot earn him God's favor. A few texts support this truth. The prophet Isaiah said, "But we are all like an unclean thing, and all our righteousnesses are like filthy rags" (Isaiah 64:6). Apostle Paul wrote: "Knowing that a man is not justified by the works of the law but by faith in Jesus Christ, even we have believed in Christ Jesus, that we might be justified by faith in Christ and not by the works of the law; for by the works of the law no flesh shall be justified" (Galatians 2:16). In Romans 3:10 we read, "There is none righteous, no, not one." And the writer of Hebrews states, "How much more shall the blood of Christ, who through the eternal Spirit offered Himself without spot to God, cleanse your conscience from dead works to serve the living God" (Hebrews 9:14).

Confession

In the process of repentance, the sinner articulates a confession of sins, agreeing with God's righteous view of sin and speaking the same. The Greek word *confession* (homologeo: logeo=say, homo=same) means "to say the same thing as". Therefore, when we confess to God, we say what He says about our sins. In other words, a sinner admits the truth about what God is saying concerning his condition. Romans 10:9 says, "If you confess with your mouth the Lord Jesus and believe in your heart that God has raised Him from the dead, you will be saved."

Theologically, there are two views of the concept of confession. In one sense, confession is the "casting off" of sin by acknowledging our transgression of God's commandments for holy living. Proverbs 28:13 states, "He who covers his sins will not prosper, but whoever confesses and forsakes them will have mercy." Paul writing to Timothy, affirms this truth, "Nevertheless the solid foundation of God stands, having this seal: 'The Lord knows those who are His,' and 'Let everyone who names the name of Christ depart from iniquity'" (2 Timothy 2:19).

In another sense, confession of sin is thanksgiving because it recognizes that forgiveness of sin is accomplished only by grace through Christ alone and by the goodness of God. Daniel said, "And I prayed to the Lord my God, and made confession, and said, 'O Lord, great and awesome God, who keeps His covenant and mercy with those who love Him, and with those who keep His commandments'" (Daniel 9:4).

Two distinct paths are provided in Scripture for the sinner and the saint to obtain the forgiveness of sins.

Sinner

The sinner initially repents from sin by acknowledging their helpless condition. On the day of Pentecost, Peter, under the anointing of the Holy Spirit, gave a powerful presentation of the Gospel to a crowd of sinners. Many were "cut to the heart" and said to Peter and the rest of the apostles, "Men and brethren, what shall we do?" Then Peter said to them, "Repent, and let every one of you be baptized in the name of Jesus Christ for the remission of sins; and you shall receive the gift of the Holy Spirit" (Acts 2:37-38). Through this process, a sinner establishes a new *relationship* with God through Jesus Christ. John says, "But as many as received Him, to them He gave the right to become children of God, to those who believe in His name" (John 1:12).

Saint

A believing sinner commits sin either knowingly or unknowingly. God understands our frail nature even though we are His children and have a personal relationship with Him. Nevertheless, He has made a provision by which we can have daily (ongoing) cleansing of our sins and trespasses. In 1 John 1:8-9, the apostle John wrote, "If we say that we have no sin, we deceive ourselves, and the truth is not in us. If we confess our sins, He is faithful and just to forgive our sins and to cleanse us from all unrighteousness." John's letter was written to Christians (saints) and not to unbelievers. Our confession is to restore fellowship with God, not to establish a relationship. This brings to an in-depth study of why man is depraved and totally helpless to save himself from sin and Satan.

The Depravity of Man

At Creation

At creation, "The Lord God formed man of the dust of the ground, and breathed into his nostrils the breath of life; and man became a living being" (Genesis 2:7). In the beginning, Adam and Eve were perfectly created and because of their perfect state, they had fellowship with God and were designed to live forever. The author of Ecclesiastes said that, "[God] put eternity in their hearts, except that no one can find out the work that God does from beginning to end" (Ecclesiastes 3:11).

Apostle Paul further elaborates on the creation story by explaining that "...your whole spirit, soul, and body be preserved blameless at the coming of our Lord Jesus Christ" (1 Thessalonians 5:23). Although this verse is a part of Paul's prayer for the Thessalonians that they may be sanctified in all aspects of their life – spirit, soul, and body – this scripture also contains an important theological lesson. At creation, man was made spirit, soul, and body. The spirit and soul of man are from above, but the body is from the dust. Elsewhere, Paul teaches that there are three types of spirits in the world. "God has revealed them to us through His Spirit. For the Spirit searches all things, yes, the deep things of God. For what man knows the things of a man except the spirit of the man which is in him?...Now we have received, not the spirit of the world, but the Spirit who is from God, that we might know the things that have been freely given to us by God" (1 Corinthians 2:10-12).

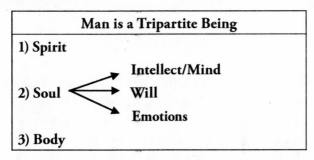

Man is a Tripartite Being
1) Spirit
2) Soul — Intellect/Mind, Will, Emotions
3) Body

The Spirit

The Bible teaches that man is made in the image and likeness of God. Since God is Person (personality), man reflects the personhood of God through his human personality, made up of intellect, emotion, will, and moral awareness. At creation, God breathed His Spirit into man (i.e., his body from the dust) and man became a living being. Then Satan came afterward and tempted Adam and Eve in the beautiful Garden of Eden. They were deceived and ate the forbidden fruit (Genesis 3:6). All of a sudden, with no one around them, they were ashamed (Genesis 2:25). Their lovely naiveté or innocence was replaced by evil thoughts, a rebellious will, and unstable emotions. Not only did man lose his sinless nature, but the Spirit of God in him. From that moment on, our first parents could not relate to God because their spirits were lifeless and a huge gap or barrier was created between man and God.

Man	Separated	God
Spirit		
Soul	Gap/Barrier	Spirit of God
Body		

Theologians have coined the word "depravity" to describe the fallen state of man. Man is totally depraved; as such he cannot even commune with God as he did before he rebelled. Man in his natural state is incapable or unable to do anything on his own to please or gain merit before God. Also, he is depraved of any urging to seek after God and lives in complete rebellion against God. By his "free will" he cannot and will never make a decision to unite and follow Christ. Furthermore, he is unable to discern the will of God, the mind of God, the truth of the Gospel, or understand when it is presented to him.

The Soul

The soul of man constitutes the intellect or mind (which is different from the brain), the will, and our emotions which are now tainted by sin. "The natural man does not receive the things of the Spirit of God, for they are foolishness to him; nor can he know them, because they are spiritually discerned" (1 Corinthians 2:14). Another reason why the natural man cannot understand the Gospel is because "it is veiled to those who are perishing, whose minds the god of this age has blinded, who do not believe..." (2 Corinthians 4:3b-4a). Not only is the mind or intellect of the natural man tainted by sin, his emotions and will are affected as well.

Apostle Paul, in his letter to the Ephesians, describes the natural man as dead in sins and separated from God (Ephesians 2:1-3).

The Body

The flesh constantly tempts our bodies toward lust, laziness, overindulgence, and sexual immorality. The flesh wants to use the body as a vehicle for its evil expressions. A classic example is the sad episode of King David and Bathsheba (2 Samuel 11:2-27). King David's lustful passion got the better part of him, and he ended up not only committing adultery and murder but devising a demonic plan to cover it all up.

God's Redemption Plan Revealed

As said earlier, the natural man's will is reflective of God's will. Man has the duty and ability to make moral choices based on his understanding and motivations. But because man's will is continually rebellious and does not understand the will of God, he does not have the capacity to repent, believe, and receive salvation. Therefore, God, in the integrity of His awesome nature, could not ask man to do what he is incapable of doing nor could He hold man responsible for all choices, whether good or evil, because the right choices are not inherent in man. Since God must judge sin, although His love constrains Him from sending man to hell, it would be contrary to God's holy character to punish man for his lack of responding to that which he could not do. In His divine and infinite wisdom and mercy, He chose a source and person outside of sinful man, the God-man Jesus the Christ. So man's salvation is predicated on faith *alone* in Christ *alone*.

At conversion, the spirit of man is regenerated as God infuses His Spirit into the human spirit. "It is the Spirit who gives life; the flesh profits nothing. The words that I speak to you are spirit, and they are life," said Jesus (John 6:63). Also at conversion, the soul of the natural man is brought back to life to relate to God. The author of Hebrews says this concerning the Word of God, "For the word of God is living and powerful, and sharper than any two-edged sword, piercing even to the division of soul and spirit, and of joints and marrow, and is a discerner of the thoughts and intents of the heart" (Hebrews 4:12). God's message is alive and active, penetrating the innermost parts of the soul. The Word of God exposes the natural and spiritual motivations of the believer as well as the unbeliever's heart. The remedy for man's dead soul is the Word of God.

At the rapture, our lowly bodies instantly will be transformed into glorified bodies to match our heavenly citizenship. Then our bodies will be glorified to be conformed to Christ's glorified body. Apostle Paul said, "For we who are in this tent groan, being burdened, not because we want to be unclothed, but further clothed, that mortality may be swallowed up by life" (2 Corinthians 5:4). Writing later to the Philippians about our mortal bodies at the rapture, Paul said, "For our citizenship is in heaven, from which we also eagerly wait for the Savior, the Lord Jesus Christ, who will transform our lowly body that it may be conformed to His glorious body, according to the working by which He is able even to subdue all things to Himself" (Philippians 3:20-21).

Rationale for Salvation?

In Ephesians 2:14-16, Paul speaks of human depravity. Sin had placed a barrier of separation between God and man. As long as this separation existed, there was no probability of fellowship between God and man. This separation, or literally the dividing wall mentioned in Ephesians 2:14 referred historically to the dividing wall in the temple in Jerusalem. This wall separated the court of the Gentiles from the rest of the temple and excluded the Gentiles from the inner sanctums. However, this wall was a picture of the spiritual barrier that stands between God and the natural man which precludes his access into God's presence. Only the Jews could go beyond the dividing wall, but this was possible because they had access through their God-given sacrificial system which eventually pointed to the person and work of Christ, the Messiah, the One who would come and take away the barrier and make peace with God for all eternity. The Bible teaches five walls of separation that Jesus had to break down to offer mankind a permanent and lasting relationship with God the Father.

Wall of Separation 1: The Holiness of God (1 Peter 1:16)

The Scriptures declare that God is love (1 John 4:8), but more is mentioned in the Bible of God's holiness than God's love. The prophet Isaiah declared that His "name is Holy" (Isaiah 57:15). Earlier, Isaiah proclaimed that the cherubim continually announce the holiness of God (Isaiah 6:3). When

Isaiah had a revelation of God's absolute holiness, he cried out, "Woe is me, for I am undone. Because I am a man of unclean lips, and I dwell in the midst of a people of unclean lips; for my eyes have seen the King; the Lord of hosts" (Isaiah 6:5). Habakkuk also spoke of the holiness of God and said, "You are of purer eyes than to behold evil, and cannot look on wickedness" (Habakkuk 1:13). Apostle Peter affirmed that, "He who called you is holy... be holy, for I [God] am holy" (1 Peter 1:15-16). John equally wrote, "God is light and in Him is no darkness at all" (1 John 1:15).

In 2 Timothy 4:8, Paul called God the righteous Judge. Even the patriarchs of the Old Testament had a revelation of God as a just God. Abraham confessed God as the judge of all the earth who had to act in accordance with His holy justice (Genesis 18:25). Moses also proclaimed God's holy character. "He is the Rock, His work is perfect; for all His ways are justice, a God of truth and without injustice; righteous and upright is He" (Deuteronomy 32:4). These and many other passages point to the perfect holiness of God and stress the fact that God cannot and will never act contrary to His holy nature. Because of God's holy nature, He cannot have fellowship and communion with sinful man or anything less than His perfect standard of holiness. It is imperative to understand that the holiness of God has two branches: perfect righteousness and perfect justice. God has revealed Himself to us as absolutely righteous and perfect. It is impossible for God to do anything wrong or to have fellowship with anything less than His perfect righteousness. Since God is also perfectly just, which acts in accord with His perfect righteousness, He cannot be partial or unfair to any creature and He must deal with all of creation in perfect justice. This means all that is unrighteous or sinful must be judged and separated from Him. Other passages that support this truth are Psalm 119:137-138; 145:17; Habakkuk 1:13; Romans 2:5-6,11; 1:18; 14:11-12; 1 Peter 4:5.

Wall of Separation 2: The Son of Man (Romans 3:23)

Scripture teaches that man is cut off from God because of his sins. Sin has created a barrier between God and man, thus hindering access to God. Romans 3:23 declares that all have sinned and fall short (missed the mark) of the glory of God (His perfect, holy character). In Isaiah 59:1-2, the prophet said, "Behold, the Lord's hand is not shortened, that it cannot save; nor His ear heavy, that it cannot hear. But your iniquities have separated you from your God; and your sins have hidden His face from you, so that He will not hear." So, the unbelievers can only come to God through Christ who alone is *the* Way, *the* Truth, and *the* Life (John 14:6; see also Acts 4:12). This also is true for the believers in Christ, even though they are saved and have unhindered access to God in Christ. Fellowship with God as His children is broken by known sin, which must be confessed so that the vital communion with God can be restored and their prayers answered (Psalm 66:18).

The Bible teaches three specific aspects of man in sin that make up this dividing wall of separation:

Imputed Sin

Romans 5:12 teaches us about imputed sin. Adam, the first parent of the human race sinned, and through our natural relationship to him, his sin is imputed (credited, reckoned) to the entire human race. Therefore, God views the human race as though we all sinned in Adam or with Adam. Another view of God, as Paul explained, is that God's grace and mercy are extended to mankind. In Romans 5:12-18, Paul said for just as Adam's sin was imputed to every man as being a descendant of Adam because of Adam's one act of sin, so Christ's righteousness is imputed to all who become children of God by faith in Christ because of His one act of righteousness. As such, Adam was a type of Christ (Romans 5:14).

Inherited Sin

The Bible teaches that as the posterity of Adam, every child is born with a sinful nature inherited from his parents. Many passages of Scripture refer to this truth. According to Ephesians 2:1-3, all are declared dead in sin and are "by nature children of wrath." Other key verses that speak to this truth are Genesis 5:3, Psalm 51:5, 58:3, 1 Peter 2:10. It is important to stress that men do not sin and become sinners, rather they sin because by nature they are sinners.

Individual or Personal Sin

Although it is biblical to view sin from the perspective of mankind as a group, the concept of personal sin is equally relevant. The actual deeds or acts of sin which the individual commits are because the person is basically sinful. References to personal sins are well documented in Romans 3:10-11, 12b, 18, 23 and Galatians 5:19-21.

Wall of Separation 3: The Penalty of Sin

Earlier, it was stated that God's holiness had two branches: perfect righteousness and perfect justice. Since God is holy and man is sinful, God's perfect justice must act against man to charge him as guilty under the penalty of sin with a debt to pay and a sentence to serve. Thus, the law of the Old Testament functions as a standard of indictment. It shows that man is guilty under the penalty of sin. This is made clear from the following passages:

- "Now we know that whatever the law says, it says to those who are under the law, that every mouth may be stopped, and all the world may become guilty before God. Therefore by the deeds of the law no flesh will be justified in His sight, for by the law is the knowledge of sin" (Romans 3:19-20).
- "What purpose then does the law serve? It was added because of transgressions, till the Seed should come to whom the promise was made; and it was appointed through angels by the hand of a mediator" (Galatians 3:19).
- "For as many of you as were baptized into Christ have put on Christ" (Galatians 3:27).
- "Having wiped out the handwriting of requirements that was against us, which was contrary to us. And He has taken it out of the way, having nailed it to the cross" (Colossians 2:14).

The "handwriting of requirements that was against us" refers to the law and its indictment that man is under the penalty of sin, which is death. Man must pay the sin debt. However, the debt cannot be paid by religion or good works or morality because the debt is so great that man is unable to pay. Man is dead (Ephesians 2:1) and incapacitated in his sinful condition (see Romans 3:9-23; Ephesians 2:1-3). Romans 1:18-3:23 teaches that all men are in the same boat, whether immoral (Romans 1:18-32) or moral (Romans 2:1-16) or religious (Romans 2:17-3:8). All have missed the mark of God's righteous standards and are under the penalty of sin, which is death (Romans 3:9-20,23; 6:23). Here is the key: Man's only hope is the righteousness of God which He supplies through faith alone in the person and work of Jesus Christ (Romans 3:21-5:21). Later, we shall discuss how the work of God in Christ breaks down all the dividing walls of hostility and builds an eternal bridge that connects man to his God forever.

Wall of Separation 4: Spiritual Death

In 1 Corinthians 15:22, Paul teaches that "in Adam all die." In other words, man's position in Adam brings spiritual death, which eventually leads to physical death, and ultimately eternal death – eternal separation from God. Romans 6:23 tells us "the wages of sin is death," and in Romans 5:12 we read, "Therefore, just as through one man sin entered the world, and death through sin, and thus death spread to all men, because all sinned." Death is a tragic consequence of sin (see Genesis 2:17; 1 Corinthians 15:21,56; Ephesians 2:1,5; Colossians 2:13). The point of these verses is that death, whether physical or spiritual, is a product of man's position in Adam and his own personal sin. This means that man in himself is without spiritual life and spiritual capacity. The result of this is spiritual bankruptcy and total failure. No matter how hard man tries, morally or religiously, he fails colossally and falls short of God's holy character and standard. Man simply cannot save himself, no matter how hard he tries and no matter how sincere he is. This is why the Savior told Nicodemus, a very religious man, "You must be born again" (John 3:3-7). Christ taught this religious man that he desperately needed spiritual renewal, a new spiritual birth from above that is accomplished only by the Spirit of God in order to see, understand, and become a part of God's kingdom people.

So man is not only separated from God by sin, by God's holy character, and by the penalty of sin, but he is faced with the problem of spiritual death and the need for spiritual life. Being spiritually dead, man needs spiritual life and eternal life which can only come through the new birth and a new position in Christ as the only source of life.

Wall of Separation 5: Unrighteousness

The prophet Isaiah writes, "But we are all like an unclean thing, and all our righteousnesses are like filthy rags; we all fade as a leaf, and our iniquities, like the wind, have taken us away" (Isaiah 64:6). Quoting Psalm 14:1-3, the apostle Paul exclaims, "As it is written: 'There is none righteous, no, not one'" (Romans 3:10). For any man to have fellowship with a righteous God, he must have a standing righteousness equal to God's. But because of man's condition, dead in sin, he can *never* establish a righteousness of his own sufficient enough to pass the righteous judgment of God.

This is the grave mistake of the typical religious person who, by his morality and religious practices, attempts to establish his own good standard before God. This mistake is two-fold: First, he does not recognize the absolute awesome holiness of God's character. For him and many others, God is simply an elevated man, as some declare—the man upstairs. Second, such a person does not see the effect of sin as deadly, which mars his or her ability to please God. Having divine clarity on this very thing, the apostle Paul had this to say in Romans 10:1-4 when he wrote of his religious brethren—the Jews: "Brethren, my heart's desire and prayer to God for Israel is that they may be saved. For I bear them witness that they have a zeal for God, but not according to knowledge. For they being ignorant of God's righteousness, and seeking to establish their own righteousness, have not submitted to the righteousness of God. For Christ is the end of the law for righteousness to everyone who believes."

Therefore, from God's standpoint, all human efforts of good or righteous practices are first dead works and worthless of acceptance by God (Romans 4:1-4; Hebrews 6:1; 9:14). What then is the solution to mankind's dilemma, of this five-fold dividing wall of separation? The only solution is God's work of grace in the person and work of the Lord Jesus Christ. This work of grace in the grand scheme of things is called reconciliation. Second Corinthians 5:18-19 says, "Now all things are of God, who has reconciled us to Himself through Jesus Christ, and has given us the ministry of reconciliation, that is, that God was in Christ reconciling the world to Himself, not imputing [recounting] their trespasses to them, and has committed to us the word of reconciliation."

The Work of Salvation
The Breaking Down of the Dividing Wall of Separation

The Concept of Reconciliation

Reconciliation in Scripture means the sinner who is separated and alienated from God can be restored to fellowship with a holy God. How? Through that which God has accomplished for man in the person and work of His Son, the Lord Jesus Christ. Remarkably, this work of God in Christ results in the reconciliation of the believing sinner to God.

The English word "reconcile" means to cause to be friendly again; to bring back to harmony, make peace – to change from enmity or disharmony to friendship and harmony. We can properly translate the word according to Paul's expressed idea of the "completeness" of reconciliation (Ephesians 2:4-6; Colossians 1:20-21). Of course, the concept of reconciliation is not limited to "reconcile" when Scripture speaks of "peace with God" (Romans 5:1), of Christ as our "peace" (Ephesians 2:15-17); this is reconciliation, the work of God in Christ to remove the enmity that exists between God and man (Romans 5:1-11).

We understand, therefore, that reconciliation is the perfect and complete work of God in Christ by which man is brought from a place of enmity to harmony or peace with God (Romans 5:1). Scripture teaches other terms of God's gracious work in Christ like redemption, justification, regeneration, and propitiation, but reconciliation, in my view, is perhaps the most all-encompassing term in Scripture of what God has done through our Lord Jesus Christ to completely eradicate the enmity or hostility or wall of separation. This is the work that sets God free to justify the believing sinner by faith in Christ alone so that there is peace with God—the change of relationship from hostility to harmony.

Who is the Source of Reconciliation?

The source of reconciliation is God and nothing else (2 Corinthians 5:18). Reconciliation is the work of God in Christ that is bathed with love, holiness, goodness, mercy, and the grace of God. It is all by His sovereign doing that a believing sinner comes to be in Christ Jesus and obtains peace with God (1 Corinthians 1:30-31).

Who is the Agent of Reconciliation?

The Agent of reconciliation is the Lord Jesus Christ. It is He who personally went to the cross of Calvary and died voluntarily for the sins of the whole world, in His own body on the tree (Romans 5:10-11; 2 Corinthians 5:18; Colossians 1:20-21; 1 Peter 2:24).

Who is the Object of Reconciliation?

Man is the one at enmity with God and who must be brought back into a complete relationship with God through Christ.

Who is the Instrument of Reconciliation?

The Instrument of reconciliation is the death of Jesus Christ on the cross. "[God] made Him who knew no sin to be sin for us, that we might become the righteousness of God in Him" (2 Corinthians 5:21). It is the death of Jesus Christ that changes man from enmity to harmony with God (Romans 5:10; Ephesians 2:13; Colossians 1:20).

What are the Results of Reconciliation?
1) The breaking down of the wall of hostility which separated man from God: sin, penalty of sin, spiritual death, and man's unrighteousness (Ephesians 2:14-18).
2) Positional sanctification and a right and perfect standing with God (Romans 5:1; 1 Corinthians 1:2; 2 Corinthians 5:17; Colossians 2:10).
3) Justification (declared righteous before God) through Christ's righteousness imputed to us (2 Corinthians 5:18-21).

What Must Ministers and Believers Do?

All believers become ministers of reconciliation. We must share the Good news entrusted to us with all people, that God wants to restore them to a right relationship with Himself (see Romans 5:8). This is the Good News that every human being on the planet must hear!

What is the Goal of Reconciliation?

One of the main goals of reconciliation is imputed righteousness or justification so that each believing sinner may have fellowship with God (2 Corinthians 5:21). Another goal of reconciliation is the transformation of a believer's character into the likeness of Christ here on earth. This is probably the emphasis in Colossians 1:21-23, according to the Colossian text.

The work of reconciliation was accomplished through the following branches in God's redemptive plan: Propitiation, Redemption, Expiation, Substitution, Regeneration, Imputation, and Justification. Through the work of God in Jesus Christ, the barriers of reconciliation are broken down by the seven components of reconciliation listed above.

The Concept of Propitiation

Propitiation is that part of the work of reconciliation which deals with the obstacle of God's holiness and the barrier caused by man's sin. Thus, the holiness of God becomes a key component in breaking down the wall of alienation or enmity against God. Holiness is the most central characteristic of God's being. Yes, it surpasses even God's love and grace. The word "holy" is found the most in Scripture when referring to His divine nature. Holy is His name. In Isaiah 57:15, the prophet wrote, "For thus says the High and Lofty [exalted] One who inhabits eternity, whose name is Holy...." Notice the following verses of scripture which affirm this fact, Exodus 15:11; Psalm 30:4; 47:8; 48:1; 89:35; Leviticus 11:44-45; 19:2; Isaiah 5:16; Revelation 15:4; 1 Peter 1:15-16. God is inherently holy and cannot approve of anything that is evil, but that which is perfect as He is perfect. Because of His perfect righteousness and perfect justice, God cannot have fellowship with anyone or anything less than His own perfect righteousness (Habakkuk 1:13; Isaiah 59:2). God is offended by man's sin. That is why when Jesus hung on the cross, He couldn't look at Him because Jesus bore the sins of mankind. Moreover, because God is also perfectly just, He must by His own character condemn, pass judgment, and place the penalty of death upon the sinner who falls short of His righteous standards (Romans 3:9-23). Therefore, propitiation is that aspect of God's work of reconciliation in Christ which deals with satisfying His holiness. Consequently, through the complete work of the person and death of Jesus Christ, God is appeased and His holiness satisfied. The believing sinner can now come boldly into God's holy presence to obtain mercy and grace (Hebrews 4:16).

Although God is rich in mercy, He cannot accept the sinner to Himself and bypass His holiness, but neither can God in His holiness bypass His love and send the sinner into the lake of fire without providing a solution. All aspects of His divine attributes must be satisfied. Therefore, in His perfect wisdom, power, love, grace, and holiness, God provided the person and work of His own Son, the Lord Jesus, who by His life and death reconciled the conflict of God's attributes. Jesus alone was God's choice because He perfectly fulfilled the law, was without sin, and lived in perfect righteousness and harmony with the will of God the Father. Only Jesus successfully and satisfactorily met the holy demands of God and was able to deal with man's sin (1 John 2:1-2; Hebrews 2:17; 1 Peter 1:18).

Jesus equally satisfied the requirements of God's justice by His death as substitutionary payment for man's sins (Romans 3:25-26). Jesus, the innocent, died for the guilty sinner. As our substitute, He bore our penalty – death, God's wrath, curse, and eternal separation from God. This single act satisfied the requirements of God's justice. In turn, this allows God to freely lavish His love on the unworthy sinner and still act in harmony with His holiness, because Jesus Christ satisfied the demands of God's holy character (Romans 3:25-26).

In the finest hour in human history, the cross symbolizes the awesome display of God's love; it also supremely displays God's absolute holiness. So, God could by no means be just and accept the sinner apart from the person, life, and death of Jesus Christ.

The Concept of Redemption

Redemption is another aspect of the overall work of God by which He has brought about our reconciliation and removal of the barriers. God was in Christ reconciling the world to Himself (2 Corinthians 5:19). Redemption deals specifically with the problem of man's sin and truth taught by Scripture that man is bound by sin (Galatians 4:3-8; 3:22). Through redemption, a great payment is made with the perfect blood of Jesus Christ – a payment that the blood of goats and bulls could not achieve. This kind of redemption is based on some great expedition of God such as it is illustrated in the following verses in the Old Testament: Exodus 6:6; 15:13: Psalm 74:2; and 78:35. Meanwhile, in the New Testament, the death of the Son of God, the Lord Jesus Christ, made it possible.

Who is the Agent of Redemption?

The agent is the Lord Jesus Christ who, in His sinless person and His death on the cross, purchased our redemption (Ephesians 1:7; Colossians 1:14; Romans 3:24). As part of the work of reconciliation, God the Father removed the sin problem through the person and work of His Son.

What is the Instrument and Point of Redemption?

It is the blood and the cross of the Lord Jesus Christ (Ephesians 1:7; 1 Peter 1:18-19). The blood stands for the fact that Christ died as the Lamb of God sacrificially and as the substitute for sinners.

Who is the Object of Redemption?

It is man's sin and slavery to sin. The object of redemption is not simply man, but man's sin problem and his bondage to sin (Ephesians 1:7; Colossians 1:14; Galatians 3:13).

What are the Results of Redemption?
a) Forgiveness of sin (Ephesians 1:7; Colossians 1:14)
b) Deliverance from the bondage of sin and the law (Galatians 3:13)
c) Provision for adoption as an adult – sons of God (Galatians 4:5-6)
d) Provision for eternal inheritance (Hebrews 9:15)
e) Provision for capacity to glorify God (1 Corinthians 6:20)

For Whom did Christ Die?

The Word of God plainly teaches that Christ died to pay the penalty for the sin of all the world for all time. And for the Savior's death to be effective for any individual, that person must personally believe or put his or her trust in the person and work of the Lord Jesus Christ. The following key verses explain this truth: 1 Timothy 4:10; John 3:18,36.

The Concept of Expiation

As redemption was that part of God's work of reconciliation that dealt with the problem of man's sin, so expiation is that component that deals with the penalty of sin that the law exacts on man, the sinner. In other words, expiation has to do with undoing the wrong done by paying or suffering the penalty for that wrong as demanded by law. In essence, expiation means to remove the penalty officially imposed by the law which indicts and proves the sinner guilty. The following key passages explain this principle: Colossians 2:14 states, "Having wiped out the handwriting of requirements that was against us, which was contrary to us. And He has taken it out of the way, having nailed it to the cross." In verse 13 Paul speaks of the regeneration and redemption of the believer when he says, "... He has made alive together with Him, having forgiven you all trespasses." Then in verse 14, he shows how the death of Christ accomplished the idea of expiation of the sinner's penalty.

It is interesting to note that the phrase "having wiped out" means "to wipe off" or "cancel out." Then "the handwriting of requirements that was against us" literally means the handwritten document in decrees or commands which was hostile to us. This refers to the Old Testament law that in revealing God's holy character, man's sinfulness also is revealed. Though that law is good and was designed to bring blessings to man, revealing God's holy character, yet it stands against man because it shows man to be a sinner under the penalty of sin, which is death (see Romans 3:19-20; 6:23; 7:7; Galatians 3:10). So because of man's condition of sin, the law is viewed as against us (Colossians 2:14), as bringing a curse (Galatians 3:10-12), as bringing death or as an administration of death (2 Corinthians 7:7-13), and as holding man bondage to sin and death (Galatians 4:3-5,9; Romans 7:10-14). No wonder the apostle Paul stressed that the law was against us and hostile to us. But Jesus "has taken it out of the way." How refreshing and glorious that is. It demonstrates how reconciliation is the work of God accomplished in Jesus Christ alone. The phrase "taken it out of the way" in the perfect tense demonstrates that the act was completed with continuing results. The wall of separation is taken out of the way.

Finally, "having nailed it to the cross" makes the point that Jesus Christ paid our certificate of debt with its charges and nailed it to His cross, showing forever that it has been paid in full. Therefore, in the doctrine of expiation, Jesus Christ is the agent, the cross is the point and place, the penalty of sin is its object, and the believing sinner, the beneficiary.

The Concept of Substitution

The doctrine of the substitutionary death of Christ is similar to the doctrine of expiation. As redemption was that component of reconciliation aimed at the problem of man's sin, and expiation was that part which dealt with the concept of the penalty that man must pay, so substitution is directed toward the specific penalty required, the penalty of death. By the substitutionary death of Christ we mean that Christ, as the innocent Lamb of God, died and suffered the penalty of death in the place of the sinner, the actual guilty party. This means He took our place and bore the penalty of God's judgment – death, which we rightly deserved. Although substitution is not specifically a biblical term, the idea that Christ is the sinner's substitute is constantly affirmed in Scripture. The following passages from the Bible describe the concept of substitution: Isaiah 53:4-11; Matthew 20:28; Philemon 13; 2 Corinthians 5:20-21; Romans 5:8; 1 Corinthians 15:3; John 1:29; Hebrews 2:9. By Christ's substitutionary death the righteous (Jesus) bore God's judgment against the unrighteous (sinner). The wonderful news of the substitution is that man will no longer die spiritually because the Savior has already borne the divine judgment against the sinner to God's full satisfaction.

The Concept of Regeneration

The concept of "regeneration" is found explicitly in Matthew 19:28 and Titus 3:5. This concept is also alluded to in many other New Testament passages. Regeneration is specifically revealed as the direct work of the Christ's Holy Spirit (John 3:3-6; Titus 3:5), but the Spirit is sent by the Father and the Son as a result of the work of Christ on the cross. It thus becomes a part of the reconciling work of Christ whereby man who is spiritually dead can have life and fellowship with God (John 7:37-39).

In relation to the wall of separation, the regeneration is that part of the reconciling work of Christ, which deals with man's spiritual death. It deals with man's need for spiritual life or the new birth (John 3:3-6; Ephesians 2:1-4). Although it is primarily the work of the Holy Spirit, all three persons of the Trinity seem to be involved in this blessed work of imparting new life. James 1:17-18 relates the Father to regeneration under the figure of being "brought forth" or "to give birth to." The Son, the Lord Jesus Christ, seems also to be involved in regeneration: "For as the Father raises the dead and gives life to them, even so the Son gives life to whom He will" (John 5:21).

Regeneration is the supernatural act of God whereby the spiritual and eternal life of the Son, the Lord Jesus Christ, is imparted to the individual through faith in Jesus Christ. It is used in Matthew 19:28 to describe the refurbished conditions that will exist during the millennial reign of Christ. But in Titus 3:5, the word is used of the bestowal of spiritual and eternal life to the believer on the basis of God's mercy. While the word regeneration itself is used for spiritual regeneration only once (Titus 3:5), the concept is clearly taught in a number of passages by a combination of other terms (see John 1:13; 3:3). Scripture also teaches three figures of regeneration:

a) *The New Birth*: As a man is born physically by natural birth to human parents, so also he must be born by spiritual birth to a spiritual parent whereby he or she becomes a child of God (Galatians 3:26; John 1:12; 3:3-6).

b) *Spiritual Resurrection*: Man is born spiritually dead in sin, but by regeneration the believer is made alive, spiritually resurrected so to speak (Ephesians 2:1; Colossians 2:13). This means he has spiritual life and can now have fellowship with God and can function for God in newness of life (Romans 6:5,13; Ephesians 2:5-10; John 5:21-23). The emphasis here is on a new kind and quality of life.

c) *A New Creation*: Regeneration also views the born-again believer as a creation, a new spiritual creation of God's, created for good works. This calls attention to our need to operate out of our new life in Christ through the power of God (Romans 6:4-14; 2 Corinthians 5:17; Ephesians 2:10).

What Regeneration is Not:

a) It is not conversion. Conversion is what man does in turning to God, while regeneration is what God does for man to give him life.

b) It also is not sanctification or justification.

What is the Process?

a) Faith is the human requirement (see John 1:12-13).

b) Scripture provides the content one must believe so that regeneration may occur (1 Peter 1:23).

c) God ultimately is the cause of regeneration. He regenerated man according to His will (John 1:13; James 1:18).

d) The Holy Spirit is the agent of regeneration (Titus 3:5; John 3:6).

e) Regeneration is instantaneous and occurs at the moment an individual places his or her faith in Christ. It is equally an instantaneous act of God which gives new and eternal life to the believer.

Results of Regeneration

a) It provides the believer with spiritual and eternal life (Ephesians 2:1; John 5:21).

b) It provides a new nature and capacity for fellowship with God (John 3:6; 2 Peter 1:3-4).

In sum, regeneration stresses man's spiritual and eternal death apart from faith in Christ and the new life He gives. In addition, regeneration emphasizes man's total helplessness to be a part of God's kingdom or to change his life without God's supernatural intervention through Christ and the work of the Spirit of God.

The Concepts of Justification and Imputation

Justification and imputation are those aspects of reconciliation that deal with the barriers of man's lack of perfect righteousness. Isaiah, under divine inspiration, declares that man's righteous deeds are as filthy rags in the sight of a perfect and holy God (Isaiah 64:6). Man does not only need to have his sins taken away but also needs the addition of God's perfect righteousness, the righteousness of Christ. God's solution to this problem is found in the doctrines of "imputation" and "justification" as set forth in the Bible.

Justification Defined

- Justification does not mean "to be righteous," rather it is God's acceptance of us because of Christ's perfect righteousness. It is a judicial act of God as the righteous judge of all the earth (Genesis 18:25; Deuteronomy 32:4; 2 Timothy 4:8).
- Scripture reveals a number of important aspects to the process of justification as defined below.
    a) The Plan and Manifestation of Justification of Righteousness (Romans 3:21)
    "But now the righteousness of God apart from the law is revealed, being witnessed by the Law and the Prophets" (Romans 3:21). And through the Gospel of the New Testament, this righteousness from God has now, since the coming of Christ, been made clearly known.

    b) The Prerequisite and Channel for Justification Righteousness (Romans 3:22a)
    "Even the righteousness of God, through faith in Jesus Christ, to all and on all who believe" (Romans 3:22a). The source of this righteousness is from God through Jesus Christ. Christ is the means or channel. Men might trust in their own works or record, but the truth of the matter, as the apostle Paul points out, is that the only means of obtaining God's righteousness is through trusting completely in Jesus Christ.

c) Reason for Justification Righteousness (Romans 3:22b-23)

"For there is no difference; for all have sinned and fall short of the glory of God" (Romans 3:22b-23). With God, there are no favorites. Man has fallen short of His holy standards, and as Judge, He must deal with sin with perfect justice.

d) The Price or Cost of Justification (Romans 3:24-25a)

"Being justified freely by His grace through the redemption that is in Christ Jesus, whom God set forth as a propitiation by His blood, through faith, to demonstrate His righteousness..." (Romans 3:24-25a). While justification is free to the believer, without cost, it was not without cost to Jesus. The price paid to redeem us from the slave block of sin was nothing short of the death of Christ who alone could satisfy (propitiate) the holy character of God.

e) The Place or Position of Justification Righteousness (2 Corinthians 5:21)

"For He made Him who knew no sin to be sin for us, that we might become the righteousness of God in Him" (2 Corinthians 5:21). Every person who receives Christ is placed into Christ. This is what makes the individual righteous. The believer is made the righteous of God in Him. This righteousness alone overcomes our desperate, sinful condition and measures up to all the demands of God's holiness.

f) The Pronouncement of Justification Righteousness (Romans 3:25b-26)

"To demonstrate His righteousness, because in His forbearance God had passed over the sins that were previously committed, to demonstrate at the present time His righteousness, that He might be just and the justifier of the one who has faith in Jesus" (Romans 3:25b-26). God must be perfectly consistent with Himself. He cannot break His own law nor violate His nature, "God is love" (1 John 4:8), and "God is light" (1 John 1:5). A God of love wants to forgive sinners, but a God of holiness must judge sin and uphold His righteous character as written in the law.

How can God be both "just and the justifier" of those who are sinners? The answer is found in the person and work of Jesus Christ. When Jesus took upon Himself the wrath of God on the cross for the sins of the whole world, He fully met the demands of God's holiness as demanded by the law. At the same time, He fully expressed the love of God's heart.

As the book of Hebrews points out, the animal sacrifices in the Old Testament never took away sin, but when Jesus died, His death was retroactive, all the way back to Adam and took care of all the sins of the past, especially of those who were believers. All the sins that mankind ever committed, is committing, and will ever commit were taken care of 2,000 years ago.

g)   The Proof of Justification Righteousness (Romans 4:24-25)

"But also for us, it shall be imputed to us who believe in Him who raised up Jesus our Lord from the dead, who was delivered up because of our offenses, and was raised because of our justification." The words "and was raised because of our justification" point to the resurrection of Jesus Christ as that momentous event following the cross which gave proof of God's acceptance of the death of Christ for our sins.

Three Levels of Sanctification			
Position	Positional sanctification	I was sanctified	Hebrews 3:1
Experience	Progressive sanctification	I am being sanctified	1 Thessalonians 5:23
Consummation	Prospective sanctification	I shall be sanctified	1 John 3:2

Justification and Sanctification Compared
a) To sanctify means "to set apart." Sanctification has three aspects: positional (unchanging), experiential (progressive), and ultimate (complete: being in God's presence).

- Positional sanctification (Romans 6:1-11) is the basis for experiential or progressive sanctification (Romans 6:12-14).
- Experiential sanctification is the process whereby God makes the believer more and more like Jesus Christ through our union with Christ and the indwelling Spirit. Just as in justification, sanctification is the exclusive work of God that must be appropriated by faith.
- Sanctification (experiential) may change from day to day. Justification never changes. When the sinner puts his trust in Christ as his Savior, God declares him to be righteous based on the work of Christ alone, and that pronouncement never will be repeated, changed, or need to be repeated.

b) Justification looks at our external position in Christ (positional sanctification), whereas sanctification, depending on the context, may look at our experiential condition from day to day.

c) Justification exempts us from the Great White Throne Judgment, whereas experiential sanctification prepares us for the Bema, the Judgment Seat of Christ, and the blessings of rewards that follow.

d) Justification removes the guilt and penalty of sin for us. Experiential sanctification removes the growth and power of sin in and over us.

In justification, Christ died for sin's penalty, whereas in sanctification He died unto sin's power.

Imputation Defined
The word "imputation" can be defined as reclaiming or charging to the account of one what properly belongs to the account of another. Because of the person and work of Christ, God imputes or credits our sin to the person of Jesus Christ and imputes His righteousness to our account through faith in Him. In Romans 4:3-8, Apostle Paul writes, "For what does the Scripture say? Abraham believed God, and it was accounted to him for righteousness.

Now to him who works, the wages are not counted as grace but as debt. But to him who does not work but believes on Him who justifies the ungodly, his faith is accounted for righteousness, just as David also describes the blessedness of the man to whom God imputes righteousness apart from works: 'Blessed are those whose lawless deeds are forgiven, and whose sins are covered; blessed is the man to whom the law shall not impute sin.'" In his letter to the Corinthians, Apostle Paul wrote, "He [God] made Him [Jesus Christ] who knew no sin to be sin for us, that we might become the righteousness of God in Him" (2 Corinthians 5:21).

Clearly, in the above passages we see both the negative, our sin imputed to Christ who was made sin for us along with the non-imputation of our sins to us, and the positive, His righteousness reckoned or imputed to the account of those who trust in Christ fully. Only the righteousness of Christ (which man can receive freely by faith) can give the believer acceptance with God.

Furthermore, the great Apostle Paul said, "But what things were gain to me, these I have counted loss for Christ. Yet indeed I also count all things loss for the excellence of the knowledge of Christ Jesus my Lord, for whom I have suffered the loss of all things, and count them as rubbish, that I may gain Christ and be found in Him, not having my own righteousness, which is from the law, but that which is through faith in Christ, the righteousness which is from God by faith" (Philippians 3:7-9). In other words, when Paul saw the glory of Jesus Christ on the Damascus Road, he came to realize that all his works of righteousness or human good were no good. As Isaiah put it, "...And all our righteousnesses are like filthy rags..." (Isaiah 64:6).

The Three Phrases (Tenses) of Salvation

Salvation is both an instantaneous event and an experiential experience in the life of the Christian. Salvation as a verb appears in Scripture in three tenses—past, present, and future.

As noted in the New King James Bible, salvation is in three tenses or phrases:

1) The child of God *has been saved* from the guilt and penalty of sin (Luke 7:50; 1 Corinthians 1:18; 2 Corinthians 2:13; Ephesians 2:5,8; 2 Timothy 1:9) and is indeed safe.

2) The believer in Jesus Christ *is being saved* from the habits, growth, and power of sin in and over the believer (Romans 6:14; 8:2; 2 Corinthians 3:18; Galatians 2:19-20; Philippians 1:20; 2:12-13; 2 Thessalonians 2:13).

3) The Christian *will be saved* at the Lord's return, from all bodily infirmities that are the result of sin and God's curse upon the wicked world (Romans 8:18-23; 1 Corinthians 15:42-44), and brought into complete conformity to Christ (Romans 13:11; Hebrews 10:36; 1 Peter 1:5; 1 John 3:2).

A Personal Application

In the preceding chapter, an attempt was made to portray the incredible provision of God whereby man might be saved. In His grace and mercy, God Himself has broken down the wall of hostility that separated man from Himself. Even though God has done this, there still remains another barrier. This is the wall of Christ Himself and His work on the cross. For unless one personally trusts in Jesus Christ and His death on the cross as the only solution for his sins, he or she remains cut off and separated from God forever.

Specifically, there is only one sin that can keep a person separated from God – the sin of rejecting Christ or the sin of unbelief in Him who is the *only* Way, the Truth, and the *only* Life. Notice the following verses from the Bible which illustrate this fact: John 3:17-18,36; 12:48; 14:12; Acts 4:12; Ephesians 2:8-9; Titus 3:5).

If you have never put your trust in Christ, may we invite you to do so right now? Jesus Christ has broken down the wall of separation between you and God the Father and provided an abundant life of fellowship and significance for you as His child. But you must personally receive Jesus Christ by faith in order to have a personal relationship with God the Father.

Pray this prayer from your heart:

Holy Father, I come to You in Jesus' name. Forgive me of all my sins and cleanse my life. Come into my heart. Be the Savior and Lord of my life in Jesus' name. I accept Your free gift of eternal life which You died to provide for me. Amen.

If you have prayed this prayer sincerely from your heart, God has forgiven all of your sins – past, present, and future. Christ has come into your life. You are now a child of God. Welcome to God's family!

Here are some passages from Scripture that will assure you of your salvation:

John 1:12

[12] But as many as received Him, to them He gave the right to become children of God, to those who believe in His name.

John 5:24, 28

[24] Most assuredly, I say to you, he who hears My word and believes in Him who sent Me has everlasting life, and shall not come into judgment, but has passed from death into life.

[28] Do not marvel at this; for the hour is coming in which all who are in the graves will hear His voice.

John 6:40, 44

[40] And this is the will of Him who sent Me, that everyone who sees the Son and believes in Him may have everlasting life; and I will raise him up at the last day.

[44] No one can come to Me unless the Father who sent Me draws him; and I will raise him up at the last day.

John 10:28-30

[28] And I give them eternal life, and they shall never perish; neither shall anyone snatch them out of My hand. [29] My Father, who has given them to Me, is greater than all; and no one is able to snatch them out of My Father's hand. [30] I and My Father are one.

Acts 3:19

[19] Repent therefore and be converted, that your sins may be blotted out, so that times of refreshing may come from the presence of the Lord.

Acts 13:39

[39] and by Him everyone who believes is justified from all things from which you could not be justified by the law of Moses.

Acts 16:31

³¹ So they said, "Believe on the Lord Jesus Christ, and you will be saved, you and your household."

Acts 20:21

²¹ testifying to Jews, and also to Greeks, repentance toward God and faith toward our Lord Jesus Christ.

Romans 2:4

⁴ Or do you despise the riches of His goodness, forbearance, and longsuffering, not knowing that the goodness of God leads you to repentance?

Romans 4:5

⁵ But to him who does not work but believes on Him who justifies the ungodly, his faith is accounted for righteousness.

Romans 8:8-9, 15-17

⁸ And there was great joy in that city. ⁹ But there was a certain man called Simon, who previously practiced sorcery in the city and astonished the people of Samaria, claiming that he was someone great,

¹⁵ who, when they had come down, prayed for them that they might receive the Holy Spirit. ¹⁶ For as yet He had fallen upon none of them. They had only been baptized in the name of the Lord Jesus. ¹⁷ Then they laid hands on them, and they received the Holy Spirit.

1 Corinthians 1:28-30

²⁸ and the base things of the world and the things which are despised God has chosen, and the things which are not, to bring to nothing the things that are, ²⁹ that no flesh should glory in His presence. ³⁰ But of Him you are in Christ Jesus, who became for us wisdom from God-- and righteousness and sanctification and redemption.

Galatians 2:16

¹⁶ knowing that a man is not justified by the works of the law but by faith in Jesus Christ, even we have believed in Christ Jesus that we might be justified by faith in Christ and not by the works of the law; for by the works of the law no flesh shall be justified.

Ephesians 2:8-9

⁸ For by grace you have been saved through faith, and that not of yourselves; it is the gift of God, ⁹ not of works, lest anyone should boast.

2 Timothy 1:12

¹² For this reason I also suffer these things; nevertheless I am not ashamed, for I know whom I have believed and am persuaded that He is able to keep what I have committed to Him until that Day.

2 Timothy 2:19, 25

¹⁹ Nevertheless the solid foundation of God stands, having this seal: "The Lord knows those who are His," and, "Let everyone who names the name of Christ depart from iniquity."
²⁵ in humility correcting those who are in opposition, if God perhaps will grant them repentance, so that they may know the truth.

2 Timothy 4:8

⁸ Finally, there is laid up for me the crown of righteousness, which the Lord, the righteous Judge, will give to me on that Day, and not to me only but also to all who have loved His appearing.

Titus 3:5

⁵ not by works of righteousness which we have done, but according to His mercy He saved us, through the washing of regeneration and renewing of the Holy Spirit.

Hebrews 7:25

²⁵ Therefore He is also able to save to the uttermost those who come to God through Him, since He always lives to make intercession for them.

Hebrews 8:12

¹² "For I will be merciful to their unrighteousness, and their sins and their lawless deeds I will remember no more."

1 John 1:8-9

⁸ If we say that we have no sin, we deceive ourselves, and the truth is not in us. ⁹ If we confess our sins, He is faithful and just to forgive us our sins and to cleanse us from all unrighteousness.

1 John 5:11-13

[11] And this is the testimony: that God has given us eternal life, and this life is in His Son. [12] He who has the Son has life; he who does not have the Son of God does not have life. [13] These things I have written to you who believe in the name of the Son of God, that you may know that you have eternal life, and that you may continue to believe in the name of the Son of God.

Jude 24

[24] Now to Him who is able to keep you from stumbling, And to present you faultless before the presence of His glory with exceeding joy,

Now that you are saved, what's next?

The acronym S.A.V.E.D. has been a useful guide in my spiritual journey. It stands for:

S – Search the Scriptures daily for the nourishment of your soul. Joshua 1:8 says, "This Book of the Law shall not depart from your mouth, but you shall meditate in it day and night, that you may observe to do according to all that is written in it. For then you will make your way prosperous, and then you will have good success."

A – Attend church regularly and be a functional part of Christ's body, the church. Share your gifts and talents with your congregation in particular and the body of Christ in general. Hebrews 10:25 says, "Not forsaking the assembling of ourselves together, as is the manner of some, but exhorting one another, and so much the more as you see the Day approaching."

V – Vow to confess Christ daily to others. Share your testimony with others about what Jesus has done for you. Daniel 12:3 says, "Those who are wise shall shine Like the brightness of the firmament, And those who turn many to righteousness Like the stars forever and ever."

E – Engage in constant prayer. Pray as if everything depends on God and work as if everything depends on you. 1 Thessalonians 5:17 says, "Pray without ceasing."

D – Depart from all sin (Proverbs 28:13) and all appearances of evil. Proverbs 28:13 says, "He who covers his sins will not prosper, But whoever confesses and forsakes them will have mercy." And 1 Thessalonians 5:22 says, "Abstain from every form of evil."

Finally, "Let us not love in word or in tongue, but in deed and in truth" as we (1 John 3:18); "But grow in the grace and knowledge of our Lord and Savior Jesus Christ. To Him be the glory both now and forever. Amen" (2 Peter 3:18).

CHAPTER 3

Faith in God

"Without faith it is impossible to please [God]."
(Hebrews 11:6)

What is Biblical Faith?

Before a clear, concise, and demonstrative definition of biblical faith is presented, let's examine what faith is *not*. There is a plethora of opinions floating in Christian circles on the concept of faith. For example, many authors and motivational speakers describe faith as a random act or leap into darkness rather than a step in the light that God has given through His Word. Some say that faith is a huge force rather than an inner assurance and confidence in God. Others mesmerize their audiences by arguing that faith is the belief in positivity or positive thinking. Still others perceive faith as common knowledge. Sitting on a chair, eating a meal, or riding in a car is an act of faith in action. Plainly speaking, faith for this example, is acting on what one believes. However, this type of faith is called common or natural faith and has nothing to do with spiritual or biblical faith. Still another misconception is the idea presented by faith teachers urging their disciples to put their faith in themselves, in others, and in the projects they embark on.

Biblical faith has nothing to do with the aforementioned. Biblical faith is the radical, unwavering trust in God, His existence, His attributes, His Word, His promises, and His will. The Word of God makes us "wise for salvation through *faith* which is in Christ Jesus" (2 Timothy 3:15). In other words, faith, according to the Scriptures, depends completely on God. He is the object of our faith, not people nor circumstances. Faith is thereby fundamental to the Christian belief and practice. It is one of the indispensable truths given in the Bible. "But without faith it is impossible to please Him, for he who comes to God must believe that He is, and that He is a rewarder of those who diligently seek Him" (Hebrews 11:6).

How Can Faith be Received?

Scriptural faith is received primarily by listening and embracing wholeheartedly the Word of God. "So then faith comes by hearing, and hearing by the word of God" (Romans 10:17). Biblical faith grows over time as the believer spends more time studying the Bible, meditating on God's promises, and seeking to please Him though obedience to His Word.

Why Must I Have Faith in God Alone?

Putting our absolute confidence in people, things, or circumstances is sheer folly. The mind of man is comprised of many inconsistencies. God alone is eternally trustworthy and infinitely loyal. God alone is faithful and keeps His covenant promises eternally. The Bible declares that even when we are faithless, vacillating, and constantly changing, God remains faithful. This is God's mode of relation toward His people and other created things. God's faithfulness is steadfast and thoroughly grounded in relation to others. This kind of fidelity or faithfulness is spoken of both in the Old and New Testaments to describe God's relation to the world and to the quality of relationship that ancient Israel and modern Christians are called upon to have with one another. A number of passages are mentioned in Scripture that highlight God's eternal faithfulness. Let's reflect on a few of them:

- "But You are the same, and Your years will have no end" (Psalm 102:27).
- "For I am the Lord, I do not change; therefore you are not consumed, O sons of Jacob" (Malachi 3:6).
- "Jesus Christ is the same yesterday, today, and forever" (Hebrews 13:8).
- "...You are from everlasting" (Psalm 93:2).
- "Every good gift and every perfect gift is from above, and comes down from the Father of lights, with whom there is no variation or shadow of turning" (James 1:17).

These verses affirm that God can be trusted completely without equivocation. Since God never changes, He will always do what is right. He remains true to His character and promises and is 100% dependable.

What is the Role of Faith in the Salvation Experience?

Faith is the central concept of Christianity. The righteousness of a believer brought about in the "salvation experience" comes by faith *alone*, in Christ Jesus *alone*. In the Christians' "Hall of Faith" (recorded in Hebrews 11), every hero of faith acts "by faith." Dating back to the origins of our existence with our first father in the faith, Abraham, we can see faith in action. (Read the section in this chapter called "Some Bible Characters and Faith.")

Faith is indispensable for salvation. The word faith comes from the Latin root, *Credere*, which has come to mean belief. Today, faith in others is perceived as loyalty to a person to whom you believe is worthy of your trust. Paul testified to the Jews about salvation saying, "Repentance [was] toward God and faith toward our Lord Jesus Christ" (Acts 20:21). Apostle John expresses a similar understanding of faith in Jesus when he declared: "This is the work of God, that you believe in Him whom He sent….Let not your heart be troubled; you believe in God, believe also in Me" (John 6:29; 14:1).

In Mark 11:22, Jesus told Peter to "have faith in God" after Peter witnessed a fig tree that had been cursed by Jesus the previous day to dry up. Jesus performed this miracle so that His listeners would place their confidence in God. With these signs, those who lack the faith before may build it through seeing Jesus' works.

In the gospels, faith is presented as an attitude toward and a relationship with God mediated by Christ Jesus. Such an attitude leads one to surrender by accepting God's gift of righteousness in Christ rather than seeking to achieve righteousness in oneself. The concept of faith is primarily that of a personal relationship with God through the adequate and finished work accomplished by Jesus in His death, burial, and resurrection. This relationship has its foundation in love—the love that is built on a personal expression of trust and dependence on Him alone.

Intellectual acknowledgement, on the other hand, is grossly inadequate in the quest for eternal bliss. Knowing that Jesus died for one's sins and pardoned the sin debt is not enough to get you to heaven, but by putting my absolute trust in Him, accepting His offer, and placing my life completely in His hands, the gift of eternal bliss is made readily available. In short, there is heart knowledge as opposed to head knowledge of Jesus Christ's atoning work. Every prospective Christian must confess with his mouth and believe in his head and heart that Jesus is the Christ. Paul said that if you confess the Lord Jesus as Christ with your mouth and believe in your heart that God has raised Him from the dead, you shall be saved (Romans 10:9). In 1 John, we read, "Whoever believes that Jesus is the Christ is born of God" (1 John 5:1); therefore, "Whoever confesses that Jesus is the Son of God, God abides in Him and he in God" (1 John 4:15). However, anyone who confesses Jesus Christ as a good teacher, prophet, and miracle worker but fails to profess Him as the Son of God, is not saved. We must confess with our lips what we deeply believe in our hearts—the truth of Jesus as the Son of God.

Faith (for the Christian) is believing that we will get what we do not see. The reward of faith is seeing what we believe. To make an even more powerful case, the author of Hebrews describes the Christian faith as being "the substance of things hoped for, the evidence of things not seen" (Hebrews 11:1). "What we hope for" and "what we do not see" refer both to God as Lord and His edicts as law. Biblical hope is a bedrock assurance based on God's Word. Faith enables us, therefore, to be confident that God exists. His promises are credible, His gifts awesome, and His life eternal through His Son Christ Jesus.

The following key concepts of the Christian message are associated with faith:

- *The State of Salvation*
  "For by grace you have been saved through faith, and that not of yourselves; it is the gift of God, not of works, lest anyone should boast" (Ephesians 2:8-9).

- *The State of Sanctification*
  "To open their eyes, in order to turn them from darkness to light, and from the power of Satan to God, that they may receive forgiveness

of sins and an inheritance among those who are sanctified by faith in Me" (Acts 26:18).

- *The State of Purification*
"And made no distinction between us and them, purifying their hearts by faith" (Acts 15:9).

- *The State of Justification*
"To him who does not work but believes on Him who justifies the ungodly, his faith is accounted for righteousness" (Romans 4:5). A sinful man in himself has no ability or resources to be righteous (holy). Like holiness, salvation is indeed the total, absolute, and complete work of the Lord Jesus Christ. On the cross of Calvary, the sinful deeds of mankind were placed on Christ Jesus, who knew and committed no sin. Second Corinthians 5:21 says, "For [God] made Him who knew no sin to be sin for us, that we might become the righteousness of God in Him." So, *only* in Christ is the sinner made righteous. How does the sinner become righteous? There are two occurrences making us eligible to achieve righteousness. First, realization of what Jesus did for us on the cross, and second, acceptance of what He is going to do for us through the Holy Spirit. These two aspects of holiness are imputed (credited) righteousness and imparted (given) righteousness. The Scriptures clearly teach both of these viewpoints of our righteousness and salvation.

In the first instance – credited righteousness – God credits sinners with the righteousness they don't possess because they believe in Jesus rather than themselves. Justification of the sinner is the work of Christ. Abraham's faith was credited as righteous even though his background was paganistic. (Romans 4:3).

In our second scenario, Christ imparts righteousness to the believer. Regeneration refers to imparted (given) righteousness. This work of grace is what Jesus does in us daily by the power of the Holy Spirit. It is something we experience when we are born again. We partake of God's divine nature (2 Peter 1:4) and have authority over sin in our lives. This knowledge is the root of our adoption.

- *The State of Adoption as Children of God*
  "For you are all sons of God through faith in Christ Jesus" (Galatians 3:26).

Each of the above salvation experiences comes only by faith that is placed in the Lord Jesus Christ. Faith is your ticket to being adopted by God. Walking by faith yields God's blessings through dependence on His Word.

What is Walking by Faith?

Walking by faith is the totality of your lifestyle that does not depend on your resources. It is casting oneself unreservedly on the merit of God, laying hold to the unfailing promises of God in Christ, relying on the finished work of Christ, and depending on the power of the awesome, indwelling Holy Spirit for daily strength. Genuine faith in God implies complete reliance and full obedience to Him. For the believer, "We walk by faith, not by sight" (2 Corinthians 5:7).

Since faith is so essential to the Christian experience, Apostle Peter addresses seven outgrowths of faith (2 Peter 1:5-7). Our faith in Jesus Christ grows as we read, meditate, and pray using the Word. This builds us into the image of our Lord Jesus. Faith in God is like a seed that must germinate and grow. So, Peter instructs us to "add to" this faith seven character traits: virtue, knowledge, temperance (self-control), patience (perseverance), godliness, brotherly kindness, and charity (agape love). Every believer who abandons himself wholly to God will experience real spiritual growth with faith being the foundation. There is a progression in faith as the follower of Christ yields completely to the indwelling Holy Spirit. The Bible presents biblical faith as a growing experience rather than a formula or mental exercise for an immediate fix.

Virtue
Adding virtue to faith allows followers of Christ to eliminate sinful actions and thoughts from their lives. The Holy Spirit brings conviction to its hosts' hearts and leads them to confess and abandon their evil ways. The host then follows a commitment to grow in the knowledge of our Lord and Savior Jesus Christ.

Knowledge

The believer adds knowledge to virtue in order to increase his or her faith in Christ. This knowledge is the desire to have a deeper understanding of the person and work of Jesus Christ. In the process of gaining this deeper understanding, the believer learns to exercise wisdom in making life's choices as well as developing a disciplined lifestyle.

Self-Control

As the believer yields by faith to the power of the indwelling Holy Spirit, he develops self- control. The believer will gradually learn to make decisions that are God-honoring, pleasing to himself or herself, and exemplary to others. Using action, the believer builds self-control, which leads to the development of patience.

Patience

It is usually in adversity that the Christian develops perseverance. Christians draw strength from the indwelling Holy Spirit, who produces the good fruit of patience. The fruit of patience leads to godliness.

Godliness

As the Christ follower develops patience through trial, temptations, and testing, he concurrently cultivates an attitude pleasing to God in how he sets his agenda, goals, and priorities. These settings are in sync with those of God the Father. The believer will seek to do that which is good by shunning evil. Pleasing God will translate into a beautiful horizontal relationship with others. The Christian's godly character will attract others to Christ.

Brotherly Kindness

As a believer develops godly characteristics, he will gradually move from a self-absorbed focus to an others-involved focus. The believer will realize that helping others is more important than being preoccupied with personal affairs. This behavior will thus translate into kindness and affection toward others, esteeming and giving preference to others above himself. Demonstrating brotherly kindness will increase the fruit of joy in the believer's life. The acronym for "JOY" is: J-Jesus, O-Others, Y-You, meaning "putting Jesus, then others, before yourself."

Charity

Last but not least is the virtue known as charity. Charity in the Greek is *agape*, meaning unconditional love. The Bible teaches three great truths of our Christian doctrine. These are faith, hope, and love. The greatest of these pillars is love. Love undergirds the previous six virtues. Faith is without meaning if it does not produce action. Love is action. Therefore, everything a Christian does must be driven by love for the Father and others. Faith is most exemplified when it is driven by love (*agape*). The above-mentioned characteristics of faith growth do not operate independently of each other; rather, these characteristics operate simultaneously as the believer yields daily to the Holy Spirit. The converse is also true. A lack of submission to the Holy Spirit's power in the life of a believer will produce stagnation in the faith walk.

Types of Faith

After examining the components that increase our faith in Jesus Christ, let's consider the different kinds of faith in the Bible. A cursory study of the types of faith revealed in God's Word shows that there are at least seven types. Biblical faith is rooted in the name of Jesus Christ. In His sermon at Solomon's portico (Acts 3:16), Peter said that the lame man who was healed received his healing "through faith in [Jesus'] name….Yes, the faith which comes through Him has given him this perfect soundness in the presence of you all."

No Faith

There are people who do not put their faith in the living God. Such, the Bible teaches, have no faith. They may have faith in themselves, others, or their circumstances, but their definition of faith is not complete. Here are some verses to support our premise:

- "For what if some did not believe?" (Romans 3:3).
- Jesus said, "Why are you so fearful? How is it that you have no faith" (Mark 4:40).
- "And if Christ is not risen, then our preaching is empty and your faith is also empty" (1 Corinthians 15:14).
- "And that we may be delivered from unreasonable and wicked men; for not all have faith" (2 Thessalonians 3:2).

Small/Little Faith

This is the gift of faith from God at conversion. In Matthew's gospel it is referred to as a small mustard seed. In a biblical scenario, the disciples could not exorcise (cast out) demons, because they failed in faith. Although the power was in them, they failed to appropriate it.

- Jesus said, "Because of your unbelief; for assuredly, I say to you, if you have faith as a mustard seed, you will say to this mountain, 'Move from here to there,' and it will move; and nothing will be impossible for you" (Matthew 17:20). This verse does not imply that it is the believer's faith that will move the mountain, but God in the believer will move the mountain. Prophet Zechariah told Zerubbabel that it was "not by might nor by power, but by [His] Spirit [our 'mountains' are moved]" (Zechariah 4:6b).
- "Now if God so clothes the grass of the field, which today is, and tomorrow is thrown into the oven, will He not much more clothe you, O you of *little faith*?" (Matthew 6:30, emphasis added; Luke 12:28).
- Jesus rescued Peter as he sank during his walk on the sea. Jesus said after Peter asked for help, "O you of *little faith*, why did you doubt?" (Matthew 14:31, emphasis added).

Great Faith

If with little faith we can move mountains, what abilities do we inherit with great faith? Matthew records an encounter between a centurion and Jesus. The centurion came to Jesus, pleading with Jesus to heal his servant. Initially, he had requested that Jesus come to his residence, but later changed his mind, asking Jesus to speak a word to his ailing servant miles away. The Bible states that when Jesus heard this, He marveled and said to those who followed, "Assuredly, I say to you, I have not found such *great faith*, not even in Israel!" (Matthew 8:10, emphasis added). Jesus then healed the man miles away because of his master's faith.

On another occasion, a Gentile woman shows remarkable faith when she cries out to Jesus to deliver her possessed daughter from a demon. In response to her plea, Jesus said, "O woman, great is your faith! Let it be to you as you desire" (Matthew 15:28).

Increasing/Growing Faith

We've gone from no faith to increasing faith. Earlier, we discussed the seven variables outlined by Peter (2 Peter 1:5-7) that are essential for our faith in Christ to grow. So, the Bible speaks of growing faith. An example of increasing faith is recorded in Luke's gospel. Jesus had been teaching on the theme of offenses and forgiveness. At the end of the presentation, the apostles requested that their faith be increased: "Increase our faith" (Luke 17:5).

In the letter to the Thessalonians (2 Thessalonians 1:3), Paul commended the brethren saying, "We are bound to thank God always for you, brethren, as it is fitting, because your faith grows exceedingly, and the love of every one of you all abounds toward each other."

Healing Faith

This brings us to the fifth kind of faith taught in the Scriptures. While every born-again child of God can exercise his or her faith to pray for others to be healed, only some in the body of Christ are granted the gift of healing. The Holy Spirit, who gives all spiritual gifts to believers, has the prerogative and power to give the gifts to whomever He chooses. Paul is an example of a believer who was granted the gift of healing. "A certain man without strength in his feet was sitting, a cripple from his mother's womb, who had never walked....Paul, observing him intently and seeing that he had faith to be healed said with a loud voice, 'Stand up straight on your feet!' And he leaped and walked" (Acts 14:8-10).

Encouraging Faith

Paul, in his epistle to the Romans, said "That I may be encouraged together with you by the mutual faith both of you and me" (Romans 1:12). Believers are expected to encourage each other in the faith as we await the day of Jesus' soon-coming rapture. A model of an encourager in the Bible is Joses, later named Barnabas by the apostles. He exercised, to the fullest, the gift of encouragement. In fact, the name Barnabas is translated to mean "son of encouragement." The following scriptures speak about Barnabas as an encourager:

- "And Joses, who was also named Barnabas by the apostles (which is translated 'Son of Encouragement'), a Levite of the country of Cyprus" (Acts 4:36).

- "Now in the church that was at Antioch there were certain prophets and teachers: Barnabas, Simeon who was called Niger, Lucius of Cyrene, Manaen who had been brought up with Herod the tetrarch, and Saul. As they ministered to the Lord and fasted, the Holy Spirit said, 'Now separate to Me Barnabas and Saul for the work to which I have called them.' Then, having fasted and prayed, and laid hands on them, they sent them away. So, being sent out by the Holy Spirit, they went down to Seleucia, and from there they sailed to Cyprus" (Acts 13:1-4).

- "Then after some days Paul said to Barnabas, 'Let us now go back and visit our brethren in every city where we have preached the word of the Lord, and see how they are doing.' Now Barnabas was determined to take with them John called Mark. But Paul insisted that they should not take with them the one who had departed from them in Pamphylia, and had not gone with them to the work. Then the contention became so sharp that they parted from one another. And so Barnabas took Mark and sailed to Cyprus; but Paul chose Silas and departed, being commended by the brethren to the grace of God. And he went through Syria and Cilicia, strengthening the churches" (Acts 15:36-41).

These references are evidence of the ministry of encouragement that Barnabas had on other Christians.

Saving Faith

At conversion, every believer receives saving faith. A follower of Christ is justified by faith when he puts his trust in the Lord Jesus Christ. "Therefore, having being justified by faith, we have peace with God through our Lord Jesus Christ" (Romans 5:1). Earlier, it was mentioned that justification is a word that refers to imputed (credited) righteousness. God "justifies the ungodly" who trust in Him (Romans 4:5). That is, God credits the believer with righteousness he does not possess, just because he trusted in Him (God) rather than in himself (man). Saving faith, therefore, is given to all who believe in the death, burial, and work of Jesus Christ. "The righteousness of God, through faith in Jesus Christ [is] to all who believe" (Romans 3:22).

Faith is a process that involves increasing degrees of trust throughout our Christian journey. Little faith hopes that God will do what He says He will do. Strong faith knows that God will do what He says He will do. Great faith believes that He has *already done* what He said He would do. In a nutshell, the Christian faith is a triumphant faith, "for whatever is born of God overcomes the world...and this is the victory that has overcome the world—our faith" (1 John 5:4).

Faith and Affliction

Our discussion will now focus on how to nurture our faith. The Christian faith is nurtured in the crucible of conflicts, problems, trials, persecutions, and all kinds of difficulties. Faith that is not tested is no faith. The psalmist said, "It is good for me that I have been afflicted, that I may learn Your statutes [commandments]" (Psalm 119:71).

God tests our faith first and foremost so that we may trust in His faithfulness. He wants to reveal to us that He is faithful. When we look to God during our troubles, we draw strength and encouragement. We are reassured that He wants us to be all that He has designed us to be in Him. When our faith is tested, our endurance is fully developed. We become strong in character and are prepared to meet with greater confidence any challenges in life.

Believing faith should never be seen as the goal, only as the beginning of a wonderful growth process of His divine nature (1 Peter 1:4-9). These types of faith will produce positive results in the life of a Christian. Here are a few examples of the power of faith under *fire*:

Effective Prayer
Faith in the Lord Jesus gives believers power for effective prayer. Remember Jesus' teaching on mountain-moving faith quoted earlier in Matthew 17:20? The secret is not that the believer will move the mountain, but prayer offered in faith will cause Jesus to move the mountain.

Effective Witness
Obeying the great commission and launching out by faith to spread the good news of the Gospel will bring thousands into the kingdom of

God. "Go therefore and make disciples of all the nations" (Matthew 28:19a). This command given by the Lord Jesus to His disciples has led to hundreds of thousands of souls saved for eternity.

Healing the Sick

Another by-product of our faith comes in the form of healing of sicknesses. Jehovah Rapha, the Lord who heals all sicknesses and diseases, wants us to participate in the healing process of the sick. In this regard, James encourages us to pray the "prayer of faith" (James 5:15) for the sick. This prayer should be rendered the prayer offered in "faith." It is this kind of prayer that will bring healing to the sick and the Lord will raise him up.

Overcoming the World

It is only by faith in God that we overcome the world system. John wrote, "And this is the victory that has overcome the world – our faith" (1 John 5:4). Since He has "overcome the world" (John 16:33), all believers who trust the Lord will also experience this victory. It is significant to note that the word "world" represents the morally evil and bankrupt system that is diametrically opposed to all that God is and holds dear. In other words, it is the satanically inspired kingdom that is at war with Christ's kingdom here on earth. However, we know what the outcome of this conflict will be because the Bible says, "The kingdoms of this world [will] become the kingdoms of our Lord and of His Christ, and He shall reign forever and ever" (Revelation 11:15). Not only does our faith in God help us to overcome the world, it is also the greatest antidote against our negative emotions—the fear of persecution, ridicule, rejection, lack of good shelter, and the future, just to mention these. A great lesson can be learned from the psalmist who said, "Whenever I am afraid, I will trust in You" (Psalm 56:3).

Patience

As stated earlier, faith that is tested produces patience. Patience is one of the more indispensable virtues necessary in the Christian walk. Listen to James: "My brethren, count it all joy when you fall into various trials, knowing that the testing of your faith produces patience. But let patience have its perfect work, that you may be perfect and complete, lacking nothing." (James 1:2-4).

Preservation

Faith in God both protects and preserves the follower of Christ. The psalmist declares, "Oh, love the Lord, all you His saints! For the Lord preserves the faithful" (Psalm 31:23) from unnecessary and unwarranted attacks.

Shield of Faith

A great benefit derived from overcoming the darts sent by the enemy (Satan and his cohorts) is to put on our shield of faith. Since our spiritual warfare is not against flesh and blood but against principalities, rulers, powers, and a host of wickedness in heavenly places, we are to put on weapons of warfare which are mighty in God. Ephesians 6:10-18 outlines these spiritual weapons. One of these mighty weapons is the shield of faith with which every believer is able to "quench all the fiery darts of the wicked one" (verse 16). Elsewhere, it is written that our heritage as servants of the Most High God is to overcome the evil one. Therefore "no weapon formed against you shall prosper, and every tongue which rises against you in judgment, you shall condemn" (Isaiah 54:17). Additionally, when believers are engaged in spiritual warfare, it is essential that they cover themselves with other pieces of the armor found in Ephesians 6. Christians will be able to resist the devil (James 4:7) and he will flee *for a while* (1 Peter 5:9-10).

Some Bible Characters and Faith

This chapter on faith will be concluded by examining some Bible characters. Those who lived by faith didn't always see quick solutions to their problems. Yet, their faith enabled them to persevere in their circumstances.

Abel

Abel's faith continued to testify after his death. "By faith Abel offered God a more excellent sacrifice than Cain, through which he obtained witness that he was righteous, God testifying of his gifts; and through it he being dead still speaks" (Hebrews 11:4). Abel's blood speaks even in his grave. His name is mentioned among the "heroes of faith" in Hebrews 11. We too can continue to testify to the coming generations by being faithful.

Abraham

Throughout the Bible (Old and New Testaments), faith is, and has always been, the way people approach God to obtain the righteousness of God through our Lord Jesus Christ. In both testaments of the Bible, righteousness has always been a gift from God. The sinful man has no resources or ability to be holy. In other words, to have a personal relationship with God, it was God who took the initiative and offered mankind His righteousness. Man has to receive His righteousness by faith. Beginning with Abraham (our father of faith) and extending to all the believers (Old and New Testament and throughout the ages), man has received accredited (imputed) and imparted (given) righteousness simply by placing his faith in God. God counted man's obedience by faith as righteousness. We are told that Abraham dwelt in the land of promise because of faith. He followed a plan he did not devise from his intellect to a destination he did not see with his naked eye. All he did was trust God to decide the plan and move him from Ur of the Chaldeans to Canaan, the land of promise. His faith was unwavering in God's Word. "Trust me Abraham, I have got it all worked out!" To this Abraham replied, "Done deal!" Abraham's faith was credited to him as "righteousness," even though he was from a pagan background (Romans 4:9).

Noah

Faith reveals itself through actions of obedience. By faith Noah, when warned about things not yet seen, in holy fear built an ark to save his family (Hebrews 11:7a). History records that Noah lived during a period in world history when it did not rain. Yet, by faith, Noah obeyed God's word that there was going to be a world-wide flood. It took 120 years to build the ark in the midst of ridicule, scorn, and disdain by his contemporaries. He was steadfast in carrying out God's order. Others who had bedrock belief in God's words were: Moses who kept the Passover; Abel who offered a better sacrifice; Rahab who aided the Jewish spies from being caught by the enemies.

Not only does faith reveal itself through obedience, a believer's faith serves as judgment on sinners. Again by faith Noah, when warned about things not yet seen, in holy fear built an ark to save his family. By faith he condemned the world and became heir of the righteousness that comes by faith (Hebrews 11:7).

Skeptics do not believe that God judges sinners nor rewards those who seek Him. But those who trust Him are rewarded. Noah and his family escaped the great flood judgment. But the ungodly were destroyed by the same flood. The truth is that those who live godly lives are already a form of God's judgment to the ungodly. In the story of Cain and Abel, the Scriptures say do not be as Cain "who was of the wicked one and murdered his brother. And why did he murder him? Because his works were evil and his brother's righteous. Do not marvel, my brethren, if the world hates you" (1 John 3:12-13). At the end of this life, God has promised a final judgment for all sinners. "Then I saw a great white throne and Him who sat on it....And I saw the dead, small and great, standing before God...and the dead were judged...each one according to his works....And anyone not found written in the Book of Life was cast into the lake of fire" (Revelation 20:11-15).

Even now, the believer shines like light in a dark world. And even now, God judges the sinners by the lives of His saints who live by faith. Let's heed the admonition that Paul wrote to the Philippians. "Do all things without complaining and disputing, that you may become blameless and harmless, children of God without fault in the midst of a crooked and perverse generation, among whom you shine as lights in the world, holding fast the word of life" (Philippians 2:14-16). Here is clearly a verdict: "Light has come into the world, and men loved darkness rather than light, because their deeds were evil" (John 3:19).

The First Hebrew Readers
The author of the book of Hebrews exhorted the first century Hebrew believers who were persecuted to walk by faith and not by sight. "Without faith it is impossible to please Him, for he who comes to God must believe that He is, and that He is a rewarder of those who diligently seek Him" (Hebrews 11:6). Perhaps the foremost duty of the believer is to please God in word, thought, and deed through the power of the Holy Spirit.

People in other religions attempt to please God through good deeds. However, faith in Jesus Christ is the only way to please God; the joy of this reward is anticipated when Christ returns. We also are comforted by the words in 2 Chronicles 16:9, "For the eyes of the Lord run to and fro throughout the whole earth, to show Himself strong on behalf of those whose heart is loyal to Him." Many people in the Scriptures were rewarded because they sought Him, such as Moses, Hannah, Hezekiah, Daniel, and all who came to Jesus for forgiveness, healing, and deliverance. But others like Abel, Isaiah, and Micah did not live to see their dreams come true. However, Jesus said, "The one who comes to Me, I will by no means cast out" (John 6:37).

To All

Many may be surprised that both Old and New Testament believers are justified only by faith. In the Old Testament we are told that Abraham "believed in the Lord; and [God] accounted it to him for righteousness" (Genesis 15:6). It can be observed that this verse is quoted in Romans 4:3. Based on the just nature of God and the fact that we are justified freely by His grace through the redemption that is in Christ Jesus (Romans 3:26), here the emphasis is on "accounted." In Galatians 3:6, the word "believed" is emphasized, couched in the book dedicated to contrast "works" and "faith." "So then those who are of faith are blessed with believing Abraham" (Galatians 3:9). The book of James was penned to encourage believers to do good works as evidence of their faith, and Genesis 15:6, quoted in James 2:23, emphasizes righteousness. "Faith without works is dead" (James 2:26).

The other Old Testament passage dealing with faith, which is quoted three times in the New Testament reads, "The just shall live by his faith" (Habakkuk 2:4). When used in Romans 1:17, just prior to the description of the evil lifestyle of the wicked (verses 18-32), the emphasis seems to be on the word "just." In Galatians 3:11, as noted above, the word "faith" is stressed. But in Hebrews 10:38 the author teaches that those who have been declared righteous by God live eternally by faith and will be able to cope with persecution (verses 34-37). Thus, the Old Testament doctrine that we are saved by faith is the work of God to solve our own problems that apply to every area of our lives and beings, including our past sins, our present and holy lives and works, and our future eternal lives.

Faith must always look toward God, rather than in other directions. "Looking unto Jesus, the author and finisher of our faith" (Hebrews 12:2). Our faith must always look toward God – that is, forward and upward. Faith sees with spiritual eyes and sees God in the future. For example, Abraham spent more time focusing on Canaan than Ur. Peter, on the other hand, was slow to learn that faith looks forward, rather than around. No wonder when he was walking on water, he looked at Jesus, but when he changed his focus from Jesus and allowed the winds to distract his faith, he started sinking.

David learned the secret of looking up even in the most challenging times of his life. "So David and his men came to the city, and there it was, burned with fire; and their wives, their sons, and their daughters had been taken captive. Then David and the people who were with him lifted up their voices and wept, until they had no more power to weep. And David's two wives, Ahinoam the Jezreelitess, and Abigail the widow of Nabal the Carmelite, had been taken captive. Now David was greatly distressed, for the people spoke of stoning him, because the soul of all the people was grieved, every man for his sons and his daughters. But David strengthened himself in the Lord his God" (1 Samuel 30:3-6). By putting his faith in God, David was able to recover his wives, children, and wealth, as well as all the possessions of his army.

While David's story of faith in God produced dramatic results of success, it is important to keep in mind that faith in God does not always guarantee worldly success. In God's economy, there are no guarantees, even for the faithful. While some believers might experience some blessings in this life, others may have to wait until the promises of God are fulfilled in glory. For example, Apostle James (brother of John) was put to death by Herod's sword (Acts 12:1-2). Around the same time Apostle Peter was delivered from death by the same sword (Acts 12:3-16). Faith in God may sometimes lead some believers to the fire and others through it. Faith may lead some to the mountain of victory, but others into the valley of death.

The author of Hebrew states, "Others were tortured, not accepting deliverance, that they might obtain a better resurrection. Still others had trial of mockings and scourgings, yes, and of chains and imprisonment. They were stoned, they were sawn in two, were tempted, were slain with the sword. They wandered about in sheepskins and goatskins, being destitute, afflicted, tormented – of whom the world was not worthy. They wandered in deserts and mountains, in dens and caves of the earth. And all these, having obtained a good testimony through faith, did not receive the promise" (Hebrews 11:35-39). Nevertheless, through faith in Christ we are more than conquerors. All believers in Christ, no matter what their earthly fate is, will enjoy eternal victory. For what is done for Christ will be rewarded in eternity. "For I am persuaded that neither death nor life, nor angels nor principalities nor powers, nor things present nor things to come, nor height nor depth, nor any other created thing, shall be able to separate us from the love of God which is in Christ Jesus our Lord" (Romans 8:38-39). Until then, let's keep living "by faith."

Application

Faith begins by knowing God and His plan. However, intellectual faith has never saved anyone although intellectual knowledge is the foundation for saving faith. Faith is also not a matter of emotions or the will; rather, it is simply casting oneself on the mercy of God and relying unreservedly in the finished work of Christ for salvation, and on the power of the indwelling Holy Spirit of God for daily strength. In all, faith is trusting God completely and obeying Him fully. Also, remember this simple acronym based on faith:

F – Forsaking
A – All
I – I
T – Trust
H – Him

The ultimate purpose of this chapter is to help Christians grow in their faith and "become mature, attaining to the whole measure of the fullness of Christ" (Ephesians 4:13 NIV).

CHAPTER 4

Instruction on Baptisms

"You are the body of Christ, and members individually."
(1 Corinthians 12:27)

The etymology, or source and history of the word "baptism" comes from the Greek word *baptizo,* which means "to dip," "to plunge under," "to immerse," or "to bury." It is best defined as being "placed under."

As with most Christian doctrines (practices and beliefs), the background of baptism lies in the practices and beliefs of the Jewish community. The church, the body of Christ, has continued this practice since its inception with the first-century church.

Notice in the title of this chapter that the author of Hebrews states "the doctrine of baptisms." The word "baptisms" is written in the plural form, indicating that there are many forms of baptisms in the Bible. This chapter will discuss the four types of baptism: Baptism into the Body of Christ, Baptism in Water, Baptism in the Holy Spirit, and Baptism into Fire (suffering). Let's examine each of these forms of baptism.

Baptismal Grid

The Four Types of Baptism in the New Testament (Hebrews 6:1-2)

	Baptism into Christ's Body (1 Corinthians 12:12-14)	Baptism in Water (Acts 2:38-45; Colossians 2:12)	Baptism in the Spirit (Acts 2:4)	Baptism of Fire (suffering, growth; Matthew 3:11; Philippians 3:10; 1 Thessalonians 3:3-4)
Middleman of Baptism	The Holy Spirit	The Minister	Jesus Christ	Jesus Christ
Nominee	The Sinner (sinner to saint)	The Believer	The Believer	The Believer
Elements into which the Nominee is Placed	Body of Christ	Water	The Holy Spirit	Trials, Tribulations, and Sufferings

Baptism into the Body of Christ (The Church)

The types of baptisms mentioned are built on the foundation of the baptism into the body of Christ. The English word "church" in the New Testament is based on the Greek word *ecclesia*, which refers to the body of all believing Christians who share similar beliefs in Christ regardless of their denominational affiliation. It is God's Word that produces church members. It is the life in the Word of God that causes spiritually dead people to become spiritually living individuals who are born again and not with corruptible human seed, but the incorruptible seed of the Holy Spirit. In 1 Peter 1:23 Peter says, "Having been born again, not of corruptible seed, but incorruptible, through the word of God which lives and abides forever." Jesus said earlier, "The words that I speak to you are spirit, and they are life," and, "It is the Spirit who gives life; the flesh profits nothing" (John 6:63).

Baptism into the body of Christ occurs at the moment of salvation. "Now you are the body of Christ, and members individually" (1 Corinthians 12:27). Although we each may fill a different role within the church, we are baptized into one body and receive the same indwelling Holy Spirit; and it is by the Spirit's conviction that we are baptized into the body of Christ. John 16:8 says, "When [the Holy Spirit] has come, He will convict the world of sin, and of righteousness, and of judgment." In the local assembly, "God has set the members, each one of them, in the body just as He pleased" (1 Corinthians 12:18). And the universal body of Christ is the total of God's people in the whole earth throughout the ages. It is also called "God's spiritual nation" in and among all nations of the earth. While the Holy Spirit acts on the Word of God to bring conviction in the human heart, it is the Lord Jesus Christ, through His death, burial, and resurrection that brought into being God's spiritual nation – the church.

The Bible uses three other concepts in the New Testament to describe the church of Jesus Christ.

The Body of Christ

"And He put all things under His feet, and gave Him to be head over all things to the church which, is His body, the fullness of Him who fills all in all" (Ephesians 1:22-23).

The Building (dwelling place of God)

"Now, therefore, you are no longer strangers and foreigners, but fellow citizens with the saints and members of the household of God, having been built on the foundation of the apostles and prophets, Jesus Christ Himself being the chief cornerstone, in whom the whole building, being fitted together, grows into a holy temple in the Lord, in whom you also are being built together for a dwelling place of God in the Spirit" (Ephesians 2:19-22).

The Bride of Christ

"For the husband is head of the wife, as also Christ is head of the church; and He is the Savior of the body. Therefore, just as the church is subject to Christ, so let the wives be to their own husbands in everything. Husbands, love your wives, just as Christ also loved the church and gave Himself for her, that He might sanctify and cleanse her with the washing of water by the word, that He might present her to Himself a glorious church, not having spot or wrinkle or any such thing, but that she should be holy and without blemish....This is a great mystery, but I speak concerning Christ and the church" (Ephesians 5:23-27,32).

Baptism of an Individual into God's Spiritual Nation – The Church

In the process of salvation, the Holy Spirit places the new convert into the body of Christ Jesus. It is through the Baptism of the Spirit that each individual is brought into union with Christ. Thus, there is a twofold identification in this baptism with Christ and with other believers. Romans 12:5 states, "So we, being many, are one body in Christ, and individually members of one another." "The body is a unit, though it is made up of many parts; and though all of its parts are many, they form one body. So it is with the church. For we were all baptized by one Spirit into one body— whether Jews or Greeks, slave or free—and we were all given the one Spirit to drink" (1 Corinthians 12:12-13 NIV). "There is neither Jew nor Greek, slave nor free, male nor female, for you are all one in Christ Jesus. If you belong to Christ, then you are Abraham's seed, and heirs according to the promise" (Galatians 3:28-29 NIV).

From the beginning of creation, God's purpose was to dwell with man and enjoy lasting fellowship with him. However, when man fell into sin, God's relationship with man was broken. In God's mercy and grace, He sent Jesus to reconcile mankind back to Him. "While we were still sinners, Christ died for us" (Romans 5:8). "God was in Christ reconciling the world to Himself" (2 Corinthians 5:19). Thus in Christ, God's initial desire to dwell with man was fulfilled when "the Word became flesh and dwelt among us" (John 1:14). Today, God dwells by His Spirit inside the bodies of Christians. "Do you not know that you are the temple of God and that the Spirit of God dwells in you?" (1 Corinthians 3:16). A realization of this truth will help the believer to keep his physical body healthy and spiritually clean. "For you were bought at a price; therefore glorify God in your body and in your spirit, which are God's" (1 Corinthians 6:20).

Elsewhere, Paul encouraged the believers to present their "bodies a living sacrifice, holy, acceptable to God, which is your reasonable service" (Romans 12:1). This means each saint ought to use his or her body to serve and obey God. Such giving of the body to God is more than a contract with a dead animal's sacrifice since we emerge from God's altar of sacrifice renewed and transformed spiritually. And Jesus promises all who come to Him: "All that the Father gives Me will come to Me, and the one who comes to Me I will by no means cast out....If anyone thirsts, let him come to Me and drink. He who believes in Me, as the Scripture has said, out of his heart will flow rivers of living water" (John 6:37; 7:37-38). The "living water" here is the indwelling Holy Spirit. Apostle John further states, "But this He [Jesus] spoke concerning the Spirit, whom those believing in Him would receive; for the Holy Spirit was not yet given, because Jesus was not yet glorified" (John 7:39). Later, when He arose from the grave in His glorified state, He breathed the Holy Spirit on them (John 20:22). Indeed, the Spirit's indwelling begins at conversion and is one of the evidences that the believer is a child of God and has eternal life. And those who do not have the indwelling Holy Spirit are not saved. "Now if anyone does not have the Spirit of Christ, he is not His" (Romans 8:9).

When a believer receives Christ at conversion, the Holy Spirit operates in at least five ways in the life of the believer. The believer is justified by regeneration, baptism, gifting, sealing, and indwelling.

Regeneration

The sinner's dead spirit is regenerated. In other words, it is the radical spiritual change in which God brings a sinner from a condition of spiritual darkness, defeat, and death to a renewed condition of holiness and life. Only God can bring about this spiritual change without a man's help. The term regeneration appears in Titus 3:5 as a description of the spiritual change which baptism symbolizes. It says, "Not by works of righteousness which we have done, but according to His mercy He saved us, through the washing of regeneration and renewing of the Holy Spirit." The idea of regeneration is also conveyed by the use of other terms related to ideas such as new birth. Jesus referred to regeneration when He told Nicodemus that he must be "born again" (John 3:3). The term "born again" may also be translated as "born from above." In 1 Peter 1:23, the term "born again" is used by Peter and carries the same meaning as expressed by Christ. All of these words describe the complete spiritual change which occurs when Christ enters the life of an individual by His Spirit.

Baptism

A similar experience is accomplished the moment an individual is justified. The concept used here is that of the "Baptism of Repentance." In Mark 1:4, John the Baptist came baptizing in the wilderness and his message was "repentance for the remission of sins." A cross reference of this phrase is also recorded in Luke 3:3.

Gifting

The moment a sinner is justified, that individual is indwelt by the Holy Spirit. Spirit gifts are deposited by the Holy Spirit in the believer. These gifts are called the fruit of the Spirit, which are "love, joy, peace, longsuffering, kindness, goodness, faithfulness, gentleness, and self-control" (Galatians 5:22-23). This fruit is the nature or character of God Himself. The Holy Spirit will use this gift in tough times to smooth away our old nature and rough edges to produce the character of God in the believer.

Sealing

During the moment of justification, the individual is sealed with the presence of the Holy Spirit. "In Him you also trusted, after you heard the word of truth, the gospel of your salvation; in whom also, having believed, you were sealed with the Holy Spirit of promise....And do not grieve the

Holy Spirit of God, by whom you were sealed for the day of redemption" (Ephesians 1:13; 4:30).

Indwelling

Finally, "That good thing which was committed to you, keep by the Holy Spirit who dwells in us" (2 Timothy 1:14). Not only does God's Spirit justify the believer, He also sanctifies the believer. Sanctification is the ongoing work of the Holy Spirit, transforming the believer daily into the likeness of Jesus Christ. Sanctification means "sanctified," "separated," or set apart from eternal death, the devil, and the world system, and set unto God – doing His will on earth. "We all, with unveiled face, beholding as in a mirror the glory of the Lord, are being transformed into the same image from glory to glory, just as by the Spirit of the Lord" (2 Corinthians 3:18; 1 Corinthians 1:30).

Consequently, we know that when a Christ-follower receives the Holy Spirit at conversion, the following things take place: He comes in immediately, produces spiritual experiences, remains permanently in the individual, and is the basis of all other ministries in the life of believers.

Baptism into Water

What is Baptism into Water?

Baptism into water is the believer's first step of obedience to the Lord's command. The servant of God places (immerses) the new convert into water. "Go therefore and make disciples of all the nations, baptizing them in the name of the Father and of the Son and of the Holy Spirit, teaching them to observe all things that I have commanded you; and lo, I am with you always, even to the end of the age" (Matthew 28:19-20). Mark echoes this same command when he wrote, "Go into all the world and preach the gospel to every creature. He who believes and is baptized will be saved; but he who does not believe will be condemned" (Mark 16:15-16).

The usual sequence of events is: the Spirit comes into an individual's life at conversion, and then the believer is baptized into water. The Holy Spirit is the gift who comes with salvation. Acts 2:38 states, "Then Peter said to them, 'Repent, and let every one of you be baptized in the name of Jesus Christ for the remission of sins; and you shall receive the gift of the

Holy Spirit.'" "And do not grieve the Holy Spirit of God, by whom you were sealed for the day of redemption" (Ephesians 4:30). Indeed, the Holy Spirit saturates the new Christian's life.

How is it to be done?

In the Old Testament, baptism of the Israelite church was symbolic of what was going to take place in the first-century church in the New Testament. God delivered Israel from Egypt by Moses. On their way to Canaan, the children of Israel "... were baptized into Moses in the cloud and in the sea" (1 Corinthians 10:2).

In the New Testament, beginning with Matthew 3:6, we read "...and [they] were baptized by him in the Jordan, confessing their sins." Matthew 3:16 says, "When He had been baptized, Jesus came up immediately from the water; and behold, the heavens were opened to Him, and He saw the Spirit of God descending like a dove and alighting upon Him." Acts 8:38-39 says: "So he commanded the chariot to stand still. And both Philip and the eunuch went down into the water, and he baptized him. Now when they came up out of the water, the Spirit of the Lord caught Philip away, so that the eunuch saw him no more; and he went on his way rejoicing." Paul states you were "...buried with Him in baptism, in which you also were raised with Him through faith in the working of God, who raised Him from the dead" (Colossians 2:12). So we see that baptism was done by immersion.

Why must we be Baptized in Water?

Primarily, there are two reasons—obeying God's command and demonstrating total identification (union) with Jesus Christ:

Obedience - We are commanded to do so. "Repent and let every one of you be baptized..." (Acts 2:38). "He who believes and is baptized will be saved..." (Mark 16:16).

Union - Through water baptism we acknowledge our total identification with Jesus Christ. "Or do you not know that as many of us as were baptized into Christ Jesus were baptized into His death? Therefore we were buried with Him through baptism into death, that just as Christ was raised from the dead by the glory of the Father, even so we also should walk in newness of life" (Romans 6:3-4).

What is the Significance of Water Baptism?

It is a demonstration of a clear conscience before God and the believer's public testimony to the world that the Christian is unashamed of his or her Lord. First Peter 3:21 says, "There is also an antitype which now saves us – baptism (not the removal of the filth of the flesh, but the answer of a good conscience toward God), through the resurrection of Jesus Christ."

Another blessing of water baptism is the joy of obedience. However, if in the act of water baptism, faith is exercised in regard to the breaking of carnal bondages in our lives, these things can, at that time, be broken. "Knowing this, that our old man was crucified with Him, that the body of sin might be done away with, that we should no longer be slaves of sin. For he who has died has been freed from sin" (Romans 6:6-7).

When should we be Baptized in Water?

We should be baptized in water as soon after our conversion as possible. Water baptism must be done wherever there is enough water for immersion. Jesus in Mark 16:16 tells us, "He who believes and is baptized will be saved...." Matthew 3:6 says that when people came confessing their sins, they were baptized in the Jordan without any delay, without any formal training in baptism. Consider a sampling of texts that cement the practice of when a new convert should be baptized:

- Acts 8:12: "But when they believed Philip as he preached the things concerning the kingdom of God and the name of Jesus Christ, both men and women were baptized."
- Acts 9:17-18: "And Ananias went his way and entered the house; and laying his hands on him he said, 'Brother Saul, the Lord Jesus, who appeared to you on the road as you came, has sent me that you may receive your sight and be filled with the Holy Spirit.' Immediately there fell from his eyes something like scales, and he received his sight at once; and he arose and was baptized."
- Acts 10:46-48: "...Then Peter answered, 'Can anyone forbid water, that these should not be baptized who have received the Holy Spirit just as we have?' And he commanded them to be baptized in the name of the Lord...."

- Act 16:25,32-33: "But at midnight Paul and Silas were praying and singing hymns to God, and the prisoners were listening to them....Then they spoke the word of the Lord to him and to all who were in his house. And he took them the same hour of the night and washed their stripes. And immediately, he and all his family were baptized."
- Acts 18:8: "Then Crispus, the ruler of the synagogue, believed on the Lord with all his household. And many of the Corinthians, hearing, believed and were baptized."
- At what age shall one be baptized? The Bible does not set specifications for an age for baptism. Rather, there is an emphasis in Scripture that water baptism be administered only after an individual has repented (able to distinguish and understand what he is doing and especially understanding who Jesus Christ is) of their sins and believed in Jesus Christ. Consider the following sampling:
    - "He who believes and is baptized will be saved" (Mark 16:16).
    - "... Repent, and let every one of you be baptized..." (Acts 2:38).
    - "But when they believed Philip as he preached the good news of the kingdom of God and the name of Jesus Christ, they were baptized, both men and women" (Acts 8:12 NIV).
    - Then Peter answered, "'Can anyone forbid water, that these should not be baptized who have received the Holy Spirit just as we have?' And he commanded them to be baptized in the name of the Lord" (Acts 10:47-48).
    - "Now a certain woman named Lydia heard us. She was a seller of purple from the city of Thyatira, who worshiped God. The Lord opened her heart to heed the things spoken by Paul. And when she and her household were baptized, she begged us saying, 'If you have judged me to be faithful to the Lord, come to my house and stay'" (Acts 16:14-15).
    - "Then Crispus, the ruler of the synagogue, believed on the Lord with all his household. And many of the Corinthians, hearing, believed and were baptized" (Acts 18:8).

Have you believed in the Lord Jesus Christ? If you have, God commands that you get baptized by immersion. Your obedience to God's command will bring to you joy unspeakable and full of glory.

The Baptism in the Holy Spirit

The third type of baptism taught in the Holy Scriptures is baptism in the Holy Spirit. First, let's discuss the "baptizer" and the "baptized." Jesus Christ, the "baptizer," baptizes the new Christian by plunging the person into the Holy Spirit's presence and power. Jesus, in John's gospel, says, "I will pray the Father, and He will give you another Helper, that He may abide with you forever – the Spirit of truth, whom the world cannot receive, because it neither sees Him nor knows Him; but you know Him, for He dwells with you and will be in you" (John 14:16-17). Later, when Peter was defending God's grace to the Gentiles before the council in Jerusalem, he said, "And as I began to speak, the Holy Spirit fell upon them, as upon us at the beginning. Then I remembered the word of the Lord, how He said, 'John indeed baptized with water, but you shall be baptized with the Holy Spirit'" (Acts 11:15-16). One may ask what is the difference between John's baptism and Jesus' baptism? The main difference between John's baptism and Jesus' baptism lies on the personal commitment to Christ and the coming of the Holy Spirit in Jesus' baptism. John 1:33 states, "I did not know Him, but He who sent me to baptize with water said to me, 'Upon whom you see the Spirit descending, and remaining on Him, this is He who baptizes with the Holy Spirit.'"

Second, the purpose of the baptism into the Holy Spirit is for empowerment to carry out the work of ministry or Christian service. In Acts 1:4-5, Jesus spoke to His disciples about the promise of the Father, "'which,' He said, 'you have heard from Me; for John truly baptized with water, but you shall be baptized with the Holy Spirit not many days from now.'" This experience is distinct from and usually subsequent to conversion in which a person receives the totality of the Spirit into his life and is thereby fully empowered for witness and service. Thus Jesus baptizes new Christians by plunging the person into the Holy Spirit's presence and power. Notice these texts: "And I will pray the Father, and He will give you another Helper, that He may abide with you forever – the Spirit of truth, whom the world cannot receive, because it neither sees Him nor knows Him; but you know Him, for He dwells with you and will be in you" (John

89

14:16-17). Also, Acts 11:15-16 states, "And as I began to speak, the Holy Spirit fell upon them, as upon us at the beginning. Then I remembered the word of the Lord, how He said, 'John indeed baptized with water, but you shall be baptized with the Holy Spirit.'"

Before Pentecost, all references to Spirit baptism were prophetic. Since it began at Pentecost, it appears that it will end at the rapture of the church. However, our conversion experience in Christ is similar to the experience of the apostles described by John in his gospel. This is where Jesus breathed the Spirit into His disciples before He was taken up to heaven. He said to them, "Receive the Holy Spirit" (John 20:22). Then at Pentecost, the Spirit descended on them (120 disciples), not only to unify them, but to equally empower them to testify of Him and perform great signs and miracles. The reception of the Spirit in John 20:22 is reminiscent of the creative breath of God into Adam in Genesis 2:7: "And the Lord God formed man of the dust of the ground, and breathed into his nostrils the breath of life; and man became a living being." It is important to note that the gift of the Spirit here was not a human spirit, but the Spirit of God, which we receive the moment we are converted to Christ.

An Overview - Baptism in the Holy Spirit
- Ever since the days of Joel, God's people have looked for the pouring out of God's Spirit. "And it shall come to pass afterward that I will pour out My Spirit on all flesh; your sons and your daughters shall prophesy, your old men shall dream dreams, your young men shall see visions. And also on My menservants and on My maidservants I will pour out My Spirit in those days. And I will show wonders in the heavens and in the earth" (Joel 2:28-30). This prophetic announcement was fulfilled in the book of Acts where baptism into the Holy Spirit was experienced. Let's consider the following sampling of the promise in the gospels:
- "I indeed baptize you with water unto repentance, but He who is coming after me is mightier than I, whose sandals I am not worthy to carry. He will baptize you with the Holy Spirit and fire" (Matthew 3:11).
- "I indeed baptized you with water, but He will baptize you with the Holy Spirit" (Mark 1:8).

- "John answered, saying to all, 'I indeed baptize you with water; but One mightier than I is coming, whose sandals strap I am not worthy to loose. He will baptize you with the Holy Spirit and fire'" (Luke 3:16).
- "I did not know Him, but He who sent me to baptize with water said to me, 'Upon whom you see the Spirit descending, and remaining on Him, this is He who baptizes with the Holy Spirit'" (John 1:33).
- "'He who believes in Me, as the Scripture has said, out of his heart will flow rivers of living water.' But this He spoke concerning the Spirit, whom those believing in Him would receive; for the Holy Spirit was not yet given, because Jesus was not yet glorified" (John 7:38-39). Jesus was glorified after His resurrection from the dead. He breathed the Holy Spirit into His disciples in John 20:22 and later baptized them at Pentecost.
- In Acts 1:5, Jesus said, "For John truly baptized with water, but you shall be baptized with the Holy Spirit not many days from now." Acts 2:1-4 describes the event of baptism into the Holy Spirit: "When the Day of Pentecost had fully come, they were all with one accord in one place. And suddenly there came a sound from heaven, as of a rushing mighty wind, and it filled the whole house where they were sitting. Then there appeared to them divided tongues, as of fire, and one sat upon each of them. And they were all filled with the Holy Spirit and began to speak with other tongues, as the Spirit gave them utterance." This is what was spoken by the prophet Joel saying, "And it shall come to pass afterward that I will pour out My Spirit on all flesh; your sons and your daughters shall prophesy, your old men shall dream dreams, your young men shall see visions" (Joel 2:28). Also, in Acts, we witness a similar presentation of the Holy Spirit's baptism. "While Peter was still speaking these words, the Holy Spirit fell upon all those who heard the word...because the gift of the Holy Spirit had been poured out on the Gentiles also. For they heard them speak with tongues and magnify God" (Acts 10:44-46). "Then I remembered the word of the Lord, how He said, 'John indeed baptized with water, but you shall be baptized with the Holy Spirit'" (Acts 11:16).

What does it Mean to be Baptized in the Holy Spirit?

It means being immersed in the presence and being of God. One immersed in the presence of God is made aware of his or her sinfulness and desires cleansing and purification. "When He [the Holy Spirit] has come, He will convict the world of sin, and of righteousness, and of judgment" (John 16:8). The result of this cleansing is living a life of righteousness in the true sense of the word. Another benefit to be derived from being baptized in the Holy Spirit is the empowerment given to the believer to do the work of ministry. "Behold, I sent the Promise of My Father upon you; but tarry in the city of Jerusalem until you are endued with power from on high," says Jesus (Luke 24:49).

The fulfillment of this promise is rendered in Acts 1:8: "But you shall receive power when the Holy Spirit has come on you; and you shall be witnesses to Me in Jerusalem, and in all Judea and Samaria, and to the end of the earth." The disciples were given a distinct mandate by the Lord Jesus Christ to carry His message throughout the world, backed by His power.

In addition, the ministries for which empowerment comes included witnessing (Acts 1:8) and working of miracles. In Acts 3, Peter and John went to the temple to pray. There was a lame man who was laid daily at the temple gate. God performed through Peter a miracle of the lame restored to full functioning capability. Furthermore, we read in Acts 5:12 that "through the hands of the apostles many signs and wonders were done among the people."

The experience of the power of the Holy Spirit was not limited to the early church; we can experience it too because "Jesus Christ is the same yesterday, today, and forever" (Hebrews 13:8), and He provides a way for the Holy Spirit's power to manifest in our lives and ministry. As part of the empowerment for ministry, believers are given the necessary spiritual gifts as recorded in the epistles.

Gifts of the Holy Spirit

In Romans 12:4-8, we find a partial list of these gifts. They are as follows: prophecy, ministry, teaching, exhorting, giving, leadership, and showing mercy. In 1 Corinthians 12:1-14, we are presented with another partial list of spiritual gifts: wisdom, word of knowledge, faith, healings, miracles, prophecy, discerning of spirits, tongues, and interpretation of tongues.

In Ephesians 4:11, we find yet another partial list: apostles, prophets, evangelists, pastors, and teachers. These gifts are given to the body of Christ for the "equipping of the saints for the work of ministry, for the edifying of the body of Christ, till we all come to the unity of the faith and of the knowledge of the Son of God, to be a perfect man, to the measure of the stature of the fullness of Christ" (Ephesians 4:12-13). In 1 Corinthians 14, Paul speaks in tongues and recognizes the value of tongues for one's personal edification, as well as for corporate encouragement. However, he reminds the brethren that the purpose of spiritual gifts, especially in public worship assembly, should have the witness to build and edify the body of Christ – the church. These gifts are to be used in humility (Romans 12:3), in faith (Romans 12:3), in unity (Romans 12:4-5), in love and sincerity (Romans 12:9), and in respect (Romans 12:10).

An extension of the baptism in the Holy Spirit is the gifts of the Spirit. These gifts are given to the body of Christ to glorify God, edify the church, evangelize the lost, and meet the needs of humanity at large.

Since every believer is a minister, the Holy Spirit gives to each one a gift as He pleases. Therefore, Peter wrote, "As each one has received a gift, minister it to one another" (1 Peter 4:10). When Christ ascended, He gave gifts to the church so that we could continue His work on earth. Therefore, every believer operates in at least one spiritual gift. Most believers operate in one or more of the service gifts. It is important to emphasize that the gift is never the end in itself; it is only a means to an end. Believers are channels through which the Holy Spirit flows. It is equally significant to note that believers do not really "have" (possess) gifts. The Holy Spirit flows through us to someone else. So, all believers must see themselves as instruments in the hand of God. Additionally, the Holy Spirit distributes spiritual gifts according to His divine grace; they cannot be earned through human effort or merit. They are received by faith, not achieved.

Human talents, gifts, and abilities inherited at birth are not adequate for spiritual service. So when we understand which spiritual gifts have been entrusted to us, we can come to understand God's perfect will for our lives.

At conversion, the Christ-follower receives the fruit (singular) of the Spirit. According to Galatians 5:22-23 the fruit is love, joy, peace, longsuffering, kindness, goodness, faithfulness, gentleness, and self-control. Fruit is a quality of life. It develops gradually and defines who the Christian is. Maturity in Christ and true spirituality is determined by the fruit. When a believer is immersed into the Holy Spirit or baptized in the Holy Spirit, one or more spiritual gifts are received. First Corinthians 12:7-11 has a list of the gifts: wisdom, knowledge, faith, healings, miracles, prophecy, discerning of spirits, tongues, and interpretation of tongues. These gifts define what a Christian does. Thus, they can be grouped as follows:

Revelation Gifts (1 Corinthians 12:8) – These express the mind of God.

Discerning of Spirits - The nature of this gift is found in the word "discerning" (Greek – *diakrosis* – meaning a judging thought). The main idea is to make a distinction or discernment whether a message is from God or from man's spirit (1 Corinthians 2:10-16). Good judgment is based on insight from God. God alone has perfect power of judging accurately 100% of the time. Peter manifested this gift when he discerned that the condition of Simon the Sorcerer's heart was not right (Acts 8:9-24). Simon the Sorcerer wanted to pay for the Holy Spirit with money for selfish reasons.

Knowledge - Knowledge is the accumulation of facts, either divinely imparted or acquired through the intellect. A word of knowledge is a Spirit-inspired utterance or acquired through formal teaching (Romans 12:6-7). Out of God's infinite store of knowledge, He chooses to reveal a small portion through a Spirit-filled believer with the word of knowledge; the word of knowledge edifies, encourages, or fortifies the church.

Wisdom - True wisdom is possessed by God alone. The Word wisdom given to a believer is a portion of that infinite wisdom of God. This kind of wisdom is distinct from human wisdom.

Speech Gifts (1 Corinthians 12:8) – These express the feeling of God's infinite heart.

Prophecy - Prophecy is seeing the world through God's eyes. The prophet sees a people and addresses the situation using God's Word. They may also use the Word of God to indicate future events. These prophecies involve forth-telling (declaring the Word of God to our hearts), and it may also involve foretelling (telling the future). First Corinthians 14:3 indicates that prophecy builds up, encourages, and comforts believers. Thus believers are urged to eagerly desire this gift. Prophecy is also useful in convicting non-believers, because the secrets of one's heart can be revealed (1 Corinthians 14:24-25). Let us echo what Moses said: "Oh, that all the Lord's people were prophets" (Numbers 11:29).

Tongues - A believer is said to have been baptized in the Spirit when the initial evidence of speaking in tongues is manifested. This gift is the distribution or the power of utterance in languages unknown to the speaker, given to certain individuals in the church by the Spirit of God and capable of interpretation. Thus we have two types of tongues. In 1 Corinthians 14, Paul speaks in tongues and recognizes the value of tongues for one's personal edification as well as for corporate encouragement. But he is reminding them of the purpose of spiritual gifts and how they are to function in public worship assemblies. Since spiritual gifts are given for the common good, the exercise of these gifts should always have the intent to build and edify the body of Christ.

Interpretation of Tongues - The gift of interpretation of tongues is synonymous with interpreting a foreign tongue into the known language of a culture by one who knows both languages.

Power Gifts (1 Corinthians 12:9-10) – These express the mighty power of God.

Faith - This comes first by hearing the Word of God (Romans 10:17). This spiritual gift must be distinguished from the faith which is impossible to please God. The powerful gift of faith described here is a special gift. When in operation, it moves the hand of God on our behalf. For example, in Matthew 17:20, Jesus said to the disciples, "Because of your unbelief; for assuredly, I say to you, if you have faith as a mustard seed, you will say to this mountain, 'Move from here to there,' and it will move; and nothing will be impossible for you.'" Mark 11:22 echoes this when he wrote the same truth about what Jesus said, "Have faith in God." In the Old Testament we witness a remarkable demonstration of faith in God by Daniel when he was thrown into the lions' den (Daniel 6:1-28).

Healings - Notice that the text presents both gifts and healings in the plural. The spiritual gifts of healings are given to glorify God, to confess the Gospel message, and to alleviate human sufferings. The administration of these gifts is done through the laying on of hands, through speaking in authority, and/or through anointing with oil. By employing any of the above means, the desired result is to bring about physical healing, emotional healing, spiritual healing, mental healing, and relational healing, just to mention these. Healings come instantly or gradually. In all, there are many ministry needs for healing.

Miracles - Miracles occur by the power of the Holy Spirit to stupefy the natural order of things and events, i.e., parting of the Red Sea, or feeding of 5,000 people, or resurrecting the dead.

Ministry Gifts (1 Corinthians 7:7; 12:8-10, 27-31; 14:26; Romans 12:7; Ephesians 4:11-13; 5:18-19; James 3:1; 1 Peter 4:9).

Every act of service, whether done through a natural ability, gift, or supernatural gift, is seen by God as valuable for ministry and for the building of the body of Christ and the Kingdom of God. Ultimately, God provides spiritual gifts for the sole purpose of service. They are not given to draw attention to believers. God intends that the ministry of His church be accomplished through spiritual gifts since human talent is grossly inadequate for supernatural service. By understanding which spiritual gifts we have been entrusted with, we can come to the understanding of God's plan and will for our lives (Romans 12:1-2). God wants to empower us for service beyond our own talents by His Holy Spirit. The list below includes fourteen concepts of ministry gifts:

Administration - This is a unique gift given to some members who have the insight and foresight to understand the overall mission of the church. Administration is also called government in the King James Version. These individuals are responsible for guiding and directing the activities of the church locally and around the world. They have offices within the local church, but their ministry is not limited to it. "And He Himself gave some to be apostles, some prophets, some evangelists, and some pastors and teachers, for the equipping of the saints for the work of ministry, for the edifying of the body of Christ, till we all come to the unity of the faith

96

and of the knowledge of the Son of God, to a perfect man, to the measure of the stature of the fullness of Christ" (Ephesians 4:11-13; see also Acts 6:1-7; 1 Corinthians 12:28; Titus 1:5). Thus, we have:

- Apostles – The word "apostle" means a messenger, one who is sent out as a missionary. Paul said in 2 Corinthians 12:12 that signs, wonders, and miracles make an apostle.
- Prophets –Their ministry is similar to those of the Old Testament.
- Evangelists – They carry the Good News to every land.
- Pastors – They shepherd the flock in the local assembly.
- Teachers – They exercise the gifted ministry of expository teaching–line by line, precept by precept.

Craftsmanship - This is a unique ability to use one's hands to make, create, construct, and repair whatever is necessary to further the work of God and bring glory to Him. "Now a certain woman named Lydia heard us. She was a seller of purple from the city of Thyatira, who worshiped God. The Lord opened her heart to heed the things spoken by Paul" (Acts 16:14; 18:3; see also Exodus 30:22-25; 31:3-11; 2 Chronicles 34:9-13).

Evangelism - This is the unique ability to share the gospel with unbelievers in such a way that they respond and become followers of Jesus Christ. "And daily in the temple, and in every house, they did not cease teaching and preaching Jesus as the Christ" (Acts 5:42; see also 8:5-6, 21:8, 6:5; Romans 10:15; Ephesians 4:11). Although all Christians are commanded to share the Good News with unbelievers, some are specially gifted to win souls to the Kingdom.

Exhortation - This is the unique ability to minister words and deeds of encouragement, comfort, and counsel to others in such a way that they feel strengthened and helped. The gift of prophecy, the gift of teaching, and the gift of exhortation all interrelate. The prophet, the teacher, and the exhorter depend upon one another to get the message across. For example, Barnabas was an encourager, Paul was a teacher, but both served the church in Antioch. "And Joses, who was also named Barnabas by the apostles (which is translated Son of Encouragement), a Levite of the country of Cyprus, having land, sold it, and brought the money and laid it at the apostles' feet"

(Acts 4:36-37; see also 11:22-26; Romans 12:8; 1 Thessalonians 2:11-12; 2 Timothy 4:2; Hebrews 10:25).

Giving - God has uniquely gifted some members in the body who have the special ability to identify a need and respond to it. They share cheerfully with their material resources and time to meet the needs of other people and advance the work of God. "He who exhorts, in exhortation; he who gives, with liberality; he who leads, with diligence; he who shows mercy, with cheerfulness" (Romans 12:8; see also Acts 4:30-37; 9:36-39; 2 Corinthians 8:1-15; 9:5-11; 1 Timothy 6:17-19).

Helping - An individual uniquely endowed with the ability to invest in the life and ministry of others in the body in order to enhance their effectiveness in service for God has the gift of helping. "At Joppa there was a certain disciple named Tabitha, which is translated Dorcas. This woman was full of good works and charitable deeds which she did" (Acts 9:36; see also Romans 16:1-2; 1 Corinthians 12:28; Philippians 2:24-30; Philemon 1:11).

Hospitality - This is the unique ability to provide a heartwarming welcome to those needing food or lodging, and to make guests and strangers feel welcome and accepted in any situation as well as help people get acquainted with others. "And when she and her household were baptized, she begged us, saying, 'If you have judged me to be faithful to the Lord, come to my house and stay.' So she persuaded us" (Acts 16:15; see also 21:4,7-8; Romans 12:13, 16:23; 1 Timothy 3:2; Hebrews 12:1-2; 1 Peter 4:9).

Intercession - This is the unique ability and calling to make petitions to God on behalf of others on a regular basis over an extended period of time, which results in specific answers. Intercessors are able to motivate others to "practice His presence" – waiting upon the Lord. "Epaphras, who is one of you, a bondservant of Christ, greets you, always laboring fervently for you in prayers, that you may stand perfect and complete in all the will of God" (Colossians 4:12; see also Acts 12:5-17; 16:25-31; 1 Timothy 2:1-8; James 5:14-16).

Leadership - This is the special ability given by the Spirit to help set goals, a course of direction, and unification of the body in accordance with God's will. Leaders are able to effectively communicate these goals to others and to motivate them to work together harmoniously to accomplish these goals for the glory of God. Servant leadership best describes God's servants placed in leadership positions in His body. "He who exhorts, in exhortation; he who gives, with liberality; he who leads, with diligence; he who shows mercy, with cheerfulness" (Romans 12:8; see also Acts 15:7-11; 1 Timothy 5:17; Hebrews 13:17).

Mercy - This is the special ability to genuinely empathize and sincerely have compassion for an individual in distressing situations and to translate that compassion into cheerfully done acts that reflect Christ's love and alleviate suffering. These members in the body show special kindness and mercy to others, inspired by Christ's example. For instance, they may aid victims. The merciful person reaches out and administers the redemption and inner healing of Jesus Christ. "But Barnabas took him and brought him to the apostles. And he declared to them how he had seen the Lord on the road, and that He had spoken to him, and how he had preached boldly at Damascus in the name of Jesus"(Acts 9:27; see also 9:36; 16:33-34; Romans 12:8).

Missionary - This unique ability God gives to members of the body of Christ is to minister in regions and other cultural settings beyond their own. "But the Lord said to him, 'Go, for he is a chosen vessel of Mine to bear My name before Gentiles, kings, and the children of Israel'" (Acts 9:15; see also 13:2-3; Romans 10:15; 1 Corinthians 9:19-23; Ephesians 3:1-7).

Music - This is a unique gift to sing or play a musical instrument in such a way that the body of Christ is edified and Jesus Christ is glorified and exalted. "And with them Heman and Jeduthun, to sound aloud with trumpets and cymbals and the musical instruments of God. Now the sons of Jeduthun were gatekeepers" (1 Chronicles 16:42; see also 2 Chronicles 5:12-13; 34:12; Psalm 101, 150; 1 Corinthians 14:26).

Serving - This is the special desire and ability to identify task-oriented needs in the body and to seek available resources to meet these needs, doing so with a willing and joyful attitude. "Now in those days, when the number of the disciples was multiplying, there arose a complaint against the Hebrews by the Hellenists, because their widows were neglected in the daily distribution. Then the twelve summoned the multitude of the disciples and said, 'It is not desirable that we should leave the word of God and serve tables. Therefore, brethren, seek out from among you seven men of good reputation, full of the Holy Spirit and wisdom, whom we may appoint over this business; but we will give ourselves continually to prayer and to the ministry of the word.' And the saying pleased the whole multitude. And they chose Stephen, a man full of faith and the Holy Spirit, and Philip, Prochorus, Nicanor, Timon, Parmenas, and Nicolas, a proselyte from Antioch, whom they set before the apostles; and when they had prayed, they laid hands on them. Then the word of God spread, and the number of the disciples multiplied greatly in Jerusalem, and a great many of the priests were obedient to the faith" (Acts 6:1-7; see also 9:36-43; Romans 12:7; 15:26-33; Galatians 6:10; 2 Timothy 1:16-18). Jesus epitomized this gift when He washed the disciples' feet. He demonstrated through His practical service the ministry of love and humility.

Teaching - Although many can teach in the secular arena, those who are baptized in the Spirit, are empowered for the service of teaching beyond their abilities. The special ability they acquire will enable them to communicate spiritual truths relevant to the needs of the body of Christ in such a way that others will be motivated to learn and to respond to the message. "And they continued steadfastly in the apostles' doctrine and fellowship, in the breaking of bread, and in prayers" (Acts 2:42; see also 15:35; 18:24-28; 19:8-10; Ephesians 4:11-15; Colossians 3:16; 1 Timothy 3:2; 2 Timothy 2:2; Titus 2:3-5; James 3:1).

Three Additional Gifts (rarely discussed) – 1 Corinthians 7:7; 1 Corinthians 13:3; 1 Peter 4:9).

Celibacy - In 1 Corinthians 7:7, Paul considers celibacy as a spiritual gift. It is the divine ability to remain single for the Gospel's sake and not suffer under sexual temptations. In this case, individuals decide to remain eunuchs for Christ's sake so that they are not entangled with family responsibility. Also in this situation, the individuals who decide to practice celibacy are not born eunuchs.

Martyrdom - Paul said in 1 Corinthians 13:3, "...Though I give my body to be burned...." Church history is replete with men and women who received this gift and offered their lives as a testimony to the ages.

Voluntary Poverty - Paul speaks about giving up worldly goods. "If I give all I possess to the poor...." In this instance, the believer is given by the Spirit the unique ability to empty him or herself of *all* their material assets for the care of others (1 Corinthians 13:3 NIV).

It is significant to observe that the greatest gift of all times, "love" (1 Corinthians 13), is sandwiched between the spiritual gifts listed in 1 Corinthians 12 and our walk with the Lord in 1 Corinthians 14. Our spirituality should never be measured by our spiritual gifts but the fruit of the Spirit we produce in our spiritual journey. All gifts are given to make us into better servants. They are not given as proprietary. A believer cannot use them as he or she pleases. Walking in the Spirit is the ongoing process of connecting and fellowshipping with the Spirit. Just as you take each step in the natural walk, so too you must depend entirely on the leadership of the Spirit to guide, lead, and use you for His glory, for His church, for the unsaved, and to meet the needs of humanity.

Is there an immediate sign of the Baptism in the Holy Spirit? Yes, the Scriptures teach that those who were baptized in the Holy Spirit "spoke with tongues." Let's consider the following sampling:

- "And they were all filled with the Holy Spirit and began to speak with other tongues, as the Spirit gave them utterance" (Acts 2:4).
- "And those of the circumcision who believed were astonished, as many as came with Peter, because the gift of the Holy Spirit had been poured out on the Gentiles also. For they heard them speak with tongues and magnify God" (Acts 10:45-46).
- "And when Paul had laid hands on them, the Holy Spirit came upon them, and they spoke with tongues and prophesied. Now the men were about twelve in all" (Acts 19:6-7).

Finally, how should seekers for baptism in the Spirit be instructed?
- They must open up their heart to the Spirit and confess all known sins (Psalm 139:23-24).
- They must earnestly expect to receive from God through His Spirit the Baptism in the Spirit.
- They must remain in obedience and submission to the will of God.
- The Holy Spirit's outpouring may come in one of three ways:
  - Solely by God (Acts 2:2, 4).
  - Through the preaching of the Word and
  - Through the laying on of hands (Acts 10:44; 8:17; 9:17; 19:6).

The Person and Work of the Holy Spirit

Jesus said, "And I will pray the Father, and He will give you another Helper, that He may abide with you forever" (John 14:16). Let's look first at what cults and false teachers teach about the Holy Spirit:

What Cults and Other Religions Teach about the Holy Spirit
- Jehovah's Witnesses say he is an invisible, active force.
- Mormons believe he is an influence or electricity-like emanation.
- Unification Church declares that he is a feminine spirit who works with Jesus.
- Christian Scientists say that he is an impersonal power.
- Unity School of Christianity declares that he is the executive power of both Father and Son: a "Definite."
- New Agers believe that he is psychic force.
- The Nation of Islam says that he is the power of God or the angel Gabriel.
- Baha'i teaches that he is the divine energy of God.
- Some followers of Judaism say God is love or power; others say it's God's activity on earth.

As a Person, the Holy Spirit is God.
- He is a Person, not a "power," but He is powerful.
- He stays alongside us; basically, He is a personal helper. "But Peter said, 'Ananias, why has Satan filled your heart to lie to the Holy Spirit....You have not lied to men, but to God'" (Acts 5:3-4). This verse clearly equates the Holy Spirit to God. "Now the Lord is the Spirit..." (2 Corinthians 3:17). "The Lord" here refers to "the Lord" in the Old Testament verse (Exodus 34:34). The Holy Spirit manifests the same attributes as the Father and the Son.
- As a Person, He has *intellect*. First Corinthians 2:11 (NIV) says, "...No one knows the thoughts of God except the Spirit of God." And Romans 8:27 (NIV) says, "He who searches our hearts knows the mind of the Spirit...." He is called alongside to help believers.
- As a Person, He has *feelings*. In Ephesians 4:30, we are told explicitly, "Do not grieve the Holy Spirit."

102

- As a Person, He has a *will* (Ephesians 1:1). First Corinthians 12:11 says that the Holy Spirit gives spiritual gifts to each as He wills. The gifts that are placed in the Body of Christ came through the marvelous working of the Holy Spirit.

In 2 Corinthians 13:14, the Spirit's association with the Father and Son is displayed: "The grace of the Lord Jesus Christ, and the love of God, and the communion of the Holy Spirit be with you all. Amen." Also, in commissioning the disciples, the Holy Spirit is mentioned in Matthew 28:19: "Go therefore and make disciples of all the nations, baptizing them in the *name* of the Father and of the Son and of the Holy Spirit" (emphasis added).

The Spirit of God also does the works of God in at least four areas:
- *He was involved in creation:* "The earth was without form, and void; and darkness was on the face of the deep. And the Spirit of God was hovering over the face of the waters" (Genesis 1:2).
- *He is involved in regeneration.* "You send forth Your Spirit, they are created; and You renew the face of the earth" (Psalm 104:30; John 3:5-6; John 20:22).
- *He is involved in giving the Scriptures:* "All Scripture is given by inspiration of God, and is profitable for doctrine, for reproof, for correction, for instruction in righteousness, that the man of God may be complete, thoroughly equipped for every good work" (2 Timothy 3:16-17).
- Finally, *He is involved in the resurrection of the dead:* "But if the Spirit of Him who raised Jesus from the dead dwells in you, He who raised Christ from the dead will also give life to your mortal bodies through His Spirit who dwells in you" (Romans 8:11).

The Scriptures also teach other significant actions that the Holy Spirit does in the life of a believer. Note carefully the following verses of Scripture which illustrate these truths:

Abides With Us Forever

"And I will pray the Father, and He will give you another Helper, that He may abide with you forever" (John 14:16).

Bears fruit

"The fruit of the Spirit is love, joy, peace, longsuffering, kindness, goodness, faithfulness, gentleness, self-control. Against such there is no law" (Galatians 5:22-23).

Bears Witness

"The Spirit Himself bears witness with our spirit that we are children of God" (Romans 8:16). "But the Holy Spirit also witnesses to us..." (Hebrews 10:15).

Brings All Things to Remembrance

"But the Helper, the Holy Spirit, whom the Father will send in My name, He will teach you all things, and bring to your remembrance all things that I said to you" (John 14:26).

Calls

"And the Spirit and the bride say, 'Come!' And let him who hears say, 'Come!' And let him who thirsts come. Whoever desires, let him take the water of life freely" (Revelation 22:17).

Comforts

"Nevertheless, I tell you the truth, it is to your advantage that I go away; for if I do not go away, the Helper will not come to you; but if I depart, I will send Him to you" (John 16:7).

Commands

"Then the Spirit said to Philip, 'Go near and overtake this chariot'" (Acts 8:29).

Convicts

"And when He has come, He will convict the world of sin, and of righteousness, and of judgment" (John 16:8).

Fills the Brethren

"And they were all filled with the Holy Spirit and began to speak with other tongues, as the Spirit gave them utterance" (Acts 2:4; see also Acts 4:8,31; 9:17; Luke 11:15,41).

Gives Discernment

"God has revealed them to us through His Spirit. For the Spirit searches all things, yes, and the deep things of God" (1 Corinthians 2:10).

Gives Gifts

"The manifestation of the Spirit is given to each one for the profit of all" – wisdom, knowledge, faith, healings, miracles, prophecy, discerning of spirits, tongues, and interpretation of tongues (1 Corinthians 12:8-10). Other gifts in New Testament (Ephesians 4:11-13; James 3:1; 1 Corinthians 7:7; 13:3; 1 Peter 4:9).

Gives Joy

"For the kingdom of God is not eating and drinking but righteousness and peace and joy in the Holy Spirit" (Romans 14:17).

Gives Power over the Devil

"...When the enemy comes in like a flood, the Spirit of the Lord will lift up a standard against him" (Isaiah 59:19).

Gives Power over Sickness, Diseases, Demons, and Death

"And when He had called His twelve disciples to Him, He gave them power over unclean spirits, to cast them out, and to heal all kinds of sickness and all kinds of disease" (Matthew 10:1; see also 2 Thessalonians 3:3; Psalm 118:17).

Gives Us Power to Endure Hardships

"You are of God, little children, and have overcome them, because He who is in you is greater than he who is in the world" (1 John 4:4).

Guides Believers

"However, when He, the Spirit of truth, has come, He will guide you into all truth; for He will not speak on His own authority, but whatever

He hears He will speak; and He will tell you things to come" (John 16:13; Romans 8:14; Acts 16:6-7).

Helps

"And I will pray the Father, and He will give you another Helper, that He may abide with you forever" (John 14:16).

Illuminates

"The God of our Lord Jesus Christ, the Father of glory, may give to you the spirit of wisdom and revelation in the knowledge of Him, the eyes of your understanding being enlightened..." (Ephesians 1:17-18; 1 Corinthians 2:12-13).

Intercedes

"Likewise the Spirit also helps in our weaknesses. For we do not know what we should pray for as we ought, but the Spirit Himself makes intercession for us with groaning which cannot be uttered" (Romans 8:26).

Opens our Minds into the Supernatural Realm

"I know a man in Christ who fourteen years ago...[was] caught up to the third heaven... he was caught up into Paradise and heard the inexpressible words, which it is not lawful for a man to utter....And lest I should be exalted above measure by the abundance of the revelations..." (2 Corinthians 12:2-4, 7).

Prays for Us

"Likewise the Spirit also helps in our weaknesses. For we do not know what we should pray for as we ought, but the Spirit Himself makes intercession for us with groanings which cannot be uttered" (Romans 8:26).

Renews

"Not by works of righteousness which we have done, but according to His mercy He saved us, though the washing of regeneration and renewing of the Holy Spirit" (Titus 3:5).

Reveals

"Who has directed the Spirit of the Lord, or as His counselor has taught Him? With whom did He take counsel, and who instructed Him, and taught Him in the path of justice? Who taught Him knowledge, and showed Him the way of understanding" (Isaiah 40:13-14; 1 Corinthians 2:10,13). "For prophecy never came by the will of man, but holy men of God spoke as they were moved by the Holy Spirit" (2 Peter 1:21).

Sanctifies

"That I might be a minister of Jesus Christ to the Gentiles, ministering the gospel of God, that the offering of the Gentiles might be acceptable, sanctified by the Holy Spirit" (Romans 15:16). "But we are bound to give thanks to God always for you, brethren beloved by the Lord, because God from the beginning chose you for salvation through sanctification by the Spirit and belief in the truth" (2 Thessalonians 2:13).

Shows Us Things to Come

"When He, the Spirit of truth, has come, He will guide you into all truth; for He will not speak on His own authority, but whatever He hears He will speak; and He will tell you things to come" (John 16:13).

Seals

"In Him you also trusted, after you heard the word of truth, the gospel of your salvation; in whom also, having believed, you were sealed with the Holy Spirit of promise" (Ephesians 1:13).

Sends Workers

"...Being sent out by the Holy Spirit, they went down to Seleucia, and from there they sailed to Cyprus" (Acts 13:2-4).

Speaks

"These things we also speak, not in words which man's wisdom teaches but which the Holy Spirit teaches, comparing spiritual things with spiritual" (1 Corinthians 2:13).

Does Not Strive

"And the Lord said, 'My Spirit shall not strive with man forever, for he is indeed flesh'" (Genesis 6:3a). Today, if you hear God's voice nudging you in your spirit, do not harden your hearts because God will not strive to claim you forever. Instead, open the door of your heart, receive Him, and He will dwell in you for eternity.

Teaches

"He will teach you all things, and bring to your remembrance all things that I said to you" (John 14:26).

Testifies

"Except that the Holy Spirit testifies in every city, saying that chains and tribulations await me" (Acts 20:23). "When the Helper comes, whom I shall send to you from the Father, the Spirit of truth who proceeds from the Father, He will testify of Me" (John 15:26).

Works

"But one and the same Spirit works all these things, distributing to each one individually as He wills" (1 Corinthians 12:11).

The Spirit's Association with the Father and Son (Godhead/Trinity)

- "When He [Jesus] had been baptized, Jesus came up immediately from the water, and behold, the heavens were opened to Him, and He saw the Spirit of God descending like a dove and alighting upon Him. And suddenly a voice came from heaven, saying, 'This is My beloved Son, in whom I am well pleased'" (Matthew 3:16-17).
- "Go therefore and make disciples of all the nations, baptizing them in the name of the Father and of the Son and of the Holy Spirit" (Matthew 28:19).
- "Therefore being exalted to the right hand of God, and having received from the Father the promise of the Holy Spirit, He poured out this which you now see and hear" (Acts 2:33).
- "The grace of the Lord Jesus Christ, and the love of God and the communion of the Holy Spirit be with you all. Amen" (2 Corinthians 13:14).
- "For there are three that bear witness in heaven: the Father, the Word, and the Holy Spirit; and these three are one" (1 John 5:7).

Offenses Against the Holy Spirit

Blaspheming
Don't blaspheme (stubborn refusal to heed the Spirit's conviction and accept the conviction that Christ offers). "Therefore I say to you, every sin and blasphemy will be forgiven men, but the blasphemy against the Spirit will not be forgiven men" (Matthew 12:31).

Grieving:
Don't grieve the Holy Spirit. "But they rebelled and grieved His Holy Spirit" (Isaiah 63:10a). "And do not grieve the Holy Spirit of God, by whom you were sealed for the day of redemption" (Ephesians 4:30).

Insulting
Don't insult the Holy Spirit. "Of how much worse punishment, do you suppose, will he be thought worthy who has trampled the Son of God underfoot, counted the blood of the covenant by which he was sanctified a common thing, and insulted the Spirit of grace" (Hebrews 10:29).

Lying
Don't lie to the Holy Spirit as Ananias did. Peter said, "Ananias, why has Satan filled your heart to lie to the Holy Spirit and keep back part of the price of land for yourself?" (Acts 5:3).

Quenching
Do not quench the Holy Spirit (1 Thessalonians 5:19).

Resisting
Don't resist the Holy Spirit. "You stiff-necked and uncircumcised in heart and ears! You always resist the Holy Spirit; as your fathers did, so do you" (Acts 7:51).

Testing
Don't test the Spirit like Ananias and Sapphira did. "Then Peter said to [Sapphira], 'How is it that you have agreed together to test the Spirit of the Lord?'" (Acts 5:9).

Some of the Symbols of the Spirit

Dividing Tongues

"Then there appeared to them divided tongues, as of fire, and one sat upon each of them....And when this sound occurred, the multitude came together, and were confused, because everyone heard them speak in his own language. Then they were all amazed and marveled, saying to one another, 'Look, are not all these who speak Galileans? And how is it that we hear, each in our own language in which we were born? Parthians and Medes and Elamites, those dwelling in Mesopotamia, Judea and Cappadocia, Pontus and Asia, Phrygia and Pamphylia, Egypt and the parts of Libya adjoining Cyrene, visitors from Rome, both Jews and proselytes, Cretans and Arabs—we hear them speaking in our own tongues the wonderful works of God'" (Acts 2:3,6-11).

Dove

The dove signifies gentleness and tenderness, and it's a universal sign of peace. "The Holy Spirit descended in bodily form like a dove upon Him, and a voice came from heaven which said, 'You are My beloved Son; in You I am well pleased'" (Luke 3:22).

Fire

Purifying - "When the Lord has washed away the filth of the daughters of Zion, and purged the blood of Jerusalem from her midst, by the spirit of judgment and by the spirit of burning" (Isaiah 4:4). "But who can endure the day of His coming? And who can stand when He appears? For He is like a refiner's fire and like launderers' soap. He will sit as a refiner and a purifier of silver; He will purify the sons of Levi, and purge them as gold and silver, that they may offer to the Lord an offering in righteousness" (Malachi 3:2-3).

Mind or Breath (Old Testament)

"The east wind carries him away, and he is gone; it sweeps him out of his place" (Job 27:21). "He causes His wind to blow, and the waters flow" (Psalm 147:18b).

Oil

Oil is a symbol of anointing and empowerment for service in Kingdom business. "The Spirit of the Lord is upon Me, because He has anointed Me to preach the gospel to the poor; He has sent Me to heal the brokenhearted, to proclaim liberty to the captives and recovery of sight to the blind, to set at liberty those who are oppressed; to proclaim the acceptable year of the Lord" (Luke 4:18-19).

Rain as Dew

"He shall come down like rain upon the grass before mowing, like showers that water the earth" (Psalm 72:6).

Seal Sign

The seal sign demonstrates ownership and a mark of authority. "In Him you also trusted, after you heard the word of truth, the gospel of your salvation; in whom also, having believed, you were sealed with the Holy Spirit of promise" (Ephesians 1:13).

Voice

"Also I heard the voice of the Lord, saying: 'Whom shall I send, and who will go for Us?' Then I said, 'Here am I! Send me'" (Isaiah 6:8).

Water

The Holy Spirit symbolizes water as an essential element to life. Jesus said, "'If anyone thirsts, let him come to Me and drink. He who believes in Me, as the Scripture has said, out of his heart will flow rivers of living water.' But this He spoke concerning the Spirit, whom those believing in Him would receive; for the Holy Spirit was not yet given, because Jesus was not yet glorified" (John 7:37-39).

Wind

In the Greek, Spirit is *pneuma*, which stands for air, breath, or wind.

Application

Instead of engaging in any of the above wrongdoings listed on page 109, let us welcome and receive Him into our lives. John writes, "As many as received Him, to them He gave the right to become children of God, to those who believed in His name" (John 1:12). John later writes, "I stand at the door and knock. If anyone hears My voice and opens the door, I will come in to him and dine with him, and he with Me" (Revelation 3:20).

For those who have received Jesus, make Him your Lord and Master so that you can live a victorious Christian life. This will happen if you totally yield to Him daily. "Do not be drunk with wine, in which is dissipation, but be filled with the Spirit" (Ephesians 5:18). For when we are filled with the Spirit, we will "walk in the Spirit...and shall not fulfill the lust of the flesh" (Galatians 5:16).

Baptism of Fire

The fourth type of baptism taught in the Scriptures is the Baptism of Fire. In Matthew 3:11, John the Baptist says, "I indeed baptize you with water unto repentance, but He who is coming after me is mightier than I, whose sandals I am not worthy to carry. He will baptize you with the Holy Spirit and fire." Here, John proclaims that it is Jesus who baptizes the believer in the Holy Spirit and fire. The baptism of fire is a separate experience from the baptism in the Holy Spirit. This baptism is the baptism into sufferings, which is inseparably connected to our salvation and calling. When believers go through trials, they are following in the footsteps of Jesus (1 Peter 2:21), participating not only in His suffering, but also in His glory (Revelation 1:7; 14:13).

Christian Calling

Suffering and evil are inevitable parts of a fallen world. The believer cannot escape or insulate himself from trials, tests, and temptations. These are integral parts of our calling as Christ-followers. Paul aptly captures this essential doctrine when he writes, "That I may know Him and the power of His resurrection, and the fellowship of His sufferings, being conformed to His death" (Philippians 3:10). Notice the expression "the fellowship of His sufferings." There are several ways a believer experiences sufferings for the sake of Christ. They may experience insults, mockery, threats, beatings, imprisonment, excommunication, and even death. In Philippians, Paul sees the value of participating in the persecutions, hardships, trials, tests, temptations, and struggles of life that naturally accompany one who is in partnership with God, living the Christian life, and sharing the Gospel message to a lost world.

With reference to Philippians 3:10, Apostle Paul earlier said to the Christ-followers, "It has been granted on behalf of Christ, not only to believe in Him, but also to suffer for His sake" (Philippians 1:29). On another occasion, when Paul wrote to the Romans, he said, we are "heirs of God and joint heirs with Christ, if indeed we suffer with Him [Christ], that we may also be glorified together" (Romans 8:17). Apostle James (the half-brother of Jesus), when writing to the twelve tribes scattered abroad (the community of believers including both Christian and non-Christian), said, "My brethren, count it all joy when you fall into various trials, knowing that the testing of your faith produces patience. But let patience have its perfect work, that you may be perfect and complete, lacking nothing" (James 1:2-4). There are benefits in open acceptance to our suffering. In this text, James describes the benefit of accepting our suffering, a subject that will be discussed in greater detail later.

Apostle Peter also points out that the Christ-follower should be encouraged to persevere in his or her calling, "For to this you were called, because Christ also suffered for us, leaving us an example, that you should follow His steps: 'who committed no sin, nor was deceit found in His mouth; who, when He was reviled, did not revile in return; when He suffered, He did not threaten, but committed Himself to Him who judges righteously; who Himself bore our sins in His own body on the tree, that we, having died to sins, might live for righteousness—by whose stripes you were healed'" (1 Peter 2:21-24). So, part of being a Christian is the challenging yet reassuring privilege of serving God faithfully in the midst of our trials even when encountering undeserved judgments by the enemies of the cross. When we observe how Christ handled unjust punishment, it gives us insight as to how we also may endure such trials.

Symbolism of Fire – What does fire symbolize in the Scripture?

In the Old and New Testaments, the word "fire" and the expression "to be baptized with fire" are certainly not to be taken literally. Rather, they often symbolize God's manifest presence, judgment, or cleansing. For example, the Lord's appearance in the burning bush was the physical manifestation of God's divine presence. In another occurrence, God led the Israelites by the pillar of fire by night (Exodus 13:21-22). Even His appearance on Mount Sinai (Exodus 19:18) attests to God's divine presence in the Old Testament. Furthermore, fire is used to symbolize Israel's worship, representing God's constant presence with Israel (Leviticus 6:12-13).

In the New Testament, the Holy Spirit is God's divine presence in the life of the believer and in the world. The believer and the world are made aware of sin, God's judgment on sin, and the need to be righteous in God's presence. God's Spirit brings the overwhelming sense of one's uncleanness and the awesome desire to be clean before a holy God. Thus, to be baptized in fire is to be convicted of sin, to be redeemed from deserved judgment, and to receive righteousness (John 16:8). The Word of God is called fire because of its judging, purifying, and consuming abilities.

Judging

In our reference text, Matthew 3:11, the baptism of fire does not imply that when Jesus comes, He will judge the believer. For "There is therefore now no condemnation to those who are in Christ Jesus" (Romans 8:1a). In Christ, we are no longer under the sentence of the law, but empowered by the Spirit within us to live for Christ. However, the works of all believers will be judged at the Bema Seat of Christ after all true believers are raptured. Again, the judgment here is one of works and has nothing to do with the believer's eternal salvation in Christ. Those whose works are approved will be rewarded. But those whose works are not approved will be burned by the fire of judgment. The fires of judgment also are reserved for all those who reject the free gift of Christ because Christ is the only means by which to obtain eternal security in heaven with God.

Purifying

The major purpose of the baptism in fire is to purify the Christ-follower. Human suffering is not always a sign of God's judgment. In this fallen world, sometimes the believer may suffer innocently. However, through that suffering, God accomplishes His good will and pleasure. "And we know that all things work together for good to those who love God, to those who are the called according to His purpose" (Romans 8:28). God is working His good purpose through this fallen world. Sometimes our suffering or the sufferings of others may blind us to the reality that the sovereign God is working out all things for His glory in His timing. In Job's case, Satan falsely accused Job of disloyalty to God. Fortunately, he later was acquitted and blessed more than before, proving God's sovereignty. Another excellent example is John's account of a man born blind. Jesus demonstrated His healing power by restoring sight to the blind man. In performing this remarkable miracle, Jesus made himself a vessel "that the works of God should be revealed in him" (John 9:3,30-33).

Consuming Fire

God speaks of Himself as a consuming fire that is a picture of His holiness and the righteousness which He demands of His people (Leviticus 11:44; 1 Peter 1:16; Matthew 5:48). Also, the expression "consuming fire" is found in both the Old and New Testaments. "Consuming fire" is further associated with God's presence (Exodus 24:17; Deuteronomy 9:3; Hebrews 12:29). In the Old Testament, God's consuming presence led the Israelites through their wilderness journey through instruction and guidance. God's presence is evident in battles against the enemies of His people in the Promised Land. On the other hand, in the New Testament (Hebrews 12:29), the reminder of God's consuming presence is urging the Christ-follower to serve God with reverential and godly fear. In light of the inevitability of human suffering, what should the believer's attitude be in response to trials, persecutions, and hardships?

A Christian's Response to Suffering

The world is a war zone. God's people should expect to suffer. Jesus said, "These things I have spoken to you, that in Me you may have peace. In the world, you will have tribulation; but be of good cheer, I have overcome the world" (John 16:33). Paul, writing to the Thessalonians, said, "That no one should be shaken by these afflictions; for you yourselves know that we are appointed to this. For, in fact, we told you before when we were with you that we would suffer tribulation, just as it happened, and you know" (1 Thessalonians 3:3-4). Without suffering, we never fully understand God's tenderness, patience, love, and overflowing compassion. We know that in the end, according to God's Word, we will ultimately triumph over our tribulation. In the end, God will keep us safe for eternity. We can remain confident of a greater reward for our agonizing heartaches. Three perspectives emerge from Scripture on sufferings as outlined in the following chart: Satan's, Man's and God's...

SATAN	MAN	GOD
Satan's primary goal in our pain and suffering is to discourage, defeat, and destroy us. Yet, we have God's word of encouragement. "We have this treasure in earthen vessels, that the excellence of the power may be of God and not of us. We are hard-pressed on every side, yet not crushed; we are perplexed, but not in despair; persecuted, but not forsaken; struck down, but not destroyed – always carrying about in the body the dying of the Lord Jesus, that the life of Jesus also may be manifested in our body. For we who live are always delivered to death for Jesus' sake, that the life of Jesus also may be manifested in our mortal flesh" (2 Corinthians 4:7-11).	Man, too, aims to discomfort us when we go through the fire of sufferings. Part of the problem with others is that they don't understand why God's people go through what everybody else goes through. Why should good people suffer? Job in the Scriptures is an excellent example. Job's pitiful friends offered counsel that aided in exacerbating Job's woes. Their counsel was most miserable at best. Because man cannot understand another person's affliction, their judgments are doomed to be skewed.	God's perspective to all human suffering is the only objective view. Suffering always must be seen through God's divine lens. Meditate on what some scriptures had to say of God's perspective on the believer's suffering.

God's Perspective

James instructs us to respond to suffering with joy. "Count it all joy when you fall into various trials" (James 1:2). Why? Because "the testing of your faith produces patience" (James 1:3). Peter echoes the same sentiments. "In [your trials] greatly rejoice, though now for a little while, if need be, you have been grieved by various trials" (1 Peter 1:6). When God's people go through fiery trials, God allows the hurt and pain to refine us. So every trial should be perceived as a magnifying process for our good. No wonder Job said, "Shall we indeed accept good from God, and shall we not accept adversity" (Job 2:10b). The psalmist said, "The counsel of the Lord stands forever, the plans of His heart [extend] to all generations" (Psalm 33:11). "Many are the afflictions of the righteous, but the Lord delivers him out of them all" (Psalm 34:19). God often does not remove our pain or hardship, nor insulate us from our tribulations; rather, He protects us in the midst of them for the following reasons:

Suffering Promotes God's Glory	First and foremost, God allows His people to suffer in order to bring glory to His name. Remember, His children's pain goes through the filter of His hands, "… that the genuineness of your faith, being much more precious than gold that perishes, though it is tested by fire, may be found to praise, honor, and glory at the revelation of Jesus Christ" (1 Peter 1:6-7).
Suffering Builds a Holy Lifestyle	God allows His children to be purified by the fires of baptism so that they may cultivate holy lifestyles. Through their afflictions, they learn as obedient children to develop a life of holiness. "As He who called you is holy, you also be holy in all your conduct" (1 Peter 1:15).

Suffering Witnesses to the World	God uses our suffering as a testimony to the world. As saints of God, Peter warns us to "abstain from fleshly lusts which war against the soul, having your conduct honorable among the Gentiles, that when they speak against you as evildoers, they may, by your good works which they observe, glorify God in the day of visitation" (1 Peter 2:11-12). Also, Christians may be ridiculed for their allegiance to Christ and harassed for their faith (Hebrews 11:35-38). Nevertheless, our suffering purifies our faith, draws us near to God, and proclaims our testimony of Christ to a lost world so that we remain faithful and joyful in our afflictions.
Suffering Develops Faith and Patience	Through our sufferings, God strengthens our faith. "My brethren, count it all joy when you fall into various trials, knowing that the testing of your faith produces patience. But let patience have its perfect work, that you may be perfect and complete, lacking nothing" (James 1:2-4). The bottom line for all hardships from God's perspective is not to destroy or afflict us, but to purge and refine His children. It is the essential ingredient for Christian maturity. That is what the words "perfect" and "complete" mean in James 1:4. Through suffering, we are able to derive full benefit of whatever we have to learn in our spiritual journey.
Suffering Builds Character	God also accomplishes His purposes through our suffering—building our character with the ultimate goal to be like Christ. Life's trials are opportunities for believers to grow, deepen our faith, and display Christ's character. In the storms of life, the Father comforts us as we share learned life lessons with others. Paul encapsulated this when he said, "Blessed be the God and Father of our Lord Jesus Christ, the Father of mercies and God of all comfort, who comforts us in all our tribulation, that we may be able to comfort those who are in any trouble, with the comfort with which we ourselves are comforted by God" (2 Corinthians 1:3-4). The experience of trials also allows His people to develop the qualities that lead to the completion of a beautiful character honoring God. God uses suffering as a tool to shape godly character within the believer.

Suffering Builds Hope	The believer's hope is not a concept, ideology, or philosophy. Rather, it is a reality that is rooted in the person of the Lord Jesus Christ. This suffering strengthens our trust in God, knowing He will never disappoint us. "Now hope does not disappoint, because the love of God has been poured out in our hearts by the Holy Spirit who was given to us" (Romans 5:5). Trials are tools in God's hands to strengthen the edges of our own imperfection and old human nature.
Suffering Corrects the Saints	Suffering is a tool God wields to correct us. God allows trials to befall us, not to impair us but to improve us. Suffering does not come to punish us. Our punishment for sin was borne on Calvary's cross by the Lord Jesus Christ. Our tests and trials are for corrective purposes only. "…My son, do not despise the chastening of the Lord, nor be discouraged when you are rebuked by Him; for whom the Lord loves He chastens, and scourges every son whom He receives" (Hebrews 12:5-6).
God Is in Our Suffering	In our suffering, God does not forsake nor forget us. He promises never to leave us nor forsake us. "But beloved, do not forget this one thing…the Lord is not slack concerning His promise, as some count slackness, but is longsuffering toward us" (2 Peter 3:8-9a). "For He Himself has said, 'I will never leave you nor forsake you'" (Hebrews 13:5b).
In Our Suffering He Gives Strength to Resist Temptation	During our time of suffering, God promises to give us divine strength. "For in that He Himself has suffered, being tempted, He is able to aid those who are tempted" (Hebrews 2:18). "Then the Lord knows how to deliver the godly out of temptations and to reserve the unjust under punishment for the day of judgment" (2 Peter 2:9). "No temptation has overtaken you except such as is common to man; but God is faithful, who will not allow you to be tempted beyond what you are able, but with the temptation will also make the way of escape, that you may be able to bear it" (1 Corinthians 10:13).

All Suffering Has an Expiration Date	All human suffering is temporal. This statement gives us courage that no matter what we are going through, it will one day end. "For our light affliction, which is but for a moment, is working for us a far more exceeding and eternal weights of glory…" (2 Corinthians 4:17-18). "I consider that the sufferings of this present time are not worthy to be compared with the glory which shall be revealed in us" (Romans 8:18).
All Suffering Has a Reward	Although Christians suffer injustice in the earth, there would come a time when God would right every wrong and reward those who have endured persecution and other hardships for His name's sake. The rewards are a testament that God feels our pain, hears our cries, sees our struggles, and faithfully listens to all our progress. "The Spirit Himself bears witness with our spirit that we are children of God, and if children, then heirs – heirs of God and joint heirs with Christ, if indeed we suffer with Him, that we may also be glorified together" (Romans 8:16-17). Paul, writing to Timothy, said, "If we endure, we shall also reign with Him" (2 Timothy 2:12).

In sum, our present suffering should focus our attention on God's loving care. We must remember His tender mercies in the past so we can willingly trust Him with our future. With this type of hope, we can renew our trust in the living God, always reminding ourselves that through our sufferings, God will protect us; through our pain, God will change us from the inside; through our outward circumstances, God will use us for His glory and finally lavish us with incredible rewards.

CHAPTER 5

Laying on of Hands

"And He took them up in His arms, laid His hands on them, and
blessed them."
(Mark 10:16)

"Laying on of hands" is a practice wherein hands are placed on a
person or animal in order to establish some spiritual fellowship. In our text
verse, the laying on of hands implied transmitting spiritual powers from
God through one of His servants to another individual. This ritual act is
found in both the Old and New Testaments.

Old Testament

In the Old Testament, laying on of hands is primarily associated with
the sacrifices prescribed in the Law of Moses. For example, a priest
making a burnt offering was to lay his hand on the animal's head that
it might be an acceptable sacrifice for his atonement. "Then he shall put
his hand on the head of the burnt offering, and it will be accepted on his
behalf to make atonement for him" (Leviticus 1:4). Other requirements
by the law were made in the same way for the peace offerings (Leviticus
3:2-13), sin offerings (Leviticus 4:4-32), "ram of consecration" or
ordination (Leviticus
8:22), and the sin offering on the annual day of atonement (Leviticus 16:21).
As prescribed by the law, the laying on of hands on the sacrificial animal
was a means of transferring one's iniquity to the animal. Leviticus 16:22
states, "The goat shall bear on itself all their iniquities to an uninhabited
land; and he shall release the goat in the wilderness." At other times, the
sins of the congregation were transferred by the elders (Leviticus 4:15) or
the high priest (Leviticus 16:21) as the people's representatives. Later, the

kings and princes acted on behalf of the nation. "Then King Hezekiah rose early, gathered the rulers of the city, and went up to the house of the Lord. And they brought seven bulls, seven rams, seven lambs, and seven male goats for a sin offering for the kingdom, for the sanctuary and for Judah. Then he commanded the priests, the sons of Aaron, to offer them on the altar of the Lord. So they killed the bulls, and the priests received the blood and sprinkled it on the altar. Likewise they killed the rams and sprinkled the blood on the altar. They also killed the lambs and sprinkled the blood on the altar. Then they brought out the male goats for the sin offering before the king and the assembly, and they laid their hands on them. And the priests killed them; and they presented their blood on the altar as a sin offering to make an atonement for all Israel, for the king commanded that the burnt offering and the sin offering be made for all Israel" (2 Chronicles 29:20-24).

When the Levites were presented to the Lord as an offering from the Jewish nation, the whole assembly laid hands on them. Numbers 8:10 instructs, "So you shall bring the Levites before the Lord, and the children of Israel shall lay their hands on the Levites." "Take outside the camp him who has cursed; then let all who heard him lay their hands on his head, and let all the congregation stone him" (Leviticus 24:14). Laying on of hands in the Old Testament had other meanings. It represented blessing, arbitration, commissioning, victory in battle, and acts of violence. Let's examine each of these.

Blessing

Jacob blessed Ephraim and Manasseh by laying his hands on their heads. Genesis 48:14 notes, "Then Israel stretched out his right hand and laid it on Ephraim's head, who was the younger, and his left hand on Manasseh's head, guiding his hands knowingly, for Manasseh was the firstborn." As an act of humility and respect, Joseph presented his sons to his father and placed his sons so that his father's right hand would rest on the head of the older son and the left hand on the younger. But Jacob deliberately reversed his hands, putting Ephraim first.

Arbitration

It is interesting to note that during Job's tribulations he longed for someone who could arbitrate between himself and God by laying "his hand on us both" (Job 9:33).

Commissioning

When Moses was passing on the mantle of authority to Joshua, he laid his hands on Joshua. "Now Joshua the son of Nun was full of the spirit of wisdom, for Moses had laid his hands on him; so the children of Israel heeded him, and did as the Lord had commanded Moses" (Deuteronomy 34:9).

Victory in Battle

An unusual event took place when prophet Elisha laid his hands on King Joash's hands as a prophetic act signifying God's promise to provide Israel victory over Syria. In 2 Kings 13:16, Elisha said to the king of Israel, "'Put your hand on the bow.' So he put his hand on it, and Elisha put his hands on the king's hands."

Violence

Mordecai, Esther's uncle discovered a plot where "Two of the king's eunuchs, Bigthan and Teresh, doorkeepers, became furious and sought to lay hands on King Ahasuerus" (Esther 2:21). Later, the matter was made known to the king, who commanded that both eunuchs be hanged on the gallows.

New Testament

Some Bible scholars view healing by the laying on of hands as an extension of the Old Testament blessing. A glaring example of this is Jesus laying His hands on children to bless them. In Mark 10:16, Jesus "took them [little children] up in His arms, laid His hands on them, and blessed them." Apart from the miraculous healings that are brought about by the laying on of hands, other benefits are documented in the New Testament.

Miraculous Healings

Jesus on several occasions performed miraculous healings when He laid His hands on the sick. On one occasion, He healed a blind man at Bethsaida. Jesus "took the blind man by the hand and led him out of the town. And when He had spit on his eyes and put His hands on him, He asked him if he saw anything. And he looked up and said, 'I see men like trees, walking.' Then He put His hands on his eyes again and made him look up. And he was restored and saw everyone clearly" (Mark 8:23-25). On another occasion, Jesus healed the sick. In His home front of Nazareth, Jesus "laid His hands on a few sick people and healed them" (Mark 6:5). Although there were few healings because of the people's unbelief. Elsewhere, Jesus healed a man with a withered hand on the Sabbath (Mark 3:1-6). Jesus' disciples continued the practice. The apostle Mark records that the disciples "will take up serpents; and if they drink anything deadly, it will by no means hurt them; they will lay hands on the sick, and they will recover" (Mark 16:18; Acts 9:12-17; 28:8).

Conferring Offices in the Local Assembly

Through the laying on of hands on "seven men of good reputation and full of faith and the Holy Spirit," the first deacon group was established to serve the needs of the widows of the Greek-speaking Jews. They set these "before the apostles; and when they had prayed, they laid hands on them" (Acts 6:6). This single act aided in the spread of the Word of God, and the community of believers greatly increased in Jerusalem.

Receiving the Holy Spirit

The act of laying on of hands was done for believers to be baptized in the Holy Spirit. At least three instances are documented. First, in Acts 8, Peter and John were sent by the Jerusalem apostles to go and encourage the brethren in Samaria where revival had taken place. The brethren had been baptized in the name of Jesus but had not been baptized in the Holy Spirit. Peter and John laid hands on the believers and "they received the Holy Spirit" (Acts 8:17). Next, Ananias, a disciple of Christ at Damascus, sought for Saul after the latter's conversion, and prayed for him to receive his sight and be filled with the Holy Spirit (Acts 9:17). Finally, Paul ministered to twelve men at Ephesus who were baptized into John's baptism but had not laid his hands on them. They all spoke with tongues and prophesied (Acts 19:6-7) when he laid his hands on them.

Conferring a Spiritual Gift

Laying on of hands is also practiced in the New Testament for conferring a spiritual gift. Paul is reminding Timothy not to neglect the gift that is in him which was given to him by prophecy "with the laying on of the hands of the eldership" (1 Timothy 4:14). Later, Paul admonishes

Timothy to stir up the gift of God which is in him through the laying on of hands (2 Timothy 1:6).

Sending Forth Missionaries

Fasting, prayer, and the laying on of hands also accompanied the appointment of Barnabas and Saul to their missionary endeavors (Acts 13:3).

Caution

Paul, in his letter to Timothy, warns against laying hands on anyone hastily to avoid acquiring sins of others. "Do not lay hands on anyone hastily, nor share in other people's sins; keep yourself pure" (1 Timothy 5:22).

In closing, our Hebrew text classified laying on of hands among the fundamental teachings of the church. Because of its usefulness, the church of Jesus Christ is blessed as persons of maturity within the body exercise this doctrine.

CHAPTER 6

Resurrection of the Dead

"I am the resurrection and the life. He who believes in Me,
though he may die, he shall live." (John 11:25)

The author of Hebrews lists the resurrection of the dead as the next
fundamental doctrine of the Christian faith. However, before a discussion
on the resurrection begins, it is absolutely essential to first explain the
notion of death because without death, there can be no resurrection.

Why Death?

In the Genesis account, we are told that God originally created a
perfect and non-decaying world. Both man and created things were not to
experience death or decay prior to the fall. Death and decay came because
of man's rebellion. To Adam, He said, "Because you have heeded the voice
of your wife, and have eaten from the tree of which I commanded you,
saying, 'You shall not eat of it': Cursed is the ground for your sake; in
toil you shall eat of it all the days of your life" (Genesis 3:17). "For the
creation was subjected to futility, not willingly, but because of Him who
subjected it in hope" (Romans 8:20).

Although man sinned and rebelled against God, God had a master
plan to redeem both man and the world as seen today. So, the ultimate
answer to death was the resurrection. The resurrection is thereby a doctrine
and act that brings persons from death to unending life.

A broad overview of the doctrine of the resurrection depicts that this
teaching is found in both the Old and New Testaments.

Old Testament

Some have argued that the doctrine of a bodily resurrection was unknown to the ancient Israelites in the Old Testament. Indeed, they claim that this was a cardinal teaching of the Sadducees even in Jesus' time. "The same day the Sadducees, who say there is no resurrection, came to Him and asked Him" (Matthew 22:23). According to the Sadducees, death was the end of human existence and the decay of living things, the end of life to all humans. But Genesis 3:19 says, "In the sweat of your face you shall eat bread till you return to the ground, for out of it you were taken; for dust you are, and to dust you shall return."

In a nutshell, the Old Testament teachings about the resurrection are scant. They do not reflect a clear theological submission. Judaism, however, gave emphases to the fact that Yahweh was sovereign over all. However, it relays no explicit statement about individual resurrection. This may have been the one reason why the Sadducees in the New Testament did not believe in the resurrection. They only believed in God as sovereign over all – even death. On the other hand, two prominent Old Testament figures taken up alive before death may have reinforced their belief against personal resurrection in the translation. "And Enoch walked with God; and he *was* not, for God took him" (Genesis 5:24). "And so it was, when they had crossed over, that Elijah said to Elisha, 'Ask! What may I do for you, before I am taken away from you?' Elisha said, 'Please let a double portion of your spirit be upon me.' So he said, 'You have asked a hard thing. *Nevertheless,* if you see me *when I am* taken from you, it shall be so for you; but if not, it shall not be so.' Then it happened, as they continued on and talked, that suddenly a chariot of fire *appeared* with horses of fire, and separated the two of them; and Elijah went up by a whirlwind into heaven" (2 Kings 2:9-11, emphasis added).

Despite the beliefs held by the Sadducees against personal resurrection, Solomon, the son of David, the son of Daniel, king of Jerusalem, said that man's spirit lives forever, since it originated in heaven. Man deposits the physical body to the ground at death, while the soul of man goes to either heaven or hell. God "made everything beautiful in its time. Also He has put eternity in their hearts, except that no one can find out the work that God does from beginning to end" (Ecclesiastes 3:11). Daniel buttresses this truth with the prediction of what will happen to man after death. "Many of those who sleep in the dust of the earth shall awake, some to everlasting life, some to shame and everlasting contempt" (Daniel 12:2). Prophet Isaiah further reiterates on a belief in the resurrection. "Your dead shall live; together with my dead body they shall arise..." (Isaiah 26:19). However, Job makes the most persuasive argument for the resurrection. "For I know that my Redeemer lives, and He shall stand at last on the earth; and after my skin is destroyed, this I know, that in my flesh I shall see God, whom I shall see for myself, and my eyes shall behold, and not another. How my heart yearns within me!" (Job 19:25-27).

New Testament

Jesus comes on the scene of the New Testament to reiterate the belief held by the Pharisees on the Resurrection of the dead. In John's gospel, Jesus declared Himself as the Resurrection and the Life. "Martha said to Him, 'I know that [Lazarus] will rise again in the Resurrection at the last day.' Jesus said to her, 'I am the Resurrection and the Life. He who believes in Me, though he may die, he shall live. And whoever lives and believes in Me shall never die. Do you believe this?'" (John 11:24-26). This earned Jesus much opposition from the Sadducee sect stemming from their unbelief in the Resurrection. Equally, the Pharisees showed contempt because Jesus declared that He was the Resurrection and the Life, equating Himself with God. Jesus equally pointed to the Resurrection of the righteous to eternal life and of the wicked to eternal punishment. "Do not marvel at this; for the hour is coming in which all who are in the graves will hear His voice and come forth— those who have done good, to the resurrection of life, and those who have done evil, to the resurrection of condemnation" (John 5:28-29). Jesus, the creator of the universe, had to become man in order to die for the sins of the world and defeat death by His own bodily resurrection. Because Jesus defeated death, He promised all who believed in Him that "because I live, you will live also" (John 14:19).

Death and Resurrection of Jesus Christ

In the gospels and in Paul's letters, there are many scriptures that attest to the death, burial, and resurrection of Jesus Christ. The most powerful evidence in the defense of Christianity is the Resurrection of Jesus Christ. His death and resurrection are the only certain hope to all Christ's followers. The evidence of Jesus Christ's resurrection from the dead is seen in the empty tomb, His appearances before His ascension to heaven, and His appearances after His ascension. Jesus had a physical as well as a spiritual body. "Then, the same day at evening, being the first day of the week, when the doors were shut where the disciples were assembled, for fear of the Jews, Jesus came and stood in the midst, and said to them, 'Peace be with you.' When He had said this, He showed them His hands and His side. Then the disciples were glad when they saw the Lord" (John 20:19-20). "And I say to you that many will come from east and west, and sit down with Abraham, Isaac, and Jacob in the kingdom of heaven. But the sons of the kingdom will be cast out into outer darkness. There will be weeping and gnashing of teeth" (Matthew 8:11-12). "When the Son of Man comes in His glory, and all the holy angels with Him, then He will sit on the throne of His glory. All the nations will be gathered before Him, and He will separate them one from another, as a shepherd divides his sheep from the goats. And He will set the sheep on His right hand, but the goats on the left. Then the King will say to those on His right hand, 'Come, you blessed of My Father, inherit the kingdom prepared for you from the foundation of the world'" (Matthew 25:31-34). "Then He will also say to those on the left hand, 'Depart from Me, you cursed, into the everlasting fire prepared for the devil and his angels: for I was hungry and you gave Me no food; I was thirsty and you gave Me no drink; I was a stranger and you did not take Me in, naked and you did not clothe Me, sick and in prison and you did not visit Me.' Then they also will answer Him, saying, 'Lord, when did we see You hungry or thirsty or a stranger or naked or sick or in prison, and did not minister to You?' Then He will answer them, saying, 'Assuredly, I say to you, inasmuch as you did not do it to one of the least of these, you did not do it to Me.' And these will go away into everlasting punishment, but the righteous into eternal life" (Matthew 25:41-46).

The foremost proponent of the doctrine of the Resurrection among the New Testament writers was Paul. "For I delivered to you first of all that which I also received: that Christ died for our sins according to the Scriptures, and that He was buried, and that He rose again the third day according to the Scriptures, and that He was seen by Cephas, then by the twelve. After that He was seen by over five hundred brethren at once, of whom the greater part remain to the present, but some have fallen asleep. After that He was seen by James, then by all the apostles. Then last of all He was seen by me also, as by one born out of due time" (1 Corinthians

15:3-8). In the above narrative, Paul emphasized Jesus' resurrection from the grave and His appearance to Cephas, the twelve, the five hundred (some of whom had died by the time Paul wrote 1 Corinthians), His appearance to James, and then He was seen by all the apostles.

After His ascension, Jesus appeared to Paul (refer to Saul's conversion story in Acts 9:1-9). Even earlier, He appeared to Stephen, the martyr, who was stoned to death for proclaiming the Good News (Acts 7:55-56). Lastly, to Apostle John who was given the revelation of the end times (Revelation 1).

It should be noted, however, that the gospel accounts also present the account of Jesus' resurrection. Matthew reported that both Mary Magdalene and Mary the mother of James and Jesus (Matthew 28:1-2; 27:56,61) came to an empty tomb. Mark's account of the resurrection (chapter 16) reports that three women came to the tomb wondering how they could apply spices to Jesus' body. But they discovered to their amazement that the stone was rolled away and a young man in white was standing by an empty grave. Luke 24 also records the visit of three women to the tomb where two angels declared that He was risen. Finally, John's gospel adds remarkable details to the other three accounts – Jesus appeared to Mary Magdalene and twice to the disciples in the Upper Room, the second time in a week for the sake of the unbelieving Thomas. In John
20:28, Apostle John retells Thomas' classic confession: "My Lord and my God," his response after he saw the nail-pierced hands of Jesus.

So we see that Jesus instructed His disciples about the prophetic and theological meanings of His death and resurrection. The resurrection of Jesus Christ involved His physical body. Paul clearly and cogently provided the first detailed account of the resurrection of Christ in 1 Corinthians 15:3-8.

In 1 Corinthians 15, Paul presents a compelling case for the Resurrection and the implication for Christ's followers. "Now if Christ is preached that He has been raised from the dead, how do some among you say that there is no resurrection of the dead? But if there is no resurrection of the dead, then Christ is not risen. And if Christ is not risen, then our preaching is empty and your faith is also empty. Yes, and we are found false witnesses of God, because we have testified of God that He raised up Christ, whom He did not raise up—if in fact the dead do not rise. For if the dead do not rise, then Christ is not risen. And if Christ is not risen, your faith is futile; you are still in your sins! Then also those who have fallen asleep in Christ have perished. If in this life only we have hope in Christ, we are of all men the most pitiable. But now Christ is risen from the dead, and has become the firstfruits of those who have fallen asleep. For since by man came death, by Man also came the resurrection of the dead. For as in Adam all die, even so in Christ all shall be made alive" (1 Corinthians 15:12-22).

In reference to Christ becoming the firstfruits of those who have fallen asleep, it may seem strange to think that we are born again "by this resurrection," but this was the instrument God used to bring about His purpose. In a real sense, Christ was "born again" with a glorified body when He arose from the dead. Since He is "the firstborn from the dead" (Colossians 1:18), many will follow, "that He might be the firstborn among many brethren" (Romans 8:29). It is equally worthy to note that the resurrected body will be a spiritual as well as physical body, although different from our present one. Furthermore, it will have continuity with the present body because Christ redeems the whole person. In this regard, Paul says, "...even we ourselves groan within ourselves, eagerly waiting for the adoption, the redemption of our body" (Romans 8:23).

As a whole, the New Testament strongly affirms the truth of the Resurrection of all persons from the dead. Those in Christ will go to a wonderful eternal reunion with Christ in a totally transformed body, but those who are not in Christ will go to an eternal life of condemnation in hell.

What Happens after Death?

We will now examine in detail what happens to four groups of people after death: the Christian, the Old Testament believer, the Tribulation believer, and the unbelievers of the Old and New Testaments. Everyone enters this life through birth and exits this life through death. The Bible says, "It is appointed for men to die once, but after this the judgment" (Hebrews 9:27).

Let's briefly examine why man must die. Romans 5:12 (NIV) provides the answer. "Sin entered the world through one man, and death through sin, and in this way death came to all men, because all sinned." If there was no sin, there would be no suffering, sorrow, death, and decay. Had there been no disobedience, there would be no disease or death. If Adam had not sinned, he and his descendants would have had bodies that no power on earth could have destroyed.

But Christ came to solve the mystery of death. Second Timothy 2:11 says, "This is a faithful saying: For if we died with Him, we shall also live with Him." Paul said in 2 Timothy 1:10 (NIV), "Christ Jesus…has destroyed death and has brought life and immortality to light through the gospel." The Lord Jesus died for our sins. When He died and destroyed death, He did not do away with death, but He made death harmless. He deprived death of its strength and sting. To illustrate this truth, a story is told of a farmer who was stung by a bee. Immediately he shouted, "Praise the Lord!" "Why?" asked a friend. "Because," he explained, "a bee only has one sting. When it stung me, it left its stinger in me. Now it cannot sting my wife or daughter. Neither can it sting any other person." Death has but one sting. It stung Christ when He died for our sins. Now it cannot sting the Christian. When we receive Christ, His death and resurrection sets us free from the penalty and the power of sin, death, decay, and hell. That is why Paul said in 2 Corinthians 5:8 that, "We are confident, yes, well pleased rather to be absent from the body and to be present with the Lord." Perhaps the single thing that unites most people from all languages, tongues, and cultures throughout history is the universal belief in life after death.

For the Christian

Once sin entered the world, both body and spirit were subject to death. It was necessary for both to be reborn. Spiritual rebirth takes place at the time an individual puts his trust for his salvation in Christ; physical rebirth will occur at the Resurrection.

For the Christian at death, the spirit and soul are escorted into the presence of Christ. But the believer's body is buried in the grave. Now, at the rapture, which is the world's next major event in God's prophetic calendar, all believers in Christ, both dead and alive, will be caught up to meet with the Lord in the air. In 1 Thessalonians 4:16-17, Paul said, "For the Lord Himself will descend from heaven with a shout, with the voice of an archangel, and with the trumpet of God. And the dead in Christ will rise first. Then we who are alive and remain shall be caught up together with them in the clouds to meet the Lord in the air. And thus we shall always be with the Lord." Second Corinthians 5:10 (NIV) declares, "For we must all appear before the judgment seat of Christ, that each one may receive what is due him for the things done while in the body, whether good or bad." When we meet with the Lord, we shall all receive one or more crowns for the works of righteousness done after our salvation experience. In the next chapter, we will discuss the different crowns that believers will receive at the Bema Seat of Christ.

At Christ's Second Coming, He will be accompanied by the believers and a host of angels to earth. Immediately following the Second Coming is His thousand-year reign on earth, which both the Old and New Testaments describe as a period of unequalled peace and joy as the world worships the Savior. "For as the lightning comes from the east and flashes to the west, so also will the coming of the Son of Man be. For wherever the carcass is, there the eagles will be gathered together. Immediately after the Tribulation of those days the sun will be darkened, and the moon will not give its light; the stars will fall from heaven, and the powers of the heavens will be shaken. Then the sign of the Son of Man will appear in heaven, and then all the tribes of the earth will mourn, and they will see the Son of Man coming on the clouds of heaven with power and great glory. And He will send His angels with a great sound of a trumpet, and they will gather together His elect from the four winds, from one end of heaven to the other" (Matthew 24:27-31).

For the Old Testament Believer

All Old Testament believers who died had their bodies buried in the grave, but their spirit and soul were escorted into Paradise, or Abraham's bosom. "So it was that the beggar died, and was carried by the angels to Abraham's bosom" (Luke 16:22). Later, at the Second Coming of Christ, these Old Testament believers will resurrect with totally transformed bodies to meet with Christ in the air and they will be with the Lord Jesus Christ forever, like the New Testament Christians.

For the Tribulation Believer

Those Christ-followers who will die during the Tribulation period will instantly be transported into Christ's presence; that is, their spirit and soul (Revelations 7). However, their bodies will be buried in the ground. At Christ's Second Coming, their spirit, soul, and body will be reunited and transformed to meet with the Lord in the air, and they too will receive their rewards and appear with Christ to judge the earth.

For the Unbeliever of All Ages

Finally, all those who rejected God in the Old Testament and refused to accept God's indescribable gift – the Lord Jesus Christ – will, at death, face the following: their bodies will be buried in the grave, but their spirit and soul will go to Sheol (or Hades) where the unbelieving dead will be temporally tormented while awaiting their final verdict at the White Throne Judgment.

Luke 16:23 speaks of Hades. Jesus narrated a popular story about a rich man and Lazarus, saying, "So it was that the beggar died, and was carried by the angels to Abraham's bosom. The rich man also died and was buried. And being in torments in Hades, he lifted up his eyes and saw Abraham afar off, and Lazarus in his bosom. Then he cried and said, 'Father Abraham, have mercy on me, and send Lazarus that he may dip the tip of his finger in the water and cool my tongue; for I am tormented in this flame.' But Abraham said, 'Son, remember that in your lifetime you received your good things, and likewise Lazarus evil things; but now he is comforted and you are tormented'" (Luke 16:22-25). The unbelieving dead will also resurrect at the end of this millennium to be judged by the righteous at the Great White Throne Judgment. "Then I saw... the lake of fire" (Revelation 20:11-15). Hell, or the lake of fire, will be the final destination for *all* unbelievers.

Conclusion

In closing, death to a Christian is like wealth to a rich man, home to a wanderer – liberty and an eternal, blissful life with the Lord. The believer will experience unending sweet fellowship with Jesus and the saints – an eternal time of uttermost bliss. Apostle Paul says in Philippians 1:21, "For to me, to live is Christ, and to die is gain." And this is what the psalmist says of your homegoing, "Precious in the sight of the Lord is the death of His saints" (Psalm 116:15). For the Christian, physical death is the gateway to live forever – physically and spiritually. God "has put eternity in their hearts" (Ecclesiastes 3:11). "For our citizenship is in heaven, from which we also eagerly wait for the Savior, the Lord Jesus Christ" (Philippians 3:20). God created us for heaven, and nothing in this earthly life can satisfy the longing of our hearts. The resurrection of Jesus Christ was central in early apostolic ministry and preaching, and indeed it remains the key tenet of our faith (Acts 3:15; 4:2,10,33; 5:30; 10:39-40). Therefore, invite Jesus into your heart today, and you will experience this resurrection power that Jesus offers.

CHAPTER 7

Eternal Judgment

"He who rejects Me, and does not receive My words, has that
which judges him—the word that I have spoken will judge
him in the last day."
(John 12:48)

From the beginning, God instituted laws to be obeyed by man. When
they were broken, He rendered righteous verdicts based on His holiness.
Thus, eternal judgment is the teaching that everyone will be judged by
the righteous Judge, the Son of Man Himself (John 12:48; 5:22) in a
future day (1 John 4:17; John 5:24-29). The Scriptures indicate that there
will be two judgments: one for believers at the Bema Seat, in which Jesus
will determine and give every believer a reward (1 Corinthians 3:12-15)
and the other, a judgment of condemnation for unbelievers (Revelation
20:11-15). The sentence to eternal damnation is irrevocable upon death (2
Thessalonians 1:6-10; Matthew 25:41; Revelation 14:10-11).

The doctrine of judgment goes back into the Old Testament. On
several occasions, the wrath of God was not only upon the nation of Israel
(disobedience or rebellion against the statutes of God's laws – 1 Chronicles
27:24; 2 Chronicles 24:18; Amos 3:2; Hosea 13:9-11) but also on her
wicked rulers (2 Kings 23:26-27; 2 Chronicles 19:2). Some individuals also
were the objects of God's wrath (Moses – Exodus 4:14, 24; Deuteronomy
1:37; Aaron – Deuteronomy 9:20; Miriam – Numbers 12:9; Nadab and
Abihu – Leviticus 10:1-2). Furthermore, the surrounding nations and
their rulers became objects of God's wrath (Psalm 2:5, 11; Isaiah
13:3,5,9; Jeremiah 50:13,15).

Building on the foundation of the Old Testament, the New Testament adds the word "eternal" to the concept of judgment. As in the Old Testament, divine judgment is both a present and future reality. Jesus' first coming represents a divine condemnation (John 3:36) and unbelievers experience in part the wrath of God (Romans 1:18-32). However, unlike unbelievers, Christ-followers are chastised for their waywardness (Hebrews 12:4-11), but that final divine verdict of judgment is yet to be carried out at a future date as mentioned earlier by Jesus Christ Himself.

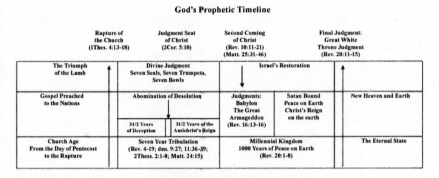

God's Prophetic Timeline

Rapture of the Church (1Thes. 4:13-18)		Judgment Seat of Christ (2Cor. 5:10)		Second Coming of Christ (Rev. 10:11-21) (Matt. 25:31-46)		Final Judgment: Great White Throne Judgment (Rev. 20:11-15)	
The Triumph of the Lamb		Divine Judgment Seven Seals, Seven Trumpets, Seven Bowls		Israel's Restoration			
Gospel Preached to the Nations		Abomination of Desolation		Judgments: Babylon The Great Armageddon (Rev. 16:13-16)	Satan Bound Peace on Earth Christ's Reign on the earth	New Heaven and Earth	
		31/2 Years of Deception	31/2 Years of the Antichrist's Reign				
Church Age From the Day of Pentecost to the Rapture		Seven Year Tribulation (Rev. 4-19; dan. 9:27; 11:36-39; 2Thess. 2:1-8; Matt. 24:15)		Millennial Kingdom 1000 Years of Peace on Earth (Rev. 20:1-8)		The Eternal State	

The Five Major Judgments

Before we delve into a discussion about the five major judgments in the Scriptures, let us examine the perennial question of how a God of love can also be a God who dispenses judgment on the humans who are the object of His eternal love. First, God's wrath is not part of His holy character; instead, it is His work of judgment because of His holiness. That work will one day be done at the White Throne Judgment where His holiness will be satisfied against all who rejected God's indescribable gift (2 Corinthians 9:15) in the person of the Lord Jesus Christ. Yet His love for them will continue forever since His love does not depend on what mankind has done or will do. The Bible teaches that, "God demonstrates [note the present tense] His love toward us [mankind], in that while we were still sinners, Christ died for us" (Romans 5:8). God is both love and a judge. His love cannot overshadow His holiness or justice. God in His own love and grace has made provision for all mankind to be saved. God put on

136

Jesus Christ the full weight of His wrath and punishment for sin because He did not create hell for man, but it was created for Satan and his cohorts. That is why God's love and judgment were fully demonstrated at the cross where both love and judgment met as Jesus Christ offered His own life for our sins. So, the choice of hell or heaven is left up to man. We choose either the devil or Christ. That is why John 3:16-19 states, "For God so loved the world that He gave His only begotten Son, that whoever believes in Him should not perish but have everlasting life. For God did not send His Son into the world to condemn the world, but that the world through Him might be saved. He who believes in Him is not condemned; but he who does not believe is condemned already, because he has not believed in the name of the only begotten Son of God. And this is the condemnation, that the light has come into the world, and men loved darkness rather than light, because their deeds were evil." Verse 36 of that same chapter says, "He who believes in the Son has everlasting life; and he who does not believe the Son shall not see life, but the wrath of God abides on him."

This leads to the second point – God's holiness ensures that His wrath is always fully just because of His infinite wisdom and knowledge. He truly renders judgment with His divine justice because He sees what all men desire. He also has the perspective of eternity that man does not have. Christians are warned not to exercise vengeance because they do not see things from an eternal perspective like God does. He is the God of infinite wisdom and knowledge, and we don't possess any of these attributes. Therefore, the appropriate response to all who hurt us is to hand them over to God, for He says, "Vengeance is Mine, I will repay" (Hebrews 10:30).

Third, judgment is God's "unusual act." Isaiah 28:21 states, "For the Lord will rise up as at Mount Perazim, He will be angry as in the Valley of Gibeon — that He may do His work, His awesome work, and bring to pass His act, His unusual act." So we see that God's justice demands that sin be judged and obedience rewarded. God's character as a holy, loving, and just God must be viewed separate from His works. His wrath is always a part of His works, not His character. The Bible gives us a clear and balanced picture of God. He harmoniously balances between His justice, grace, and works. Let's now turn to our discussion of the five major judgments, divided into past and future judgments.

Past Judgments

Flood Judgment

An account of the flood judgment is presented in the book of Genesis. The first account is recorded in Genesis 7:1-12. "Then the Lord said to Noah, 'Come into the ark, you and all your household, because I have seen that you are righteous before Me in this generation. You shall take with you seven each of every clean animal, a male and his female; two each of animals that are unclean, a male and his female; also seven each of birds of the air, male and female, to keep the species alive on the face of the earth. For after seven more days I will cause it to rain on the earth forty days and forty nights, and I will destroy from the face of the earth all living things that I have made.' And Noah did according to all that the Lord commanded him. Noah was six hundred years old when the floodwaters were on the earth. So Noah, with his sons, his wife, and his sons' wives, went into the ark because of the waters of the flood. Of clean animals, of animals that are unclean, of birds, and of everything that creeps on the earth, two by two they went into the ark to Noah, male and female, as God had commanded Noah. And it came to pass after seven days that the waters of the flood were on the earth. In the six hundredth year of Noah's life, in the second month, the seventeenth day of the month, on that day all the foundations of the great deep were broken up, and the windows of heaven were opened. And the rain was on the earth forty days and forty nights."

This great flood was a period in ancient history that God punished the earth by destroying it with a deluge of water. Why did God do such a terrible thing? Because the "wickedness of man was great in the earth, and that every intent of the thoughts of his heart was only evil continually" (Genesis 6:5). In other words, God took account of the earth's wickedness, the persistent and willful bend toward evil and corruption that filled the earth with injustice. However, God did not only see the wickedness on earth, but also saw the righteous Noah – blameless in his generation as one who walked with God. So, He announced His intention to Noah and instructed him to build a gigantic ark for himself, his family, and all creeping animals, even the unclean ones.

After the flood, Noah offered a sacrifice to Yahweh. This act moved God to vow never to destroy the earth again with water. "...Then the Lord said in His heart, 'I will never again curse the ground for man's sake, although the imagination of man's heart is evil from his youth; nor will I again destroy every living thing as I have done'" (Genesis 8:21).

As a sign of the vow God made, He established the rainbow. "'The rainbow shall be in the cloud, and I will look on it to remember the everlasting covenant between God and every living creature of all flesh that is on the earth.' And God said to Noah, 'This is the sign of the covenant which I have established between Me and all flesh that is on the earth'" (Genesis 9:16-17).

Cross Judgment

The second major past judgment is the judgment on the cross. This judgment was usually associated with capital punishment or crucifixion.

Brief Background on the Cross

Crucifixion developed into a form of capital punishment to penalize the enemies of the state or captives of war. According to Jewish law (Deuteronomy 21:22-23), hardened criminals were hung on a tree, which meant they were the accursed of God and outside the covenant people of God. Such offenders were to be removed from the cross before nightfall lest they "defile the land." On the whole, the Jews condemned and seldom used this hideous method of punishment. Summarily, the practice was abolished after the "conversion" of the emperor, Constantine, to Christianity. The Sanhedrin no longer was allowed to carry out capital punishment by the Roman authorities.

Crucifixion

Before an overview is presented on the eyewitness accounts of the four gospel writers on the crucifixion of Jesus, a quick examination of the way the Romans carried out this type of capital punishment is essential. In Jesus' day, a person crucified was, first of all, scourged (beaten with a whip with pieces of metal or bone attached to its end) or at least flogged until blood flowed. This was not just done out of cruelty, but was designed to hasten death and lessen prolonged pain of the ordeal. After the beating, the victim was forced to bear the crossbeam to the execution site in order to indicate life was over and to break the will to live. A tablet detailing the crimes of the accused was placed around the criminal's neck and then fastened to the cross. At the site of the crucifixion the victim was often tied, or sometimes nailed (if a quicker death was desired). Then the nail would be driven through the wrist rather than the palms, since the smaller bones of the hand could not support the weight of the body. The beam with the body was then lifted and tied to the already affixed upright pole. Finally, the feet were tied or nailed to the pole. Death ensued as a result of the loss of blood circulation and heart failure.

Jesus' Crucifixion

Jesus was handed over to the Roman soldiers by the Sanhedrin. Roman customs used the following pattern: scourging, mock enthronement, carrying the crossbeam, then crucifixion. Gospel writers look at Jesus' crucifixion from four vantage points highlighting diverse aspects of the significance of His death. For instance, Mark and Matthew focused on the horrors of putting the Son of God to death. However, Mark emphasized the Messianic meaning using sarcastic remarks of the crowds to "save Yourself" (Mark 15:30-31), pointing subconsciously to His resurrection. Matthew extends Mark's comments by pointing to Jesus as the royal Messiah who faced His demise in complete control of the situation.

Jesus Himself had predicted His death, not only in rending of the temple veil and the centurion's testimony (Matthew 27:51,54) but in the remarkable raising of the Old Testament saints (verses 52-53), which links the Resurrection to the open tomb. For Matthew, the cross rendered the power of death ineffective and ushered in an outpouring of salvation to all people. Luke probably has the most unique portrayal, with two outstanding emphases: Jesus as the righteous martyr who forgave His enemies, and the crucifixion as an awesome scene of reverence and worship. He completely omitted the negative aspect of the crucifixion (earthquakes, wine with myrrh, cry of abandonment). Instead, he wrote about the crowd returning home, beating their breasts (Luke 23:48) and included three words of Jesus which relate to prayer (found only in Luke): "Father, forgive them" (verse 34, a contrast to the ridicules); "Today you will be with Me in Paradise" (verse 43, in response to the criminal's plea); and "Father, into Your hands I commit My spirit" (verse 46). John, in his account, is perhaps the most compelling, upbeat disciple even moreso than Luke. Jesus' sovereign control of the entire scene is at the heart of his narrative. The cross, from John's perspective, becomes His throne. John states that the inscription on the cross (*JESUS OF NAZARETH, THE KING OF THE JEWS*) was written in Aramaic, Latin, and Greek (John 19:19-20), thereby changing it (the cross) into a universal proclamation of Jesus' royal status. From the beginning of His crucifixion to the final cry, "It is finished" (verse 30), Jesus was in absolute control of Himself and His circumstances.

Paul, a non-eyewitness of the events of the cross, lucidly states that he had "received" and then "delivered" to the Corinthians the truth that Jesus died for our sins according to the Scriptures (1 Corinthians 15:3-5). Paul highlights three great and insightful themes about the theology of the cross: Jesus' death as our substitute (Isaiah 53:5; Mark 10:45; 14:24), Jesus' death and resurrection as fulfilling the Scripture, and Jesus' vindication and exaltation by God.

a) *Jesus' Death as our Substitute*
The cross of Jesus is symbolic of God's love and forgiveness. According to Paul, "the message of the cross" (1 Corinthians 1:18) is the heart of the Gospel, and the preaching of the Cross is the soul of the church's mission. The Cross was the central event in human history, the one moment which demonstrated God's love, forgiveness, and control, as well as His involvement in human history. It is only in the Cross that salvation can be found, and only in the "foolish" preaching of the cross and "weakness" can the power of God be seen (1 Corinthians 1:21,25). In Romans 4:25, Paul notes that the Cross is the basis of our salvation as well as the Resurrection of Jesus Christ. The three major terms of our salvation are: *redemption,* emphasizing the *ransom payment* made by Jesus' blood in delivering us from sin (Titus 2:14; 1 Peter 1:18); *propitiation,* which stands for Jesus' death as *satisfying* God's righteous wrath (Romans 3:5; Hebrews 2:17), and *justification,* referring to the result of the cross, the complete *acquittal* (declaring the repentant sinner righteous) of all guilt (Romans 3:24; 4:25; Galatians 2:16-21; 3:24).

b) *Jesus' Death and Resurrection as Fulfilling the Scripture*
Besides the grace of salvation given to mankind, the Cross has forged a new union between Jew and Gentile by breaking down "the dividing wall of hostility" and made the two one (Ephesians 2:14-15 NIV), thereby providing "peace" and creating a new access to the Father (verse 18). In addition, the Cross "disarmed" the demonic power and forged the final defeat over Satan and his cohorts (Colossians 2:15). Satan made the

greatest mistake by underestimating the incredible power of the Cross of Calvary; he did not foresee that Jesus' death would lead to His predicted resurrection.

c) *Jesus' Vindication and Exaltation by God*

Because Jesus was completely obedient to God the Father, He was raised from the dead. He was subsequently highly elevated to sit at the right hand of God the Father, far above all principalities or powers (Philippians 2:8-11).

Lessons for Christ-followers

By dying in our place, Jesus taught us some valuable lessons of the way of the Cross. First, Jesus gave His life as an offering to the Father (John 19:17-30). Thus, the Cross symbolizes self-denial, surrender, and total commitment to God. We as Christ-followers are challenged to also take up our cross and follow Jesus' example (Mark 8:34; 10:38; Matthew 16:24; Luke 9:23; 14:27). Next, closely related to Paul's symbolism of a crucified life, is a life totally yielded to God (Galatians 2:20). Self-centered desires are nailed to the cross daily (Galatians 5:24), and worldly interests die along with them (Galatians 6:14). In addition, accepting all sorts of ridicule for Christ's sake by loving our enemies (Matthew 5:44) is the way of the Cross. The believer relives the death and resurrection of Christ by putting to death the old self and putting on the new man.

Future Judgments

In addition to the two past judgments, a discussion of three future judgments will follow. These universal judgments include: The Judgment Seat of Christ (Bema Seat Judgment), the Tribulation, and the Great White Throne Judgment.

The Judgment Seat of Christ (Bema Seat)

Currently, the church is in the period of "grace" in which she is commanded to reach the world with the Gospel. But once the Rapture occurs, the grace period ends. So the next major world event will be of cataclysmic proportions in which Christ will return in the clouds to meet His bride (the church). This event will be called "the Rapture." The word

Rapture means "taken out from among or caught up together with them." According to the clear teachings of the Scriptures, believers from the Old and New Testaments will be snatched from planet earth. "Listen, I tell you a mystery: We will not all sleep, but we will all be changed— in a flash, in the twinkling of an eye, at the last trumpet. For the trumpet will sound, the dead will be raised imperishable, and we will be changed" (1 Corinthians 15:51-52 NIV). This event is the fulfillment of Jesus' promise in John 14:2-3 (NIV),which says, "In my Father's house are many rooms; if it were not so, I would have told you. I am going there to prepare a place for you. And if I go and prepare a place for you, I will come back and take you to be with me that you also may be where I am."

Some significant pointers are to be discussed. First, all living and dead believers in Christ will be removed physically from the earth. Second, only unbelievers will be left behind. This is how the rapture will unfold. Listen to Paul's words: "For the Lord himself will come down from heaven, with a loud command, with the voice of the archangel and with the trumpet call of God, and the dead in Christ will rise first. After that, we who are still alive and are left will be caught up together with them in the clouds to meet the Lord in the air. And so we will be with the Lord forever" (1 Thessalonians 4:16-17 NIV). Scriptures also make it clear that believers will not experience the Tribulation, a period of unparalleled suffering on earth. "Because you have kept My command to persevere, I also will keep you from the hour of trial [the Tribulation] which shall come upon the whole world, to test those who dwell on the earth" (Revelation 3:10).

Fellow believers, this is great news to be excited about. Before the rapture takes place, the living and dead believers shall be changed instantly and permanently as Christians go home to meet with the Lord eternally. Believers shall leave behind chaos, otherwise known as the Tribulation – a seven-year period in which the first three-and-one-half years will reveal the antichrist and his deceitful alliance with Israel. Then, followed by another three-and-one-half-year period just before the Second Coming of Christ, a time of trouble unsurpassed in all human history, "… there will be great distress, unequaled from the beginning of the world until now—and never to be equaled again. If those days had not been cut short, no one would survive, but for the sake of the elect those days will be shortened" (Matthew 24:21-22 NIV). There will be turmoil, total confusion in homes, churches, schools, businesses, governments, and nations.

We know, according to Scripture, that "God is not a man, that He should lie, nor a son of man, that He should repent. Has He said, and will He not do? Or has He spoken, and will He not make it good" (Numbers 23:19).

Again, according to Scripture, we are in the Church Age, a period of time when all believers are encouraged to preach the Gospel or Good News to all nations. In God's timing, Christians will be physically taken out of the earth and will see the glory of Christ immediately (1 John 3:2). At the same time, they will be transformed into His likeness (1 Corinthians 15:51-53), while the world will not see the glory of Christ until the Second Coming.

When is the rapture to take place? It is imminent and could occur any day. It is going to happen without warning. The idea of an imminent coming of Christ for the believer is called pre-Tribulation.

After believers are raptured, they will appear before the judgment seat of Christ. "...We shall all stand before the judgment seat of Christ" (Romans 14:10). Paul, writing to the Corinthians, also said, "So we make it our goal to please him, whether we are at home in the body or away from it. For we must all appear before the judgment seat of Christ, that each one may receive what is due him for the things done while in the body, whether good or bad" (2 Corinthians 5:9-10 NIV). At His judgment, Jesus will evaluate each believer's faithfulness to Him and reward each person appropriately. "For no one can lay any foundation other than the one already laid, which is Jesus Christ. If any man builds on this foundation using gold, silver, costly stones, wood, hay or straw, his work will be shown for what it is, because the Day will bring it to light. It will be revealed with fire, and the fire will test the quality of each man's work. If what he has built survives, then he will receive his reward. If it is burned up, he himself will be saved, but only as one escaping through the flames" (1 Corinthians 3:11-15 NIV).

It should be stressed that the reward will not be a determination of one's eternal destiny. That issue is decided the moment an individual puts his or her faith in Jesus Christ at conversion. The presiding judge will be Jesus Christ and it will take place in heaven (1 Corinthians 5:8), when all Christians are gathered in heaven around the throne of Christ.

Another question worthy of consideration is: What is the nature of these eternal rewards? Two main points emerge from the Bible concerning rewards. First are the various "crowns" mentioned in the New Testament as rewards. These rewards affirm the words of Jesus when He said, "'Blessed are the dead who die in the Lord from now on.' 'Yes,' says the Spirit, 'that they [believers] may rest from their labors, and their works follow them'" (Revelation 14:13). So these five crowns are:

Crown of Exultation (Rejoicing)

"For what is our hope, our joy, or the crown in which we will glory in the presence of our Lord Jesus when he comes? Is it not you?" (1 Thessalonians 2:19 NIV). "...And those who turn many to righteousness [are] like the stars forever and ever" (Daniel 12:3). Finally, "He who win souls is wise" (Proverbs 11:30).

Crown of Righteousness

"Now there is in store for me the crown of righteousness, which the Lord, the righteous Judge, will award to me on that day—and not only to me, but also to all who have longed for his appearing" (2 Timothy 4:8 NIV). All believers who look forward to Christ's appearing purify themselves from sin and unrighteousness.

Crown of Life

"Blessed is the man who endures temptation..." (James 1:12). This crown is for all those who suffer persecution for the sake of the Gospel (Revelation 2:10; 3:11).

Crown of Imperishability

"And everyone who competes for the prize is temperate in all things. Now they do it to obtain a perishable crown, but we for an imperishable crown" (1 Corinthians 9:25). This crown is reserved for all who run the race of life well.

Crown of Glory

"And when the Chief Shepherd appears, you will receive the crown of glory that does not fade away" (1 Peter 5:4). In this verse, Jesus is referred to as the Chief Shepherd. Elsewhere, Jesus is called the Shepherd (1 Peter 2:25), the Good Shepherd (John 10:11,14), and the Great Shepherd

(Hebrews 13:20). It must be emphasized that God guarantees that these ministers who serve faithfully, not "lording over" His people, not serving by compulsion, but willingly from their hearts, not working out of duty, but out of devotion, and being examples to the flock will receive an eternal reward in Christ's coming kingdom.

It must be pointed out that every believer will lay his crown(s) at the feet of Jesus. Probably, this act is done to show that the believer's good works were done by the power of God in Christ. Another major point of interest as a reward to believers is the prospect of serving and ruling in eternity with Christ in exchange for the believer's faithfulness to Him on earth (Matthew 25:21,23; Revelation 22:3,5).

Some believers' work will be burned (1 Corinthians 3:15). Fire is the instrument that God will use to evaluate everyone's work. While fire proves the quality of gold, on the one hand, it consumes wood and hay (physically) and (spiritually) things motivated by selfish desire and wrong motives. But all who served God with pure motives will be praised and rewarded. The true value of such services will become obvious to all in the day of God's judgment.

Finally, how can believers stay ready for the rapture? Three words provide the answer: Proclaim, Purify, and Watch!

Proclaim
Believers should tirelessly share the news of salvation to others. "Brethren, do not grow weary in doing good" (2 Thessalonians 3:13). Christians must live responsibly, work diligently, and invest their time, talent, and treasure wisely as good stewards.

Purify
There is one thing all Christ-followers must maintain – personal purity. In light of the disintegration of everything in the end times, Peter admonishes believers to live a holy life (2 Peter 3:11-12).

Watch
On several occasions, Christ warns His followers to stay on the alert (Mark 13:22-27). Believers are to live each day as if it were their last, but plan as though their world might last a hundred years. Christ-followers

also should echo the words of Paul, "I have fought the good fight, I have finished the race, I have kept the faith. Finally, there is laid up for me the crown of righteousness, which the Lord, the righteous Judge, will give to me on that Day, and not to me only but also to all who have loved His appearing" (2 Timothy 4:7-8), fixing our eyes on Jesus, the author and finisher of our faith (Hebrews 12:2).

The period of the end times extends about seven years from the time of the Rapture to the time of the Second Coming of Christ. The book of Revelation makes it clear that the world ruler, the antichrist, will emerge on the world scene and will dominate the earth for three-and-one-half years prior to the Second Coming. He will seek to kill everyone who does not acknowledge him as God (Revelation 13:7,10,15). Revelation 7:9-17 describes a multitude of martyrs in heaven from every nation, tribe, people, and language. They are described as those who came out of the Great Tribulation. These are saints who are saved after the rapture and who seal their testimony with their own blood in the Great Tribulation.

The Tribulation Period

The next major future judgment that will sweep across the globe is the Tribulation. Jesus Christ, the righteous Judge, will punish earth dwellers from heaven. It will be a time of particularly great suffering associated with the events of the end times. The term "Tribulation" can be gleaned from passages in the Old and New Testaments. An alternative name for it is the "time of trouble" (Jeremiah 30:7,11; Daniel 12:1). Daniel says that this coming time will be such as never occurred before, probably in scope and intensity. His prophecy was affirmed by Jesus in Matthew 24:15-28. The period begins with the rapture of the church, followed by a revelation of the antichrist, and ends with the Second Coming of the King of Kings, the Lord Jesus Christ, to establish the millennial reign on earth. The period of the end time extends for approximately seven years from the time of the rapture to the time of the Second Coming.

Three Views about the Tribulation:

Pre-Tribulation Rapture

This view of the timing of the rapture described in 1 Thessalonians 4:17 teaches that before the seven-year Tribulation, true believers will be taken out from the earth and saved from the wrath of God that will come.

Mid-Tribulation Rapture

This view of the timing of the Rapture (1 Thessalonians 4:17) teaches that in the middle of the future seven-year Tribulation, true believers will be "caught up" from the earth to heaven, saved from the direct wrath of God that comes during the Great Tribulation.

Post-Tribulation Rapture

This view of timing of the Rapture described in I Thessalonians 4:17 teaches that after the future seven-year Tribulation, true believers who survived the persecution and martyrdom will be "caught up" from the earth to heaven to reign with Christ during the Millennium.

Before we delve into the Tribulation narrative, it is imperative that we answer the question, "Will the church go through the Tribulation?" The answer is a resounding *"No!"* The Bible teaches that the Day of the Lord will come "like a thief in the night" (1 Thessalonians 5:1-2). It states explicitly in 1 Thessalonians 5:9 (NIV) that the church will not be subjected to the wrath of the period. "For God did not appoint us to suffer wrath, but to receive salvation through our Lord Jesus Christ." Although 1 Thessalonians 5:9 denies that the church will experience this time of wrath, many will come to faith in Christ even during the Tribulation period. These future believers will experience persecution during the Great Tribulation. It is for their sake that Christ will shorten the time of their great suffering (Matthew 24:22).

Another confirmation that the church will not go through the Tribulation is the Day of the Lord, which begins at the time of the rapture. It is important that we take note of the expression "the Day of the Lord," a familiar Old Testament term which refers to any period of time where God deals in direct judgment with Israel because of their waywardness (Joel 1:1-2:17; 3:14-16). Currently, the church is in a period of grace and God is not dishing out direct judgment. But once the Rapture occurs, the grace period ends. The beginning of the Rapture will also be the start of the Tribulation time until the millennial kingdom, where Christ will rule for 1,000 years, followed by Satan's last- ditch rebellion which will be put down, and sin will be judged in a drastic and final way.

A second question which begs an answer: "Why does God judge the earth and which groups are involved?" The motive of judgment is an answer to the prayers of the martyred saints (Revelation 5:8). In addition, God's righteous vengeance is particularly directed toward those who oppose His work and reject the gift of Jesus Christ. Furthermore, the purpose of the judgment is to release the wrath of God on wickedness and bring about repentance for some. The two major groups that will go through the Great Tribulation are the nations of Israel and the unbelieving Gentiles who rejected the Gospel.

Soon after the Rapture, the Antichrist will rise to power and enter into a covenant with Israel. Putting together all scriptures that bear on the Tribulation, Revelation implies that the Roman Empire has to be revived in the end times. According to Daniel 7:7, ten nations band together in what may look like a "United States of the World," or a modern revived ancient Roman Empire. This may begin as a friendly alliance, but once it is formed, a dictator arises (Daniel 7:8). Finally, he is regarded as the dominant leader throughout Europe and the Middle East.

During this rise to power, the Antichrist enters with the covenant of Daniel 9:27, which describes a seven-year period leading up to the Second Coming of Christ. It begins as a peace treaty between Israel and her neighbors enforced by the ruler, who is generally identified as the Antichrist. For the first half of the seven years, he protects Israel. This peace is suddenly broken when Israel is attacked by an alliance of nations led by a ruler from the north (Ezekiel 38-39). God will intervene and rescue Israel by helping them destroy the invaders. Note also that the Old Testament saints will be judged. "At that time Michael shall stand up, the great prince who stands watch over the sons of your people; and there shall be a time of trouble, such as never was since there was a nation, even to that time. And at that time your people shall be delivered, everyone who is found written in the book. And many of those who sleep in the dust of the earth shall awake, some to everlasting life, some to shame and everlasting contempt. Those who are wise shall shine like the brightness of the firmament, and those who turn many to righteousness like the stars forever and ever" (Daniel 12:1-3).

The Bible states that in the middle of the last seven years, the Antichrist will break his covenant with Israel and become their persecutor. He will attempt to kill all the Jews and Gentile believers who have chosen to be identified with God rather than to worship him. This begins the period referred to by Scripture as the Great Tribulation. According to Matthew

24:15, Christ said it would begin with the desecration of a Jewish temple which is yet to be built, but which will be in operation at that time. The Antichrist will change the temple into a shrine devoted to the worship of himself. Since his purpose is to kill all who will not worship him as god, God pours out the terrible judgments of Revelation 6-18, which will effectively wipe out the world's population and destroy civilization as a whole.

During the Great Tribulation, God will release three major judgments upon the earth: seven seals, seven trumpets, and seven bowls. The first of these accompanies the breaking of the seven seals (Revelation 6:1-17; 8:1-2) on a small scroll which may be the title deed of the world. The second judgment accompanies the sounding of seven trumpets (Revelation 8:2-9:21; 11:15-19), while the final series of judgment occurs as seven angels empty vials (Revelation 16:1-21) of the wrath of God upon the world. These judgments will last for approximately seven years, but for the intervention of Jesus (Matthew 24:22).

Each series describes unique events of the coming Tribulation; the effects of the judgments overlap so that they intensify toward the end and culminate at the return of Christ. A cursory reading of the chapters 6-18 in Revelation reveals how terrible and catastrophic it will be. For example, the fourth seal, which represents an early phase of this judgment, speaks of the earth being wiped out (Revelation 6:7-8). The seal judgments in chapters 6:1-8:1 are followed by a series of punishments announced by the sounding of seven trumpets. The sixth trumpet adds another terrible fact that one-third of the remaining population of the earth will be killed (Revelation 9:15). These seven trumpets in turn are followed by the final bowls of God's wrath (Revelation 16:1-21), each of which is still another terrible judgment on planet earth. The seventh and final bowl of wrath is described as an earthquake that is greater than any in history. It will split "the great city" (probably Jerusalem) into three parts, and "the city of nations" will collapse (Revelation 16:19). In other words, the nations of the Gentile world will be destroyed by this great earthquake. It is described further as a time in which islands and mountains disappear and the whole earth is in literal convulsion. Added to all this, a supernatural storm will pelt the earth with 100-pound hailstones. It will be an unimaginable scene to witness all the horrific things that will happen to human life and vegetation. Two-thirds of the nation of Israel will die (Zechariah 13:8-9). The rest of Israel will be saved (Revelation 7:8). Also, millions of the unbelieving Gentile world will be killed.

In Revelation 7:9-17, the Scriptures describe a countless multitude of Gentile believers who survive the Tribulation. Thus, the Bible clearly teaches that during the Tribulation, many Jews and Gentiles will be saved (Zechariah 12:10-12; Romans 11:26; Galatians 3:16). It is only after these judgments of God that Jesus Christ will come again and reveal His power and great glory to stop the carnage which, if allowed to continue, would destroy every human being.

In closing, one would wonder if all this bloodshed makes sense. It does because a just and righteous God must punish sin and disobedience. The benefit of judgment is that many Gentiles, as well as Jews, will repent and become members of the Kingdom of God.

Great White Throne Judgment
The last and final future judgment recorded in the Scriptures is the Great White Throne Judgment. This is the climax of human history where all the dead who were wicked will be raised to life to stand before the Great White Throne presided over by the Lord Jesus Christ (Revelation 20:12).

This event will take place at the end of the 1,000-year reign of Christ. Prior to this judgment will be a period when there will be a worldwide rebellion against God (Revelation 20:7-9) led by Satan. This revolt will be crushed by God when He sends fire out of heaven to devour Satan and the nations that rejected God (Revelation 20:9). Summarily, Satan and his demons will be judged and sentenced to the everlasting lake of fire prepared for them from the foundations of the world. "The devil, who deceived them, was cast into the lake of fire and brimstone where the beast and the false prophet are. And they will be tormented day and night forever and ever" (Revelation 20:10). "And the angels who did not keep their proper domain, but left their own abode, He has reserved in everlasting chains under darkness for the judgment of the great day" (Jude 6).

Standing before the White Throne Judgment will be unbelievers consigned to hell based on their evil works and rejection of God. The reader should be reminded that the saved are already enjoying fellowship with Christ. However, at the Great White Throne Judgment, a determination will be made as to the severity of punishment the unbelievers will receive based upon their deeds when the Book of Life is opened (Revelation 20:12b). Some will receive harsher sentences, while others will receive a lesser degree of eternal suffering in hell. All those condemned will be summarily cast "into the lake of fire" (Revelation 20:14), where they will join Satan, the Antichrist, the False Prophet, and every evil person, according to their personally assigned judgments. At last, God's perfect justice will be accomplished, and no evil will reign in heaven where the righteous will be with God for all eternity.

APPENDIX 1

A Model Church Worth Emulating

Acts 2 is perhaps the best biblical church model that exists. It began with 120 disciples gathering for fervent prayer while awaiting the promise of the Holy Spirit (Acts 2:1). When God poured out His Spirit upon them, "They were all filled with the Holy Spirit and began to speak with other tongues, as the Spirit gave them utterance" (Acts 2:4,11). Henceforth, this radically transformed first-century disciples operated in the power of the Holy Spirit. What the Spirit did *then*, He can do *today*.

Acts 2:42 succinctly outlines the four practices of the first-century church. Scripture declares that the first-century Christian "continued steadfastly in the apostles' doctrine [teaching] and fellowship, in the breaking of bread, and in prayers." Thus, the Acts 2 church existed to:

Teach

The early church continued in the teachings of the Word of God as set forth by the apostles. They paid great attention to the apostles' teaching, gave honor to God by their obedience to the Word, and were built up in their most holy faith. Not only did the early church grow quantitatively through evangelism, it grew qualitatively through discipleship (Matthew 28:19-20). Later in the book of Acts, the Berean Christians were noted for "search[ing] the Scriptures daily to find out whether [the things taught] were so" (Acts 17:11).

Fellowship

Another vibrant characteristic (hallmark) of the first-century believers was the loving community they created. They were all in one accord, not discord or strife. Their love for each other was pure and contagious. They valued people over possession (John 13:35) through the enabling of the

Holy Spirit. They were cheerful and genuine in their love and affection for each other, hence were liberal in giving to the needs of poor brethren among them. They were living the reality of Christ, and His resurrection power was at work in and through them. Fellowship for these saints meant much more than "being together." It meant "having in common with," which indeed refers to sharing material goods and services. Such behavior continued well into the second century.

Break Bread

Not only did the first-century Christians continue in the teachings of the apostles and fellowship with each other, they regularly observed the ordinances of the Lord's Supper – Holy Communion or Eucharist. Whenever they met either in the temple or in domestic chapels (private homes), they celebrated in the sharing of the "body" and "blood" of Jesus Christ. Bread and wine were common fare at a Jewish memorial of the Lord's death, burial, and resurrection. They made it a habitual practice because it was instituted by Christ Jesus Himself. Not only did they practice in the celebration of Eucharist, they passed this holy activity to succeeding generations of the church. Such table fellowship was done with joyful worship in private residences and fostered intimacy among the believers.

Pray

Prayer was the fourth holy practice to which the early saints devoted themselves. Even after the Spirit was poured into them, their prayer habits were never superseded until they came to be swallowed up into everlasting praise. It is interesting to note that the breaking of bread comes between their work and prayer, for it has reference to both and is a catalyst to both.

The results of the practices of the Acts 2 church are well-documented in the verses that follow (starting with Acts 2:42). First, the fear of God pervaded the communities and undeniable miracles were "done through the apostles" (Acts 2:43). Second, the saints were unified and had all things in common (2:44). Third, the believers were magnified – they found favor with all people (Acts 2:47a). Finally, "the Lord added to the church daily" those who were being saved.

In closing, emulating the Acts 2 model for the church of today probably will produce similar results. Through the grace of God and the power of the Holy Spirit, the contemporary church can experience change. Any church empowered and driven by the Holy Spirit, along with adopting the model of the Acts 2 Church, might experience the life-changing power of God.

APPENDIX 2

The Names of God

Hebrew	Meaning	Significance	Reference
1. Elohim	The Creator	He is my Maker	Genesis 1:1,26 NIV
2. Yahweh/Jehovah	The Lord is Self-Existent	He is my Rock	Exodus 3:14 NIV
3. Jehovah-Tsidkenu	The Lord is Righteous	He is my Righteousness	Jeremiah 23:6 NIV
4. Jehovah-M'kaddesh	The Lord is [my] Sanctifier	He is my Sanctification	Exodus 31:13 NKJV
5. Jehovah-Jehozabed	The Lord Satisfies	He satisfies my heart's deepest desires	Psalm 145:16 NKJV
6. Jehovah-Jireh	The Lord Provides	He provides for my physical needs	Genesis 22:14 NKJV
7. Jehovah-El Elyon	The Lord Most High	He protects me from all evil	Daniel 4:34 NIV
8. Jehovah-El Shaddai	The Lord Almighty	He is my Sufficiency	Genesis 17:2 NIV
9. Jehovah-Adonai	The Sovereign Ruler	He is my Master	Isaiah 6:8 NIV
10. Jehovah Shalom	The Lord is Peace	He is my Peace	Judges 6:24 NIV

11. Jehovah Shammah	The Lord is everywhere present	He lives in me	Ezekiel 48:35 NKJV
12. Jehovah Sabaoth	The Lord of Hosts	He fights my battles	1 Samuel 17:45 NIV
13. Jehovah Gibbor	The Lord all Powerful	He is my Strength	Psalm 24:8 NKJV
14. Jehovah-Rapha	The Lord is [my] Healer	He heals all my diseases	Exodus 15:26 NKJV
15. Jehovah-Nissi	The Lord is [my] Banner	He gives me victory over everything	Exodus 17:10-15 NIV
16. Jehovah-Rohi	The Lord is [my] Shepherd	He keeps me from wandering	Psalm 23 NKJV
17. Jehovah-Baal Perazim	The Lord who breaks through	He opens doors for us	2 Samuel 5:20 NKJV
18. Jehovah-Olam	The Lord is Everlasting	He gives me eternal life	Genesis 21:33; John 3:16 NKJV
19. Jehovah-Roi	The Lord Sees	He is my Security	Genesis 16:13 NKJV
20. Jehovah-El Elohe Israel	The Lord of Israel	He is the God of Israel	Genesis 33:20 NKJV

APPENDIX 3

The Attributes of God

God has chosen to reveal Himself through His unique and divine attributes. The Bible, the source of this revelation, did not come by the will of man, but God (2 Timothy 3:16; 2 Peter 1:20-21). God is invisible, personal, and a living Spirit. These personal characteristics define what God is and can be grouped into six major categories: immutable, cognitive, moral, emotional, existential, and relational.

Immutable
- God is self-existent – God has life in Himself (John 5:26).
- God is Spirit (John 4:24).
- God is invisible (1 Timothy 6:16).
- God is a living and active Spirit (Hebrews 4:12).
- God is self-sufficient (Acts 17:25).
- God is eternal (Exodus 3:14; Psalm 48:14).
- God is omnipresent (Ezekiel 48:35).
- God is enthroned as King forever (Psalm 29:10).
- God is unchanging in nature, desire, and purpose (Psalm 102:25-27; James 1:17; 1 Samuel 15:29; Numbers 23:19).
- God's counsel stands forever (Psalm 33:11).
- God's Word will never fail (Matthew 5:18; 24:35).
- God is unlimited, infinite, free, and self-determined.

Cognitive
- God differs from other spirits not only in being immutable, but He also has unlimited intellectual capabilities. He uses them fully and perfectly.
- God is omniscient:
  ○ He knows all things (1 John 3:20).

- ° He knows our inward thoughts and outward acts thoroughly (Hebrews 4:13).
- ° He knows all of history at once, simultaneously, since He is not limited by time, space, and succession. He knows the past, present, and future all at once.
- • God is wise (Romans 16:27).

Moral
- • God is different from any other created thing, not only in being immutable, and having cognition, but also morally. He is morally perfect in character, words, and actions.
- • God is holy and free from all evil (Isaiah 6:3; 40:25; Hebrews 1:13).
- • God is just and righteous altogether (Jeremiah 33:6).
- • God is faithful and true (Revelation 19:11; Hebrews 10:23).
- • In mercy, He withholds or modifies deserved judgments, and in grace He freely gives undeserved benefits to whom He chooses – His *agape* (unconditional) love.

Emotional
- • God has feelings, but His emotions are immutable; His feelings are never out of control and are not driven by circumstances (Ephesians 4:30).
- • God hates evil, but is longsuffering, merciful, forgiving, gracious, and abounding in goodness and truth (Exodus 34:6-7; Psalm 80:15; 2 Peter 3:9).
- • Although the Lord is slow to anger, He will in no way leave the guilty unpunished. He will pour His fury on them in the Great Tribulation (Nahum 1:3).

Existential
- • As an essential part of life, God is the creator of everything seen and unseen, is free, authentic, and omnipotent (all powerful).
- • God is free and not inhabited by any external or internal forces.
- • God is self-determined, but He cannot contradict His divine nature – i.e., He is not free to sin, to be unloving, to be unwise, to be uncompassionate, or to be unmerciful.

- God is free to be Himself – immutable, cognitive, moral, emotional, personal, eternal, living, and volitional.
- God is authentic – true to Himself. There exists no molecule of hypocrisy in Him.
- God's purposes are known completely by Him (1 Corinthians 2:11). Therefore, He has a keen sense of identity, meaning, and purpose.
- God is omnipotent (Mark 14:36; Luke 1:37). He is able to do whatever He wants, whenever He wills to do it.
- God's eternal purpose for history can never be thwarted, but must be accomplished according to His plan (Ephesians 1:11).
- In a nutshell, God not only has the power to effect all His purposes, but the authority to do whatever He wills because nothing exists independent of His divine sovereignty.

Relational

- God is relational and transcendent in being, present universally in providential activity, and always active in the lives of His people in redemptive activity.
- God is transcendent, meaning He is uniquely other than everything in creation. He is over all and above created things in the universe.
- God is faithful, true, keeps His promises (Hebrews 10:23; Revelation 19:11), never fails (1 Kings 8:50), forgives sins (1 John. 1:9), sanctifies believers until the return of Christ (1 Thessalonians 5:23-24), strengthens and protects His children from the evil one (2 Thessalonians 3:3), and will not allow any temptation beyond what we can bear (1 Corinthians 10:13). In addition, even if we are faithless, He remains faithful, for He cannot disown Himself (2 Timothy 2:13).
- When a person bows to the transcendent Lord of glory, that individual is free from bowing to every finite, fallen creature.

- God is imminent in the lives of His people who repent of their sins and live by faith to accomplish the purposes preplanned by God (Isaiah 57:15; Jeremiah 29:11).
- Furthermore, God is graciously present in forgiving sinners when they repent and dwell in Him forever.
- In the final analysis, God created mankind to be in perpetual relationship with Him and enjoy the unity shared by other members of Christ's body forever (Ephesians 4:1-24).

APPENDIX 4

Scripture Reference Guide

Scriptures referenced in *Seven Pillars of Christianity* are listed here by chapter in the order they are mentioned, except for those printed out in the text of the chapter and except those referencing an entire Bible chapter. Our purpose in this is to make this book a comprehensive reference tool, where the reader has all scriptures used in these teachings readily available.

INTRODUCTION

Matthew 7:22-23
22 Many will say to Me in that day, 'Lord, Lord, have we not prophesied in Your name, cast out demons in Your name, and done many wonders in Your name?' 23 And then I will declare to them, 'I never knew you; depart from Me, you who practice lawlessness!'

2 Peter 1:3
3 as His divine power has given to us all things that pertain to life and godliness, through the knowledge of Him who called us by glory and virtue.

Ephesians 6:11,13
11 Put on the whole armor of God, that you may be able to stand against the wiles of the devil. 13 Therefore take up the whole armor of God, that you may be able to withstand in the evil day, and having done all, to stand.

2 Timothy 3:16

[16] All Scripture is given by inspiration of God, and is profitable for doctrine, for reproof, for correction, for instruction in righteousness.

2 Corinthians 4:3-4

[3] But even if our gospel is veiled, it is veiled to those who are perishing, [4] whose minds the god of this age has blinded, who do not believe, lest the light of the gospel of the glory of Christ, who is the image of God, should shine on them.

Luke 24:45

[45] And He opened their understanding, that they might comprehend the Scriptures.

Ephesians 1:10-18

[10] that in the dispensation of the fullness of the times He might gather together in one all things in Christ, both which are in heaven and which are on earth--in Him. [11] In Him also we have obtained an inheritance, being predestined according to the purpose of Him who works all things according to the counsel of His will, [12] that we who first trusted in Christ should be to the praise of His glory. [13] In Him you also trusted, after you heard the word of truth, the gospel of your salvation; in whom also, having believed, you were sealed with the Holy Spirit of promise, [14] who is the guarantee of our inheritance until the redemption of the purchased possession, to the praise of His glory. [15] Therefore I also, after I heard of your faith in the Lord Jesus and your love for all the saints, [16] do not cease to give thanks for you, making mention of you in my prayers: [17] that the God of our Lord Jesus Christ, the Father of glory, may give to you the spirit of wisdom and revelation in the knowledge of Him, [18] the eyes of your understanding being enlightened; that you may know what is the hope of His calling, what are the riches of the glory of His inheritance in the saints.

Isaiah 7:14

[14] Therefore the Lord Himself will give you a sign: Behold, the virgin shall conceive and bear a Son, and shall call His name Immanuel.

Luke 1:26-35

26 Now in the sixth month the angel Gabriel was sent by God to a city of Galilee named Nazareth, 27 to a virgin betrothed to a man whose name was Joseph, of the house of David. The virgin's name was Mary. 28 And having come in, the angel said to her, "Rejoice, highly favored one, the Lord is with you; blessed are you among women!" 29 But when she saw him, she was troubled at his saying, and considered what manner of greeting this was. 30 Then the angel said to her, "Do not be afraid, Mary, for you have found favor with God. 31 And behold, you will conceive in your womb and bring forth a Son, and shall call His name Jesus. 32 He will be great, and will be called the Son of the Highest; and the Lord God will give Him the throne of His father David. 33 And He will reign over the house of Jacob forever, and of His kingdom there will be no end." 34 Then Mary said to the angel, "How can this be, since I do not know a man?" 35 And the angel answered and said to her, "The Holy Spirit will come upon you, and the power of the Highest will overshadow you; therefore, also, that Holy One who is to be born will be called the Son of God."

Micah 5:2

2 "But you, Bethlehem Ephrathah, Though you are little among the thousands of Judah, Yet out of you shall come forth to Me The One to be Ruler in Israel, Whose goings forth are from of old, From everlasting."

Matthew 2:1

1 Now after Jesus was born in Bethlehem of Judea in the days of Herod the king, behold, wise men from the East came to Jerusalem"

Matthew 1:23

23 "Behold, the virgin shall be with child, and bear a Son, and they shall call His name Immanuel," which is translated, "God with us."

Isaiah 9:1-2

1 Nevertheless the gloom will not be upon her who is distressed, As when at first He lightly esteemed The land of Zebulun and the land of Naphtali, And afterward more heavily oppressed her, By the way of the sea, beyond the Jordan, In Galilee of the Gentiles. 2 The people who walked in darkness Have seen a great light; Those who dwelt in the land of the shadow of death, Upon them a light has shined.

Matthew 4:12-16

[12] Now when Jesus heard that John had been put in prison, He departed to Galilee. [13] And leaving Nazareth, He came and dwelt in Capernaum, which is by the sea, in the regions of Zebulun and Naphtali, [14] that it might be fulfilled which was spoken by Isaiah the prophet, saying: [15] "The land of Zebulun and the land of Naphtali, By the way of the sea, beyond the Jordan, Galilee of the Gentiles: [16] The people who sat in darkness have seen a great light, And upon those who sat in the region and shadow of death Light has dawned."

Zechariah 9:9

[9] "Rejoice greatly, O daughter of Zion! Shout, O daughter of Jerusalem! Behold, your King is coming to you; He is just and having salvation, Lowly and riding on a donkey, A colt, the foal of a donkey."

Matthew 21:1-11

[1] Now when they drew near Jerusalem, and came to Bethphage, at the Mount of Olives, then Jesus sent two disciples, [2] saying to them, "Go into the village opposite you, and immediately you will find a donkey tied, and a colt with her. Loose them and bring them to Me. [3] And if anyone says anything to you, you shall say, 'The Lord has need of them,' and immediately he will send them." [4] All this was done that it might be fulfilled which was spoken by the prophet, saying: [5] "Tell the daughter of Zion, 'Behold, your King is coming to you, Lowly, and sitting on a donkey, A colt, the foal of a donkey.'" [6] So the disciples went and did as Jesus commanded them. [7] They brought the donkey and the colt, laid their clothes on them, and set Him on them. [8] And a very great multitude spread their clothes on the road; others cut down branches from the trees and spread them on the road. [9] Then the multitudes who went before and those who followed cried out, saying: "Hosanna to the Son of David! 'Blessed is He who comes in the name of the Lord!' Hosanna in the highest!" [10] And when He had come into Jerusalem, all the city was moved, saying, "Who is this?" [11] So the multitudes said, "This is Jesus, the prophet from Nazareth of Galilee."

Genesis 1:1

[1] In the beginning God created the heavens and the earth.

Hebrews 1:3

[3] who being the brightness of His glory and the express image of His person, and upholding all things by the word of His power, when He had by Himself purged our sins, sat down at the right hand of the Majesty on high,

Romans 1:18-25

[18] For the wrath of God is revealed from heaven against all ungodliness and unrighteousness of men, who suppress the truth in unrighteousness, [19] because what may be known of God is manifest in them, for God has shown it to them. [20] For since the creation of the world His invisible attributes are clearly seen, being understood by the things that are made, even His eternal power and Godhead, so that they are without excuse, [21] because, although they knew God, they did not glorify Him as God, nor were thankful, but became futile in their thoughts, and their foolish hearts were darkened. [22] Professing to be wise, they became fools, [23] and changed the glory of the incorruptible God into an image made like corruptible man--and birds and four-footed animals and creeping things. [24] Therefore God also gave them up to uncleanness, in the lusts of their hearts, to dishonor their bodies among themselves, [25] who exchanged the truth of God for the lie, and worshiped and served the creature rather than the Creator, who is blessed forever. Amen.

1 Corinthians 2:14

[14] But the natural man does not receive the things of the Spirit of God, for they are foolishness to him; nor can he know them, because they are spiritually discerned.

Philippians 2:16

[16] holding fast the word of life, so that I may rejoice in the day of Christ that I have not run in vain or labored in vain.

Romans 1:16

[16] For I am not ashamed of the gospel of Christ, for it is the power of God to salvation for everyone who believes, for the Jew first and also for the Greek.

John 16:8

[8] And when He has come, He will convict the world of sin, and of righteousness, and of judgment:

Proverbs 4:22
> 22 For they are life to those who find them, And health to all their flesh.

Mark 7:13
> 13 making the word of God of no effect through your tradition which you have handed down. And many such things you do."

John 10:35
> 35 If He called them gods, to whom the word of God came (and the Scripture cannot be broken),

Luke 4:21
> 21 And He began to say to them, "Today this Scripture is fulfilled in your hearing."

Luke 5:39
> 39 And no one, having drunk old wine, immediately desires new; for he says, 'The old is better.'"

Mark 7:8
> 8 "For laying aside the commandment of God, you hold the tradition of men --the washing of pitchers and cups, and many other such things you do."

Matthew 19:4-5
> 4 And He answered and said to them, "Have you not read that He who made them at the beginning 'made them male and female,' 5 and said, 'For this reason a man shall leave his father and mother and be joined to his wife, and the two shall become one flesh'?

Matthew 24:37-39
> 37 But as the days of Noah were, so also will the coming of the Son of Man be. 38 For as in the days before the flood, they were eating and drinking, marrying and giving in marriage, until the day that Noah entered the ark, 39 and did not know until the flood came and took them all away, so also will the coming of the Son of Man be.

Luke 17:28-32
> 28 Likewise as it was also in the days of Lot: They ate, they drank, they bought, they sold, they planted, they built; 29 but on the day that Lot went out of Sodom it rained fire and brimstone from heaven

and destroyed them all. [30] Even so will it be in the day when the Son of Man is revealed. [31] In that day, he who is on the housetop, and his goods are in the house, let him not come down to take them away. And likewise the one who is in the field, let him not turn back. [32] Remember Lot's wife.

Matthew 12:38-41

[38] Then some of the scribes and Pharisees answered, saying, "Teacher, we want to see a sign from You." [39] But He answered and said to them, "An evil and adulterous generation seeks after a sign, and no sign will be given to it except the sign of the prophet Jonah. [40] For as Jonah was three days and three nights in the belly of the great fish, so will the Son of Man be three days and three nights in the heart of the earth. [41] The men of Nineveh will rise up in the judgment with this generation and condemn it, because they repented at the preaching of Jonah; and indeed a greater than Jonah is here.

John 12:48-49

[48] He who rejects Me, and does not receive My words, has that which judges him--the word that I have spoken will judge him in the last day. [49] For I have not spoken on My own authority; but the Father who sent Me gave Me a command, what I should say and what I should speak.

Matthew 12:3

[3] But He said to them, "Have you not read what David did when he was hungry, he and those who were with him:

John 10:34

[34] Jesus answered them, "Is it not written in your law, 'I said, "You are gods"'?

Psalm 82:6

[6] I said, "You are gods, And all of you are children of the Most High.

Matthew 22:32

[32] 'I am the God of Abraham, the God of Isaac, and the God of Jacob'? God is not the God of the dead, but of the living."

Exodus 3:6,15

[6] Moreover He said, "I am the God of your father--the God of Abraham, the God of Isaac, and the God of Jacob." And Moses hid his face, for he was afraid to look upon God.

[15] Moreover God said to Moses, "Thus you shall say to the children of Israel: 'The Lord God of your fathers, the God of Abraham, the God of Isaac, and the God of Jacob, has sent me to you. This is My name forever, and this is My memorial to all generations.'

Matthew 22:42-44

[42] saying, "What do you think about the Christ? Whose Son is He?" They said to Him, "The Son of David." [43] He said to them, "How then does David in the Spirit call Him 'Lord '"saying: [44] 'The Lord said to my Lord, "Sit at My right hand, Till I make Your enemies Your footstool"'?

Psalm 110:1

[1] A Psalm of David. The Lord said to my Lord, "Sit at My right hand, Till I make Your enemies Your footstool."

Matthew 4:4,7,10

[4] But He answered and said, "It is written, 'Man shall not live by bread alone, but by every word that proceeds from the mouth of God.'"

[7] Jesus said to him, "It is written again, 'You shall not tempt the Lord your God.'"

[10] Then Jesus said to him, "Away with you, Satan! For it is written, 'You shall worship the Lord your God, and Him only you shall serve.'"

Daniel 9:2

[2] in the first year of his reign I, Daniel, understood by the books the number of the years specified by the word of the Lord through Jeremiah the prophet, that He would accomplish seventy years in the desolations of Jerusalem.

2 Peter 1:20-21

[20] knowing this first, that no prophecy of Scripture is of any private interpretation, [21] for prophecy never came by the will of man, but holy men of God spoke as they were moved by the Holy Spirit.

2 Peter 3:16

[16] as also in all his epistles, speaking in them of these things, in which are some things hard to understand, which untaught and unstable people twist to their own destruction, as they do also the rest of the Scriptures.

Isaiah 1:2

[2] Hear, O heavens, and give ear, O earth! For the Lord has spoken: "I have nourished and brought up children, And they have rebelled against Me;

Ezekiel 3:11

[11] And go, get to the captives, to the children of your people, and speak to them and tell them, 'Thus says the Lord God,' whether they hear, or whether they refuse."

Galatians 1:11-12

[11] But I make known to you, brethren, that the gospel which was preached by me is not according to man. [12] For I neither received it from man, nor was I taught it, but it came through the revelation of Jesus Christ.

1 Thessalonians 2:13

[13] For this reason we also thank God without ceasing, because when you received the word of God which you heard from us, you welcomed it not as the word of men, but as it is in truth, the word of God, which also effectively works in you who believe.

Genesis 3:15

[15] And I will put enmity Between you and the woman, And between your seed and her Seed; He shall bruise your head, And you shall bruise His heel."

Luke 22:20

[20] Likewise He also took the cup after supper, saying, "This cup is the new covenant in My blood, which is shed for you.

Genesis 4:4

[4] Abel also brought of the firstborn of his flock and of their fat. And the Lord respected Abel and his offering,

Jeremiah 31:31-34

[31] "Behold, the days are coming, says the Lord, when I will make a new covenant with the house of Israel and with the house of Judah-- [32] not according to the covenant that I made with their fathers in the day that I took them by the hand to lead them out of the land of Egypt, My covenant which they broke, though I was a husband to them, says the Lord. [33] But this is the covenant that I will make with the house of Israel after those days, says the Lord: I will put My law in their minds, and write it on their hearts; and I will be their God, and they shall be My people. [34] No more shall every man teach his neighbor, and every man his brother, saying, 'Know the Lord,' for they all shall know Me, from the least of them to the greatest of them, says the Lord. For I will forgive their iniquity, and their sin I will remember no more."

John 3:1-8

[1] There was a man of the Pharisees named Nicodemus, a ruler of the Jews. [2] This man came to Jesus by night and said to Him, "Rabbi, we know that You are a teacher come from God; for no one can do these signs that You do unless God is with him." [3] Jesus answered and said to him, "Most assuredly, I say to you, unless one is born again, he cannot see the kingdom of God." [4] Nicodemus said to Him, "How can a man be born when he is old? Can he enter a second time into his mother's womb and be born?" [5] Jesus answered, "Most assuredly, I say to you, unless one is born of water and the Spirit, he cannot enter the kingdom of God. [6] That which is born of the flesh is flesh, and that which is born of the Spirit is spirit. [7] Do not marvel that I said to you, 'You must be born again.' [8] The wind blows where it wishes, and you hear the sound of it, but cannot tell where it comes from and where it goes. So is everyone who is born of the Spirit."

Luke 22:20

[20] Likewise He also took the cup after supper, saying, "This cup is the new covenant in My blood, which is shed for you.

Acts 6:7

[7] Then the word of God spread, and the number of the disciples multiplied greatly in Jerusalem, and a great many of the priests were obedient to the faith.

Acts 9:31

[31] Then the churches throughout all Judea, Galilee, and Samaria had peace and were edified. And walking in the fear of the Lord and in the comfort of the Holy Spirit, they were multiplied.

Acts 12:24

[24] But the word of God grew and multiplied.

Acts 16:5

[5] So the churches were strengthened in the faith, and increased in number daily.

Acts 19:20

[20] So the word of the Lord grew mightily and prevailed.

Acts 28:30-31

[30] Then Paul dwelt two whole years in his own rented house, and received all who came to him, [31] preaching the kingdom of God and teaching the things which concern the Lord Jesus Christ with all confidence, no one forbidding him.

CHAPTER 1

Luke 24:27

[27] And beginning at Moses and all the Prophets, He expounded to them in all the Scriptures the things concerning Himself.

John 5:39

[39] You search the Scriptures, for in them you think you have eternal life; and these are they which testify of Me. [40]

Colossians 1:16

[16] For by Him all things were created that are in heaven and that are on earth, visible and invisible, whether thrones or dominions or principalities or powers. All things were created through Him and for Him.

Genesis 11:6-9

[6] And the Lord said, "Indeed the people are one and they all have one language, and this is what they begin to do; now nothing that they propose to do will be withheld from them. [7] Come, let Us go down

and there confuse their language, that they may not understand one another's speech." ⁸ So the Lord scattered them abroad from there over the face of all the earth, and they ceased building the city. ⁹ Therefore its name is called Babel, because there the Lord confused the language of all the earth; and from there the Lord scattered them abroad over the face of all the earth.

Isaiah 6:1-8

¹ In the year that King Uzziah died, I saw the Lord sitting on a throne, high and lifted up, and the train of His robe filled the temple. ² Above it stood seraphim; each one had six wings: with two he covered his face, with two he covered his feet, and with two he flew. ³ And one cried to another and said: "Holy, holy, holy is the Lord of hosts; The whole earth is full of His glory!" ⁴ And the posts of the door were shaken by the voice of him who cried out, and the house was filled with smoke. ⁵ So I said: "Woe is me, for I am undone! Because I am a man of unclean lips, And I dwell in the midst of a people of unclean lips; For my eyes have seen the King, The Lord of hosts." ⁶ Then one of the seraphim flew to me, having in his hand a live coal which he had taken with the tongs from the altar. ⁷ And he touched my mouth with it, and said: "Behold, this has touched your lips; Your iniquity is taken away, And your sin purged." ⁸ Also I heard the voice of the Lord, saying: "Whom shall I send, And who will go for Us?" Then I said, "Here am I! Send me."

Genesis 3:15

¹⁵ And I will put enmity Between you and the woman, And between your seed and her Seed; He shall bruise your head, And you shall bruise His heel."

Exodus 17:6

⁶ Behold, I will stand before you there on the rock in Horeb; and you shall strike the rock, and water will come out of it, that the people may drink." And Moses did so in the sight of the elders of Israel.

1 Corinthians 10:4

⁴ and all drank the same spiritual drink. For they drank of that spiritual Rock that followed them, and that Rock was Christ.

Exodus 12:11

11 And thus you shall eat it: with a belt on your waist, your sandals on your feet, and your staff in your hand. So you shall eat it in haste. It is the Lord's Passover.

John 1:36

36 And looking at Jesus as He walked, he said, "Behold the Lamb of God!"

John 19:36

36 For these things were done that the Scripture should be fulfilled, "Not one of His bones shall be broken."

1 Corinthians 10:4

4 and all drank the same spiritual drink. For they drank of that spiritual Rock that followed them, and that Rock was Christ.

John 3:14-15

14 And as Moses lifted up the serpent in the wilderness, even so must the Son of Man be lifted up, 15 that whoever believes in Him should not perish but have eternal life.

Deuteronomy 18:15-22

15 "The Lord your God will raise up for you a Prophet like me from your midst, from your brethren. Him you shall hear, 16 according to all you desired of the Lord your God in Horeb in the day of the assembly, saying, 'Let me not hear again the voice of the Lord my God, nor let me see this great fire anymore, lest I die.' 17 And the Lord said to me: 'What they have spoken is good. 18 I will raise up for them a Prophet like you from among their brethren, and will put My words in His mouth, and He shall speak to them all that I command Him. 19 And it shall be that whoever will not hear My words, which He speaks in My name, I will require it of him. 20 But the prophet who presumes to speak a word in My name, which I have not commanded him to speak, or who speaks in the name of other gods, that prophet shall die.' 21 And if you say in your heart, 'How shall we know the word which the Lord has not spoken?'-- 22 when a prophet speaks in the name of the Lord, if the thing does not happen or come to pass, that is the thing which the Lord has not spoken; the prophet has spoken it presumptuously; you shall not be afraid of him.

Acts 3:22

²² For Moses truly said to the fathers, 'The Lord your God will raise up for you a Prophet like me from your brethren. Him you shall hear in all things, whatever He says to you.

Acts 7:37

³⁷ "This is that Moses who said to the children of Israel, 'The Lord your God will raise up for you a Prophet like me from your brethren. Him you shall hear.'

Deuteronomy 21:23

²³ his body shall not remain overnight on the tree, but you shall surely bury him that day, so that you do not defile the land which the Lord your God is giving you as an inheritance; for he who is hanged is accursed of God.

Galatians 3:13

¹³ Christ has redeemed us from the curse of the law, having become a curse for us (for it is written, "Cursed is everyone who hangs on a tree"),

Joshua 5:15

¹⁵ Then the Commander of the Lord's army said to Joshua, "Take your sandal off your foot, for the place where you stand is holy." And Joshua did so.

Luke 11:31

³¹ The queen of the South will rise up in the judgment with the men of this generation and condemn them, for she came from the ends of the earth to hear the wisdom of Solomon; and indeed a greater than Solomon is here.

Luke 24:19

¹⁹ And He said to them, "What things?" So they said to Him, "The things concerning Jesus of Nazareth, who was a Prophet mighty in deed and word before God and all the people,

2 Kings 8:19

¹⁹ Yet the Lord would not destroy Judah, for the sake of his servant David, as He promised him to give a lamp to him and his sons forever.

Revelation 21:23

23 The city had no need of the sun or of the moon to shine in it, for the glory of God illuminated it. The Lamb is its light.

1 Chronicles 17:13

13 I will be his Father, and he shall be My son; and I will not take My mercy away from him, as I took it from him who was before you.

Luke 1:32-33

32 He will be great, and will be called the Son of the Highest; and the Lord God will give Him the throne of His father David. 33 And He will reign over the house of Jacob forever, and of His kingdom there will be no end."

Hebrews 1:5

5 For to which of the angels did He ever say: "You are My Son, Today I have begotten You"? And again: "I will be to Him a Father, And He shall be to Me a Son"?

1 Chronicles 29:10-13

10 Therefore David blessed the Lord before all the assembly; and David said: "Blessed are You, Lord God of Israel, our Father, forever and ever. 11 Yours, O Lord, is the greatness, The power and the glory, The victory and the majesty; For all that is in heaven and in earth is Yours; Yours is the kingdom, O Lord, And You are exalted as head over all. 12 Both riches and honor come from You, And You reign over all. In Your hand is power and might; In Your hand it is to make great And to give strength to all. 13 "Now therefore, our God, We thank You And praise Your glorious name.

Revelation 5:12-13

12 saying with a loud voice: "Worthy is the Lamb who was slain To receive power and riches and wisdom, And strength and honor and glory and blessing!" 13 And every creature which is in heaven and on the earth and under the earth and such as are in the sea, and all that are in them, I heard saying: "Blessing and honor and glory and power Be to Him who sits on the throne, And to the Lamb, forever and ever!"

Luke 4:18

18 "The Spirit of the Lord is upon Me, Because He has anointed Me To preach the gospel to the poor; He has sent Me to heal the

brokenhearted, To proclaim liberty to the captives And recovery of sight to the blind, To set at liberty those who are oppressed;

Luke 11:49

[49] Therefore the wisdom of God also said, 'I will send them prophets and apostles, and some of them they will kill and persecute,'

Hebrews 1:2-3

[2] has in these last days spoken to us by His Son, whom He has appointed heir of all things, through whom also He made the worlds; [3] who being the brightness of His glory and the express image of His person, and upholding all things by the word of His power, when He had by Himself purged our sins, sat down at the right hand of the Majesty on high,

John 15:5

[5] I am the vine, you are the branches. He who abides in Me, and I in him, bears much fruit; for without Me you can do nothing.

Ephesians 5:32

[32] This is a great mystery, but I speak concerning Christ and the church.

Isaiah 7:14

[14] Therefore the Lord Himself will give you a sign: Behold, the virgin shall conceive and bear a Son, and shall call His name Immanuel.

Isaiah 52:13-15

[13] Behold, My Servant shall deal prudently; He shall be exalted and extolled and be very high. [14] Just as many were astonished at you, So His visage was marred more than any man, And His form more than the sons of men; [15] So shall He sprinkle many nations. Kings shall shut their mouths at Him; For what had not been told them they shall see, And what they had not heard they shall consider.

Isaiah 53:1-12

[1] Who has believed our report? And to whom has the arm of the Lord been revealed? [2] For He shall grow up before Him as a tender plant, And as a root out of dry ground. He has no form or comeliness; And when we see Him, There is no beauty that we should desire Him. [3] He is despised and rejected by men, A Man of sorrows and acquainted with

grief. And we hid, as it were, our faces from Him; He was despised, and we did not esteem Him. [4] Surely He has borne our griefs And carried our sorrows; Yet we esteemed Him stricken, Smitten by God, and afflicted. [5] But He was wounded for our transgressions, He was bruised for our iniquities; The chastisement for our peace was upon Him, And by His stripes we are healed. [6] All we like sheep have gone astray; We have turned, every one, to his own way; And the Lord has laid on Him the iniquity of us all. [7] He was oppressed and He was afflicted, Yet He opened not His mouth; He was led as a lamb to the slaughter, And as a sheep before its shearers is silent, So He opened not His mouth. [8] He was taken from prison and from judgment, And who will declare His generation? For He was cut off from the land of the living; For the transgressions of My people He was stricken. [9] And they made His grave with the wicked-- But with the rich at His death, Because He had done no violence, Nor was any deceit in His mouth. [10] Yet it pleased the Lord to bruise Him; He has put Him to grief. When You make His soul an offering for sin, He shall see His seed, He shall prolong His days, And the pleasure of the Lord shall prosper in His hand. [11] He shall see the labor of His soul, and be satisfied. By His knowledge My righteous Servant shall justify many, For He shall bear their iniquities. [12] Therefore I will divide Him a portion with the great, And He shall divide the spoil with the strong, Because He poured out His soul unto death, And He was numbered with the transgressors, And He bore the sin of many, And made intercession for the transgressors.

Matthew 1:23

[23] "Behold, the virgin shall be with child, and bear a Son, and they shall call His name Immanuel," which is translated, "God with us."

Matthew 16:21

[21] From that time Jesus began to show to His disciples that He must go to Jerusalem, and suffer many things from the elders and chief priests and scribes, and be killed, and be raised the third day.

Jeremiah 9:1

[1] Oh, that my head were waters, And my eyes a fountain of tears, That I might weep day and night For the slain of the daughter of my people!

Luke 19:41

⁴¹ Now as He drew near, He saw the city and wept over it,

Jeremiah 7:11-15

¹¹ Has this house, which is called by My name, become a den of thieves in your eyes? Behold, I, even I, have seen it," says the Lord. ¹² "But go now to My place which was in Shiloh, where I set My name at the first, and see what I did to it because of the wickedness of My people Israel. ¹³ And now, because you have done all these works," says the Lord, "and I spoke to you, rising up early and speaking, but you did not hear, and I called you, but you did not answer, ¹⁴ therefore I will do to the house which is called by My name, in which you trust, and to this place which I gave to you and your fathers, as I have done to Shiloh. ¹⁵ And I will cast you out of My sight, as I have cast out all your brethren--the whole posterity of Ephraim.

Matthew 21:1-2

¹ Now when they drew near Jerusalem, and came to Bethphage, at the Mount of Olives, then Jesus sent two disciples, ² saying to them, "Go into the village opposite you, and immediately you will find a donkey tied, and a colt with her. Loose them and bring them to Me.

Matthew 2:15

¹⁵ and was there until the death of Herod, that it might be fulfilled which was spoken by the Lord through the prophet, saying, "Out of Egypt I called My Son."

Hosea 11:1

¹ "When Israel was a child, I loved him, And out of Egypt I called My son.

1 Thessalonians 5:2

² For you yourselves know perfectly that the day of the Lord so comes as a thief in the night.

2 Peter 3:10

¹⁰ But the day of the Lord will come as a thief in the night, in which the heavens will pass away with a great noise, and the elements will melt with fervent heat; both the earth and the works that are in it will be burned up.

Acts 2:16-21

[16] But this is what was spoken by the prophet Joel: [17] 'And it shall come to pass in the last days, says God, That I will pour out of My Spirit on all flesh; Your sons and your daughters shall prophesy, Your young men shall see visions, Your old men shall dream dreams. [18] And on My menservants and on My maidservants I will pour out My Spirit in those days; And they shall prophesy. [19] I will show wonders in heaven above And signs in the earth beneath: Blood and fire and vapor of smoke. [20] The sun shall be turned into darkness, And the moon into blood, Before the coming of the great and awesome day of the Lord. [21] And it shall come to pass That whoever calls on the name of the Lord Shall be saved.'

Luke 11:29-32

[29] And while the crowds were thickly gathered together, He began to say, "This is an evil generation. It seeks a sign, and no sign will be given to it except the sign of Jonah the prophet. [30] For as Jonah became a sign to the Ninevites, so also the Son of Man will be to this generation. [31] The queen of the South will rise up in the judgment with the men of this generation and condemn them, for she came from the ends of the earth to hear the wisdom of Solomon; and indeed a greater than Solomon is here. [32] The men of Nineveh will rise up in the judgment with this generation and condemn it, for they repented at the preaching of Jonah; and indeed a greater than Jonah is here.

Matthew 2:6

[6] 'But you, Bethlehem, in the land of Judah, Are not the least among the rulers of Judah; For out of you shall come a Ruler Who will shepherd My people Israel.'"

Nahum 1:15

[15] Behold, on the mountains The feet of him who brings good tidings, Who proclaims peace! O Judah, keep your appointed feasts, Perform your vows. For the wicked one shall no more pass through you; He is utterly cut off.

Acts 10:36

[36] The word which God sent to the children of Israel, preaching peace through Jesus Christ--He is Lord of all--

Nahum 1:4

⁴ He rebukes the sea and makes it dry, And dries up all the rivers. Bashan and Carmel wither, And the flower of Lebanon wilts.

Matthew 8:26

²⁶ But He said to them, "Why are you fearful, O you of little faith?" Then He arose and rebuked the winds and the sea, and there was a great calm.

Habakkuk 3:17-18

¹⁷ Though the fig tree may not blossom, Nor fruit be on the vines; Though the labor of the olive may fail, And the fields yield no food; Though the flock may be cut off from the fold, And there be no herd in the stalls-- ¹⁸ Yet I will rejoice in the Lord, I will joy in the God of my salvation.

Revelation 1:17

¹⁷ And when I saw Him, I fell at His feet as dead. But He laid His right hand on me, saying to me, "Do not be afraid; I am the First and the Last.

Zephaniah 3:15

¹⁵ The Lord has taken away your judgments, He has cast out your enemy. The King of Israel, the Lord, is in your midst; You shall see disaster no more.

Mark 15:26

²⁶ And the inscription of His accusation was written above: THE KING OF THE JEWS.

Haggai 2:6-7

⁶ "For thus says the Lord of hosts: 'Once more (it is a little while) I will shake heaven and earth, the sea and dry land; ⁷ and I will shake all nations, and they shall come to the Desire of All Nations, and I will fill this temple with glory,' says the Lord of hosts.

Luke 2:32

³² A light to bring revelation to the Gentiles, And the glory of Your people Israel."

Zechariah 12:10

[10] "And I will pour on the house of David and on the inhabitants of Jerusalem the Spirit of grace and supplication; then they will look on Me whom they pierced. Yes, they will mourn for Him as one mourns for his only son, and grieve for Him as one grieves for a firstborn.

John 19:34,37

[34] But one of the soldiers pierced His side with a spear, and immediately blood and water came out. [37] And again another Scripture says, "They shall look on Him whom they pierced."

Revelation 1:7

[7] Behold, He is coming with clouds, and every eye will see Him, even they who pierced Him. And all the tribes of the earth will mourn because of Him. Even so, Amen.

Matthew 27:37

[37] And they put up over His head the accusation written against Him: THIS IS JESUS THE KING OF THE JEWS.

Mark 10:45

[45] For even the Son of Man did not come to be served, but to serve, and to give His life a ransom for many."

Romans 1:3-4

[3] concerning His Son Jesus Christ our Lord, who was born of the seed of David according to the flesh, [4] and declared to be the Son of God with power according to the Spirit of holiness, by the resurrection from the dead.

1 Corinthians 1:18,24

[18] For the message of the cross is foolishness to those who are perishing, but to us who are being saved it is the power of God. [24] but to those who are called, both Jews and Greeks, Christ the power of God and the wisdom of God.

1 Corinthians 1:21,24,30

[21] For since, in the wisdom of God, the world through wisdom did not know God, it pleased God through the foolishness of the message preached to save those who believe. [24] but to those who are called, both Jews and Greeks, Christ the power of God and the wisdom of God.

³⁰ But of Him you are in Christ Jesus, who became for us wisdom from God--and righteousness and sanctification and redemption--

Galatians 3:13

¹³ Christ has redeemed us from the curse of the law, having become a curse for us (for it is written, "Cursed is everyone who hangs on a tree"),

Galatians 2:19-20

¹⁹ For I through the law died to the law that I might live to God. ²⁰ I have been crucified with Christ; it is no longer I who live, but Christ lives in me; and the life which I now live in the flesh I live by faith in the Son of God, who loved me and gave Himself for me.

2 Timothy 1:12

¹² For this reason I also suffer these things; nevertheless I am not ashamed, for I know whom I have believed and am persuaded that He is able to keep what I have committed to Him until that Day.

Titus 2:14

¹⁴ who gave Himself for us, that He might redeem us from every lawless deed and purify for Himself His own special people, zealous for good works.

Titus 2:13

¹³ looking for the blessed hope and glorious appearing of our great God and Savior Jesus Christ,

2 Peter 1:17

¹⁷ For He received from God the Father honor and glory when such a voice came to Him from the Excellent Glory: "This is My beloved Son, in whom I am well pleased."

1 John 1:3

³ that which we have seen and heard we declare to you, that you also may have fellowship with us; and truly our fellowship is with the Father and with His Son Jesus Christ.

1 John 1:7

⁷ But if we walk in the light as He is in the light, we have fellowship with one another, and the blood of Jesus Christ His Son cleanses us from all sin.

Jude 21

²¹ keep yourselves in the love of God, looking for the mercy of our Lord Jesus Christ unto eternal life.

Hebrews 6:1

¹ Therefore, leaving the discussion of the elementary principles of Christ, let us go on to perfection, not laying again the foundation of repentance from dead works and of faith toward God,

2 John 9

⁹ Whoever transgresses and does not abide in the doctrine of Christ does not have God. He who abides in the doctrine of Christ has both the Father and the Son.

2 John 7

⁷ For many deceivers have gone out into the world who do not confess Jesus Christ as coming in the flesh. This is a deceiver and an antichrist.

2 John 10-11

¹⁰ If anyone comes to you and does not bring this doctrine, do not receive him into your house nor greet him; ¹¹ for he who greets him shares in his evil deeds.

John 10:36

³⁶ do you say of Him whom the Father sanctified and sent into the world, 'You are blaspheming,' because I said, 'I am the Son of God'?

Acts 2:22

²² "Men of Israel, hear these words: Jesus of Nazareth, a Man attested by God to you by miracles, wonders, and signs which God did through Him in your midst, as you yourselves also know--

Matthew 8:16-17,28-34

¹⁶ When evening had come, they brought to Him many who were demon-possessed. And He cast out the spirits with a word, and healed all who were sick, ¹⁷ that it might be fulfilled which was spoken by Isaiah the prophet, saying: "He Himself took our infirmities And bore our sicknesses."
²⁸ When He had come to the other side, to the country of the Gergesenes, there met Him two demon-possessed men, coming

out of the tombs, exceedingly fierce, so that no one could pass that way. [29] And suddenly they cried out, saying, "What have we to do with You, Jesus, You Son of God? Have You come here to torment us before the time?" [30] Now a good way off from them there was a herd of many swine feeding. [31] So the demons begged Him, saying, "If You cast us out, permit us to go away into the herd of swine." [32] And He said to them, "Go." So when they had come out, they went into the herd of swine. And suddenly the whole herd of swine ran violently down the steep place into the sea, and perished in the water. [33] Then those who kept them fled; and they went away into the city and told everything, including what had happened to the demon-possessed men. [34] And behold, the whole city came out to meet Jesus. And when they saw Him, they begged Him to depart from their region.

Matthew 8:18-22

[18] And when Jesus saw great multitudes about Him, He gave a command to depart to the other side. [19] Then a certain scribe came and said to Him, "Teacher, I will follow You wherever You go." [20] And Jesus said to him, "Foxes have holes and birds of the air have nests, but the Son of Man has nowhere to lay His head." [21] Then another of His disciples said to Him, "Lord, let me first go and bury my father." [22] But Jesus said to him, "Follow Me, and let the dead bury their own dead."

Matthew 9:9

[9] As Jesus passed on from there, He saw a man named Matthew sitting at the tax office. And He said to him, "Follow Me." So he arose and followed Him.

Matthew 8:23-27

[23] Now when He got into a boat, His disciples followed Him. [24] And suddenly a great tempest arose on the sea, so that the boat was covered with the waves. But He was asleep. [25] Then His disciples came to Him and awoke Him, saying, "Lord, save us! We are perishing!" [26] But He said to them, "Why are you fearful, O you of little faith?" Then He arose and rebuked the winds and the sea, and there was a great calm. [27] So the men marveled, saying, "Who can this be, that even the winds and the sea obey Him?"

Matthew 8:1-15

¹ When He had come down from the mountain, great multitudes followed Him. ² And behold, a leper came and worshiped Him, saying, "Lord, if You are willing, You can make me clean." ³ Then Jesus put out His hand and touched him, saying, "I am willing; be cleansed." Immediately his leprosy was cleansed. ⁴ And Jesus said to him, "See that you tell no one; but go your way, show yourself to the priest, and offer the gift that Moses commanded, as a testimony to them." ⁵ Now when Jesus had entered Capernaum, a centurion came to Him, pleading with Him, ⁶ saying, "Lord, my servant is lying at home paralyzed, dreadfully tormented." ⁷ And Jesus said to him, "I will come and heal him." ⁸ The centurion answered and said, "Lord, I am not worthy that You should come under my roof. But only speak a word, and my servant will be healed. ⁹ For I also am a man under authority, having soldiers under me. And I say to this one, 'Go,' and he goes; and to another, 'Come,' and he comes; and to my servant, 'Do this,' and he does it." ¹⁰ When Jesus heard it, He marveled, and said to those who followed, "Assuredly, I say to you, I have not found such great faith, not even in Israel! ¹¹ And I say to you that many will come from east and west, and sit down with Abraham, Isaac, and Jacob in the kingdom of heaven. ¹² But the sons of the kingdom will be cast out into outer darkness. There will be weeping and gnashing of teeth." ¹³ Then Jesus said to the centurion, "Go your way; and as you have believed, so let it be done for you." And his servant was healed that same hour. ¹⁴ Now when Jesus had come into Peter's house, He saw his wife's mother lying sick with a fever. ¹⁵ So He touched her hand, and the fever left her. And she arose and served them.

Matthew 8:24

²⁴ And suddenly a great tempest arose on the sea, so that the boat was covered with the waves. But He was asleep.

Matthew 8:26-27

²⁶ But He said to them, "Why are you fearful, O you of little faith?" Then He arose and rebuked the winds and the sea, and there was a great calm. ²⁷ So the men marveled, saying, "Who can this be, that even the winds and the sea obey Him?"

1 John 1:1-4

[1] That which was from the beginning, which we have heard, which we have seen with our eyes, which we have looked upon, and our hands have handled, concerning the Word of life-- [2] the life was manifested, and we have seen, and bear witness, and declare to you that eternal life which was with the Father and was manifested to us-- [3] that which we have seen and heard we declare to you, that you also may have fellowship with us; and truly our fellowship is with the Father and with His Son Jesus Christ. [4] And these things we write to you that your joy may be full.

Luke 23:46

[46] And when Jesus had cried out with a loud voice, He said, "Father, 'into Your hands I commit My spirit.'" Having said this, He breathed His last.

John 12:44-45

[44] Then Jesus cried out and said, "He who believes in Me, believes not in Me but in Him who sent Me. [45] And he who sees Me sees Him who sent Me.

John 17:11-12

[11] Now I am no longer in the world, but these are in the world, and I come to You. Holy Father, keep through Your name those whom You have given Me, that they may be one as We are. [12] While I was with them in the world, I kept them in Your name. Those whom You gave Me I have kept; and none of them is lost except the son of perdition, that the Scripture might be fulfilled.

John 16:5-15

[5] "But now I go away to Him who sent Me, and none of you asks Me, 'Where are You going?' [6] But because I have said these things to you, sorrow has filled your heart. [7] Nevertheless I tell you the truth. It is to your advantage that I go away; for if I do not go away, the Helper will not come to you; but if I depart, I will send Him to you. [8] And when He has come, He will convict the world of sin, and of righteousness, and of judgment: [9] of sin, because they do not believe in Me; [10] of righteousness, because I go to My Father and you see Me no more; [11] of judgment, because the ruler of this world is judged. [12] I still have many things to say to you, but you cannot bear them now. [13] However, when

He, the Spirit of truth, has come, He will guide you into all truth; for He will not speak on His own authority, but whatever He hears He will speak; and He will tell you things to come. [14] He will glorify Me, for He will take of what is Mine and declare it to you. [15] All things that the Father has are Mine. Therefore I said that He will take of Mine and declare it to you.

Luke 1:31,34-35

[31] And behold, you will conceive in your womb and bring forth a Son, and shall call His name Jesus. [34] Then Mary said to the angel, "How can this be, since I do not know a man?" [35] And the angel answered and said to her, "The Holy Spirit will come upon you, and the power of the Highest will overshadow you; therefore, also, that Holy One who is to be born will be called the Son of God.

Genesis 3:15

[15] And I will put enmity Between you and the woman, And between your seed and her Seed; He shall bruise your head, And you shall bruise His heel."

Galatians 4:4

[4] But when the fullness of the time had come, God sent forth His Son, born of a woman, born under the law,

Genesis 12:3

[3] I will bless those who bless you, And I will curse him who curses you; And in you all the families of the earth shall be blessed."

Matthew 1:1

[1] The book of the genealogy of Jesus Christ, the Son of David, the Son of Abraham:

Genesis 17:19

[19] Then God said: "No, Sarah your wife shall bear you a son, and you shall call his name Isaac; I will establish My covenant with him for an everlasting covenant, and with his descendants after him.

Luke 3:34

[34] the son of Jacob, the son of Isaac, the son of Abraham, the son of Terah, the son of Nahor,

Numbers 24:17

[17] "I see Him, but not now; I behold Him, but not near; A Star shall come out of Jacob; A Scepter shall rise out of Israel, And batter the brow of Moab, And destroy all the sons of tumult.

Matthew 1:2

[2] Abraham begot Isaac, Isaac begot Jacob, and Jacob begot Judah and his brothers.

Matthew 2:2

[2] saying, "Where is He who has been born King of the Jews? For we have seen His star in the East and have come to worship Him."

Genesis 49:10

[10] The scepter shall not depart from Judah, Nor a lawgiver from between his feet, Until Shiloh comes; And to Him shall be the obedience of the people.

Luke 3:33

[33] the son of Amminadab, the son of Ram, the son of Hezron, the son of Perez, the son of Judah,

Isaiah 9:7

[7] Of the increase of His government and peace There will be no end, Upon the throne of David and over His kingdom, To order it and establish it with judgment and justice From that time forward, even forever. The zeal of the Lord of hosts will perform this.

Luke 1:32-33

[32] He will be great, and will be called the Son of the Highest; and the Lord God will give Him the throne of His father David. [33] And He will reign over the house of Jacob forever, and of His kingdom there will be no end."

Micah 5:2

[2] "But you, Bethlehem Ephrathah, Though you are little among the thousands of Judah, Yet out of you shall come forth to Me The One to be Ruler in Israel, Whose goings forth are from of old, From everlasting."

Luke 2:4-5,7

[4] Joseph also went up from Galilee, out of the city of Nazareth, into Judea, to the city of David, which is called Bethlehem, because he was of the house and lineage of David, [5] to be registered with Mary, his betrothed wife, who was with child. [7] And she brought forth her firstborn Son, and wrapped Him in swaddling cloths, and laid Him in a manger, because there was no room for them in the inn.

Isaiah 7:14

[14] Therefore the Lord Himself will give you a sign: Behold, the virgin shall conceive and bear a Son, and shall call His name Immanuel.

Luke 1:26-27,30-31

[26] Now in the sixth month the angel Gabriel was sent by God to a city of Galilee named Nazareth, [27] to a virgin betrothed to a man whose name was Joseph, of the house of David. The virgin's name was Mary. [30] Then the angel said to her, "Do not be afraid, Mary, for you have found favor with God. [31] And behold, you will conceive in your womb and bring forth a Son, and shall call His name Jesus.

Jeremiah 31:15

[15] Thus says the Lord: "A voice was heard in Ramah, Lamentation and bitter weeping, Rachel weeping for her children, Refusing to be comforted for her children, Because they are no more."

Matthew 2:16-18

[16] Then Herod, when he saw that he was deceived by the wise men, was exceedingly angry; and he sent forth and put to death all the male children who were in Bethlehem and in all its districts, from two years old and under, according to the time which he had determined from the wise men. [17] Then was fulfilled what was spoken by Jeremiah the prophet, saying: [18] "A voice was heard in Ramah, Lamentation, weeping, and great mourning, Rachel weeping for her children, Refusing to be comforted, Because they are no more."

Hosea 11:1

[1] "When Israel was a child, I loved him, And out of Egypt I called My son.

Matthew 24:14-15

[14] And this gospel of the kingdom will be preached in all the world as a witness to all the nations, and then the end will come. [15] "Therefore when you see the 'abomination of desolation,' spoken of by Daniel the prophet, standing in the holy place" (whoever reads, let him understand),

Zechariah 11:12-13

[12] Then I said to them, "If it is agreeable to you, give me my wages; and if not, refrain." So they weighed out for my wages thirty pieces of silver. [13] And the Lord said to me, "Throw it to the potter"--that princely price they set on me. So I took the thirty pieces of silver and threw them into the house of the Lord for the potter.

Matthew 27:5,7-8

[5] Then he threw down the pieces of silver in the temple and departed, and went and hanged himself. [7] And they consulted together and bought with them the potter's field, to bury strangers in. [8] Therefore that field has been called the Field of Blood to this day.

Psalm 118:26

[26] Blessed is he who comes in the name of the Lord! We have blessed you from the house of the Lord.

Matthew 21:1-10

[1] Now when they drew near Jerusalem, and came to Bethphage, at the Mount of Olives, then Jesus sent two disciples, [2] saying to them, "Go into the village opposite you, and immediately you will find a donkey tied, and a colt with her. Loose them and bring them to Me. [3] And if anyone says anything to you, you shall say, 'The Lord has need of them,' and immediately he will send them." [4] All this was done that it might be fulfilled which was spoken by the prophet, saying: [5] "Tell the daughter of Zion, 'Behold, your King is coming to you, Lowly, and sitting on a donkey, A colt, the foal of a donkey.'" [6] So the disciples went and did as Jesus commanded them. [7] They brought the donkey and the colt, laid their clothes on them, and set Him on them. [8] And a very great multitude spread their clothes on the road; others cut down branches from the trees and spread them on the road. [9] Then the multitudes who went before and those who followed cried out, saying: "Hosanna to the Son of David! 'Blessed is He who comes in the name

of the Lord!' Hosanna in the highest!" [10] And when He had come into Jerusalem, all the city was moved, saying, "Who is this?"

Isaiah 53:9

[9] And they made His grave with the wicked-- But with the rich at His death, Because He had done no violence, Nor was any deceit in His mouth.

John 19:38-42

[38] After this, Joseph of Arimathea, being a disciple of Jesus, but secretly, for fear of the Jews, asked Pilate that he might take away the body of Jesus; and Pilate gave him permission. So he came and took the body of Jesus. [39] And Nicodemus, who at first came to Jesus by night, also came, bringing a mixture of myrrh and aloes, about a hundred pounds. [40] Then they took the body of Jesus, and bound it in strips of linen with the spices, as the custom of the Jews is to bury. [41] Now in the place where He was crucified there was a garden, and in the garden a new tomb in which no one had yet been laid. [42] So there they laid Jesus, because of the Jews' Preparation Day, for the tomb was nearby.

Exodus 12:46

[46] In one house it shall be eaten; you shall not carry any of the flesh outside the house, nor shall you break one of its bones.

John 19:31-36

[31] Therefore, because it was the Preparation Day, that the bodies should not remain on the cross on the Sabbath (for that Sabbath was a high day), the Jews asked Pilate that their legs might be broken, and that they might be taken away. [32] Then the soldiers came and broke the legs of the first and of the other who was crucified with Him. [33] But when they came to Jesus and saw that He was already dead, they did not break His legs. [34] But one of the soldiers pierced His side with a spear, and immediately blood and water came out. [35] And he who has seen has testified, and his testimony is true; and he knows that he is telling the truth, so that you may believe. [36] For these things were done that the Scripture should be fulfilled, "Not one of His bones shall be broken."

Isaiah 53:12

[12] Therefore I will divide Him a portion with the great, And He shall divide the spoil with the strong, Because He poured out His soul unto

death, And He was numbered with the transgressors, And He bore the sin of many, And made intercession for the transgressors.

Romans 5:15-19

[15] But the free gift is not like the offense. For if by the one man's offense many died, much more the grace of God and the gift by the grace of the one Man, Jesus Christ, abounded to many. [16] And the gift is not like that which came through the one who sinned. For the judgment which came from one offense resulted in condemnation, but the free gift which came from many offenses resulted in justification. [17] For if by the one man's offense death reigned through the one, much more those who receive abundance of grace and of the gift of righteousness will reign in life through the One, Jesus Christ.) [18] Therefore, as through one man's offense judgment came to all men, resulting in condemnation, even so through one Man's righteous act the free gift came to all men, resulting in justification of life. [19] For as by one man's disobedience many were made sinners, so also by one Man's obedience many will be made righteous.

Mark 15:27-28

[27] With Him they also crucified two robbers, one on His right and the other on His left. [28] So the Scripture was fulfilled which says, "And He was numbered with the transgressors."

Luke 22:37

[37] For I say to you that this which is written must still be accomplished in Me: 'And He was numbered with the transgressors.' For the things concerning Me have an end."

Psalm 16:10

[10] For You will not leave my soul in Sheol, Nor will You allow Your Holy One to see corruption.

Matthew 27:53

[53] and coming out of the graves after His resurrection, they went into the holy city and appeared to many.

Acts 2:24-31

[24] whom God raised up, having loosed the pains of death, because it was not possible that He should be held by it. [25] For David says

concerning Him: 'I foresaw the Lord always before my face, For He is at my right hand, that I may not be shaken. [26] Therefore my heart rejoiced, and my tongue was glad; Moreover my flesh also will rest in hope. [27] For You will not leave my soul in Hades, Nor will You allow Your Holy One to see corruption. [28] You have made known to me the ways of life; You will make me full of joy in Your presence.' [29] "Men and brethren, let me speak freely to you of the patriarch David, that he is both dead and buried, and his tomb is with us to this day. [30] Therefore, being a prophet, and knowing that God had sworn with an oath to him that of the fruit of his body, according to the flesh, He would raise up the Christ to sit on his throne, [31] he, foreseeing this, spoke concerning the resurrection of the Christ, that His soul was not left in Hades, nor did His flesh see corruption.

Acts 13:35-37

[35] Therefore He also says in another Psalm: 'You will not allow Your Holy One to see corruption.' [36] "For David, after he had served his own generation by the will of God, fell asleep, was buried with his fathers, and saw corruption; [37] but He whom God raised up saw no corruption.

Psalm 22:1

[1] To the Chief Musician. Set to 'The Deer of the Dawn.' A Psalm of David. My God, My God, why have You forsaken Me? Why are You so far from helping Me, And from the words of My groaning?

Matthew 27:38-46

[38] Then two robbers were crucified with Him, one on the right and another on the left. [39] And those who passed by blasphemed Him, wagging their heads [40] and saying, "You who destroy the temple and build it in three days, save Yourself! If You are the Son of God, come down from the cross." [41] Likewise the chief priests also, mocking with the scribes and elders, said, [42] "He saved others; Himself He cannot save. If He is the King of Israel, let Him now come down from the cross, and we will believe Him. [43] He trusted in God; let Him deliver Him now if He will have Him; for He said, 'I am the Son of God.'" [44] Even the robbers who were crucified with Him reviled Him with the same thing. [45] Now from the sixth hour until the ninth hour there was darkness over all the land. [46] And about the ninth hour Jesus cried

out with a loud voice, saying, "Eli, Eli, lama sabachthani?" that is, "My God, My God, why have You forsaken Me?"

Isaiah 52:13
[13] Behold, My Servant shall deal prudently; He shall be exalted and extolled and be very high.

Philippians 2:9
[9] Therefore God also has highly exalted Him and given Him the name which is above every name,

Psalm 110:1
[1] A Psalm of David. The Lord said to my Lord, "Sit at My right hand, Till I make Your enemies Your footstool."

Mark 16:19
[19] So then, after the Lord had spoken to them, He was received up into heaven, and sat down at the right hand of God.

Luke 20:42
[42] Now David himself said in the Book of Psalms: 'The Lord said to my Lord, "Sit at My right hand,

1 John 3:5
[5] And you know that He was manifested to take away our sins, and in Him there is no sin.

Isaiah 53:9
[9] And they made His grave with the wicked-- But with the rich at His death, Because He had done no violence, Nor was any deceit in His mouth.

Matthew 9:1-8
[1] So He got into a boat, crossed over, and came to His own city. [2] Then behold, they brought to Him a paralytic lying on a bed. When Jesus saw their faith, He said to the paralytic, "Son, be of good cheer; your sins are forgiven you." [3] And at once some of the scribes said within themselves, "This Man blasphemes!" [4] But Jesus, knowing their thoughts, said, "Why do you think evil in your hearts? [5] For which is easier, to say, 'Your sins are forgiven you,' or to say, 'Arise and walk'? [6] But that you may know that the Son of Man has power on earth to forgive sins"--then He said to the paralytic, "Arise, take up your bed,

and go to your house." [7] And he arose and departed to his house. [8] Now when the multitudes saw it, they marveled and glorified God, who had given such power to men.

Colossians 1:16

[16] For by Him all things were created that are in heaven and that are on earth, visible and invisible, whether thrones or dominions or principalities or powers. All things were created through Him and for Him.

Matthew 20:28

[28] just as the Son of Man did not come to be served, but to serve, and to give His life a ransom for many."

John 17:2-3

[2] as You have given Him authority over all flesh, that He should give eternal life to as many as You have given Him. [3] And this is eternal life, that they may know You, the only true God, and Jesus Christ whom You have sent.

1 John 5:11

[11] And this is the testimony: that God has given us eternal life, and this life is in His Son.

Matthew 28:17-18

[17] When they saw Him, they worshiped Him; but some doubted. [18] And Jesus came and spoke to them, saying, "All authority has been given to Me in heaven and on earth.

John 5:22-23

[22] For the Father judges no one, but has committed all judgment to the Son, [23] that all should honor the Son just as they honor the Father. He who does not honor the Son does not honor the Father who sent Him.

John 9:38

[38] Then he said, "Lord, I believe!" And he worshiped Him.

John 17:5

[5] And now, O Father, glorify Me together with Yourself, with the glory which I had with You before the world was.

John 5:16-23

> 16 For this reason the Jews persecuted Jesus, and sought to kill Him, because He had done these things on the Sabbath. 17 But Jesus answered them, "My Father has been working until now, and I have been working." 18 Therefore the Jews sought all the more to kill Him, because He not only broke the Sabbath, but also said that God was His Father, making Himself equal with God. 19 Then Jesus answered and said to them, "Most assuredly, I say to you, the Son can do nothing of Himself, but what He sees the Father do; for whatever He does, the Son also does in like manner. 20 For the Father loves the Son, and shows Him all things that He Himself does; and He will show Him greater works than these, that you may marvel. 21 For as the Father raises the dead and gives life to them, even so the Son gives life to whom He will. 22 For the Father judges no one, but has committed all judgment to the Son, 23 that all should honor the Son just as they honor the Father. He who does not honor the Son does not honor the Father who sent Him.

John 10:30

> 30 I and My Father are one."

John 19:7

> 7 The Jews answered him, "We have a law, and according to our law He ought to die, because He made Himself the Son of God."

Genesis 1:1

> 1 In the beginning God created the heavens and the earth.

Psalm 102:25

> 25 Of old You laid the foundation of the earth, And the heavens are the work of Your hands.

Isaiah 44:24

> 24 Thus says the Lord, your Redeemer, And He who formed you from the womb: "I am the Lord, who makes all things, Who stretches out the heavens all alone, Who spreads abroad the earth by Myself;

John 1:3

> 3 All things were made through Him, and without Him nothing was made that was made.

Colossians 1:16

¹⁶ For by Him all things were created that are in heaven and that are on earth, visible and invisible, whether thrones or dominions or principalities or powers. All things were created through Him and for Him.

Hebrews 1:2,10

² has in these last days spoken to us by His Son, whom He has appointed heir of all things, through whom also He made the worlds;
¹⁰ And: "You, Lord, in the beginning laid the foundation of the earth, And the heavens are the work of Your hands.

Isaiah 44:6

⁶ "Thus says the Lord, the King of Israel, And his Redeemer, the Lord of hosts: 'I am the First and I am the Last; Besides Me there is no God.

Revelation 1:17

¹⁷ And when I saw Him, I fell at His feet as dead. But He laid His right hand on me, saying to me, "Do not be afraid; I am the First and the Last.

Revelation 22:13

¹³ I am the Alpha and the Omega, the Beginning and the End, the First and the Last."

Deuteronomy 10:17

¹⁷ For the Lord your God is God of gods and Lord of lords, the great God, mighty and awesome, who shows no partiality nor takes a bribe.

Psalm 136:3

³ Oh, give thanks to the Lord of lords! For His mercy endures forever:

1 Timothy 6:15

¹⁵ which He will manifest in His own time, He who is the blessed and only Potentate, the King of kings and Lord of lords,

Revelation 17:14

14 These will make war with the Lamb, and the Lamb will overcome them, for He is Lord of lords and King of kings; and those who are with Him are called, chosen, and faithful."

Revelation 19:16

16 And He has on His robe and on His thigh a name written: KING OF KINGS AND LORD OF LORDS.

Psalm 90:2

2 Before the mountains were brought forth, Or ever You had formed the earth and the world, Even from everlasting to everlasting, You are God.

Psalm 102:26-27

26 They will perish, but You will endure; Yes, they will all grow old like a garment; Like a cloak You will change them, And they will be changed. 27 But You are the same, And Your years will have no end.

Malachi 3:6

6 "For I am the Lord, I do not change; Therefore you are not consumed, O sons of Jacob.

John 8:58

58 Jesus said to them, "Most assuredly, I say to you, before Abraham was, I AM."

Colossians 1:17

17 And He is before all things, and in Him all things consist.

Hebrews 1:11-12

11 They will perish, but You remain; And they will all grow old like a garment; 12 Like a cloak You will fold them up, And they will be changed. But You are the same, And Your years will not fail."

Hebrews 13:8

8 Jesus Christ is the same yesterday, today, and forever.

Isaiah 43:11

11 I, even I, am the Lord, And besides Me there is no savior.

Isaiah 45:21-22

[21] Tell and bring forth your case; Yes, let them take counsel together. Who has declared this from ancient time? Who has told it from that time? Have not I, the Lord? And there is no other God besides Me, A just God and a Savior; There is none besides Me. [22] "Look to Me, and be saved, All you ends of the earth! For I am God, and there is no other.

Hosea 13:4

[4] "Yet I am the Lord your God Ever since the land of Egypt, And you shall know no God but Me; For there is no Savior besides Me.

John 4:42

[42] Then they said to the woman, "Now we believe, not because of what you said, for we ourselves have heard Him and we know that this is indeed the Christ, the Savior of the world."

Acts 4:12

[12] Nor is there salvation in any other, for there is no other name under heaven given among men by which we must be saved."

Titus 2:13

[13] looking for the blessed hope and glorious appearing of our great God and Savior Jesus Christ,

1 John 4:4

[4] You are of God, little children, and have overcome them, because He who is in you is greater than he who is in the world.

Exodus 19:5

[5] Now therefore, if you will indeed obey My voice and keep My covenant, then you shall be a special treasure to Me above all people; for all the earth is Mine.

Psalm 130:7-8

[7] O Israel, hope in the Lord; For with the Lord there is mercy, And with Him is abundant redemption. [8] And He shall redeem Israel From all his iniquities.

Ezekiel 37:23

[23] They shall not defile themselves anymore with their idols, nor with their detestable things, nor with any of their transgressions; but I will

deliver them from all their dwelling places in which they have sinned, and will cleanse them. Then they shall be My people, and I will be their God.

Titus 2:14

[14] who gave Himself for us, that He might redeem us from every lawless deed and purify for Himself His own special people, zealous for good works.

Psalm 86:5-7

[5] For You, Lord, are good, and ready to forgive, And abundant in mercy to all those who call upon You. [6] Give ear, O Lord, to my prayer; And attend to the voice of my supplications. [7] In the day of my trouble I will call upon You, For You will answer me.

Isaiah 55:6-7

[6] Seek the Lord while He may be found, Call upon Him while He is near. [7] Let the wicked forsake his way, And the unrighteous man his thoughts; Let him return to the Lord, And He will have mercy on him; And to our God, For He will abundantly pardon.

Jeremiah 33:3

[3] 'Call to Me, and I will answer you, and show you great and mighty things, which you do not know.'

Joel 2:32

[32] And it shall come to pass That whoever calls on the name of the Lord Shall be saved. For in Mount Zion and in Jerusalem there shall be deliverance, As the Lord has said, Among the remnant whom the Lord calls.

Isaiah 65:24

[24] "It shall come to pass That before they call, I will answer; And while they are still speaking, I will hear.

John 14:14

[14] If you ask anything in My name, I will do it.

Romans 10:12-13

[12] For there is no distinction between Jew and Greek, for the same Lord over all is rich to all who call upon Him. [13] For "whoever calls on the name of the Lord shall be saved."

2 Corinthians 12:8-9

8 Concerning this thing I pleaded with the Lord three times that it might depart from me. 9 And He said to me, "My grace is sufficient for you, for My strength is made perfect in weakness." Therefore most gladly I will rather boast in my infirmities, that the power of Christ may rest upon me.

1 Peter 3:12

12 For the eyes of the Lord are on the righteous, And His ears are open to their prayers; But the face of the Lord is against those who do evil."

Isaiah 42:8

8 I am the Lord, that is My name; And My glory I will not give to another, Nor My praise to carved images.

Isaiah 48:11

11 For My own sake, for My own sake, I will do it; For how should My name be profaned? And I will not give My glory to another.

Psalm 97:7

7 Let all be put to shame who serve carved images, Who boast of idols. Worship Him, all you gods.

John 17:5

5 And now, O Father, glorify Me together with Yourself, with the glory which I had with You before the world was.

Hebrews 1:6

6 But when He again brings the firstborn into the world, He says: "Let all the angels of God worship Him."

Luke 2:40,52

40 And the Child grew and became strong in spirit, filled with wisdom; and the grace of God was upon Him.
52 And Jesus increased in wisdom and stature, and in favor with God and men.

Matthew 4:2

2 And when He had fasted forty days and forty nights, afterward He was hungry.

John 4:6

⁶ Now Jacob's well was there. Jesus therefore, being wearied from His journey, sat thus by the well. It was about the sixth hour.

John 19:28

²⁸ After this, Jesus, knowing that all things were now accomplished, that the Scripture might be fulfilled, said, "I thirst!"

Matthew 8:24

²⁴ And suddenly a great tempest arose on the sea, so that the boat was covered with the waves. But He was asleep.

Luke 22:44

⁴⁴ And being in agony, He prayed more earnestly. Then His sweat became like great drops of blood falling down to the ground.

Matthew 8:23-27

²³ Now when He got into a boat, His disciples followed Him. ²⁴ And suddenly a great tempest arose on the sea, so that the boat was covered with the waves. But He was asleep. ²⁵ Then His disciples came to Him and awoke Him, saying, "Lord, save us! We are perishing!" ²⁶ But He said to them, "Why are you fearful, O you of little faith?" Then He arose and rebuked the winds and the sea, and there was a great calm. ²⁷ So the men marveled, saying, "Who can this be, that even the winds and the sea obey Him?"

Matthew 14:22,33

²² Immediately Jesus made His disciples get into the boat and go before Him to the other side, while He sent the multitudes away.
³³ Then those who were in the boat came and worshiped Him, saying, "Truly You are the Son of God."

Mark 2:1-12

¹ And again He entered Capernaum after some days, and it was heard that He was in the house. ² Immediately many gathered together, so that there was no longer room to receive them, not even near the door. And He preached the word to them. ³ Then they came to Him, bringing a paralytic who was carried by four men. ⁴ And when they could not come near Him because of the crowd, they uncovered the roof where He was. So when they had broken through, they let down the bed on which the paralytic was lying. ⁵ When Jesus saw their faith,

He said to the paralytic, "Son, your sins are forgiven you." [6] And some of the scribes were sitting there and reasoning in their hearts, [7] "Why does this Man speak blasphemies like this? Who can forgive sins but God alone?" [8] But immediately, when Jesus perceived in His spirit that they reasoned thus within themselves, He said to them, "Why do you reason about these things in your hearts? [9] Which is easier, to say to the paralytic, 'Your sins are forgiven you,' or to say, 'Arise, take up your bed and walk'? [10] But that you may know that the Son of Man has power on earth to forgive sins"--He said to the paralytic, [11] I say to you, arise, take up your bed, and go to your house." [12] Immediately he arose, took up the bed, and went out in the presence of them all, so that all were amazed and glorified God, saying, "We never saw anything like this!"

John 5:17-18

[17] But Jesus answered them, "My Father has been working until now, and I have been working." [18] Therefore the Jews sought all the more to kill Him, because He not only broke the Sabbath, but also said that God was His Father, making Himself equal with God.

John 5:19-23

[19] Then Jesus answered and said to them, "Most assuredly, I say to you, the Son can do nothing of Himself, but what He sees the Father do; for whatever He does, the Son also does in like manner. [20] For the Father loves the Son, and shows Him all things that He Himself does; and He will show Him greater works than these, that you may marvel. [21] For as the Father raises the dead and gives life to them, even so the Son gives life to whom He will. [22] For the Father judges no one, but has committed all judgment to the Son, [23] that all should honor the Son just as they honor the Father. He who does not honor the Son does not honor the Father who sent Him.

Acts 20:28

[28] Therefore take heed to yourselves and to all the flock, among which the Holy Spirit has made you overseers, to shepherd the church of God which He purchased with His own blood.

Colossians 2:9

[9] For in Him dwells all the fullness of the Godhead bodily;

Mark 1:38

[38] But He said to them, "Let us go into the next towns, that I may preach there also, because for this purpose I have come forth."

Revelation 11:15

[15] Then the seventh angel sounded: And there were loud voices in heaven, saying, "The kingdoms of this world have become the kingdoms of our Lord and of His Christ, and He shall reign forever and ever!"

Luke 9:1-2

[1] Then He called His twelve disciples together and gave them power and authority over all demons, and to cure diseases. [2] He sent them to preach the kingdom of God and to heal the sick.

Luke 19:10

[10] for the Son of Man has come to seek and to save that which was lost."

1 John 3:8

[8] He who sins is of the devil, for the devil has sinned from the beginning. For this purpose the Son of God was manifested, that He might destroy the works of the devil.

Mark 10:45

[45] For even the Son of Man did not come to be served, but to serve, and to give His life a ransom for many."

Hebrews 9:24-25

[24] For Christ has not entered the holy places made with hands, which are copies of the true, but into heaven itself, now to appear in the presence of God for us; [25] not that He should offer Himself often, as the high priest enters the Most Holy Place every year with blood of another--

Hebrews 9:12

[12] Not with the blood of goats and calves, but with His own blood He entered the Most Holy Place once for all, having obtained eternal redemption.

2 Corinthians 5:19

[19] that is, that God was in Christ reconciling the world to Himself, not imputing their trespasses to them, and has committed to us the word of reconciliation.

Romans 16:26-27

[26] but now has been made manifest, and by the prophetic Scriptures has been made known to all nations, according to the commandment of the everlasting God, for obedience to the faith-- [27] to God, alone wise, be glory through Jesus Christ forever. Amen.

Revelation 1:17

[17] And when I saw Him, I fell at His feet as dead. But He laid His right hand on me, saying to me, "Do not be afraid; I am the First and the Last.

Hebrews 9:14

[14] how much more shall the blood of Christ, who through the eternal Spirit offered Himself without spot to God, cleanse your conscience from dead works to serve the living God?

Psalm 100:3

[3] Know that the Lord, He is God; It is He who has made us, and not we ourselves; We are His people and the sheep of His pasture.

Colossians 1:16

[16] For by Him all things were created that are in heaven and that are on earth, visible and invisible, whether thrones or dominions or principalities or powers. All things were created through Him and for Him.

Psalm 104:30

[30] You send forth Your Spirit, they are created; And You renew the face of the earth.

Genesis 1:11-31

[11] Then God said, "Let the earth bring forth grass, the herb that yields seed, and the fruit tree that yields fruit according to its kind, whose seed is in itself, on the earth"; and it was so. [12] And the earth brought forth grass, the herb that yields seed according to its kind, and the tree that yields fruit, whose seed is in itself according to its kind. And God saw that it was good. [13] So the evening and the morning were the third day. [14] Then God said, "Let there be lights in the firmament of the heavens to divide the day from the night; and let them be for signs and seasons, and for days and years; [15] and let them be for lights in the firmament of the heavens to give light on the earth"; and it was

so. ¹⁶ Then God made two great lights: the greater light to rule the day, and the lesser light to rule the night. He made the stars also. ¹⁷ God set them in the firmament of the heavens to give light on the earth, ¹⁸ and to rule over the day and over the night, and to divide the light from the darkness. And God saw that it was good. ¹⁹ So the evening and the morning were the fourth day. ²⁰ Then God said, "Let the waters abound with an abundance of living creatures, and let birds fly above the earth across the face of the firmament of the heavens." ²¹ So God created great sea creatures and every living thing that moves, with which the waters abounded, according to their kind, and every winged bird according to its kind. And God saw that it was good. ²² And God blessed them, saying, "Be fruitful and multiply, and fill the waters in the seas, and let birds multiply on the earth." ²³ So the evening and the morning were the fifth day. ²⁴ Then God said, "Let the earth bring forth the living creature according to its kind: cattle and creeping thing and beast of the earth, each according to its kind"; and it was so. ²⁵ And God made the beast of the earth according to its kind, cattle according to its kind, and everything that creeps on the earth according to its kind. And God saw that it was good. ²⁶ Then God said, "Let Us make man in Our image, according to Our likeness; let them have dominion over the fish of the sea, over the birds of the air, and over the cattle, over all the earth and over every creeping thing that creeps on the earth." ²⁷ So God created man in His own image; in the image of God He created him; male and female He created them. ²⁸ Then God blessed them, and God said to them, "Be fruitful and multiply; fill the earth and subdue it; have dominion over the fish of the sea, over the birds of the air, and over every living thing that moves on the earth." ²⁹ And God said, "See, I have given you every herb that yields seed which is on the face of all the earth, and every tree whose fruit yields seed; to you it shall be for food. ³⁰ Also, to every beast of the earth, to every bird of the air, and to everything that creeps on the earth, in which there is life, I have given every green herb for food"; and it was so. ³¹ Then God saw everything that He had made, and indeed it was very good. So the evening and the morning were the sixth day.

John 5:21

²¹ For as the Father raises the dead and gives life to them, even so the Son gives life to whom He will.

John 1:4

4 In Him was life, and the life was the light of men.

Romans 8:10-11

10 And if Christ is in you, the body is dead because of sin, but the Spirit is life because of righteousness. 11 But if the Spirit of Him who raised Jesus from the dead dwells in you, He who raised Christ from the dead will also give life to your mortal bodies through His Spirit who dwells in you.

John 3:8

8 The wind blows where it wishes, and you hear the sound of it, but cannot tell where it comes from and where it goes. So is everyone who is born of the Spirit."

Ephesians 1:5

5 having predestined us to adoption as sons by Jesus Christ to Himself, according to the good pleasure of His will,

Matthew 8:31

31 So the demons begged Him, saying, "If You cast us out, permit us to go away into the herd of swine."

1 Corinthians 12:11

11 But one and the same Spirit works all these things, distributing to each one individually as He wills.

Psalm 138:3

3 In the day when I cried out, You answered me, And made me bold with strength in my soul.

Philippians 4:13

13 I can do all things through Christ who strengthens me.

Ephesians 3:16

16 that He would grant you, according to the riches of His glory, to be strengthened with might through His Spirit in the inner man,

Jeremiah 23:24

24 Can anyone hide himself in secret places, So I shall not see him?" says the Lord; "Do I not fill heaven and earth?" says the Lord.

Ephesians 1:23

²³ which is His body, the fullness of Him who fills all in all.

Psalm 139:7

⁷ Where can I go from Your Spirit? Or where can I flee from Your presence?

1 John 3:20

²⁰ For if our heart condemns us, God is greater than our heart, and knows all things.

John 21:17

17 He said to him the third time, "Simon, son of Jonah, do you love Me?" Peter was grieved because He said to him the third time, "Do you love Me?" And he said to Him, "Lord, You know all things; You know that I love You." Jesus said to him, "Feed My sheep."

1 Corinthians 2:10

¹⁰ But God has revealed them to us through His Spirit. For the Spirit searches all things, yes, the deep things of God.

1 Corinthians 15:24

²⁴ Then comes the end, when He delivers the kingdom to God the Father, when He puts an end to all rule and all authority and power.

John 5:16-23

¹⁶ For this reason the Jews persecuted Jesus, and sought to kill Him, because He had done these things on the Sabbath. ¹⁷ But Jesus answered them, "My Father has been working until now, and I have been working." ¹⁸ Therefore the Jews sought all the more to kill Him, because He not only broke the Sabbath, but also said that God was His Father, making Himself equal with God. ¹⁹ Then Jesus answered and said to them, "Most assuredly, I say to you, the Son can do nothing of Himself, but what He sees the Father do; for whatever He does, the Son also does in like manner. ²⁰ For the Father loves the Son, and shows Him all things that He Himself does; and He will show Him greater works than these, that you may marvel. ²¹ For as the Father raises the dead and gives life to them, even so the Son gives life to whom He will. ²² For the Father judges no one, but has committed all judgment to the Son, ²³ that all should honor the Son just as they

honor the Father. He who does not honor the Son does not honor the Father who sent Him.

Acts 5:3-4

³ But Peter said, "Ananias, why has Satan filled your heart to lie to the Holy Spirit and keep back part of the price of the land for yourself? ⁴ While it remained, was it not your own? And after it was sold, was it not in your own control? Why have you conceived this thing in your heart? You have not lied to men but to God."

John 16:30

³⁰ Now we are sure that You know all things, and have no need that anyone should question You. By this we believe that You came forth from God."

Matthew 28:20

²⁰ teaching them to observe all things that I have commanded you; and lo, I am with you always, even to the end of the age." Amen.

Matthew 28:18

¹⁸ And Jesus came and spoke to them, saying, "All authority has been given to Me in heaven and on earth.

Hebrews 13:8

Jesus Christ is the same yesterday, today, and forever.

Revelation 1:17

¹⁷ And when I saw Him, I fell at His feet as dead. But He laid His right hand on me, saying to me, "Do not be afraid; I am the First and the Last.

John 19:30,34

³⁰ So when Jesus had received the sour wine, He said, "It is finished!" And bowing His head, He gave up His spirit.
³⁴ But one of the soldiers pierced His side with a spear, and immediately blood and water came out.

John 19:41-42

⁴¹ Now in the place where He was crucified there was a garden, and in the garden a new tomb in which no one had yet been laid. ⁴² So there they laid Jesus, because of the Jews' Preparation Day, for the tomb was nearby.

Matthew 27:57-61

⁵⁷ Now when evening had come, there came a rich man from Arimathea, named Joseph, who himself had also become a disciple of Jesus. ⁵⁸ This man went to Pilate and asked for the body of Jesus. Then Pilate commanded the body to be given to him. ⁵⁹ When Joseph had taken the body, he wrapped it in a clean linen cloth, ⁶⁰ and laid it in his new tomb which he had hewn out of the rock; and he rolled a large stone against the door of the tomb, and departed. ⁶¹ And Mary Magdalene was there, and the other Mary, sitting opposite the tomb.

Mark 15:42-47

⁴² Now when evening had come, because it was the Preparation Day, that is, the day before the Sabbath, ⁴³ Joseph of Arimathea, a prominent council member, who was himself waiting for the kingdom of God, coming and taking courage, went in to Pilate and asked for the body of Jesus. ⁴⁴ Pilate marveled that He was already dead; and summoning the centurion, he asked him if He had been dead for some time. ⁴⁵ So when he found out from the centurion, he granted the body to Joseph. ⁴⁶ Then he bought fine linen, took Him down, and wrapped Him in the linen. And he laid Him in a tomb which had been hewn out of the rock, and rolled a stone against the door of the tomb. ⁴⁷ And Mary Magdalene and Mary the mother of Joses observed where He was laid.

Luke 23:50-56

⁵⁰ Now behold, there was a man named Joseph, a council member, a good and just man. ⁵¹ He had not consented to their decision and deed. He was from Arimathea, a city of the Jews, who himself was also waiting for the kingdom of God. ⁵² This man went to Pilate and asked for the body of Jesus. ⁵³ Then he took it down, wrapped it in linen, and laid it in a tomb that was hewn out of the rock, where no one had ever lain before. ⁵⁴ That day was the Preparation, and the Sabbath drew near. ⁵⁵ And the women who had come with Him from Galilee followed after, and they observed the tomb and how His body was laid. ⁵⁶ Then they returned and prepared spices and fragrant oils. And they rested on the Sabbath according to the commandment.

Matthew 28:6-7

⁶ He is not here; for He is risen, as He said. Come, see the place where the Lord lay. ⁷ And go quickly and tell His disciples that He is risen

from the dead, and indeed He is going before you into Galilee; there you will see Him. Behold, I have told you."

Luke 24:39-43

[39] Behold My hands and My feet, that it is I Myself. Handle Me and see, for a spirit does not have flesh and bones as you see I have." [40] When He had said this, He showed them His hands and His feet. [41] But while they still did not believe for joy, and marveled, He said to them, "Have you any food here?" [42] So they gave Him a piece of a broiled fish and some honeycomb. [43] And He took it and ate in their presence.

John 20:27-29

[27] Then He said to Thomas, "Reach your finger here, and look at My hands; and reach your hand here, and put it into My side. Do not be unbelieving, but believing." [28] And Thomas answered and said to Him, "My Lord and my God!" [29] Jesus said to him, "Thomas, because you have seen Me, you have believed. Blessed are those who have not seen and yet have believed."

Acts 10:41

[41] not to all the people, but to witnesses chosen before by God, even to us who ate and drank with Him after He arose from the dead.

Mark 16:9

[9] Now when He rose early on the first day of the week, He appeared first to Mary Magdalene, out of whom He had cast seven demons.

John 20:11-18

[11] But Mary stood outside by the tomb weeping, and as she wept she stooped down and looked into the tomb. [12] And she saw two angels in white sitting, one at the head and the other at the feet, where the body of Jesus had lain. [13] Then they said to her, "Woman, why are you weeping?" She said to them, "Because they have taken away my Lord, and I do not know where they have laid Him." [14] Now when she had said this, she turned around and saw Jesus standing there, and did not know that it was Jesus. [15] Jesus said to her, "Woman, why are you weeping? Whom are you seeking?" She, supposing Him to be the gardener, said to Him, "Sir, if You have carried Him away, tell me where You have laid Him, and I will take Him away." [16] Jesus said to her, "Mary! She turned and said to Him, "Rabboni!" (which is to say,

Teacher). [17] Jesus said to her, "Do not cling to Me, for I have not yet ascended to My Father; but go to My brethren and say to them, 'I am ascending to My Father and your Father, and to My God and your God.'" [18] Mary Magdalene came and told the disciples that she had seen the Lord, and that He had spoken these things to her.

Matthew 28:8-10

[8] So they went out quickly from the tomb with fear and great joy, and ran to bring His disciples word. [9] And as they went to tell His disciples, behold, Jesus met them, saying, "Rejoice!" So they came and held Him by the feet and worshiped Him. [10] Then Jesus said to them, "Do not be afraid. Go and tell My brethren to go to Galilee, and there they will see Me."

Luke 24:34

[34] saying, "The Lord is risen indeed, and has appeared to Simon!"

Luke 24:36-43

[36] Now as they said these things, Jesus Himself stood in the midst of them, and said to them, "Peace to you." [37] But they were terrified and frightened, and supposed they had seen a spirit. [38] And He said to them, "Why are you troubled? And why do doubts arise in your hearts? [39] Behold My hands and My feet, that it is I Myself. Handle Me and see, for a spirit does not have flesh and bones as you see I have." [40] When He had said this, He showed them His hands and His feet. [41] But while they still did not believe for joy, and marveled, He said to them, "Have you any food here?" [42] So they gave Him a piece of a broiled fish and some honeycomb. [43] And He took it and ate in their presence.

John 20:19-25

[19] Then, the same day at evening, being the first day of the week, when the doors were shut where the disciples were assembled, for fear of the Jews, Jesus came and stood in the midst, and said to them, "Peace be with you." [20] When He had said this, He showed them His hands and His side. Then the disciples were glad when they saw the Lord. [21] So Jesus said to them again, "Peace to you! As the Father has sent Me, I also send you." [22] And when He had said this, He breathed on them, and said to them, "Receive the Holy Spirit. [23] If you forgive the sins of any, they are forgiven them; if you retain the sins of any, they are retained." [24] Now Thomas, called the Twin, one of the twelve, was

not with them when Jesus came. [25] The other disciples therefore said to him, "We have seen the Lord." So he said to them, "Unless I see in His hands the print of the nails, and put my finger into the print of the nails, and put my hand into His side, I will not believe."

Mark 16:14

[14] Later He appeared to the eleven as they sat at the table; and He rebuked their unbelief and hardness of heart, because they did not believe those who had seen Him after He had risen.

John 20:26-29

[26] And after eight days His disciples were again inside, and Thomas with them. Jesus came, the doors being shut, and stood in the midst, and said, "Peace to you!" [27] Then He said to Thomas, "Reach your finger here, and look at My hands; and reach your hand here, and put it into My side. Do not be unbelieving, but believing." [28] And Thomas answered and said to Him, "My Lord and my God!" [29] Jesus said to him, "Thomas, because you have seen Me, you have believed. Blessed are those who have not seen and yet have believed."

Mark 16:12-13

[12] After that, He appeared in another form to two of them as they walked and went into the country. [13] And they went and told it to the rest, but they did not believe them either.

Luke 24:13-35

[13] Now behold, two of them were traveling that same day to a village called Emmaus, which was seven miles from Jerusalem. [14] And they talked together of all these things which had happened. [15] So it was, while they conversed and reasoned, that Jesus Himself drew near and went with them. [16] But their eyes were restrained, so that they did not know Him. [17] And He said to them, "What kind of conversation is this that you have with one another as you walk and are sad?" [18] Then the one whose name was Cleopas answered and said to Him, "Are You the only stranger in Jerusalem, and have You not known the things which happened there in these days?" [19] And He said to them, "What things?" So they said to Him, "The things concerning Jesus of Nazareth, who was a Prophet mighty in deed and word before God and all the people, [20] and how the chief priests and our rulers delivered Him to be condemned to death, and crucified Him. [21] But we were hoping that it was He who

was going to redeem Israel. Indeed, besides all this, today is the third day since these things happened. ²² Yes, and certain women of our company, who arrived at the tomb early, astonished us. ²³ When they did not find His body, they came saying that they had also seen a vision of angels who said He was alive. ²⁴ And certain of those who were with us went to the tomb and found it just as the women had said; but Him they did not see." ²⁵ Then He said to them, "O foolish ones, and slow of heart to believe in all that the prophets have spoken! ²⁶ Ought not the Christ to have suffered these things and to enter into His glory?" ²⁷ And beginning at Moses and all the Prophets, He expounded to them in all the Scriptures the things concerning Himself. ²⁸ Then they drew near to the village where they were going, and He indicated that He would have gone farther. ²⁹ But they constrained Him, saying, "Abide with us, for it is toward evening, and the day is far spent." And He went in to stay with them. ³⁰ Now it came to pass, as He sat at the table with them, that He took bread, blessed and broke it, and gave it to them. ³¹ Then their eyes were opened and they knew Him; and He vanished from their sight. ³² And they said to one another, "Did not our heart burn within us while He talked with us on the road, and while He opened the Scriptures to us?" ³³ So they rose up that very hour and returned to Jerusalem, and found the eleven and those who were with them gathered together, ³⁴ saying, "The Lord is risen indeed, and has appeared to Simon!" ³⁵ And they told about the things that had happened on the road, and how He was known to them in the breaking of bread.

Matthew 28:16-20

¹⁶ Then the eleven disciples went away into Galilee, to the mountain which Jesus had appointed for them. ¹⁷ When they saw Him, they worshiped Him; but some doubted. ¹⁸ And Jesus came and spoke to them, saying, "All authority has been given to Me in heaven and on earth. ¹⁹ Go therefore and make disciples of all the nations, baptizing them in the name of the Father and of the Son and of the Holy Spirit, ²⁰ teaching them to observe all things that I have commanded you; and lo, I am with you always, even to the end of the age." Amen.

John 21:1-24

¹ After these things Jesus showed Himself again to the disciples at the Sea of Tiberias, and in this way He showed Himself: ² Simon Peter, Thomas called the Twin, Nathanael of Cana in Galilee, the sons of Zebedee, and two others of His disciples were together. ³ Simon Peter

said to them, "I am going fishing." They said to him, "We are going with you also." They went out and immediately got into the boat, and that night they caught nothing. ⁴ But when the morning had now come, Jesus stood on the shore; yet the disciples did not know that it was Jesus. ⁵ Then Jesus said to them, "Children, have you any food?" They answered Him, "No." ⁶ And He said to them, "Cast the net on the right side of the boat, and you will find some." So they cast, and now they were not able to draw it in because of the multitude of fish. ⁷ Therefore that disciple whom Jesus loved said to Peter, "It is the Lord!" Now when Simon Peter heard that it was the Lord, he put on his outer garment (for he had removed it), and plunged into the sea. ⁸ But the other disciples came in the little boat (for they were not far from land, but about two hundred cubits), dragging the net with fish. ⁹ Then, as soon as they had come to land, they saw a fire of coals there, and fish laid on it, and bread. ¹⁰ Jesus said to them, "Bring some of the fish which you have just caught." ¹¹ Simon Peter went up and dragged the net to land, full of large fish, one hundred and fifty-three; and although there were so many, the net was not broken. ¹² Jesus said to them, "Come and eat breakfast." Yet none of the disciples dared ask Him, "Who are You?" --knowing that it was the Lord. ¹³ Jesus then came and took the bread and gave it to them, and likewise the fish. ¹⁴ This is now the third time Jesus showed Himself to His disciples after He was raised from the dead. ¹⁵ So when they had eaten breakfast, Jesus said to Simon Peter, "Simon, son of Jonah, do you love Me more than these?" He said to Him, "Yes, Lord; You know that I love You." He said to him, "Feed My lambs." ¹⁶ He said to him again a second time, "Simon, son of Jonah, do you love Me?" He said to Him, "Yes, Lord; You know that I love You." He said to him, "Tend My sheep." ¹⁷ He said to him the third time, "Simon, son of Jonah, do you love Me?" Peter was grieved because He said to him the third time, "Do you love Me?" And he said to Him, "Lord, You know all things; You know that I love You." Jesus said to him, "Feed My sheep. ¹⁸ Most assuredly, I say to you, when you were younger, you girded yourself and walked where you wished; but when you are old, you will stretch out your hands, and another will gird you and carry you where you do not wish." ¹⁹ This He spoke, signifying by what death he would glorify God. And when He had spoken this, He said to him, "Follow Me." ²⁰ Then Peter, turning around, saw the disciple whom Jesus loved following, who also had leaned on His breast at the supper, and said, "Lord, who is the one who betrays You?" [21] Peter, seeing him, said to Jesus, "But Lord, what about this man?" [22] Jesus said to him, "If I will that he remain till I come, what is that to you? You follow Me." [23] Then this saying went out among the brethren that this disciple would not die. Yet Jesus did not say to him that he would not die, but, "If I will that he remain till I come, what is that to you?" [24] This is the disciple who testifies of these things, and wrote these things; and we know that his testimony is true.

1 Corinthians 15:6

[6] After that He was seen by over five hundred brethren at once, of whom the greater part remain to the present, but some have fallen asleep.

1 Corinthians 15:7

[7] After that He was seen by James, then by all the apostles.

Mark 16:19-20

[19] So then, after the Lord had spoken to them, He was received up into heaven, and sat down at the right hand of God. [20] And they went out and preached everywhere, the Lord working with them and confirming the word through the accompanying signs. Amen.

Luke 24:50-53

[50] And He led them out as far as Bethany, and He lifted up His hands and blessed them. [51] Now it came to pass, while He blessed them, that He was parted from them and carried up into heaven. [52] And they worshiped Him, and returned to Jerusalem with great joy, [53] and were continually in the temple praising and blessing God. Amen.

Acts 1:9-11

[9] Now when He had spoken these things, while they watched, He was taken up, and a cloud received Him out of their sight. [10] And while they looked steadfastly toward heaven as He went up, behold, two men stood by them in white apparel, [11] who also said, "Men of Galilee, why do you stand gazing up into heaven? This same Jesus, who was taken up from you into heaven, will so come in like manner as you saw Him go into heaven."

Acts 9:1-6

¹ Then Saul, still breathing threats and murder against the disciples of the Lord, went to the high priest ² and asked letters from him to the synagogues of Damascus, so that if he found any who were of the Way, whether men or women, he might bring them bound to Jerusalem.
³ As he journeyed he came near Damascus, and suddenly a light shone around him from heaven. ⁴ Then he fell to the ground, and heard a voice saying to him, "Saul, Saul, why are you persecuting Me?" ⁵ And he said, "Who are You, Lord?" Then the Lord said, "I am Jesus, whom you are persecuting. It is hard for you to kick against the goads." ⁶ So he, trembling and astonished, said, "Lord, what do You want me to do?" Then the Lord said to him, "Arise and go into the city, and you will be told what you must do."

Acts 22:1-10

¹ "Brethren and fathers, hear my defense before you now." ² And when they heard that he spoke to them in the Hebrew language, they kept all the more silent. Then he said: ³ "I am indeed a Jew, born in Tarsus of Cilicia, but brought up in this city at the feet of Gamaliel, taught according to the strictness of our fathers' law, and was zealous toward God as you all are today. ⁴ I persecuted this Way to the death, binding and delivering into prisons both men and women, ⁵ as also the high priest bears me witness, and all the council of the elders, from whom I also received letters to the brethren, and went to Damascus to bring in chains even those who were there to Jerusalem to be punished. ⁶ Now it happened, as I journeyed and came near Damascus at about noon, suddenly a great light from heaven shone around me. ⁷ And I fell to the ground and heard a voice saying to me, 'Saul, Saul, why are you persecuting Me?' ⁸ So I answered, 'Who are You, Lord?' And He said to me, 'I am Jesus of Nazareth, whom you are persecuting.' ⁹ And those who were with me indeed saw the light and were afraid, but they did not hear the voice of Him who spoke to me. ¹⁰ So I said, 'What shall I do, Lord?' And the Lord said to me, 'Arise and go into Damascus, and there you will be told all things which are appointed for you to do.'

Acts 26:12-18

¹² "While thus occupied, as I journeyed to Damascus with authority and commission from the chief priests, ¹³ at midday, O king, along the road I saw a light from heaven, brighter than the sun, shining

around me and those who journeyed with me. [14] And when we all had fallen to the ground, I heard a voice speaking to me and saying in the Hebrew language, 'Saul, Saul, why are you persecuting Me? It is hard for you to kick against the goads.' [15] So I said, 'Who are You, Lord?' And He said, 'I am Jesus, whom you are persecuting. [16] But rise and stand on your feet; for I have appeared to you for this purpose, to make you a minister and a witness both of the things which you have seen and of the things which I will yet reveal to you. [17] I will deliver you from the Jewish people, as well as from the Gentiles, to whom I now send you, [18] to open their eyes, in order to turn them from darkness to light, and from the power of Satan to God, that they may receive forgiveness of sins and an inheritance among those who are sanctified by faith in Me.'

1 Corinthians 15:8

[8] Then last of all He was seen by me also, as by one born out of due time.

Genesis 1:1

[1] In the beginning God created the heavens and the earth.

Hebrews 1:3

[3] who being the brightness of His glory and the express image of His person, and upholding all things by the word of His power, when He had by Himself purged our sins, sat down at the right hand of the Majesty on high,

John 1:3

[3] All things were made through Him, and without Him nothing was made that was made.

CHAPTER 2

Hebrews 6:10

[10] For God is not unjust to forget your work and labor of love which you have shown toward His name, in that you have ministered to the saints, and do minister.

Genesis 3:6

6 So when the woman saw that the tree was good for food, that it was pleasant to the eyes, and a tree desirable to make one wise, she took of its fruit and ate. She also gave to her husband with her, and he ate.

Genesis 2:25

25 And they were both naked, the man and his wife, and were not ashamed.

Ephesians 2:1-3

1 And you He made alive, who were dead in trespasses and sins, 2 in which you once walked according to the course of this world, according to the prince of the power of the air, the spirit who now works in the sons of disobedience, 3 among whom also we all once conducted ourselves in the lusts of our flesh, fulfilling the desires of the flesh and of the mind, and were by nature children of wrath, just as the others.

2 Samuel 11:2-27

2 Then it happened one evening that David arose from his bed and walked on the roof of the king's house. And from the roof he saw a woman bathing, and the woman was very beautiful to behold. 3 So David sent and inquired about the woman. And someone said, "Is this not Bathsheba, the daughter of Eliam, the wife of Uriah the Hittite?" 4 Then David sent messengers, and took her; and she came to him, and he lay with her, for she was cleansed from her impurity; and she returned to her house. 5 And the woman conceived; so she sent and told David, and said, "I am with child." 6 Then David sent to Joab, saying, "Send me Uriah the Hittite." And Joab sent Uriah to David. 7 When Uriah had come to him, David asked how Joab was doing, and how the people were doing, and how the war prospered. 8 And David said to Uriah, "Go down to your house and wash your feet." So Uriah departed from the king's house, and a gift of food from the king followed him. 9 But Uriah slept at the door of the king's house with all the servants of his lord, and did not go down to his house. 10 So when they told David, saying, "Uriah did not go down to his house," David said to Uriah, "Did you not come from a journey? Why did you not go down to your house?" 11 And Uriah said to David, "The ark and Israel and Judah are dwelling in tents, and my lord Joab and the servants of

my lord are encamped in the open fields. Shall I then go to my house to eat and drink, and to lie with my wife? As you live, and as your soul lives, I will not do this thing." [12] Then David said to Uriah, "Wait here today also, and tomorrow I will let you depart." So Uriah remained in Jerusalem that day and the next. [13] Now when David called him, he ate and drank before him; and he made him drunk. And at evening he went out to lie on his bed with the servants of his lord, but he did not go down to his house. [14] In the morning it happened that David wrote a letter to Joab and sent it by the hand of Uriah. [15] And he wrote in the letter, saying, "Set Uriah in the forefront of the hottest battle, and retreat from him, that he may be struck down and die." [16] So it was, while Joab besieged the city, that he assigned Uriah to a place where he knew there were valiant men. [17] Then the men of the city came out and fought with Joab. And some of the people of the servants of David fell; and Uriah the Hittite died also. [18] Then Joab sent and told David all the things concerning the war, [19] and charged the messenger, saying, "When you have finished telling the matters of the war to the king, [20] if it happens that the king's wrath rises, and he says to you: 'Why did you approach so near to the city when you fought? Did you not know that they would shoot from the wall? [21] Who struck Abimelech the son of Jerubbesheth? Was it not a woman who cast a piece of a millstone on him from the wall, so that he died in Thebez? Why did you go near the wall?'--then you shall say, 'Your servant Uriah the Hittite is dead also.'" [22] So the messenger went, and came and told David all that Joab had sent by him. [23] And the messenger said to David, "Surely the men prevailed against us and came out to us in the field; then we drove them back as far as the entrance of the gate. [24] The archers shot from the wall at your servants; and some of the king's servants are dead, and your servant Uriah the Hittite is dead also." [25] Then David said to the messenger, "Thus you shall say to Joab: 'Do not let this thing displease you, for the sword devours one as well as another. Strengthen your attack against the city, and overthrow it.' So encourage him." [26] When the wife of Uriah heard that Uriah her husband was dead, she mourned for her husband. [27] And when her mourning was over, David sent and brought her to his house, and she became his wife and bore him a son. But the thing that David had done displeased the Lord.

Ephesians 2:14-16

¹⁴ For He Himself is our peace, who has made both one, and has broken down the middle wall of separation, ¹⁵ having abolished in His flesh the enmity, that is, the law of commandments contained in ordinances, so as to create in Himself one new man from the two, thus making peace, ¹⁶ and that He might reconcile them both to God in one body through the cross, thereby putting to death the enmity.

1 Peter 1:16

¹⁶ because it is written, "Be holy, for I am holy."

1 John 4:8

⁸ He who does not love does not know God, for God is love.

Isaiah 57:15

¹⁵ For thus says the High and Lofty One Who inhabits eternity, whose name is Holy: "I dwell in the high and holy place, With him who has a contrite and humble spirit, To revive the spirit of the humble, And to revive the heart of the contrite ones.

Isaiah 6:3

³ And one cried to another and said: "Holy, holy, holy is the Lord of hosts; The whole earth is full of His glory!"

2 Timothy 4:8

⁸ Finally, there is laid up for me the crown of righteousness, which the Lord, the righteous Judge, will give to me on that Day, and not to me only but also to all who have loved His appearing.

Genesis 18:25

²⁵ Far be it from You to do such a thing as this, to slay the righteous with the wicked, so that the righteous should be as the wicked; far be it from You! Shall not the Judge of all the earth do right?"

Psalm 119:137-138

¹³⁷ Righteous are You, O Lord, And upright are Your judgments. ¹³⁸ Your testimonies, which You have commanded, Are righteous and very faithful.

Psalm 145:17

¹⁷ The Lord is righteous in all His ways, Gracious in all His works.

Habakkuk 1:13

13 You are of purer eyes than to behold evil, And cannot look on wickedness. Why do You look on those who deal treacherously, And hold Your tongue when the wicked devours A person more righteous than he?

Romans 2:5-6,11

5 But in accordance with your hardness and your impenitent heart you are treasuring up for yourself wrath in the day of wrath and revelation of the righteous judgment of God, 6 who "will render to each one according to his deeds":
11 For there is no partiality with God.

Romans 1:18

18 For the wrath of God is revealed from heaven against all ungodliness and unrighteousness of men, who suppress the truth in unrighteousness,

Romans 14:11-12

11 For it is written: "As I live, says the Lord, Every knee shall bow to Me, And every tongue shall confess to God." 12 So then each of us shall give account of himself to God.

1 Peter 4:5

5 They will give an account to Him who is ready to judge the living and the dead.

Romans 3:23

23 for all have sinned and fall short of the glory of God,

John 14:6

6 Jesus said to him, "I am the way, the truth, and the life. No one comes to the Father except through Me.

Acts 4:12

12 Nor is there salvation in any other, for there is no other name under heaven given among men by which we must be saved."

Psalm 66:18

18 If I regard iniquity in my heart, The Lord will not hear.

Romans 5:12-18

[12] Therefore, just as through one man sin entered the world, and death through sin, and thus death spread to all men, because all sinned-- [13] (For until the law sin was in the world, but sin is not imputed when there is no law. [14] Nevertheless death reigned from Adam to Moses, even over those who had not sinned according to the likeness of the transgression of Adam, who is a type of Him who was to come. [15] But the free gift is not like the offense. For if by the one man's offense many died, much more the grace of God and the gift by the grace of the one Man, Jesus Christ, abounded to many. [16] And the gift is not like that which came through the one who sinned. For the judgment which came from one offense resulted in condemnation, but the free gift which came from many offenses resulted in justification. [17] For if by the one man's offense death reigned through the one, much more those who receive abundance of grace and of the gift of righteousness will reign in life through the One, Jesus Christ.) [18] Therefore, as through one man's offense judgment came to all men, resulting in condemnation, even so through one Man's righteous act the free gift came to all men, resulting in justification of life.

Ephesians 2:1-3

[1] And you He made alive, who were dead in trespasses and sins, [2] in which you once walked according to the course of this world, according to the prince of the power of the air, the spirit who now works in the sons of disobedience, [3] among whom also we all once conducted ourselves in the lusts of our flesh, fulfilling the desires of the flesh and of the mind, and were by nature children of wrath, just as the others.

Genesis 5:3

[3] And Adam lived one hundred and thirty years, and begot a son in his own likeness, after his image, and named him Seth.

Psalm 51:5

[5] Behold, I was brought forth in iniquity, And in sin my mother conceived me.

Psalm 58:3

[3] The wicked are estranged from the womb; They go astray as soon as they are born, speaking lies.

1 Peter 2:10

[10] who once were not a people but are now the people of God, who had not obtained mercy but now have obtained mercy.

Romans 3:10-12,18,23

[10] As it is written: "There is none righteous, no, not one; [11] There is none who understands; There is none who seeks after God. [12] They have all turned aside; They have together become unprofitable; There is none who does good, no, not one."
[18] "There is no fear of God before their eyes."
[23] for all have sinned and fall short of the glory of God,

Galatians 5:19-21

[19] Now the works of the flesh are evident, which are: adultery, fornication, uncleanness, lewdness, [20] idolatry, sorcery, hatred, contentions, jealousies, outbursts of wrath, selfish ambitions, dissensions, heresies, [21] envy, murders, drunkenness, revelries, and the like; of which I tell you beforehand, just as I also told you in time past, that those who practice such things will not inherit the kingdom of God.

Ephesians 2:1-3

[1] And you He made alive, who were dead in trespasses and sins, [2] in which you once walked according to the course of this world, according to the prince of the power of the air, the spirit who now works in the sons of disobedience, [3] among whom also we all once conducted ourselves in the lusts of our flesh, fulfilling the desires of the flesh and of the mind, and were by nature children of wrath, just as the others.

Romans 3:9-23

[9] What then? Are we better than they? Not at all. For we have previously charged both Jews and Greeks that they are all under sin. [10] As it is written: "There is none righteous, no, not one; [11] There is none who understands; There is none who seeks after God. [12] They have all turned aside; They have together become unprofitable; There is none who does good, no, not one." [13] "Their throat is an open tomb; With their tongues they have practiced deceit"; "The poison of asps is under their lips"; [14] "Whose mouth is full of cursing and bitterness." [15] "Their feet are swift to shed blood; [16] Destruction and misery are in their ways; [17] And the way of peace they have not known." [18] "There is no

fear of God before their eyes." [19] Now we know that whatever the law says, it says to those who are under the law, that every mouth may be stopped, and all the world may become guilty before God. [20] Therefore by the deeds of the law no flesh will be justified in His sight, for by the law is the knowledge of sin. [21] But now the righteousness of God apart from the law is revealed, being witnessed by the Law and the Prophets, [22] even the righteousness of God, through faith in Jesus Christ, to all and on all who believe. For there is no difference; [23] for all have sinned and fall short of the glory of God,

Romans 1:18-32

[18] For the wrath of God is revealed from heaven against all ungodliness and unrighteousness of men, who suppress the truth in unrighteousness, [19] because what may be known of God is manifest in them, for God has shown it to them. [20] For since the creation of the world His invisible attributes are clearly seen, being understood by the things that are made, even His eternal power and Godhead, so that they are without excuse, [21] because, although they knew God, they did not glorify Him as God, nor were thankful, but became futile in their thoughts, and their foolish hearts were darkened. [22] Professing to be wise, they became fools, [23] and changed the glory of the incorruptible God into an image made like corruptible man--and birds and four-footed animals and creeping things. [24] Therefore God also gave them up to uncleanness, in the lusts of their hearts, to dishonor their bodies among themselves, [25] who exchanged the truth of God for the lie, and worshiped and served the creature rather than the Creator, who is blessed forever. Amen. [26] For this reason God gave them up to vile passions. For even their women exchanged the natural use for what is against nature. [27] Likewise also the men, leaving the natural use of the woman, burned in their lust for one another, men with men committing what is shameful, and receiving in themselves the penalty of their error which was due. [28] And even as they did not like to retain God in their knowledge, God gave them over to a debased mind, to do those things which are not fitting; [29] being filled with all unrighteousness, sexual immorality, wickedness, covetousness, maliciousness; full of envy, murder, strife, deceit, evil-mindedness; they are whisperers, [30] backbiters, haters of God, violent, proud, boasters, inventors of evil things, disobedient to parents, [31] undiscerning, untrustworthy, unloving, unforgiving, unmerciful; [32] who, knowing the righteous judgment of God, that those who practice such things are

deserving of death, not only do the same but also approve of those who practice them.

Romans 2:1-16

[1] Therefore you are inexcusable, O man, whoever you are who judge, for in whatever you judge another you condemn yourself; for you who judge practice the same things. [2] But we know that the judgment of God is according to truth against those who practice such things. [3] And do you think this, O man, you who judge those practicing such things, and doing the same, that you will escape the judgment of God? [4] Or do you despise the riches of His goodness, forbearance, and longsuffering, not knowing that the goodness of God leads you to repentance? [5] But in accordance with your hardness and your impenitent heart you are treasuring up for yourself wrath in the day of wrath and revelation of the righteous judgment of God, [6] who "will render to each one according to his deeds": [7] eternal life to those who by patient continuance in doing good seek for glory, honor, and immortality; [8] but to those who are self-seeking and do not obey the truth, but obey unrighteousness--indignation and wrath, [9] tribulation and anguish, on every soul of man who does evil, of the Jew first and also of the Greek; [10] but glory, honor, and peace to everyone who works what is good, to the Jew first and also to the Greek. [11] For there is no partiality with God. [12] For as many as have sinned without law will also perish without law, and as many as have sinned in the law will be judged by the law [13] (for not the hearers of the law are just in the sight of God, but the doers of the law will be justified; [14] for when Gentiles, who do not have the law, by nature do the things in the law, these, although not having the law, are a law to themselves, [15] who show the work of the law written in their hearts, their conscience also bearing witness, and between themselves their thoughts accusing or else excusing them) [16] in the day when God will judge the secrets of men by Jesus Christ, according to my gospel.

Romans 2:17-29

[17] Indeed you are called a Jew, and rest on the law, and make your boast in God, [18] and know His will, and approve the things that are excellent, being instructed out of the law, [19] and are confident that you yourself are a guide to the blind, a light to those who are in darkness, [20] an instructor of the foolish, a teacher of babes, having the form of knowledge and truth in the law. [21] You, therefore, who teach another,

do you not teach yourself? You who preach that a man should not steal, do you steal? [22] You who say, "Do not commit adultery," do you commit adultery? You who abhor idols, do you rob temples? [23] You who make your boast in the law, do you dishonor God through breaking the law? [24] For "the name of God is blasphemed among the Gentiles because of you," as it is written. [25] For circumcision is indeed profitable if you keep the law; but if you are a breaker of the law, your circumcision has become uncircumcision. [26] Therefore, if an uncircumcised man keeps the righteous requirements of the law, will not his uncircumcision be counted as circumcision? [27] And will not the physically uncircumcised, if he fulfills the law, judge you who, even with your written code and circumcision, are a transgressor of the law? [28] For he is not a Jew who is one outwardly, nor is circumcision that which is outward in the flesh; [29] but he is a Jew who is one inwardly; and circumcision is that of the heart, in the Spirit, not in the letter; whose praise is not from men but from God.

Romans 3:1-8

[1] What advantage then has the Jew, or what is the profit of circumcision? [2] Much in every way! Chiefly because to them were committed the oracles of God. [3] For what if some did not believe? Will their unbelief make the faithfulness of God without effect? [4] Certainly not! Indeed, let God be true but every man a liar. As it is written: "That You may be justified in Your words, And may overcome when You are judged." [5] But if our unrighteousness demonstrates the righteousness of God, what shall we say? Is God unjust who inflicts wrath? (I speak as a man.) [6] Certainly not! For then how will God judge the world? [7] For if the truth of God has increased through my lie to His glory, why am I also still judged as a sinner? [8] And why not say, "Let us do evil that good may come"?--as we are slanderously reported and as some affirm that we say. Their condemnation is just.

Romans 6:23

[23] For the wages of sin is death, but the gift of God is eternal life in Christ Jesus our Lord.

1 Corinthians 15:22

[22] For as in Adam all die, even so in Christ all shall be made alive.

Genesis 2:17

[17] but of the tree of the knowledge of good and evil you shall not eat, for in the day that you eat of it you shall surely die."

1 Corinthians 15:21,56

[21] For since by man came death, by Man also came the resurrection of the dead.
[56] The sting of death is sin, and the strength of sin is the law.

Ephesians 2:1,5

[1] And you He made alive, who were dead in trespasses and sins,
[5] even when we were dead in trespasses, made us alive together with Christ (by grace you have been saved),

Colossians 2:13

[13] But now in Christ Jesus you who once were far off have been brought near by the blood of Christ.

John 3:3-7

[3] Jesus answered and said to him, "Most assuredly, I say to you, unless one is born again, he cannot see the kingdom of God." [4] Nicodemus said to Him, "How can a man be born when he is old? Can he enter a second time into his mother's womb and be born?" [5] Jesus answered, "Most assuredly, I say to you, unless one is born of water and the Spirit, he cannot enter the kingdom of God. [6] That which is born of the flesh is flesh, and that which is born of the Spirit is spirit. [7] Do not marvel that I said to you, 'You must be born again.'

Psalm 14:1-3

[1] To the Chief Musician. A Psalm of David. The fool has said in his heart, "There is no God." They are corrupt, They have done abominable works, There is none who does good. [2] The Lord looks down from heaven upon the children of men, To see if there are any who understand, who seek God. [3] They have all turned aside, They have together become corrupt; There is none who does good, No, not one.

Romans 4:1-4

[1] What then shall we say that Abraham our father has found according to the flesh? [2] For if Abraham was justified by works, he has something to boast about, but not before God. [3] For what does the Scripture say? "Abraham believed God, and it was accounted to him for

righteousness." ⁴ Now to him who works, the wages are not counted as grace but as debt.

Hebrews 6:1

¹ Therefore, leaving the discussion of the elementary principles of Christ, let us go on to perfection, not laying again the foundation of repentance from dead works and of faith toward God,

Hebrews 9:14

¹⁴ how much more shall the blood of Christ, who through the eternal Spirit offered Himself without spot to God, cleanse your conscience from dead works to serve the living God?

Ephesians 2:4-6

⁴ But God, who is rich in mercy, because of His great love with which He loved us, ⁵ even when we were dead in trespasses, made us alive together with Christ (by grace you have been saved), ⁶ and raised us up together, and made us sit together in the heavenly places in Christ Jesus,

Colossians 1:20-21

²⁰ and by Him to reconcile all things to Himself, by Him, whether things on earth or things in heaven, having made peace through the blood of His cross. ²¹ And you, who once were alienated and enemies in your mind by wicked works, yet now He has reconciled

Romans 5:1-11

¹ Therefore, having been justified by faith, we have peace with God through our Lord Jesus Christ, ² through whom also we have access by faith into this grace in which we stand, and rejoice in hope of the glory of God. ³ And not only that, but we also glory in tribulations, knowing that tribulation produces perseverance; ⁴ and perseverance, character; and character, hope. ⁵ Now hope does not disappoint, because the love of God has been poured out in our hearts by the Holy Spirit who was given to us. ⁶ For when we were still without strength, in due time Christ died for the ungodly. ⁷ For scarcely for a righteous man will one die; yet perhaps for a good man someone would even dare to die. ⁸ But God demonstrates His own love toward us, in that while we were still sinners, Christ died for us. ⁹ Much more then, having now been justified by His blood, we shall be saved from wrath through Him. ¹⁰ For if when we were enemies we were reconciled to God through

the death of His Son, much more, having been reconciled, we shall be saved by His life. [11] And not only that, but we also rejoice in God through our Lord Jesus Christ, through whom we have now received the reconciliation.

Ephesians 2:15-17

[15] having abolished in His flesh the enmity, that is, the law of commandments contained in ordinances, so as to create in Himself one new man from the two, thus making peace, [16] and that He might reconcile them both to God in one body through the cross, thereby putting to death the enmity. [17] And He came and preached peace to you who were afar off and to those who were near.

2 Corinthians 5:18

[18] Now all things are of God, who has reconciled us to Himself through Jesus Christ, and has given us the ministry of reconciliation,

1 Corinthians 1:30-31

[30] But of Him you are in Christ Jesus, who became for us wisdom from God--and righteousness and sanctification and redemption-- [31] that, as it is written, "He who glories, let him glory in the Lord."

1 Peter 2:24

[24] who Himself bore our sins in His own body on the tree, that we, having died to sins, might live for righteousness--by whose stripes you were healed.

Ephesians 2:13

[13] But now in Christ Jesus you who once were far off have been brought near by the blood of Christ.

Ephesians 2:14-18

[14] For He Himself is our peace, who has made both one, and has broken down the middle wall of separation, [15] having abolished in His flesh the enmity, that is, the law of commandments contained in ordinances, so as to create in Himself one new man from the two, thus making peace, [16] and that He might reconcile them both to God in one body through the cross, thereby putting to death the enmity. [17] And He came and preached peace to you who were afar off and to those who were near. [18] For through Him we both have access by one Spirit to the Father.

1 Corinthians 1:2

2 To the church of God which is at Corinth, to those who are sanctified in Christ Jesus, called to be saints, with all who in every place call on the name of Jesus Christ our Lord, both theirs and ours:

2 Corinthians 5:17

17 Therefore, if anyone is in Christ, he is a new creation; old things have passed away; behold, all things have become new.

Colossians 2:10

10 and you are complete in Him, who is the head of all principality and power.

2 Corinthians 5:18-21

18 Now all things are of God, who has reconciled us to Himself through Jesus Christ, and has given us the ministry of reconciliation, 19 that is, that God was in Christ reconciling the world to Himself, not imputing their trespasses to them, and has committed to us the word of reconciliation. 20 Now then, we are ambassadors for Christ, as though God were pleading through us: we implore you on Christ's behalf, be reconciled to God. 21 For He made Him who knew no sin to be sin for us, that we might become the righteousness of God in Him.

Colossians 1:21-23

21 And you, who once were alienated and enemies in your mind by wicked works, yet now He has reconciled 22 in the body of His flesh through death, to present you holy, and blameless, and above reproach in His sight-- 23 if indeed you continue in the faith, grounded and steadfast, and are not moved away from the hope of the gospel which you heard, which was preached to every creature under heaven, of which I, Paul, became a minister.

Exodus 15:11

11 "Who is like You, O Lord, among the gods? Who is like You, glorious in holiness, Fearful in praises, doing wonders?

Psalm 30:4

4 Sing praise to the Lord, You saints of His, And give thanks at the remembrance of His holy name.

Psalm 47:8

⁸ God reigns over the nations; God sits on His holy throne.

Psalm 48:1

¹ A song. A Psalm of the sons of Korah. Great is the Lord, and greatly to be praised In the city of our God, In His holy mountain.

Psalm 89:35

³⁵ Once I have sworn by My holiness; I will not lie to David:

Leviticus 11:44-45

⁴⁴ For I am the Lord your God. You shall therefore consecrate yourselves, and you shall be holy; for I am holy. Neither shall you defile yourselves with any creeping thing that creeps on the earth. ⁴⁵ For I am the Lord who brings you up out of the land of Egypt, to be your God. You shall therefore be holy, for I am holy.

Leviticus 19:2

² "Speak to all the congregation of the children of Israel, and say to them: 'You shall be holy, for I the Lord your God am holy.

Isaiah 5:16

¹⁶ But the Lord of hosts shall be exalted in judgment, And God who is holy shall be hallowed in righteousness.

Revelation 15:4

⁴ Who shall not fear You, O Lord, and glorify Your name? For You alone are holy. For all nations shall come and worship before You, For Your judgments have been manifested."

1 Peter 1:15-16

¹⁵ but as He who called you is holy, you also be holy in all your conduct, ¹⁶ because it is written, "Be holy, for I am holy."

Habakkuk 1:13

¹³ You are of purer eyes than to behold evil, And cannot look on wickedness. Why do You look on those who deal treacherously, And hold Your tongue when the wicked devours A person more righteous than he?

Isaiah 59:2

² But your iniquities have separated you from your God; And your sins have hidden His face from you, So that He will not hear.

Romans 3:9-23

⁹ What then? Are we better than they? Not at all. For we have previously charged both Jews and Greeks that they are all under sin. ¹⁰ As it is written: "There is none righteous, no, not one; ¹¹ There is none who understands; There is none who seeks after God. ¹² They have all turned aside; They have together become unprofitable; There is none who does good, no, not one." ¹³ "Their throat is an open tomb; With their tongues they have practiced deceit"; "The poison of asps is under their lips"; ¹⁴ "Whose mouth is full of cursing and bitterness." ¹⁵ "Their feet are swift to shed blood; ¹⁶ Destruction and misery are in their ways; ¹⁷ And the way of peace they have not known." ¹⁸ "There is no fear of God before their eyes." ¹⁹ Now we know that whatever the law says, it says to those who are under the law, that every mouth may be stopped, and all the world may become guilty before God. ²⁰ Therefore by the deeds of the law no flesh will be justified in His sight, for by the law is the knowledge of sin. ²¹ But now the righteousness of God apart from the law is revealed, being witnessed by the Law and the Prophets, ²² even the righteousness of God, through faith in Jesus Christ, to all and on all who believe. For there is no difference; ²³ for all have sinned and fall short of the glory of God,

Hebrews 4:16

¹⁶ Let us therefore come boldly to the throne of grace, that we may obtain mercy and find grace to help in time of need.

1 John 2:1-2

¹ My little children, these things I write to you, so that you may not sin. And if anyone sins, we have an Advocate with the Father, Jesus Christ the righteous. ² And He Himself is the propitiation for our sins, and not for ours only but also for the whole world.

Hebrews 2:17

¹⁷ Therefore, in all things He had to be made like His brethren, that He might be a merciful and faithful High Priest in things pertaining to God, to make propitiation for the sins of the people.

1 Peter 1:18

[18] knowing that you were not redeemed with corruptible things, like silver or gold, from your aimless conduct received by tradition from your fathers,

Romans 3:25-26

[25] whom God set forth as a propitiation by His blood, through faith, to demonstrate His righteousness, because in His forbearance God had passed over the sins that were previously committed, [26] to demonstrate at the present time His righteousness, that He might be just and the justifier of the one who has faith in Jesus.

Galatians 4:3-8

[3] Even so we, when we were children, were in bondage under the elements of the world. [4] But when the fullness of the time had come, God sent forth His Son, born of a woman, born under the law, [5] to redeem those who were under the law, that we might receive the adoption as sons. [6] And because you are sons, God has sent forth the Spirit of His Son into your hearts, crying out, "Abba, Father!" [7] Therefore you are no longer a slave but a son, and if a son, then an heir of God through Christ. [8] But then, indeed, when you did not know God, you served those which by nature are not gods.

Galatians 3:22

[22] But the Scripture has confined all under sin, that the promise by faith in Jesus Christ might be given to those who believe.

Exodus 6:6

[6] Therefore say to the children of Israel: 'I am the Lord; I will bring you out from under the burdens of the Egyptians, I will rescue you from their bondage, and I will redeem you with an outstretched arm and with great judgments.

Exodus 15:13

[13] You in Your mercy have led forth The people whom You have redeemed; You have guided them in Your strength To Your holy habitation.

Psalm 74:2

² Remember Your congregation, which You have purchased of old, The tribe of Your inheritance, which You have redeemed-- This Mount Zion where You have dwelt.

Psalm 78:35

³⁵ Then they remembered that God was their rock, And the Most High God their Redeemer.

Ephesians 1:7

⁷ In Him we have redemption through His blood, the forgiveness of sins, according to the riches of His grace.

Colossians 1:14

¹⁴ in whom we have redemption through His blood, the forgiveness of sins.

Romans 3:24

²⁴ being justified freely by His grace through the redemption that is in Christ Jesus,

1 Peter 1:18-19

¹⁸ knowing that you were not redeemed with corruptible things, like silver or gold, from your aimless conduct received by tradition from your fathers, ¹⁹ but with the precious blood of Christ, as of a lamb without blemish and without spot.

Galatians 3:13

¹³ Christ has redeemed us from the curse of the law, having become a curse for us (for it is written, "Cursed is everyone who hangs on a tree"),

Hebrews 9:15

¹⁵ And for this reason He is the Mediator of the new covenant, by means of death, for the redemption of the transgressions under the first covenant, that those who are called may receive the promise of the eternal inheritance.

1 Corinthians 6:20

²⁰ For you were bought at a price; therefore glorify God in your body and in your spirit, which are God's.

1 Timothy 4:10

¹⁰ For to this end we both labor and suffer reproach, because we trust in the living God, who is the Savior of all men, especially of those who believe.

John 3:18,36

¹⁸ He who believes in Him is not condemned; but he who does not believe is condemned already, because he has not believed in the name of the only begotten Son of God.

³⁶ He who believes in the Son has everlasting life; and he who does not believe the Son shall not see life, but the wrath of God abides on him."

Romans 3:19-20

¹⁹ Now we know that whatever the law says, it says to those who are under the law, that every mouth may be stopped, and all the world may become guilty before God. ²⁰ Therefore by the deeds of the law no flesh will be justified in His sight, for by the law is the knowledge of sin.

Romans 6:23

²³ For the wages of sin is death, but the gift of God is eternal life in Christ Jesus our Lord.

Romans 7:7

⁷ What shall we say then? Is the law sin? Certainly not! On the contrary, I would not have known sin except through the law. For I would not have known covetousness unless the law had said, "You shall not covet."

Galatians 3:10-12

¹⁰ For as many as are of the works of the law are under the curse; for it is written, "Cursed is everyone who does not continue in all things which are written in the book of the law, to do them." ¹¹ But that no one is justified by the law in the sight of God is evident, for "the just shall live by faith." ¹² Yet the law is not of faith, but "the man who does them shall live by them."

Colossians 2:14

¹⁴ having wiped out the handwriting of requirements that was against us, which was contrary to us. And He has taken it out of the way, having nailed it to the cross.

2 Corinthians 7:7-13

[7] and not only by his coming, but also by the consolation with which he was comforted in you, when he told us of your earnest desire, your mourning, your zeal for me, so that I rejoiced even more. [8] For even if I made you sorry with my letter, I do not regret it; though I did regret it. For I perceive that the same epistle made you sorry, though only for a while. [9] Now I rejoice, not that you were made sorry, but that your sorrow led to repentance. For you were made sorry in a godly manner, that you might suffer loss from us in nothing. [10] For godly sorrow produces repentance leading to salvation, not to be regretted; but the sorrow of the world produces death. [11] For observe this very thing, that you sorrowed in a godly manner: What diligence it produced in you, what clearing of yourselves, what indignation, what fear, what vehement desire, what zeal, what vindication! In all things you proved yourselves to be clear in this matter. [12] Therefore, although I wrote to you, I did not do it for the sake of him who had done the wrong, nor for the sake of him who suffered wrong, but that our care for you in the sight of God might appear to you. [13] Therefore we have been comforted in your comfort. And we rejoiced exceedingly more for the joy of Titus, because his spirit has been refreshed by you all.

Galatians 4:3-5,9

[3] Even so we, when we were children, were in bondage under the elements of the world. [4] But when the fullness of the time had come, God sent forth His Son, born of a woman, born under the law, [5] to redeem those who were under the law, that we might receive the adoption as sons.

[9] But now after you have known God, or rather are known by God, how is it that you turn again to the weak and beggarly elements, to which you desire again to be in bondage?

Romans 7:10-14

[10] And the commandment, which was to bring life, I found to bring death. [11] For sin, taking occasion by the commandment, deceived me, and by it killed me. [12] Therefore the law is holy, and the commandment holy and just and good. [13] Has then what is good become death to me? Certainly not! But sin, that it might appear sin, was producing death in me through what is good, so that sin through the commandment might become exceedingly sinful. [14] For we know that the law is spiritual, but I am carnal, sold under sin.

Isaiah 53:4-11

4 Surely He has borne our griefs And carried our sorrows; Yet we esteemed Him stricken, Smitten by God, and afflicted. 5 But He was wounded for our transgressions, He was bruised for our iniquities; The chastisement for our peace was upon Him, And by His stripes we are healed. 6 All we like sheep have gone astray; We have turned, every one, to his own way; And the Lord has laid on Him the iniquity of us all. 7 He was oppressed and He was afflicted, Yet He opened not His mouth; He was led as a lamb to the slaughter, And as a sheep before its shearers is silent, So He opened not His mouth. 8 He was taken from prison and from judgment, And who will declare His generation? For He was cut off from the land of the living; For the transgressions of My people He was stricken. 9 And they made His grave with the wicked-- But with the rich at His death, Because He had done no violence, Nor was any deceit in His mouth. 10 Yet it pleased the Lord to bruise Him; He has put Him to grief. When You make His soul an offering for sin, He shall see His seed, He shall prolong His days, And the pleasure of the Lord shall prosper in His hand. 11 He shall see the labor of His soul, and be satisfied. By His knowledge My righteous Servant shall justify many, For He shall bear their iniquities.

Matthew 20:28

28 just as the Son of Man did not come to be served, but to serve, and to give His life a ransom for many."

Philemon 13

13 whom I wished to keep with me, that on your behalf he might minister to me in my chains for the gospel.

2 Corinthians 5:20-21

20 Now then, we are ambassadors for Christ, as though God were pleading through us: we implore you on Christ's behalf, be reconciled to God. 21 For He made Him who knew no sin to be sin for us, that we might become the righteousness of God in Him.

Romans 5:8

8 But God demonstrates His own love toward us, in that while we were still sinners, Christ died for us.

1 Corinthians 15:3

³ For I delivered to you first of all that which I also received: that Christ died for our sins according to the Scriptures,

John 1:29

²⁹ The next day John saw Jesus coming toward him, and said, "Behold! The Lamb of God who takes away the sin of the world!

Hebrews 2:9

⁹ But we see Jesus, who was made a little lower than the angels, for the suffering of death crowned with glory and honor, that He, by the grace of God, might taste death for everyone.

Matthew 19:28

²⁸ So Jesus said to them, "Assuredly I say to you, that in the regeneration, when the Son of Man sits on the throne of His glory, you who have followed Me will also sit on twelve thrones, judging the twelve tribes of Israel.

Titus 3:5

⁵ not by works of righteousness which we have done, but according to His mercy He saved us, through the washing of regeneration and renewing of the Holy Spirit,

John 3:3-6

³ Jesus answered and said to him, "Most assuredly, I say to you, unless one is born again, he cannot see the kingdom of God." ⁴ Nicodemus said to Him, "How can a man be born when he is old? Can he enter a second time into his mother's womb and be born?" ⁵ Jesus answered, "Most assuredly, I say to you, unless one is born of water and the Spirit, he cannot enter the kingdom of God. ⁶ That which is born of the flesh is flesh, and that which is born of the Spirit is spirit.

John 7:37-39

³⁷ On the last day, that great day of the feast, Jesus stood and cried out, saying, "If anyone thirsts, let him come to Me and drink. ³⁸ He who believes in Me, as the Scripture has said, out of his heart will flow rivers of living water." ³⁹ But this He spoke concerning the Spirit, whom those believing in Him would receive; for the Holy Spirit was not yet given, because Jesus was not yet glorified.

Ephesians 2:1-4

[1] And you He made alive, who were dead in trespasses and sins, [2] in which you once walked according to the course of this world, according to the prince of the power of the air, the spirit who now works in the sons of disobedience, [3] among whom also we all once conducted ourselves in the lusts of our flesh, fulfilling the desires of the flesh and of the mind, and were by nature children of wrath, just as the others. [4] But God, who is rich in mercy, because of His great love with which He loved us,

James 1:17-18

[17] Every good gift and every perfect gift is from above, and comes down from the Father of lights, with whom there is no variation or shadow of turning. [18] Of His own will He brought us forth by the word of truth, that we might be a kind of firstfruits of His creatures.

Matthew 19:28

[28] So Jesus said to them, "Assuredly I say to you, that in the regeneration, when the Son of Man sits on the throne of His glory, you who have followed Me will also sit on twelve thrones, judging the twelve tribes of Israel.

John 1:13

[13] who were born, not of blood, nor of the will of the flesh, nor of the will of man, but of God.

John 3:3

[3] Jesus answered and said to him, "Most assuredly, I say to you, unless one is born again, he cannot see the kingdom of God."

Galatians 3:26

[26] For you are all sons of God through faith in Christ Jesus.

John 1:12

[12] But as many as received Him, to them He gave the right to become children of God, to those who believe in His name:

John 3:3-6

[3] Jesus answered and said to him, "Most assuredly, I say to you, unless one is born again, he cannot see the kingdom of God." [4] Nicodemus said to Him, "How can a man be born when he is old? Can he enter a

second time into his mother's womb and be born?" [5] Jesus answered, "Most assuredly, I say to you, unless one is born of water and the Spirit, he cannot enter the kingdom of God. [6] That which is born of the flesh is flesh, and that which is born of the Spirit is spirit.

Colossians 2:13

[13] And you, being dead in your trespasses and the uncircumcision of your flesh, He has made alive together with Him, having forgiven you all trespasses,

Romans 6:5,13

[5] For if we have been united together in the likeness of His death, certainly we also shall be in the likeness of His resurrection,
[13] And do not present your members as instruments of unrighteousness to sin, but present yourselves to God as being alive from the dead, and your members as instruments of righteousness to God.

Ephesians 2:5-10

[5] even when we were dead in trespasses, made us alive together with Christ (by grace you have been saved), [6] and raised us up together, and made us sit together in the heavenly places in Christ Jesus, [7] that in the ages to come He might show the exceeding riches of His grace in His kindness toward us in Christ Jesus. [8] For by grace you have been saved through faith, and that not of yourselves; it is the gift of God, [9] not of works, lest anyone should boast. [10] For we are His workmanship, created in Christ Jesus for good works, which God prepared beforehand that we should walk in them.

John 5:21-23

[21] For as the Father raises the dead and gives life to them, even so the Son gives life to whom He will. [22] For the Father judges no one, but has committed all judgment to the Son, [23] that all should honor the Son just as they honor the Father. He who does not honor the Son does not honor the Father who sent Him.

Romans 6:4-14

[4] Therefore we were buried with Him through baptism into death, that just as Christ was raised from the dead by the glory of the Father, even so we also should walk in newness of life. [5] For if we have been united together in the likeness of His death, certainly we also shall be in the likeness of His resurrection, [6] knowing this, that our old man

was crucified with Him, that the body of sin might be done away with, that we should no longer be slaves of sin. [7] For he who has died has been freed from sin. [8] Now if we died with Christ, we believe that we shall also live with Him, [9] knowing that Christ, having been raised from the dead, dies no more. Death no longer has dominion over Him. [10] For the death that He died, He died to sin once for all; but the life that He lives, He lives to God. [11] Likewise you also, reckon yourselves to be dead indeed to sin, but alive to God in Christ Jesus our Lord. [12] Therefore do not let sin reign in your mortal body, that you should obey it in its lusts. [13] And do not present your members as instruments of unrighteousness to sin, but present yourselves to God as being alive from the dead, and your members as instruments of righteousness to God. [14] For sin shall not have dominion over you, for you are not under law but under grace.

2 Corinthians 5:17

[17] Therefore, if anyone is in Christ, he is a new creation; old things have passed away; behold, all things have become new.

Ephesians 2:10

[10] For we are His workmanship, created in Christ Jesus for good works, which God prepared beforehand that we should walk in them.

John 1:12-13

[12] But as many as received Him, to them He gave the right to become children of God, to those who believe in His name: [13] who were born, not of blood, nor of the will of the flesh, nor of the will of man, but of God.

1 Peter 1:23

[23] having been born again, not of corruptible seed but incorruptible, through the word of God which lives and abides forever,

2 Peter 1:3-4

[3] as His divine power has given to us all things that pertain to life and godliness, through the knowledge of Him who called us by glory and virtue, [4] by which have been given to us exceedingly great and precious promises, that through these you may be partakers of the divine nature, having escaped the corruption that is in the world through lust.

Isaiah 64:6

⁶ But we are all like an unclean thing, And all our righteousnesses are like filthy rags; We all fade as a leaf, And our iniquities, like the wind, Have taken us away.

Genesis 18:25

²⁵ Far be it from You to do such a thing as this, to slay the righteous with the wicked, so that the righteous should be as the wicked; far be it from You! Shall not the Judge of all the earth do right?"

Deuteronomy 32:4

⁴ He is the Rock, His work is perfect; For all His ways are justice, A God of truth and without injustice; Righteous and upright is He.

2 Timothy 4:8

⁸ Finally, there is laid up for me the crown of righteousness, which the Lord, the righteous Judge, will give to me on that Day, and not to me only but also to all who have loved His appearing.

Romans 3:21-25

²¹ But now the righteousness of God apart from the law is revealed, being witnessed by the Law and the Prophets, ²² even the righteousness of God, through faith in Jesus Christ, to all and on all who believe. For there is no difference; ²³ for all have sinned and fall short of the glory of God, ²⁴ being justified freely by His grace through the redemption that is in Christ Jesus, ²⁵ whom God set forth as a propitiation by His blood, through faith, to demonstrate His righteousness, because in His forbearance God had passed over the sins that were previously committed,

2 Corinthians 5:21

²¹ For He made Him who knew no sin to be sin for us, that we might become the righteousness of God in Him.

Romans 3:25-26

²⁵ whom God set forth as a propitiation by His blood, through faith, to demonstrate His righteousness, because in His forbearance God had passed over the sins that were previously committed, ²⁶ to demonstrate at the present time His righteousness, that He might be just and the justifier of the one who has faith in Jesus. ²⁷ Where is boasting then?

It is excluded. By what law? Of works? No, but by the law of faith. [28] Therefore

1 John 4:8

[8] He who does not love does not know God, for God is love.

1 John 1:5

[5] This is the message which we have heard from Him and declare to you, that God is light and in Him is no darkness at all.

Hebrews 3:1

[1] Therefore, holy brethren, partakers of the heavenly calling, consider the Apostle and High Priest of our confession, Christ Jesus,

1 Thessalonians 5:23

[23] Now may the God of peace Himself sanctify you completely; and may your whole spirit, soul, and body be preserved blameless at the coming of our Lord Jesus Christ.

1 John 3:2

[2] Beloved, now we are children of God; and it has not yet been revealed what we shall be, but we know that when He is revealed, we shall be like Him, for we shall see Him as He is.

Romans 6:1-11

[1] What shall we say then? Shall we continue in sin that grace may abound? [2] Certainly not! How shall we who died to sin live any longer in it? [3] Or do you not know that as many of us as were baptized into Christ Jesus were baptized into His death? [4] Therefore we were buried with Him through baptism into death, that just as Christ was raised from the dead by the glory of the Father, even so we also should walk in newness of life. [5] For if we have been united together in the likeness of His death, certainly we also shall be in the likeness of His resurrection, [6] knowing this, that our old man was crucified with Him, that the body of sin might be done away with, that we should no longer be slaves of sin. [7] For he who has died has been freed from sin. [8] Now if we died with Christ, we believe that we shall also live with Him, [9] knowing that Christ, having been raised from the dead, dies no more. Death no longer has dominion over Him. [10] For the death that He died, He died to sin once for all; but the life that He lives, He lives to

God. [11] Likewise you also, reckon yourselves to be dead indeed to sin, but alive to God in Christ Jesus our Lord.

Romans 6:12-14

[12] Therefore do not let sin reign in your mortal body, that you should obey it in its lusts. [13] And do not present your members as instruments of unrighteousness to sin, but present yourselves to God as being alive from the dead, and your members as instruments of righteousness to God. [14] For sin shall not have dominion over you, for you are not under law but under grace.

Isaiah 64:6

[6] But we are all like an unclean thing, And all our righteousnesses are like filthy rags; We all fade as a leaf, And our iniquities, like the wind, Have taken us away.

Luke 7:50

[50] Then He said to the woman, "Your faith has saved you. Go in peace."
Luke 7:50 (NKJV)

1 Corinthians 1:18

[18] For the message of the cross is foolishness to those who are perishing, but to us who are being saved it is the power of God.

2 Corinthians 2:13

[13] I had no rest in my spirit, because I did not find Titus my brother; but taking my leave of them, I departed for Macedonia.

Ephesians 2:5,8

[5] even when we were dead in trespasses, made us alive together with Christ (by grace you have been saved),
[8] For by grace you have been saved through faith, and that not of yourselves; it is the gift of God,

2 Timothy 1:9

[9] who has saved us and called us with a holy calling, not according to our works, but according to His own purpose and grace which was given to us in Christ Jesus before time began,

Romans 6:14

14 For sin shall not have dominion over you, for you are not under law but under grace.

Romans 8:2

2 For the law of the Spirit of life in Christ Jesus has made me free from the law of sin and death.

2 Corinthians 3:18

18 But we all, with unveiled face, beholding as in a mirror the glory of the Lord, are being transformed into the same image from glory to glory, just as by the Spirit of the Lord.

Galatians 2:19-20

19 For I through the law died to the law that I might live to God. 20 I have been crucified with Christ; it is no longer I who live, but Christ lives in me; and the life which I now live in the flesh I live by faith in the Son of God, who loved me and gave Himself for me.

Philippians 1:20

20 according to my earnest expectation and hope that in nothing I shall be ashamed, but with all boldness, as always, so now also Christ will be magnified in my body, whether by life or by death.

Philippians 2:12-13

12 Therefore, my beloved, as you have always obeyed, not as in my presence only, but now much more in my absence, work out your own salvation with fear and trembling; 13 for it is God who works in you both to will and to do for His good pleasure.

2 Thessalonians 2:13

13 But we are bound to give thanks to God always for you, brethren beloved by the Lord, because God from the beginning chose you for salvation through sanctification by the Spirit and belief in the truth,

Romans 8:18-23

18 For I consider that the sufferings of this present time are not worthy to be compared with the glory which shall be revealed in us. 19 For the earnest expectation of the creation eagerly waits for the revealing of the sons of God. 20 For the creation was subjected to futility, not willingly, but because of Him who subjected it in hope; 21 because the creation

itself also will be delivered from the bondage of corruption into the glorious liberty of the children of God. [22] For we know that the whole creation groans and labors with birth pangs together until now. [23] Not only that, but we also who have the firstfruits of the Spirit, even we ourselves groan within ourselves, eagerly waiting for the adoption, the redemption of our body.

1 Corinthians 15:42-44

[42] So also is the resurrection of the dead. The body is sown in corruption, it is raised in incorruption. [43] It is sown in dishonor, it is raised in glory. It is sown in weakness, it is raised in power. [44] It is sown a natural body, it is raised a spiritual body. There is a natural body, and there is a spiritual body.

Romans 13:11

[11] And do this, knowing the time, that now it is high time to awake out of sleep; for now our salvation is nearer than when we first believed.

Hebrews 10:36

[36] For you have need of endurance, so that after you have done the will of God, you may receive the promise:

1 Peter 1:5

[5] who are kept by the power of God through faith for salvation ready to be revealed in the last time.

1 John 3:2

[2] Beloved, now we are children of God; and it has not yet been revealed what we shall be, but we know that when He is revealed, we shall be like Him, for we shall see Him as He is.

John 3:17-18,36

[17] For God did not send His Son into the world to condemn the world, but that the world through Him might be saved. [18] He who believes in Him is not condemned; but he who does not believe is condemned already, because he has not believed in the name of the only begotten Son of God.
[36] He who believes in the Son has everlasting life; and he who does not believe the Son shall not see life, but the wrath of God abides on him."

John 12:48

[48] He who rejects Me, and does not receive My words, has that which judges him--the word that I have spoken will judge him in the last day.

John 14:12

[12] "Most assuredly, I say to you, he who believes in Me, the works that I do he will do also; and greater works than these he will do, because I go to My Father.

Acts 4:12

[12] Nor is there salvation in any other, for there is no other name under heaven given among men by which we must be saved."

Ephesians 2:8-9

[8] For by grace you have been saved through faith, and that not of yourselves; it is the gift of God, [9] not of works, lest anyone should boast.

Titus 3:5

[5] not by works of righteousness which we have done, but according to His mercy He saved us, through the washing of regeneration and renewing of the Holy Spirit,

CHAPTER 3

2 Timothy 3:15

[15] and that from childhood you have known the Holy Scriptures, which are able to make you wise for salvation through faith which is in Christ Jesus.

Psalm 93:2

[2] Your throne is established from of old; You are from everlasting.

John 14:1

[1] "Let not your heart be troubled; you believe in God, believe also in Me.

Mark 11:22

[22] So Jesus answered and said to them, "Have faith in God."

Romans 10:9

9 that if you confess with your mouth the Lord Jesus and believe in your heart that God has raised Him from the dead, you will be saved.

Romans 4:3

3 For what does the Scripture say? "Abraham believed God, and it was accounted to him for righteousness."

2 Peter 1:4

4 by which have been given to us exceedingly great and precious promises, that through these you may be partakers of the divine nature, having escaped the corruption that is in the world through lust.

2 Peter 1:5-7

5 But also for this very reason, giving all diligence, add to your faith virtue, to virtue knowledge, 6 to knowledge self-control, to self-control perseverance, to perseverance godliness, 7 to godliness brotherly kindness, and to brotherly kindness love.

Acts 3:16

16 And His name, through faith in His name, has made this man strong, whom you see and know. Yes, the faith which comes through Him has given him this perfect soundness in the presence of you all.

Romans 4:5

5 But to him who does not work but believes on Him who justifies the ungodly, his faith is accounted for righteousness,

1 Peter 1:4-9

4 to an inheritance incorruptible and undefiled and that does not fade away, reserved in heaven for you, 5 who are kept by the power of God through faith for salvation ready to be revealed in the last time. 6 In this you greatly rejoice, though now for a little while, if need be, you have been grieved by various trials, 7 that the genuineness of your faith, being much more precious than gold that perishes, though it is tested by fire, may be found to praise, honor, and glory at the revelation of Jesus Christ, 8 whom having not seen you love. Though now you do not see Him, yet believing, you rejoice with joy inexpressible and full of glory, 9 receiving the end of your faith--the salvation of your souls.

Matthew 17:20

²⁰ So Jesus said to them, "Because of your unbelief; for assuredly, I say to you, if you have faith as a mustard seed, you will say to this mountain, 'Move from here to there,' and it will move; and nothing will be impossible for you.

James 5:15

¹⁵ And the prayer of faith will save the sick, and the Lord will raise him up. And if he has committed sins, he will be forgiven.

John 16:33

³³ These things I have spoken to you, that in Me you may have peace. In the world you will have tribulation; but be of good cheer, I have overcome the world."

Ephesians 6:10-18

¹⁰ Finally, my brethren, be strong in the Lord and in the power of His might. ¹¹ Put on the whole armor of God, that you may be able to stand against the wiles of the devil. ¹² For we do not wrestle against flesh and blood, but against principalities, against powers, against the rulers of the darkness of this age, against spiritual hosts of wickedness in the heavenly places. ¹³ Therefore take up the whole armor of God, that you may be able to withstand in the evil day, and having done all, to stand. ¹⁴ Stand therefore, having girded your waist with truth, having put on the breastplate of righteousness, ¹⁵ and having shod your feet with the preparation of the gospel of peace; ¹⁶ above all, taking the shield of faith with which you will be able to quench all the fiery darts of the wicked one. ¹⁷ And take the helmet of salvation, and the sword of the Spirit, which is the word of God; ¹⁸ praying always with all prayer and supplication in the Spirit, being watchful to this end with all perseverance and supplication for all the saints--

James 4:7

⁷ Therefore submit to God. Resist the devil and he will flee from you.

1 Peter 5:9-10

⁹ Resist him, steadfast in the faith, knowing that the same sufferings are experienced by your brotherhood in the world. ¹⁰ But may the God of all grace, who called us to His eternal glory by Christ Jesus, after you have suffered a while, perfect, establish, strengthen, and settle you.

Romans 4:9

9 Does this blessedness then come upon the circumcised only, or upon the uncircumcised also? For we say that faith was accounted to Abraham for righteousness.

Hebrews 11:7

7 By faith Noah, being divinely warned of things not yet seen, moved with godly fear, prepared an ark for the saving of his household, by which he condemned the world and became heir of the righteousness which is according to faith.

Revelation 20:11-15

11 Then I saw a great white throne and Him who sat on it, from whose face the earth and the heaven fled away. And there was found no place for them. 12 And I saw the dead, small and great, standing before God, and books were opened. And another book was opened, which is the Book of Life. And the dead were judged according to their works, by the things which were written in the books. 13 The sea gave up the dead who were in it, and Death and Hades delivered up the dead who were in them. And they were judged, each one according to his works. 14 Then Death and Hades were cast into the lake of fire. This is the second death. 15 And anyone not found written in the Book of Life was cast into the lake of fire.

Romans 3:26

26 to demonstrate at the present time His righteousness, that He might be just and the justifier of the one who has faith in Jesus.

Genesis 15:6

6 And he believed in the Lord, and He accounted it to him for righteousness.

James 2:23

23 And the Scripture was fulfilled which says, "Abraham believed God, and it was accounted to him for righteousness." And he was called the friend of God.

Romans 1:17-32

17 For in it the righteousness of God is revealed from faith to faith; as it is written, "The just shall live by faith." 18 For the wrath of God is revealed from heaven against all ungodliness and unrighteousness

of men, who suppress the truth in unrighteousness, [19] because what may be known of God is manifest in them, for God has shown it to them. [20] For since the creation of the world His invisible attributes are clearly seen, being understood by the things that are made, even His eternal power and Godhead, so that they are without excuse, [21] because, although they knew God, they did not glorify Him as God, nor were thankful, but became futile in their thoughts, and their foolish hearts were darkened. [22] Professing to be wise, they became fools, [23] and changed the glory of the incorruptible God into an image made like corruptible man--and birds and four-footed animals and creeping things. [24] Therefore God also gave them up to uncleanness, in the lusts of their hearts, to dishonor their bodies among themselves, [25] who exchanged the truth of God for the lie, and worshiped and served the creature rather than the Creator, who is blessed forever. Amen. [26] For this reason God gave them up to vile passions. For even their women exchanged the natural use for what is against nature. [27] Likewise also the men, leaving the natural use of the woman, burned in their lust for one another, men with men committing what is shameful, and receiving in themselves the penalty of their error which was due. [28] And even as they did not like to retain God in their knowledge, God gave them over to a debased mind, to do those things which are not fitting; [29] being filled with all unrighteousness, sexual immorality, wickedness, covetousness, maliciousness; full of envy, murder, strife, deceit, evil-mindedness; they are whisperers, [30] backbiters, haters of God, violent, proud, boasters, inventors of evil things, disobedient to parents, [31] undiscerning, untrustworthy, unloving, unforgiving, unmerciful; [32] who, knowing the righteous judgment of God, that those who practice such things are deserving of death, not only do the same but also approve of those who practice them.

Galatians 3:11

[11] But that no one is justified by the law in the sight of God is evident, for "the just shall live by faith."

Hebrews 10:38

[38] Now the just shall live by faith; But if anyone draws back, My soul has no pleasure in him."

Hebrews 10:34-37

[34] for you had compassion on me in my chains, and joyfully accepted the plundering of your goods, knowing that you have a better and an enduring possession for yourselves in heaven. [35] Therefore do not cast away your confidence, which has great reward. [36] For you have need of endurance, so that after you have done the will of God, you may receive the promise: [37] "For yet a little while, And He who is coming will come and will not tarry.

Hebrews 12:2

[2] looking unto Jesus, the author and finisher of our faith, who for the joy that was set before Him endured the cross, despising the shame, and has sat down at the right hand of the throne of God.

Acts 12:1-2

[1] Now about that time Herod the king stretched out his hand to harass some from the church. [2] Then he killed James the brother of John with the sword.

Acts 12:3-16

[3] And because he saw that it pleased the Jews, he proceeded further to seize Peter also. Now it was during the Days of Unleavened Bread. [4] So when he had arrested him, he put him in prison, and delivered him to four squads of soldiers to keep him, intending to bring him before the people after Passover. [5] Peter was therefore kept in prison, but constant prayer was offered to God for him by the church. [6] And when Herod was about to bring him out, that night Peter was sleeping, bound with two chains between two soldiers; and the guards before the door were keeping the prison. [7] Now behold, an angel of the Lord stood by him, and a light shone in the prison; and he struck Peter on the side and raised him up, saying, "Arise quickly!" And his chains fell off his hands. [8] Then the angel said to him, "Gird yourself and tie on your sandals"; and so he did. And he said to him, "Put on your garment and follow me." [9] So he went out and followed him, and did not know that what was done by the angel was real, but thought he was seeing a vision. [10] When they were past the first and the second guard posts, they came to the iron gate that leads to the city, which opened to them of its own accord; and they went out and went down one street, and immediately the angel departed from him. [11] And when Peter had come to himself, he said, "Now I know for certain that

the Lord has sent His angel, and has delivered me from the hand of Herod and from all the expectation of the Jewish people." [12] So, when he had considered this, he came to the house of Mary, the mother of John whose surname was Mark, where many were gathered together praying. [13] And as Peter knocked at the door of the gate, a girl named Rhoda came to answer. [14] When she recognized Peter's voice, because of her gladness she did not open the gate, but ran in and announced that Peter stood before the gate. [15] But they said to her, "You are beside yourself!" Yet she kept insisting that it was so. So they said, "It is his angel." [16] Now Peter continued knocking; and when they opened the door and saw him, they were astonished.

Ephesians 4:13 (NIV)

"Until we all reach unity in the faith and in the knowledge of the Son of God and become mature, attaining to the whole measure of the fullness of Christ."

CHAPTER 4

1 Corinthians 12:12-14

[12] For as the body is one and has many members, but all the members of that one body, being many, are one body, so also is Christ. [13] For by one Spirit we were all baptized into one body--whether Jews or Greeks, whether slaves or free--and have all been made to drink into one Spirit. [14] For in fact the body is not one member but many.

Acts 2:38-45

[38] Then Peter said to them, "Repent, and let every one of you be baptized in the name of Jesus Christ for the remission of sins; and you shall receive the gift of the Holy Spirit. [39] For the promise is to you and to your children, and to all who are afar off, as many as the Lord our God will call." [40] And with many other words he testified and exhorted them, saying, "Be saved from this perverse generation." [41] Then those who gladly received his word were baptized; and that day about three thousand souls were added to them. [42] And they continued steadfastly in the apostles' doctrine and fellowship, in the breaking of bread, and in prayers. [43] Then fear came upon every soul, and many wonders and signs were done through the apostles. [44] Now all who believed were

together, and had all things in common, ⁴⁵ and sold their possessions and goods, and divided them among all, as anyone had need.

Colossians 2:12

¹² buried with Him in baptism, in which you also were raised with Him through faith in the working of God, who raised Him from the dead.

Acts 2:4

⁴ And they were all filled with the Holy Spirit and began to speak with other tongues, as the Spirit gave them utterance.

Matthew 3:11

¹¹ I indeed baptize you with water unto repentance, but He who is coming after me is mightier than I, whose sandals I am not worthy to carry. He will baptize you with the Holy Spirit and fire.

Philippians 3:10

¹⁰ that I may know Him and the power of His resurrection, and the fellowship of His sufferings, being conformed to His death,

1 Thessalonians 3:3-4

³ that no one should be shaken by these afflictions; for you yourselves know that we are appointed to this. ⁴ For, in fact, we told you before when we were with you that we would suffer tribulation, just as it happened, and you know.

John 20:22

²² And when He had said this, He breathed on them, and said to them, "Receive the Holy Spirit.

John 3:3

³ Jesus answered and said to him, "Most assuredly, I say to you, unless one is born again, he cannot see the kingdom of God."

1 Peter 1:23

²³ having been born again, not of corruptible seed but incorruptible, through the word of God which lives and abides forever,

Mark 1:4

⁴ John came baptizing in the wilderness and preaching a baptism of repentance for the remission of sins.

Luke 3:3

³ And he went into all the region around the Jordan, preaching a baptism of repentance for the remission of sins,

Galatians 5:22-23

²² But the fruit of the Spirit is love, joy, peace, longsuffering, kindness, goodness, faithfulness, ²³ gentleness, self-control. Against such there is no law.

1 Corinthians 1:30

³⁰ But of Him you are in Christ Jesus, who became for us wisdom from God--and righteousness and sanctification and redemption--

Acts 2:38

³⁸ Then Peter said to them, "Repent, and let every one of you be baptized in the name of Jesus Christ for the remission of sins; and you shall receive the gift of the Holy Spirit.

Mark 16:16

¹⁶ He who believes and is baptized will be saved; but he who does not believe will be condemned.

Matthew 3:6

⁶ and were baptized by him in the Jordan, confessing their sins.

Acts 1:4-5

⁴ And being assembled together with them, He commanded them not to depart from Jerusalem, but to wait for the Promise of the Father, "which," He said, "you have heard from Me; ⁵ for John truly baptized with water, but you shall be baptized with the Holy Spirit not many days from now."

John 20:22

²² And when He had said this, He breathed on them, and said to them, "Receive the Holy Spirit.

Acts 5:12

¹² And through the hands of the apostles many signs and wonders were done among the people. And they were all with one accord in Solomon's Porch.

Hebrews 12:4-8

⁴ For as we have many members in one body, but all the members do not have the same function, ⁵ so we, being many, are one body in Christ, and individually members of one another. ⁶ Having then gifts differing according to the grace that is given to us, let us use them: if prophecy, let us prophesy in proportion to our faith; ⁷ or ministry, let us use it in our ministering; he who teaches, in teaching; ⁸ he who exhorts, in exhortation; he who gives, with liberality; he who leads, with diligence; he who shows mercy, with cheerfulness.

1 Corinthians 12:1-14

¹ Now concerning spiritual gifts, brethren, I do not want you to be ignorant: ² You know that you were Gentiles, carried away to these dumb idols, however you were led. ³ Therefore I make known to you that no one speaking by the Spirit of God calls Jesus accursed, and no one can say that Jesus is Lord except by the Holy Spirit. ⁴ There are diversities of gifts, but the same Spirit. ⁵ There are differences of ministries, but the same Lord. ⁶ And there are diversities of activities, but it is the same God who works all in all. ⁷ But the manifestation of the Spirit is given to each one for the profit of all: ⁸ for to one is given the word of wisdom through the Spirit, to another the word of knowledge through the same Spirit, ⁹ to another faith by the same Spirit, to another gifts of healings by the same Spirit, ¹⁰ to another the working of miracles, to another prophecy, to another discerning of spirits, to another different kinds of tongues, to another the interpretation of tongues. ¹¹ But one and the same Spirit works all these things, distributing to each one individually as He wills. ¹² For as the body is one and has many members, but all the members of that one body, being many, are one body, so also is Christ. ¹³ For by one Spirit we were all baptized into one body--whether Jews or Greeks, whether slaves or free--and have all been made to drink into one Spirit. ¹⁴ For in fact the body is not one member but many.

Ephesians 4:11-13

And He Himself gave some to be apostles, some prophets, some evangelists, and some pastors and teachers, ¹² for the equipping of the saints for the work of ministry, for the edifying of the body of Christ, ¹³ till we all come to the unity of the faith and of the knowledge of the Son of God, to a perfect man, to the measure of the stature of the fullness of Christ;

Romans 12:3-5

3 For I say, through the grace given to me, to everyone who is among you, not to think of himself more highly than he ought to think, but to think soberly, as God has dealt to each one a measure of faith. 4 For as we have many members in one body, but all the members do not have the same function,

Romans 12:9-10

9 Let love be without hypocrisy. Abhor what is evil. Cling to what is good. 10 Be kindly affectionate to one another with brotherly love, in honor giving preference to one another;

1 Corinthians 12:8

8 for to one is given the word of wisdom through the Spirit, to another the word of knowledge through the same Spirit, 9

1 Corinthians 2:10-16

10 But God has revealed them to us through His Spirit. For the Spirit searches all things, yes, the deep things of God. 11 For what man knows the things of a man except the spirit of the man which is in him? Even so no one knows the things of God except the Spirit of God. 12 Now we have received, not the spirit of the world, but the Spirit who is from God, that we might know the things that have been freely given to us by God. 13 These things we also speak, not in words which man's wisdom teaches but which the Holy Spirit teaches, comparing spiritual things with spiritual. 14 But the natural man does not receive the things of the Spirit of God, for they are foolishness to him; nor can he know them, because they are spiritually discerned. 15 But he who is spiritual judges all things, yet he himself is rightly judged by no one. 16 For "who has known the mind of the Lord that he may instruct Him?" But we have the mind of Christ.

Acts 8:9-24

9 But there was a certain man called Simon, who previously practiced sorcery in the city and astonished the people of Samaria, claiming that he was someone great, 10 to whom they all gave heed, from the least to the greatest, saying, "This man is the great power of God." 11 And they heeded him because he had astonished them with his sorceries for a long time. 12 But when they believed Philip as he preached the things concerning the kingdom of God and the name of Jesus Christ,

both men and women were baptized. [13] Then Simon himself also believed; and when he was baptized he continued with Philip, and was amazed, seeing the miracles and signs which were done. [14] Now when the apostles who were at Jerusalem heard that Samaria had received the word of God, they sent Peter and John to them, [15] who, when they had come down, prayed for them that they might receive the Holy Spirit. [16] For as yet He had fallen upon none of them. They had only been baptized in the name of the Lord Jesus. [17] Then they laid hands on them, and they received the Holy Spirit. [18] And when Simon saw that through the laying on of the apostles' hands the Holy Spirit was given, he offered them money, [19] saying, "Give me this power also, that anyone on whom I lay hands may receive the Holy Spirit." [20] But Peter said to him, "Your money perish with you, because you thought that the gift of God could be purchased with money! [21] You have neither part nor portion in this matter, for your heart is not right in the sight of God. [22] Repent therefore of this your wickedness, and pray God if perhaps the thought of your heart may be forgiven you. [23] For I see that you are poisoned by bitterness and bound by iniquity." [24] Then Simon answered and said, "Pray to the Lord for me, that none of the things which you have spoken may come upon me."

Romans 12:6-7

[6] Having then gifts differing according to the grace that is given to us, let us use them: if prophecy, let us prophesy in proportion to our faith; [7] or ministry, let us use it in our ministering; he who teaches, in teaching;

1 Corinthians 12:8

[8] for to one is given the word of wisdom through the Spirit, to another the word of knowledge through the same Spirit,

1 Corinthians 14:3

[3] But he who prophesies speaks edification and exhortation and comfort to men.

1 Corinthians 14:24-25

[24] But if all prophesy, and an unbeliever or an uninformed person comes in, he is convinced by all, he is convicted by all. [25] And thus the secrets of his heart are revealed; and so, falling down on his face, he will worship God and report that God is truly among you.

Numbers 11:29

²⁹ Then Moses said to him, "Are you zealous for my sake? Oh, that all the Lord's people were prophets and that the Lord would put His Spirit upon them!"

1 Corinthians 12:9-10

⁹ to another faith by the same Spirit, to another gifts of healings by the same Spirit, ¹⁰ to another the working of miracles, to another prophecy, to another discerning of spirits, to another different kinds of tongues, to another the interpretation of tongues.

Romans 10:17

¹⁷ So then faith comes by hearing, and hearing by the word of God.

1 Corinthians 7:7

⁷ For I wish that all men were even as I myself. But each one has his own gift from God, one in this manner and another in that.

1 Corinthians 12:8-10,27-31

⁸ for to one is given the word of wisdom through the Spirit, to another the word of knowledge through the same Spirit, ⁹ to another faith by the same Spirit, to another gifts of healings by the same Spirit, ¹⁰ to another the working of miracles, to another prophecy, to another discerning of spirits, to another different kinds of tongues, to another the interpretation of tongues.

²⁷ Now you are the body of Christ, and members individually. ²⁸ And God has appointed these in the church: first apostles, second prophets, third teachers, after that miracles, then gifts of healings, helps, administrations, varieties of tongues. ²⁹ Are all apostles? Are all prophets? Are all teachers? Are all workers of miracles? ³⁰ Do all have gifts of healings? Do all speak with tongues? Do all interpret? ³¹ But earnestly desire the best gifts. And yet I show you a more excellent way.

1 Corinthians 14:26

²⁶ How is it then, brethren? Whenever you come together, each of you has a psalm, has a teaching, has a tongue, has a revelation, has an interpretation. Let all things be done for edification.

Romans 12:7

⁷ or ministry, let us use it in our ministering; he who teaches, in teaching;

Ephesians 4:11-13

¹¹ And He Himself gave some to be apostles, some prophets, some evangelists, and some pastors and teachers, ¹² for the equipping of the saints for the work of ministry, for the edifying of the body of Christ, ¹³ till we all come to the unity of the faith and of the knowledge of the Son of God, to a perfect man, to the measure of the stature of the fullness of Christ;

Ephesians 5:18-19

¹⁸ And do not be drunk with wine, in which is dissipation; but be filled with the Spirit, ¹⁹ speaking to one another in psalms and hymns and spiritual songs, singing and making melody in your heart to the Lord,

James 3:1

¹ My brethren, let not many of you become teachers, knowing that we shall receive a stricter judgment.

1 Peter 4:9

⁹ Be hospitable to one another without grumbling.

Romans 12:1-2

¹ I beseech you therefore, brethren, by the mercies of God, that you present your bodies a living sacrifice, holy, acceptable to God, which is your reasonable service. ² And do not be conformed to this world, but be transformed by the renewing of your mind, that you may prove what is that good and acceptable and perfect will of God.

Acts 6:1-7

¹ Now in those days, when the number of the disciples was multiplying, there arose a complaint against the Hebrews by the Hellenists, because their widows were neglected in the daily distribution. ² Then the twelve summoned the multitude of the disciples and said, "It is not desirable that we should leave the word of God and serve tables. ³ Therefore, brethren, seek out from among you seven men of good reputation, full of the Holy Spirit and wisdom, whom we may appoint over this business; ⁴ but we will give ourselves continually to prayer and to the ministry of the word." ⁵ And the saying pleased the whole multitude. And they chose Stephen, a man full of faith and the Holy Spirit, and Philip, Prochorus, Nicanor, Timon, Parmenas, and Nicolas, a proselyte from Antioch, ⁶ whom they set before the apostles; and when they had

prayed, they laid hands on them. ⁷ Then the word of God spread, and the number of the disciples multiplied greatly in Jerusalem, and a great many of the priests were obedient to the faith.

1 Corinthians 12:28

²⁸ And God has appointed these in the church: first apostles, second prophets, third teachers, after that miracles, then gifts of healings, helps, administrations, varieties of tongues.

Titus 1:5

⁵ For this reason I left you in Crete, that you should set in order the things that are lacking, and appoint elders in every city as I commanded you--

2 Corinthians 12:1

¹² Truly the signs of an apostle were accomplished among you with all perseverance, in signs and wonders and mighty deeds.

Acts 18:3

³ So, because he was of the same trade, he stayed with them and worked; for by occupation they were tentmakers.

Exodus 30:22-25

²² Moreover the Lord spoke to Moses, saying: ²³ "Also take for yourself quality spices--five hundred shekels of liquid myrrh, half as much sweet-smelling cinnamon (two hundred and fifty shekels), two hundred and fifty shekels of sweet-smelling cane, ²⁴ five hundred shekels of cassia, according to the shekel of the sanctuary, and a hin of olive oil. ²⁵ And you shall make from these a holy anointing oil, an ointment compounded according to the art of the perfumer. It shall be a holy anointing oil.

Exodus 31:3-11

³ And I have filled him with the Spirit of God, in wisdom, in understanding, in knowledge, and in all manner of workmanship, ⁴ to design artistic works, to work in gold, in silver, in bronze, ⁵ in cutting jewels for setting, in carving wood, and to work in all manner of workmanship. ⁶ And I, indeed I, have appointed with him Aholiab the son of Ahisamach, of the tribe of Dan; and I have put wisdom in the hearts of all who are gifted artisans, that they may make all that I have commanded you: ⁷ the tabernacle of meeting, the ark of the Testimony

and the mercy seat that is on it, and all the furniture of the tabernacle--
⁸ the table and its utensils, the pure gold lampstand with all its utensils, the altar of incense, ⁹ the altar of burnt offering with all its utensils, and the laver and its base-- ¹⁰ the garments of ministry, the holy garments for Aaron the priest and the garments of his sons, to minister as priests, ¹¹ and the anointing oil and sweet incense for the holy place. According to all that I have commanded you they shall do."

2 Chronicles 34:9-13

⁹ When they came to Hilkiah the high priest, they delivered the money that was brought into the house of God, which the Levites who kept the doors had gathered from the hand of Manasseh and Ephraim, from all the remnant of Israel, from all Judah and Benjamin, and which they had brought back to Jerusalem. ¹⁰ Then they put it in the hand of the foremen who had the oversight of the house of the Lord; and they gave it to the workmen who worked in the house of the Lord, to repair and restore the house. ¹¹ They gave it to the craftsmen and builders to buy hewn stone and timber for beams, and to floor the houses which the kings of Judah had destroyed. ¹² And the men did the work faithfully. Their overseers were Jahath and Obadiah the Levites, of the sons of Merari, and Zechariah and Meshullam, of the sons of the Kohathites, to supervise. Others of the Levites, all of whom were skillful with instruments of music, ¹³ were over the burden bearers and were overseers of all who did work in any kind of service. And some of the Levites were scribes, officers, and gatekeepers.

Acts 8:5-6

⁵ Then Philip went down to the city of Samaria and preached Christ to them. ⁶ And the multitudes with one accord heeded the things spoken by Philip, hearing and seeing the miracles which he did.

Acts 21:8

⁸ On the next day we who were Paul's companions departed and came to Caesarea, and entered the house of Philip the evangelist, who was one of the seven, and stayed with him.

Acts 6:5

⁵ And the saying pleased the whole multitude. And they chose Stephen, a man full of faith and the Holy Spirit, and Philip, Prochorus, Nicanor, Timon, Parmenas, and Nicolas, a proselyte from Antioch,

Romans 10:15

¹⁵ And how shall they preach unless they are sent? As it is written: "How beautiful are the feet of those who preach the gospel of peace, Who bring glad tidings of good things!"

Ephesians 4:11

¹¹ And He Himself gave some to be apostles, some prophets, some evangelists, and some pastors and teachers,

Acts 11:22-26

²² Then news of these things came to the ears of the church in Jerusalem, and they sent out Barnabas to go as far as Antioch. ²³ When he came and had seen the grace of God, he was glad, and encouraged them all that with purpose of heart they should continue with the Lord. ²⁴ For he was a good man, full of the Holy Spirit and of faith. And a great many people were added to the Lord. ²⁵ Then Barnabas departed for Tarsus to seek Saul. ²⁶ And when he had found him, he brought him to Antioch. So it was that for a whole year they assembled with the church and taught a great many people. And the disciples were first called Christians in Antioch.

Romans 12:8

⁸ he who exhorts, in exhortation; he who gives, with liberality; he who leads, with diligence; he who shows mercy, with cheerfulness.

1 Thessalonians 2:11-12

¹¹ as you know how we exhorted, and comforted, and charged every one of you, as a father does his own children, ¹² that you would walk worthy of God who calls you into His own kingdom and glory.

2 Timothy 4:2

² Preach the word! Be ready in season and out of season. Convince, rebuke, exhort, with all longsuffering and teaching.

Hebrews 10:25

²⁵ not forsaking the assembling of ourselves together, as is the manner of some, but exhorting one another, and so much the more as you see the Day approaching.

Acts 4:30-37

[30] by stretching out Your hand to heal, and that signs and wonders may be done through the name of Your holy Servant Jesus." [31] And when they had prayed, the place where they were assembled together was shaken; and they were all filled with the Holy Spirit, and they spoke the word of God with boldness. [32] Now the multitude of those who believed were of one heart and one soul; neither did anyone say that any of the things he possessed was his own, but they had all things in common. [33] And with great power the apostles gave witness to the resurrection of the Lord Jesus. And great grace was upon them all. [34] Nor was there anyone among them who lacked; for all who were possessors of lands or houses sold them, and brought the proceeds of the things that were sold, [35] and laid them at the apostles' feet; and they distributed to each as anyone had need. [36] And Joses, who was also named Barnabas by the apostles (which is translated Son of Encouragement), a Levite of the country of Cyprus, [37] having land, sold it, and brought the money and laid it at the apostles' feet.

Acts 9:36-39

[36] At Joppa there was a certain disciple named Tabitha, which is translated Dorcas. This woman was full of good works and charitable deeds which she did. [37] But it happened in those days that she became sick and died. When they had washed her, they laid her in an upper room. [38] And since Lydda was near Joppa, and the disciples had heard that Peter was there, they sent two men to him, imploring him not to delay in coming to them. [39] Then Peter arose and went with them. When he had come, they brought him to the upper room. And all the widows stood by him weeping, showing the tunics and garments which Dorcas had made while she was with them.

2 Corinthians 8:1-15

[1] Moreover, brethren, we make known to you the grace of God bestowed on the churches of Macedonia: [2] that in a great trial of affliction the abundance of their joy and their deep poverty abounded in the riches of their liberality. [3] For I bear witness that according to their ability, yes, and beyond their ability, they were freely willing, [4] imploring us with much urgency that we would receive the gift and the fellowship of the ministering to the saints. [5] And not only as we had hoped, but they first gave themselves to the Lord, and then to us by the will of God. [6] So we urged Titus, that as he had begun, so he would also complete

this grace in you as well. [7] But as you abound in everything--in faith, in speech, in knowledge, in all diligence, and in your love for us--see that you abound in this grace also. [8] I speak not by commandment, but I am testing the sincerity of your love by the diligence of others. [9] For you know the grace of our Lord Jesus Christ, that though He was rich, yet for your sakes He became poor, that you through His poverty might become rich. [10] And in this I give advice: It is to your advantage not only to be doing what you began and were desiring to do a year ago; [11] but now you also must complete the doing of it; that as there was a readiness to desire it, so there also may be a completion out of what you have. [12] For if there is first a willing mind, it is accepted according to what one has, and not according to what he does not have. [13] For I do not mean that others should be eased and you burdened; [14] but by an equality, that now at this time your abundance may supply their lack, that their abundance also may supply your lack--that there may be equality. [15] As it is written, "He who gathered much had nothing left over, and he who gathered little had no lack."

2 Corinthians 5:9-11

[9] Therefore we make it our aim, whether present or absent, to be well pleasing to Him. [10] For we must all appear before the judgment seat of Christ, that each one may receive the things done in the body, according to what he has done, whether good or bad. [11] Knowing, therefore, the terror of the Lord, we persuade men; but we are well known to God, and I also trust are well known in your consciences.

1 Timothy 6:17-19

[17] Command those who are rich in this present age not to be haughty, nor to trust in uncertain riches but in the living God, who gives us richly all things to enjoy. [18] Let them do good, that they be rich in good works, ready to give, willing to share, [19] storing up for themselves a good foundation for the time to come, that they may lay hold on eternal life.

Romans 16:1-2

[1] I commend to you Phoebe our sister, who is a servant of the church in Cenchrea, [2] that you may receive her in the Lord in a manner worthy of the saints, and assist her in whatever business she has need of you; for indeed she has been a helper of many and of myself also.

1 Corinthians 12:28

[28] And God has appointed these in the church: first apostles, second prophets, third teachers, after that miracles, then gifts of healings, helps, administrations, varieties of tongues.

Philippians 2:24-30

[24] But I trust in the Lord that I myself shall also come shortly. [25] Yet I considered it necessary to send to you Epaphroditus, my brother, fellow worker, and fellow soldier, but your messenger and the one who ministered to my need; [26] since he was longing for you all, and was distressed because you had heard that he was sick. [27] For indeed he was sick almost unto death; but God had mercy on him, and not only on him but on me also, lest I should have sorrow upon sorrow. [28] Therefore I sent him the more eagerly, that when you see him again you may rejoice, and I may be less sorrowful. [29] Receive him therefore in the Lord with all gladness, and hold such men in esteem; [30] because for the work of Christ he came close to death, not regarding his life, to supply what was lacking in your service toward me.

Philemon 1:11

[11] who once was unprofitable to you, but now is profitable to you and to me.

Acts 21:4,7-8

[4] And finding disciples, we stayed there seven days. They told Paul through the Spirit not to go up to Jerusalem.

[7] And when we had finished our voyage from Tyre, we came to Ptolemais, greeted the brethren, and stayed with them one day. [8] On the next day we who were Paul's companions departed and came to Caesarea, and entered the house of Philip the evangelist, who was one of the seven, and stayed with him.

Romans 12:13

[13] distributing to the needs of the saints, given to hospitality.

Romans 16:23

[23] Gaius, my host and the host of the whole church, greets you. Erastus, the treasurer of the city, greets you, and Quartus, a brother.

1 Timothy 3:2

² A bishop then must be blameless, the husband of one wife, temperate, sober-minded, of good behavior, hospitable, able to teach;

Hebrews 12:1-2

¹ Therefore we also, since we are surrounded by so great a cloud of witnesses, let us lay aside every weight, and the sin which so easily ensnares us, and let us run with endurance the race that is set before us, ² looking unto Jesus, the author and finisher of our faith, who for the joy that was set before Him endured the cross, despising the shame, and has sat down at the right hand of the throne of God.

1 Peter 4:9

⁹ Be hospitable to one another without grumbling.

Acts 12:15-17

¹⁵ But they said to her, "You are beside yourself!" Yet she kept insisting that it was so. So they said, "It is his angel." ¹⁶ Now Peter continued knocking; and when they opened the door and saw him, they were astonished. ¹⁷ But motioning to them with his hand to keep silent, he declared to them how the Lord had brought him out of the prison. And he said, "Go, tell these things to James and to the brethren." And he departed and went to another place.

Acts 16:25-31

²⁵ But at midnight Paul and Silas were praying and singing hymns to God, and the prisoners were listening to them. ²⁶ Suddenly there was a great earthquake, so that the foundations of the prison were shaken; and immediately all the doors were opened and everyone's chains were loosed. ²⁷ And the keeper of the prison, awaking from sleep and seeing the prison doors open, supposing the prisoners had fled, drew his sword and was about to kill himself. ²⁸ But Paul called with a loud voice, saying, "Do yourself no harm, for we are all here." ²⁹ Then he called for a light, ran in, and fell down trembling before Paul and Silas. ³⁰ And he brought them out and said, "Sirs, what must I do to be saved?" ³¹ So they said, "Believe on the Lord Jesus Christ, and you will be saved, you and your household."

1 Timothy 2:1-8

¹ Therefore I exhort first of all that supplications, prayers, intercessions, and giving of thanks be made for all men, ² for kings and all who are

in authority, that we may lead a quiet and peaceable life in all godliness and reverence. [3] For this is good and acceptable in the sight of God our Savior, [4] who desires all men to be saved and to come to the knowledge of the truth. [5] For there is one God and one Mediator between God and men, the Man Christ Jesus, [6] who gave Himself a ransom for all, to be testified in due time, [7] for which I was appointed a preacher and an apostle--I am speaking the truth in Christ and not lying--a teacher of the Gentiles in faith and truth. [8] I desire therefore that the men pray everywhere, lifting up holy hands, without wrath and doubting;

James 5:14-16

[14] Is anyone among you sick? Let him call for the elders of the church, and let them pray over him, anointing him with oil in the name of the Lord. [15] And the prayer of faith will save the sick, and the Lord will raise him up. And if he has committed sins, he will be forgiven. [16] Confess your trespasses to one another, and pray for one another, that you may be healed. The effective, fervent prayer of a righteous man avails much.

Romans 12:8

[8] he who exhorts, in exhortation; he who gives, with liberality; he who leads, with diligence; he who shows mercy, with cheerfulness.

Acts 15:7-11

[7] And when there had been much dispute, Peter rose up and said to them: "Men and brethren, you know that a good while ago God chose among us, that by my mouth the Gentiles should hear the word of the gospel and believe. [8] So God, who knows the heart, acknowledged them by giving them the Holy Spirit, just as He did to us, [9] and made no distinction between us and them, purifying their hearts by faith. [10] Now therefore, why do you test God by putting a yoke on the neck of the disciples which neither our fathers nor we were able to bear? [11] But we believe that through the grace of the Lord Jesus Christ we shall be saved in the same manner as they."

1 Timothy 5:17

[17] Let the elders who rule well be counted worthy of double honor, especially those who labor in the word and doctrine.

Hebrews 13:17

[17] Obey those who rule over you, and be submissive, for they watch out for your souls, as those who must give account. Let them do so with joy and not with grief, for that would be unprofitable for you.

Acts 9:36

[36] At Joppa there was a certain disciple named Tabitha, which is translated Dorcas. This woman was full of good works and charitable deeds which she did.

Acts 16:33-34

[33] And he took them the same hour of the night and washed their stripes. And immediately he and all his family were baptized. [34] Now when he had brought them into his house, he set food before them; and he rejoiced, having believed in God with all his household.

Romans 12:8

[8] he who exhorts, in exhortation; he who gives, with liberality; he who leads, with diligence; he who shows mercy, with cheerfulness.

Acts 13:2-3

[2] As they ministered to the Lord and fasted, the Holy Spirit said, "Now separate to Me Barnabas and Saul for the work to which I have called them." [3] Then, having fasted and prayed, and laid hands on them, they sent them away.

Romans 10:15

[15] And how shall they preach unless they are sent? As it is written: "How beautiful are the feet of those who preach the gospel of peace, Who bring glad tidings of good things!"

1 Corinthians 9:19-23

[19] For though I am free from all men, I have made myself a servant to all, that I might win the more; [20] and to the Jews I became as a Jew, that I might win Jews; to those who are under the law, as under the law, that I might win those who are under the law; [21] to those who are without law, as without law (not being without law toward God, but under law toward Christ), that I might win those who are without law; [22] to the weak I became as weak, that I might win the weak. I have become all things to all men, that I might by all means save some. [23] Now this I do for the gospel's sake, that I may be partaker of it with you.

Ephesians 3:1-7

¹ For this reason I, Paul, the prisoner of Christ Jesus for you Gentiles-- ² if indeed you have heard of the dispensation of the grace of God which was given to me for you, ³ how that by revelation He made known to me the mystery (as I have briefly written already, ⁴ by which, when you read, you may understand my knowledge in the mystery of Christ), ⁵ which in other ages was not made known to the sons of men, as it has now been revealed by the Spirit to His holy apostles and prophets: ⁶ that the Gentiles should be fellow heirs, of the same body, and partakers of His promise in Christ through the gospel, ⁷ of which I became a minister according to the gift of the grace of God given to me by the effective working of His power.

2 Chronicles 5:12-13

¹² and the Levites who were the singers, all those of Asaph and Heman and Jeduthun, with their sons and their brethren, stood at the east end of the altar, clothed in white linen, having cymbals, stringed instruments and harps, and with them one hundred and twenty priests sounding with trumpets-- ¹³ indeed it came to pass, when the trumpeters and singers were as one, to make one sound to be heard in praising and thanking the Lord, and when they lifted up their voice with the trumpets and cymbals and instruments of music, and praised the Lord, saying: "For He is good, For His mercy endures forever," that the house, the house of the Lord, was filled with a cloud,

2 Chronicles 34:12

¹² And the men did the work faithfully. Their overseers were Jahath and Obadiah the Levites, of the sons of Merari, and Zechariah and Meshullam, of the sons of the Kohathites, to supervise. Others of the Levites, all of whom were skillful with instruments of music,

Psalm 101

¹ A Psalm of David. I will sing of mercy and justice; To You, O Lord, I will sing praises. ² I will behave wisely in a perfect way. Oh, when will You come to me? I will walk within my house with a perfect heart. ³ I will set nothing wicked before my eyes; I hate the work of those who fall away; It shall not cling to me. ⁴ A perverse heart shall depart from me; I will not know wickedness. ⁵ Whoever secretly slanders his neighbor, Him I will destroy; The one who has a haughty look and a proud heart, Him I will not endure. ⁶ My eyes shall be on the faithful

of the land, That they may dwell with me; He who walks in a perfect way, He shall serve me. ⁷ He who works deceit shall not dwell within my house; He who tells lies shall not continue in my presence. ⁸ Early I will destroy all the wicked of the land, That I may cut off all the evildoers from the city of the Lord.

Psalm 150

¹ Praise the Lord! Praise God in His sanctuary; Praise Him in His mighty firmament! ² Praise Him for His mighty acts; Praise Him according to His excellent greatness! ³ Praise Him with the sound of the trumpet; Praise Him with the lute and harp! ⁴ Praise Him with the timbrel and dance; Praise Him with stringed instruments and flutes! ⁵ Praise Him with loud cymbals; Praise Him with clashing cymbals! ⁶ Let everything that has breath praise the Lord. Praise the Lord!

1 Corinthians 14:26

²⁶ How is it then, brethren? Whenever you come together, each of you has a psalm, has a teaching, has a tongue, has a revelation, has an interpretation. Let all things be done for edification.

Acts 9:36-43

³⁶ At Joppa there was a certain disciple named Tabitha, which is translated Dorcas. This woman was full of good works and charitable deeds which she did. ³⁷ But it happened in those days that she became sick and died. When they had washed her, they laid her in an upper room. ³⁸ And since Lydda was near Joppa, and the disciples had heard that Peter was there, they sent two men to him, imploring him not to delay in coming to them. ³⁹ Then Peter arose and went with them. When he had come, they brought him to the upper room. And all the widows stood by him weeping, showing the tunics and garments which Dorcas had made while she was with them. ⁴⁰ But Peter put them all out, and knelt down and prayed. And turning to the body he said, "Tabitha, arise." And she opened her eyes, and when she saw Peter she sat up. ⁴¹ Then he gave her his hand and lifted her up; and when he had called the saints and widows, he presented her alive. ⁴² And it became known throughout all Joppa, and many believed on the Lord. ⁴³ So it was that he stayed many days in Joppa with Simon, a tanner.

Romans 12:7

7 or ministry, let us use it in our ministering; he who teaches, in teaching;

Romans 15:26-33

26 For it pleased those from Macedonia and Achaia to make a certain contribution for the poor among the saints who are in Jerusalem. 27 It pleased them indeed, and they are their debtors. For if the Gentiles have been partakers of their spiritual things, their duty is also to minister to them in material things. 28 Therefore, when I have performed this and have sealed to them this fruit, I shall go by way of you to Spain. 29 But I know that when I come to you, I shall come in the fullness of the blessing of the gospel of Christ. 30 Now I beg you, brethren, through the Lord Jesus Christ, and through the love of the Spirit, that you strive together with me in prayers to God for me, 31 that I may be delivered from those in Judea who do not believe, and that my service for Jerusalem may be acceptable to the saints, 32 that I may come to you with joy by the will of God, and may be refreshed together with you. 33 Now the God of peace be with you all. Amen.

Galatians 6:10

10 Therefore, as we have opportunity, let us do good to all, especially to those who are of the household of faith.

2 Timothy 1:16-18

16 The Lord grant mercy to the household of Onesiphorus, for he often refreshed me, and was not ashamed of my chain; 17 but when he arrived in Rome, he sought me out very zealously and found me. 18 The Lord grant to him that he may find mercy from the Lord in that Day--and you know very well how many ways he ministered to me at Ephesus.

Acts 15:35

35 Paul and Barnabas also remained in Antioch, teaching and preaching the word of the Lord, with many others also.

Acts 18:24-28

24 Now a certain Jew named Apollos, born at Alexandria, an eloquent man and mighty in the Scriptures, came to Ephesus. 25 This man had been instructed in the way of the Lord; and being fervent in spirit, he spoke and taught accurately the things of the Lord, though he knew only the baptism of John. 26 So he began to speak boldly in the

synagogue. When Aquila and Priscilla heard him, they took him aside and explained to him the way of God more accurately. [27] And when he desired to cross to Achaia, the brethren wrote, exhorting the disciples to receive him; and when he arrived, he greatly helped those who had believed through grace; [28] for he vigorously refuted the Jews publicly, showing from the Scriptures that Jesus is the Christ.

Acts 19:8-10

[8] And he went into the synagogue and spoke boldly for three months, reasoning and persuading concerning the things of the kingdom of God. [9] But when some were hardened and did not believe, but spoke evil of the Way before the multitude, he departed from them and withdrew the disciples, reasoning daily in the school of Tyrannus. [10] And this continued for two years, so that all who dwelt in Asia heard the word of the Lord Jesus, both Jews and Greeks.

Ephesians 4:11-15

[11] And He Himself gave some to be apostles, some prophets, some evangelists, and some pastors and teachers, [12] for the equipping of the saints for the work of ministry, for the edifying of the body of Christ, [13] till we all come to the unity of the faith and of the knowledge of the Son of God, to a perfect man, to the measure of the stature of the fullness of Christ; [14] that we should no longer be children, tossed to and fro and carried about with every wind of doctrine, by the trickery of men, in the cunning craftiness of deceitful plotting, [15] but, speaking the truth in love, may grow up in all things into Him who is the head--Christ--

Colossians 3:16

[16] Let the word of Christ dwell in you richly in all wisdom, teaching and admonishing one another in psalms and hymns and spiritual songs, singing with grace in your hearts to the Lord.

1 Timothy 3:2

[2] A bishop then must be blameless, the husband of one wife, temperate, sober-minded, of good behavior, hospitable, able to teach;

2 Timothy 2:2

[2] And the things that you have heard from me among many witnesses, commit these to faithful men who will be able to teach others also.

Titus 2:3-5

3 the older women likewise, that they be reverent in behavior, not slanderers, not given to much wine, teachers of good things-- 4 that they admonish the young women to love their husbands, to love their children, 5 to be discreet, chaste, homemakers, good, obedient to their own husbands, that the word of God may not be blasphemed.

James 3:1

1 My brethren, let not many of you become teachers, knowing that we shall receive a stricter judgment.

1 Corinthians 7:7

7 For I wish that all men were even as I myself. But each one has his own gift from God, one in this manner and another in that.

1 Corinthians 13:3

3 And though I bestow all my goods to feed the poor, and though I give my body to be burned, but have not love, it profits me nothing.

1 Peter 4:9

9 Be hospitable to one another without grumbling. 1

1 Corinthians 7:7

7 For I wish that all men were even as I myself. But each one has his own gift from God, one in this manner and another in that.

Psalm 139:23-24

23 Search me, O God, and know my heart; Try me, and know my anxieties; 24 And see if there is any wicked way in me, And lead me in the way everlasting.

Acts 2:2,4

2 And suddenly there came a sound from heaven, as of a rushing mighty wind, and it filled the whole house where they were sitting. 4 And they were all filled with the Holy Spirit and began to speak with other tongues, as the Spirit gave them utterance.

Acts 10:44

44 While Peter was still speaking these words, the Holy Spirit fell upon all those who heard the word.

Acts 8:17

[17] Then they laid hands on them, and they received the Holy Spirit.

Acts 9:17

[17] And Ananias went his way and entered the house; and laying his hands on him he said, "Brother Saul, the Lord Jesus, who appeared to you on the road as you came, has sent me that you may receive your sight and be filled with the Holy Spirit."

Acts 19:6

[6] And when Paul had laid hands on them, the Holy Spirit came upon them, and they spoke with tongues and prophesied.

Matthew 28:19

[19] Go therefore and make disciples of all the nations, baptizing them in the name of the Father and of the Son and of the Holy Spirit,

Matthew 3:16-17

[16] When He had been baptized, Jesus came up immediately from the water; and behold, the heavens were opened to Him, and He saw the Spirit of God descending like a dove and alighting upon Him. [17] And suddenly a voice came from heaven, saying, "This is My beloved Son, in whom I am well pleased."

Acts 2:33

[33] Therefore being exalted to the right hand of God, and having received from the Father the promise of the Holy Spirit, He poured out this which you now see and hear.

1 John 5:7

[7] For there are three that bear witness in heaven: the Father, the Word, and the Holy Spirit; and these three are one.

2 Corinthians 13:14

[14] The grace of the Lord Jesus Christ, and the love of God, and the communion of the Holy Spirit be with you all. Amen.

Hebrews 9:14

[14] how much more shall the blood of Christ, who through the eternal Spirit offered Himself without spot to God, cleanse your conscience from dead works to serve the living God?

John 14:21

²¹ He who has My commandments and keeps them, it is he who loves Me. And he who loves Me will be loved by My Father, and I will love him and manifest Myself to him."

John 16:12-13

¹² I still have many things to say to you, but you cannot bear them now. ¹³ However, when He, the Spirit of truth, has come, He will guide you into all truth; for He will not speak on His own authority, but whatever He hears He will speak; and He will tell you things to come.

1 Corinthians 2:10-11

¹⁰ But God has revealed them to us through His Spirit. For the Spirit searches all things, yes, the deep things of God. ¹¹ For what man knows the things of a man except the spirit of the man which is in him? Even so no one knows the things of God except the Spirit of God.

Luke 1:35,37

³⁵ And the angel answered and said to her, "The Holy Spirit will come upon you, and the power of the Highest will overshadow you; therefore, also, that Holy One who is to be born will be called the Son of God.
³⁷ For with God nothing will be impossible."

Psalm 139:7-10

⁷ Where can I go from Your Spirit? Or where can I flee from Your presence? ⁸ If I ascend into heaven, You are there; If I make my bed in hell, behold, You are there. ⁹ If I take the wings of the morning, And dwell in the uttermost parts of the sea, ¹⁰ Even there Your hand shall lead me, And Your right hand shall hold me.

Genesis 1:2

² The earth was without form, and void; and darkness was on the face of the deep. And the Spirit of God was hovering over the face of the waters.

Psalm 104:30

³⁰ You send forth Your Spirit, they are created; And You renew the face of the earth.

John 3:5-6

[5] Jesus answered, "Most assuredly, I say to you, unless one is born of water and the Spirit, he cannot enter the kingdom of God. [6] That which is born of the flesh is flesh, and that which is born of the Spirit is spirit.

John 20:22

[22] And when He had said this, He breathed on them, and said to them, "Receive the Holy Spirit.

2 Timothy 3:16-17

[16] All Scripture is given by inspiration of God, and is profitable for doctrine, for reproof, for correction, for instruction in righteousness, [17] that the man of God may be complete, thoroughly equipped for every good work.

Romans 8:11

[11] But if the Spirit of Him who raised Jesus from the dead dwells in you, He who raised Christ from the dead will also give life to your mortal bodies through His Spirit who dwells in you.

Acts 5:3-4

[3] But Peter said, "Ananias, why has Satan filled your heart to lie to the Holy Spirit and keep back part of the price of the land for yourself? [4] While it remained, was it not your own? And after it was sold, was it not in your own control? Why have you conceived this thing in your heart? You have not lied to men but to God."

2 Corinthians 3:17

[17] Now the Lord is the Spirit; and where the Spirit of the Lord is, there is liberty.

Exodus 34:34

[34] But whenever Moses went in before the Lord to speak with Him, he would take the veil off until he came out; and he would come out and speak to the children of Israel whatever he had been commanded.

Ephesians 1:1

[1] Paul, an apostle of Jesus Christ by the will of God,

1 Corinthians 12:11

[11] But one and the same Spirit works all these things, distributing to each one individually as He wills.

John 3:5-6

[5] Jesus answered, "Most assuredly, I say to you, unless one is born of water and the Spirit, he cannot enter the kingdom of God. [6] That which is born of the flesh is flesh, and that which is born of the Spirit is spirit.

John 20:22

[22] And when He had said this, He breathed on them, and said to them, "Receive the Holy Spirit.

Acts 4:8,31

[8] Then Peter, filled with the Holy Spirit, said to them, "Rulers of the people and elders of Israel:
[31] And when they had prayed, the place where they were assembled together was shaken; and they were all filled with the Holy Spirit, and they spoke the word of God with boldness.

Acts 9:17

[17] And Ananias went his way and entered the house; and laying his hands on him he said, "Brother Saul, the Lord Jesus, who appeared to you on the road as you came, has sent me that you may receive your sight and be filled with the Holy Spirit."

Luke 11:15,41

[15] But some of them said, "He casts out demons by Beelzebub , the ruler of the demons."
[41] But rather give alms of such things as you have; then indeed all things are clean to you.

Ephesians 4:11-13

[11] And He Himself gave some to be apostles, some prophets, some evangelists, and some pastors and teachers, [12] for the equipping of the saints for the work of ministry, for the edifying of the body of Christ,
[13] till we all come to the unity of the faith and of the knowledge of the Son of God, to a perfect man, to the measure of the stature of the fullness of Christ;

James 3:1

¹ My brethren, let not many of you become teachers, knowing that we shall receive a stricter judgment.

1 Corinthians 7:7

⁷ For I wish that all men were even as I myself. But each one has his own gift from God, one in this manner and another in that.

1 Corinthians 13:3

³ And though I bestow all my goods to feed the poor, and though I give my body to be burned, but have not love, it profits me nothing.

1 Peter 4:9

⁹ Be hospitable to one another without grumbling.

2 Thessalonians 3:3

³ But the Lord is faithful, who will establish you and guard you from the evil one.

Psalm 118:17

¹⁷ I shall not die, but live, And declare the works of the Lord.

Romans 8:14

¹⁴ For as many as are led by the Spirit of God, these are sons of God.

Acts 16:6-7

⁶ Now when they had gone through Phrygia and the region of Galatia, they were forbidden by the Holy Spirit to preach the word in Asia. ⁷ After they had come to Mysia, they tried to go into Bithynia, but the Spirit did not permit them.

1 Corinthians 2:12-13

¹² Now we have received, not the spirit of the world, but the Spirit who is from God, that we might know the things that have been freely given to us by God. ¹³ These things we also speak, not in words which man's wisdom teaches but which the Holy Spirit teaches, comparing spiritual things with spiritual.

1 Corinthians 2:10,13

¹⁰ But God has revealed them to us through His Spirit. For the Spirit searches all things, yes, the deep things of God.

[13] These things we also speak, not in words which man's wisdom teaches but which the Holy Spirit teaches, comparing spiritual things with spiritual.

Acts 13:2-4

[2] As they ministered to the Lord and fasted, the Holy Spirit said, "Now separate to Me Barnabas and Saul for the work to which I have called them." [3] Then, having fasted and prayed, and laid hands on them, they sent them away. [4] So, being sent out by the Holy Spirit, they went down to Seleucia, and from there they sailed to Cyprus.

1 Thessalonians 5:19

Do not quench the Spirit.

1 Corinthians 12:13

[13] For by one Spirit we were all baptized into one body--whether Jews or Greeks, whether slaves or free--and have all been made to drink into one Spirit.

Acts 13:2-4

[2] As they ministered to the Lord and fasted, the Holy Spirit said, "Now separate to Me Barnabas and Saul for the work to which I have called them." [3] Then, having fasted and prayed, and laid hands on them, they sent them away. [4] So, being sent out by the Holy Spirit, they went down to Seleucia, and from there they sailed to Cyprus.

2 Samuel 23:2

[2] "The Spirit of the Lord spoke by me, And His word was on my tongue.

Nehemiah 9:30

[30] Yet for many years You had patience with them, And testified against them by Your Spirit in Your prophets. Yet they would not listen; Therefore You gave them into the hand of the peoples of the lands.

Zechariah 7:12

[12] Yes, they made their hearts like flint, refusing to hear the law and the words which the Lord of hosts had sent by His Spirit through the former prophets. Thus great wrath came from the Lord of hosts.

John 14:17

[17] the Spirit of truth, whom the world cannot receive, because it neither sees Him nor knows Him; but you know Him, for He dwells with you and will be in you.

Exodus 31:2-3

[2] "See, I have called by name Bezalel the son of Uri, the son of Hur, of the tribe of Judah. [3] And I have filled him with the Spirit of God, in wisdom, in understanding, in knowledge, and in all manner of workmanship,

Judges 13:25

[25] And the Spirit of the Lord began to move upon him at Mahaneh Dan between Zorah and Eshtaol.

Acts 1:8

[8] But you shall receive power when the Holy Spirit has come upon you; and you shall be witnesses to Me in Jerusalem, and in all Judea and Samaria, and to the end of the earth."

Luke 4:1

[1] Then Jesus, being filled with the Holy Spirit, returned from the Jordan and was led by the Spirit into the wilderness,

Acts 2:4

[4] And they were all filled with the Holy Spirit and began to speak with other tongues, as the Spirit gave them utterance.

Ephesians 5:18

[18] And do not be drunk with wine, in which is dissipation; but be filled with the Spirit,

2 Corinthians 1:22

[22] who also has sealed us and given us the Spirit in our hearts as a guarantee.

Ephesians 5:5

[5] For this you know, that no fornicator, unclean person, nor covetous man, who is an idolater, has any inheritance in the kingdom of Christ and God.

Ephesians1:14

[14] who is the guarantee of our inheritance until the redemption of the purchased possession, to the praise of His glory.

2 Timothy 1:14

[14] That good thing which was committed to you, keep by the Holy Spirit who dwells in us.

John 14:16,26

[16] And I will pray the Father, and He will give you another Helper, that He may abide with you forever--
[26] But the Helper, the Holy Spirit, whom the Father will send in My name, He will teach you all things, and bring to your remembrance all things that I said to you.

John 15:26

[26] "But when the Helper comes, whom I shall send to you from the Father, the Spirit of truth who proceeds from the Father, He will testify of Me.

John 16:7

[7] Nevertheless I tell you the truth. It is to your advantage that I go away; for if I do not go away, the Helper will not come to you; but if I depart, I will send Him to you.

1 Corinthians 2:10-13

[10] But God has revealed them to us through His Spirit. For the Spirit searches all things, yes, the deep things of God. [11] For what man knows the things of a man except the spirit of the man which is in him? Even so no one knows the things of God except the Spirit of God. [12] Now we have received, not the spirit of the world, but the Spirit who is from God, that we might know the things that have been freely given to us by God. [13] These things we also speak, not in words which man's wisdom teaches but which the Holy Spirit teaches, comparing spiritual things with spiritual.

Romans 8:9-11

[9] But you are not in the flesh but in the Spirit, if indeed the Spirit of God dwells in you. Now if anyone does not have the Spirit of Christ, he is not His. [10] And if Christ is in you, the body is dead because of sin, but the Spirit is life because of righteousness. [11] But if the Spirit

of Him who raised Jesus from the dead dwells in you, He who raised Christ from the dead will also give life to your mortal bodies through His Spirit who dwells in you.

1 Corinthians 3:16

[16] Do you not know that you are the temple of God and that the Spirit of God dwells in you?

1 Corinthians 6:19

[19] Or do you not know that your body is the temple of the Holy Spirit who is in you, whom you have from God, and you are not your own?

Romans 8:26-28

[26] Likewise the Spirit also helps in our weaknesses. For we do not know what we should pray for as we ought, but the Spirit Himself makes intercession for us with groanings which cannot be uttered. [27] Now He who searches the hearts knows what the mind of the Spirit is, because He makes intercession for the saints according to the will of God. [28] And we know that all things work together for good to those who love God, to those who are the called according to His purpose.

Galatians 5:22-23

[22] But the fruit of the Spirit is love, joy, peace, longsuffering, kindness, goodness, faithfulness, [23] gentleness, self-control. Against such there is no law.

Galatians 5:16,18,25

[16] I say then: Walk in the Spirit, and you shall not fulfill the lust of the flesh.
[18] But if you are led by the Spirit, you are not under the law.
[25] If we live in the Spirit, let us also walk in the Spirit.

John 3:5-6,8

[5] Jesus answered, "Most assuredly, I say to you, unless one is born of water and the Spirit, he cannot enter the kingdom of God. [6] That which is born of the flesh is flesh, and that which is born of the Spirit is spirit.
[8] The wind blows where it wishes, and you hear the sound of it, but cannot tell where it comes from and where it goes. So is everyone who is born of the Spirit."

Genesis 6:3

³ And the Lord said, "My Spirit shall not strive with man forever, for he is indeed flesh; yet his days shall be one hundred and twenty years."

John 16:8-10

⁸ And when He has come, He will convict the world of sin, and of righteousness, and of judgment: ⁹ of sin, because they do not believe in Me; ¹⁰ of righteousness, because I go to My Father and you see Me no more;

Acts 7:51

⁵¹ "You stiffnecked and uncircumcised in heart and ears! You always resist the Holy Spirit; as your fathers did, so do you.

Romans 15:16

¹⁶ that I might be a minister of Jesus Christ to the Gentiles, ministering the gospel of God, that the offering of the Gentiles might be acceptable, sanctified by the Holy Spirit.

1 Corinthians 6:11

¹¹ And such were some of you. But you were washed, but you were sanctified, but you were justified in the name of the Lord Jesus and by the Spirit of our God.

2 Thessalonians 2:13

¹³ But we are bound to give thanks to God always for you, brethren beloved by the Lord, because God from the beginning chose you for salvation through sanctification by the Spirit and belief in the truth,

2 Corinthians 1:22

²² who also has sealed us and given us the Spirit in our hearts as a guarantee.

Ephesians 1:14

¹⁴ who is the guarantee of our inheritance until the redemption of the purchased possession, to the praise of His glory.

Ephesians 4:30

³⁰ And do not grieve the Holy Spirit of God, by whom you were sealed for the day of redemption.

Acts 20:28

²⁸ Therefore take heed to yourselves and to all the flock, among which the Holy Spirit has made you overseers, to shepherd the church of God which He purchased with His own blood.

2 Corinthians 13:14

¹⁴ The grace of the Lord Jesus Christ, and the love of God, and the communion of the Holy Spirit be with you all. Amen.

Philippians 2:1

¹ Therefore if there is any consolation in Christ, if any comfort of love, if any fellowship of the Spirit, if any affection and mercy,

1 Peter 2:21

²¹ For to this you were called, because Christ also suffered for us, leaving us an example, that you should follow His steps:

Revelation 1:7

⁷ Behold, He is coming with clouds, and every eye will see Him, even they who pierced Him. And all the tribes of the earth will mourn because of Him. Even so, Amen.

Revelation 14:13

¹³ Then I heard a voice from heaven saying to me, "Write: 'Blessed are the dead who die in the Lord from now on.'" "Yes," says the Spirit, "that they may rest from their labors, and their works follow them."

Philippians 3:10

¹⁰ that I may know Him and the power of His resurrection, and the fellowship of His sufferings, being conformed to His death,

Exodus 13:21-22

²¹ And the Lord went before them by day in a pillar of cloud to lead the way, and by night in a pillar of fire to give them light, so as to go by day and night. ²² He did not take away the pillar of cloud by day or the pillar of fire by night from before the people.

Exodus 19:18

¹⁸ Now Mount Sinai was completely in smoke, because the Lord descended upon it in fire. Its smoke ascended like the smoke of a furnace, and the whole mountain quaked greatly.

Leviticus 6:12-13

¹² And the fire on the altar shall be kept burning on it; it shall not be put out. And the priest shall burn wood on it every morning, and lay the burnt offering in order on it; and he shall burn on it the fat of the peace offerings. ¹³ A fire shall always be burning on the altar; it shall never go out.

John 16:8

⁸ And when He has come, He will convict the world of sin, and of righteousness, and of judgment:

Matthew 3:11

¹¹ I indeed baptize you with water unto repentance, but He who is coming after me is mightier than I, whose sandals I am not worthy to carry. He will baptize you with the Holy Spirit and fire.

John 9:3,30-33

³ Jesus answered, "Neither this man nor his parents sinned, but that the works of God should be revealed in him.
³⁰ The man answered and said to them, "Why, this is a marvelous thing, that you do not know where He is from; yet He has opened my eyes! ³¹ Now we know that God does not hear sinners; but if anyone is a worshiper of God and does His will, He hears him. ³² Since the world began it has been unheard of that anyone opened the eyes of one who was born blind. ³³ If this Man were not from God, He could do nothing."

Leviticus 11:44

⁴⁴ For I am the Lord your God. You shall therefore consecrate yourselves, and you shall be holy; for I am holy. Neither shall you defile yourselves with any creeping thing that creeps on the earth.

1 Peter 1:16

¹⁶ because it is written, "Be holy, for I am holy."

Matthew 5:48

⁴⁸ Therefore you shall be perfect, just as your Father in heaven is perfect.

Exodus 24:17

[17] The sight of the glory of the Lord was like a consuming fire on the top of the mountain in the eyes of the children of Israel.

Deuteronomy 9:3

[3] Therefore understand today that the Lord your God is He who goes over before you as a consuming fire. He will destroy them and bring them down before you; so you shall drive them out and destroy them quickly, as the Lord has said to you.

Hebrews 12:29

[29] For our God is a consuming fire.

Hebrews 11:35-38

[35] Women received their dead raised to life again. And others were tortured, not accepting deliverance, that they might obtain a better resurrection. [36] Still others had trial of mockings and scourgings, yes, and of chains and imprisonment. [37] They were stoned, they were sawn in two, were tempted, were slain with the sword. They wandered about in sheepskins and goatskins, being destitute, afflicted, tormented-- [38] of whom the world was not worthy. They wandered in deserts and mountains, in dens and caves of the earth.

2 Corinthians 4:17-18

[17] For our light affliction, which is but for a moment, is working for us a far more exceeding and eternal weight of glory, [18] while we do not look at the things which are seen, but at the things which are not seen. For the things which are seen are temporary, but the things which are not seen are eternal.

CHAPTER 5

Leviticus 3:2-13

[2] And he shall lay his hand on the head of his offering, and kill it at the door of the tabernacle of meeting; and Aaron's sons, the priests, shall sprinkle the blood all around on the altar. [3] Then he shall offer from the sacrifice of the peace offering an offering made by fire to the Lord. The fat that covers the entrails and all the fat that is on the entrails, [4] the two kidneys and the fat that is on them by the flanks, and the fatty lobe attached to the liver above the kidneys, he shall remove;

[5] and Aaron's sons shall burn it on the altar upon the burnt sacrifice, which is on the wood that is on the fire, as an offering made by fire, a sweet aroma to the Lord. [6] 'If his offering as a sacrifice of a peace offering to the Lord is of the flock, whether male or female, he shall offer it without blemish. [7] If he offers a lamb as his offering, then he shall offer it before the Lord. [8] And he shall lay his hand on the head of his offering, and kill it before the tabernacle of meeting; and Aaron's sons shall sprinkle its blood all around on the altar. [9] Then he shall offer from the sacrifice of the peace offering, as an offering made by fire to the Lord, its fat and the whole fat tail which he shall remove close to the backbone. And the fat that covers the entrails and all the fat that is on the entrails, [10] the two kidneys and the fat that is on them by the flanks, and the fatty lobe attached to the liver above the kidneys, he shall remove; [11] and the priest shall burn them on the altar as food, an offering made by fire to the Lord. [12] 'And if his offering is a goat, then he shall offer it before the Lord. [13] He shall lay his hand on its head and kill it before the tabernacle of meeting; and the sons of Aaron shall sprinkle its blood all around on the altar.

Leviticus 4:4-32

[4] He shall bring the bull to the door of the tabernacle of meeting before the Lord, lay his hand on the bull's head, and kill the bull before the Lord. [5] Then the anointed priest shall take some of the bull's blood and bring it to the tabernacle of meeting. [6] The priest shall dip his finger in the blood and sprinkle some of the blood seven times before the Lord, in front of the veil of the sanctuary. [7] And the priest shall put some of the blood on the horns of the altar of sweet incense before the Lord, which is in the tabernacle of meeting; and he shall pour the remaining blood of the bull at the base of the altar of the burnt offering, which is at the door of the tabernacle of meeting. [8] He shall take from it all the fat of the bull as the sin offering. The fat that covers the entrails and all the fat which is on the entrails, [9] the two kidneys and the fat that is on them by the flanks, and the fatty lobe attached to the liver above the kidneys, he shall remove, [10] as it was taken from the bull of the sacrifice of the peace offering; and the priest shall burn them on the altar of the burnt offering. [11] But the bull's hide and all its flesh, with its head and legs, its entrails and offal-- [12] the whole bull he shall carry outside the camp to a clean place, where the ashes are poured out, and burn it on wood with fire; where the ashes are poured out it shall be burned.

 ¹³ 'Now if the whole congregation of Israel sins unintentionally, and the thing is hidden from the eyes of the assembly, and they have done something against any of the commandments of the Lord in anything which should not be done, and are guilty; ¹⁴ when the sin which they have committed becomes known, then the assembly shall offer a young bull for the sin, and bring it before the tabernacle of meeting. ¹⁵ And the elders of the congregation shall lay their hands on the head of the bull before the Lord. Then the bull shall be killed before the Lord. ¹⁶ The anointed priest shall bring some of the bull's blood to the tabernacle of meeting. ¹⁷ Then the priest shall dip his finger in the blood and sprinkle it seven times before the Lord, in front of the veil. ¹⁸ And he shall put some of the blood on the horns of the altar which is before the Lord, which is in the tabernacle of meeting; and he shall pour the remaining blood at the base of the altar of burnt offering, which is at the door of the tabernacle of meeting. ¹⁹ He shall take all the fat from it and burn it on the altar. ²⁰ And he shall do with the bull as he did with the bull as a sin offering; thus he shall do with it. So the priest shall make atonement for them, and it shall be forgiven them. ²¹ Then he shall carry the bull outside the camp, and burn it as he burned the first bull. It is a sin offering for the assembly. ²² 'When a ruler has sinned, and done something unintentionally against any of the commandments of the Lord his God in anything which should not be done, and is guilty, ²³ or if his sin which he has committed comes to his knowledge, he shall bring as his offering a kid of the goats, a male without blemish. ²⁴ And he shall lay his hand on the head of the goat, and kill it at the place where they kill the burnt offering before the Lord. It is a sin offering. ²⁵ The priest shall take some of the blood of the sin offering with his finger, put it on the horns of the altar of burnt offering, and pour its blood at the base of the altar of burnt offering. ²⁶ And he shall burn all its fat on the altar, like the fat of the sacrifice of the peace offering. So the priest shall make atonement for him concerning his sin, and it shall be forgiven him. ²⁷ 'If anyone of the common people sins unintentionally by doing something against any of the commandments of the Lord in anything which ought not to be done, and is guilty, ²⁸ or if his sin which he has committed comes to his knowledge, then he shall bring as his offering a kid of the goats, a female without blemish, for his sin which he has committed. ²⁹ And he shall lay his hand on the head of the sin offering, and kill the sin

offering at the place of the burnt offering. ³⁰ Then the priest shall take some of its blood with his finger, put it on the horns of the altar of burnt offering, and pour all the remaining blood at the base of the altar. ³¹ He shall remove all its fat, as fat is removed from the sacrifice of the peace offering; and the priest shall burn it on the altar for a sweet aroma to the Lord. So the priest shall make atonement for him, and it shall be forgiven him. ³² 'If he brings a lamb as his sin offering, he shall bring a female without blemish.

Leviticus 8:22

²² And he brought the second ram, the ram of consecration. Then Aaron and his sons laid their hands on the head of the ram,

Leviticus 16:21

²¹ Aaron shall lay both his hands on the head of the live goat, confess over it all the iniquities of the children of Israel, and all their transgressions, concerning all their sins, putting them on the head of the goat, and shall send it away into the wilderness by the hand of a suitable man.

Job 9:33

³³ Nor is there any mediator between us, Who may lay his hand on us both.

Mark 6:5

⁵ Now He could do no mighty work there, except that He laid His hands on a few sick people and healed them.

Mark 3:1-6

¹ And He entered the synagogue again, and a man was there who had a withered hand. ² So they watched Him closely, whether He would heal him on the Sabbath, so that they might accuse Him. ³ And He said to the man who had the withered hand, "Step forward." ⁴ Then He said to them, "Is it lawful on the Sabbath to do good or to do evil, to save life or to kill?" But they kept silent. ⁵ And when He had looked around at them with anger, being grieved by the hardness of their hearts, He said to the man, "Stretch out your hand." And he stretched it out, and his hand was restored as whole as the other. ⁶ Then the Pharisees went out and immediately plotted with the Herodians against Him, how they might destroy Him.

Acts 9:12-17

[12] And in a vision he has seen a man named Ananias coming in and putting his hand on him, so that he might receive his sight." [13] Then Ananias answered, "Lord, I have heard from many about this man, how much harm he has done to Your saints in Jerusalem. [14] And here he has authority from the chief priests to bind all who call on Your name." [15] But the Lord said to him, "Go, for he is a chosen vessel of Mine to bear My name before Gentiles, kings, and the children of Israel. [16] For I will show him how many things he must suffer for My name's sake." [17] And Ananias went his way and entered the house; and laying his hands on him he said, "Brother Saul, the Lord Jesus, who appeared to you on the road as you came, has sent me that you may receive your sight and be filled with the Holy Spirit."

Acts 28:8

[8] And it happened that the father of Publius lay sick of a fever and dysentery. Paul went in to him and prayed, and he laid his hands on him and healed him.

Acts 8:17

[17] Then they laid hands on them, and they received the Holy Spirit.

Acts 9:17

[17] And Ananias went his way and entered the house; and laying his hands on him he said, "Brother Saul, the Lord Jesus, who appeared to you on the road as you came, has sent me that you may receive your sight and be filled with the Holy Spirit."

Acts 19:6-7

[6] And when Paul had laid hands on them, the Holy Spirit came upon them, and they spoke with tongues and prophesied. [7] Now the men were about twelve in all.

2 Timothy 1:6

[6] Therefore I remind you to stir up the gift of God which is in you through the laying on of my hands.

Acts 13:3

[3] Then, having fasted and prayed, and laid hands on them, they sent them away.

CHAPTER 6

John 14:19

[19] "A little while longer and the world will see Me no more, but you will see Me. Because I live, you will live also.

Acts 9:1-9

[1] Then Saul, still breathing threats and murder against the disciples of the Lord, went to the high priest [2] and asked letters from him to the synagogues of Damascus, so that if he found any who were of the Way, whether men or women, he might bring them bound to Jerusalem. [3] As he journeyed he came near Damascus, and suddenly a light shone around him from heaven. [4] Then he fell to the ground, and heard a voice saying to him, "Saul, Saul, why are you persecuting Me?" [5] And he said, "Who are You, Lord?" Then the Lord said, "I am Jesus, whom you are persecuting. It is hard for you to kick against the goads." [6] So he, trembling and astonished, said, "Lord, what do You want me to do?" Then the Lord said to him, "Arise and go into the city, and you will be told what you must do." [7] And the men who journeyed with him stood speechless, hearing a voice but seeing no one. [8] Then Saul arose from the ground, and when his eyes were opened he saw no one. But they led him by the hand and brought him into Damascus. [9] And he was three days without sight, and neither ate nor drank.

Acts 7:55-56

[55] But he, being full of the Holy Spirit, gazed into heaven and saw the glory of God, and Jesus standing at the right hand of God, [56] and said, "Look! I see the heavens opened and the Son of Man standing at the right hand of God!"

Matthew 28:1-2

[1] Now after the Sabbath, as the first day of the week began to dawn, Mary Magdalene and the other Mary came to see the tomb. [2] And behold, there was a great earthquake; for an angel of the Lord descended from heaven, and came and rolled back the stone from the door, and sat on it.

Matthew 27:56,61

[56] among whom were Mary Magdalene, Mary the mother of James and Joses, and the mother of Zebedee's sons.

⁶¹ And Mary Magdalene was there, and the other Mary, sitting opposite the tomb.

John 20:28

²⁸ And Thomas answered and said to Him, "My Lord and my God!"

1 Corinthians 5:3-8

³ For I indeed, as absent in body but present in spirit, have already judged (as though I were present) him who has so done this deed. ⁴ In the name of our Lord Jesus Christ, when you are gathered together, along with my spirit, with the power of our Lord Jesus Christ, ⁵ deliver such a one to Satan for the destruction of the flesh, that his spirit may be saved in the day of the Lord Jesus. ⁶ Your glorying is not good. Do you not know that a little leaven leavens the whole lump? ⁷ Therefore purge out the old leaven, that you may be a new lump, since you truly are unleavened. For indeed Christ, our Passover, was sacrificed for us. ⁸ Therefore let us keep the feast, not with old leaven, nor with the leaven of malice and wickedness, but with the unleavened bread of sincerity and truth.

Colossians 1:18

¹⁸ And He is the head of the body, the church, who is the beginning, the firstborn from the dead, that in all things He may have the preeminence.

Romans 8:29

²⁹ For whom He foreknew, He also predestined to be conformed to the image of His Son, that He might be the firstborn among many brethren.

Revelation 20:11-15

¹¹ Then I saw a great white throne and Him who sat on it, from whose face the earth and the heaven fled away. And there was found no place for them. ¹² And I saw the dead, small and great, standing before God, and books were opened. And another book was opened, which is the Book of Life. And the dead were judged according to their works, by the things which were written in the books. ¹³ The sea gave up the dead who were in it, and Death and Hades delivered up the dead who were in them. And they were judged, each one according to his works. ¹⁴ Then Death and Hades were cast into the lake of fire. This is the second death. ¹⁵ And anyone not found written in the Book of Life was cast into the lake of fire.

Ecclesiastes 3:11

[11] He has made everything beautiful in its time. Also He has put eternity in their hearts, except that no one can find out the work that God does from beginning to end.

Acts 3:15

[15] and killed the Prince of life, whom God raised from the dead, of which we are witnesses.

[2] being greatly disturbed that they taught the people and preached in Jesus the resurrection from the dead.

Acts 4:2,10,33

[2] being greatly disturbed that they taught the people and preached in Jesus the resurrection from the dead.

[10] let it be known to you all, and to all the people of Israel, that by the name of Jesus Christ of Nazareth, whom you crucified, whom God raised from the dead, by Him this man stands here before you whole.

[33] And with great power the apostles gave witness to the resurrection of the Lord Jesus. And great grace was upon them all.

Acts 5:30

[30] The God of our fathers raised up Jesus whom you murdered by hanging on a tree.

Acts 10:39-40

[39] And we are witnesses of all things which He did both in the land of the Jews and in Jerusalem, whom they killed by hanging on a tree.

[40] Him God raised up on the third day, and showed Him openly,

CHAPTER 7

John 5:22

[22] For the Father judges no one, but has committed all judgment to the Son,

1 John 4:17

[17] Love has been perfected among us in this: that we may have boldness in the day of judgment; because as He is, so are we in this world.

John 5:24-29

[24] "Most assuredly, I say to you, he who hears My word and believes in Him who sent Me has everlasting life, and shall not come into judgment, but has passed from death into life. [25] Most assuredly, I say to you, the hour is coming, and now is, when the dead will hear the voice of the Son of God; and those who hear will live. [26] For as the Father has life in Himself, so He has granted the Son to have life in Himself, [27] and has given Him authority to execute judgment also, because He is the Son of Man. [28] Do not marvel at this; for the hour is coming in which all who are in the graves will hear His voice [29] and come forth--those who have done good, to the resurrection of life, and those who have done evil, to the resurrection of condemnation.

1 Corinthians 3:12-15

[12] Now if anyone builds on this foundation with gold, silver, precious stones, wood, hay, straw, [13] each one's work will become clear; for the Day will declare it, because it will be revealed by fire; and the fire will test each one's work, of what sort it is. [14] If anyone's work which he has built on it endures, he will receive a reward. [15] If anyone's work is burned, he will suffer loss; but he himself will be saved, yet so as through fire.

Revelation 20:11-15

[11] Then I saw a great white throne and Him who sat on it, from whose face the earth and the heaven fled away. And there was found no place for them. [12] And I saw the dead, small and great, standing before God, and books were opened. And another book was opened, which is the Book of Life. And the dead were judged according to their works, by the things which were written in the books. [13] The sea gave up the dead who were in it, and Death and Hades delivered up the dead who were in them. And they were judged, each one according to his works. [14] Then Death and Hades were cast into the lake of fire. This is the second death. [15] And anyone not found written in the Book of Life was cast into the lake of fire.

[6] since it is a righteous thing with God to repay with tribulation those who trouble you, [7] and to give you who are troubled rest with us when the Lord Jesus is revealed from heaven with His mighty angels, [8] in flaming fire taking vengeance on those who do not know God, and on those who do not obey the gospel of our Lord Jesus Christ. [9] These shall be punished with everlasting destruction from the presence of the

Lord and from the glory of His power, [10] when He comes, in that Day, to be glorified in His saints and to be admired among all those who believe, because our testimony among you was believed.

Matthew 25:41

[41] Then He will also say to those on the left hand, 'Depart from Me, you cursed, into the everlasting fire prepared for the devil and his angels:

Revelation 14:10-11

[10] he himself shall also drink of the wine of the wrath of God, which is poured out full strength into the cup of His indignation. He shall be tormented with fire and brimstone in the presence of the holy angels and in the presence of the Lamb. [11] And the smoke of their torment ascends forever and ever; and they have no rest day or night, who worship the beast and his image, and whoever receives the mark of his name."

1 Chronicles 27:24

[24] Joab the son of Zeruiah began a census, but he did not finish, for wrath came upon Israel because of this census; nor was the number recorded in the account of the chronicles of King David.

2 Chronicles 24:18

[18] Therefore they left the house of the Lord God of their fathers, and served wooden images and idols; and wrath came upon Judah and Jerusalem because of their trespass.

Amos 3:2

[2] "You only have I known of all the families of the earth; Therefore I will punish you for all your iniquities."

Hosea 13:9-11

[9] "O Israel, you are destroyed, But your help is from Me. [10] I will be your King; Where is any other, That he may save you in all your cities? And your judges to whom you said, 'Give me a king and princes'? [11] I gave you a king in My anger, And took him away in My wrath.

2 Kings 23:26-27

[26] Nevertheless the Lord did not turn from the fierceness of His great wrath, with which His anger was aroused against Judah, because of all

the provocations with which Manasseh had provoked Him. ²⁷ And the Lord said, "I will also remove Judah from My sight, as I have removed Israel, and will cast off this city Jerusalem which I have chosen, and the house of which I said, 'My name shall be there.'"

2 Chronicles 19:2

² And Jehu the son of Hanani the seer went out to meet him, and said to King Jehoshaphat, "Should you help the wicked and love those who hate the Lord? Therefore the wrath of the Lord is upon you.

Exodus 4:14,24

¹⁴ So the anger of the Lord was kindled against Moses, and He said: "Is not Aaron the Levite your brother? I know that he can speak well. And look, he is also coming out to meet you. When he sees you, he will be glad in his heart.
²⁴ And it came to pass on the way, at the encampment, that the Lord met him and sought to kill him.

Deuteronomy 1:37

³⁷ The Lord was also angry with me for your sakes, saying, 'Even you shall not go in there;

Deuteronomy 9:20

²⁰ And the Lord was very angry with Aaron and would have destroyed him; so I prayed for Aaron also at the same time.

Numbers 12:9

⁹ So the anger of the Lord was aroused against them, and He departed.

Leviticus 10:1-2

¹ Then Nadab and Abihu, the sons of Aaron, each took his censer and put fire in it, put incense on it, and offered profane fire before the Lord, which He had not commanded them. ² So fire went out from the Lord and devoured them, and they died before the Lord.

Psalm 2:5,11

⁵ Then He shall speak to them in His wrath, And distress them in His deep displeasure:
¹¹ Serve the Lord with fear, And rejoice with trembling.

Isaiah 13:3,5,9

³ I have commanded My sanctified ones; I have also called My mighty ones for My anger-- Those who rejoice in My exaltation."

⁵ They come from a far country, From the end of heaven-- The Lord and His weapons of indignation, To destroy the whole land.

⁹ Behold, the day of the Lord comes, Cruel, with both wrath and fierce anger, To lay the land desolate; And He will destroy its sinners from it.

Isaiah 50:13,15

¹³ Because of the wrath of the Lord She shall not be inhabited, But she shall be wholly desolate. Everyone who goes by Babylon shall be horrified And hiss at all her plagues.

¹⁵ Shout against her all around; She has given her hand, Her foundations have fallen, Her walls are thrown down; For it is the vengeance of the Lord. Take vengeance on her. As she has done, so do to her.

John 3:36

³⁶ He who believes in the Son has everlasting life; and he who does not believe the Son shall not see life, but the wrath of God abides on him."

Romans 1:18-32

¹⁸ For the wrath of God is revealed from heaven against all ungodliness and unrighteousness of men, who suppress the truth in unrighteousness, ¹⁹ because what may be known of God is manifest in them, for God has shown it to them. ²⁰ For since the creation of the world His invisible attributes are clearly seen, being understood by the things that are made, even His eternal power and Godhead, so that they are without excuse, ²¹ because, although they knew God, they did not glorify Him as God, nor were thankful, but became futile in their thoughts, and their foolish hearts were darkened. ²² Professing to be wise, they became fools, ²³ and changed the glory of the incorruptible God into an image made like corruptible man--and birds and four-footed animals and creeping things. ²⁴ Therefore God also gave them up to uncleanness, in the lusts of their hearts, to dishonor their bodies among themselves, ²⁵ who exchanged the truth of God for the lie, and worshiped and served the creature rather than the Creator, who is blessed forever. Amen. ²⁶ For this reason God gave them up to vile passions. For even their women exchanged the natural use for what is against nature. ²⁷ Likewise also the

men, leaving the natural use of the woman, burned in their lust for one another, men with men committing what is shameful, and receiving in themselves the penalty of their error which was due. [28] And even as they did not like to retain God in their knowledge, God gave them over to a debased mind, to do those things which are not fitting; [29] being filled with all unrighteousness, sexual immorality, wickedness, covetousness, maliciousness; full of envy, murder, strife, deceit, evil-mindedness; they are whisperers, [30] backbiters, haters of God, violent, proud, boasters, inventors of evil things, disobedient to parents, [31] undiscerning, untrustworthy, unloving, unforgiving, unmerciful; [32] who, knowing the righteous judgment of God, that those who practice such things are deserving of death, not only do the same but also approve of those who practice them.

Hebrews 12:4-11

[4] You have not yet resisted to bloodshed, striving against sin. [5] And you have forgotten the exhortation which speaks to you as to sons: "My son, do not despise the chastening of the Lord, Nor be discouraged when you are rebuked by Him; [6] For whom the Lord loves He chastens, And scourges every son whom He receives." [7] If you endure chastening, God deals with you as with sons; for what son is there whom a father does not chasten? [8] But if you are without chastening, of which all have become partakers, then you are illegitimate and not sons. [9] Furthermore, we have had human fathers who corrected us, and we paid them respect. Shall we not much more readily be in subjection to the Father of spirits and live? [10] For they indeed for a few days chastened us as seemed best to them, but He for our profit, that we may be partakers of His holiness. [11] Now no chastening seems to be joyful for the present, but painful; nevertheless, afterward it yields the peaceable fruit of righteousness to those who have been trained by it.

2 Corinthians 9:15

[15] Thanks be to God for His indescribable gift!

Deuteronomy 21:22-23

[22] "If a man has committed a sin deserving of death, and he is put to death, and you hang him on a tree, [23] his body shall not remain overnight on the tree, but you shall surely bury him that day, so that you do not defile the land which the Lord your God is giving you as an inheritance; for he who is hanged is accursed of God.

Mark 15:30-31

[30] save Yourself, and come down from the cross!" [31] Likewise the chief priests also, mocking among themselves with the scribes, said, "He saved others; Himself He cannot save.

Matthew 27:51-54

[51] Then, behold, the veil of the temple was torn in two from top to bottom; and the earth quaked, and the rocks were split, [52] and the graves were opened; and many bodies of the saints who had fallen asleep were raised; [53] and coming out of the graves after His resurrection, they went into the holy city and appeared to many. [54] So when the centurion and those with him, who were guarding Jesus, saw the earthquake and the things that had happened, they feared greatly, saying, "Truly this was the Son of God!"

Luke 23:48

[48] And the whole crowd who came together to that sight, seeing what had been done, beat their breasts and returned.

Luke 23:34

[34] Then Jesus said, "Father, forgive them, for they do not know what they do." And they divided His garments and cast lots.

Luke 23:43

[43] And Jesus said to him, "Assuredly, I say to you, today you will be with Me in Paradise."

Luke 23:46

[46] And when Jesus had cried out with a loud voice, He said, "Father, 'into Your hands I commit My spirit.'" Having said this, He breathed His last.

John 19:19-20

[19] Now Pilate wrote a title and put it on the cross. And the writing was: JESUS OF NAZARETH, THE KING OF THE JEWS. [20] Then many of the Jews read this title, for the place where Jesus was crucified was near the city; and it was written in Hebrew, Greek, and Latin.

John 19:30

[30] So when Jesus had received the sour wine, He said, "It is finished!" And bowing His head, He gave up His spirit.

1 Corinthians 15:3-5

³ For I delivered to you first of all that which I also received: that Christ died for our sins according to the Scriptures, ⁴ and that He was buried, and that He rose again the third day according to the Scriptures, ⁵ and that He was seen by Cephas, then by the twelve.

Isaiah 53:5

⁵ But He was wounded for our transgressions, He was bruised for our iniquities; The chastisement for our peace was upon Him, And by His stripes we are healed.

Mark 10:45

⁴⁵ For even the Son of Man did not come to be served, but to serve, and to give His life a ransom for many."

Mark 14:24

²⁴ And He said to them, "This is My blood of the new covenant, which is shed for many.

1 Corinthians 1:18

¹⁸ For the message of the cross is foolishness to those who are perishing, but to us who are being saved it is the power of God.

1 Corinthians 1:21,25

²¹ For since, in the wisdom of God, the world through wisdom did not know God, it pleased God through the foolishness of the message preached to save those who believe.
²⁵ Because the foolishness of God is wiser than men, and the weakness of God is stronger than men.

Romans 4:25

²⁵ who was delivered up because of our offenses, and was raised because of our justification.

Titus 2:14

¹⁴ who gave Himself for us, that He might redeem us from every lawless deed and purify for Himself His own special people, zealous for good works.

1 Peter 1:18

¹⁸ knowing that you were not redeemed with corruptible things, like silver or gold, from your aimless conduct received by tradition from your fathers,

Romans 3:5

⁵ But if our unrighteousness demonstrates the righteousness of God, what shall we say? Is God unjust who inflicts wrath? (I speak as a man.)

Hebrews 2:17

¹⁷ Therefore, in all things He had to be made like His brethren, that He might be a merciful and faithful High Priest in things pertaining to God, to make propitiation for the sins of the people.

Romans 3:24

²⁴ being justified freely by His grace through the redemption that is in Christ Jesus,

Romans 4:25

²⁵ who was delivered up because of our offenses, and was raised because of our justification.

Galatians 2:16-21

¹⁶ knowing that a man is not justified by the works of the law but by faith in Jesus Christ, even we have believed in Christ Jesus, that we might be justified by faith in Christ and not by the works of the law; for by the works of the law no flesh shall be justified. ¹⁷ But if, while we seek to be justified by Christ, we ourselves also are found sinners, is Christ therefore a minister of sin? Certainly not! ¹⁸ For if I build again those things which I destroyed, I make myself a transgressor. ¹⁹ For I through the law died to the law that I might live to God. ²⁰ I have been crucified with Christ; it is no longer I who live, but Christ lives in me; and the life which I now live in the flesh I live by faith in the Son of God, who loved me and gave Himself for me. ²¹ I do not set aside the grace of God; for if righteousness comes through the law, then Christ died in vain."

Galatians 3:24

²⁴ Therefore the law was our tutor to bring us to Christ, that we might be justified by faith.

Ephesians 2:14-15 NIV

[14] For he himself is our peace, who has made the two one and has destroyed the barrier, the dividing wall of hostility, [15] by abolishing in his flesh the law with its commandments and regulations. His purpose was to create in himself one new man out of the two, thus making peace,

Ephesians 2:18 NIV

[18] For through him we both have access to the Father by one Spirit.

Colossians 2:15

[15] Having disarmed principalities and powers, He made a public spectacle of them, triumphing over them in it.

Philippians 2:8-11

[8] And being found in appearance as a man, He humbled Himself and became obedient to the point of death, even the death of the cross. [9] Therefore God also has highly exalted Him and given Him the name which is above every name, [10] that at the name of Jesus every knee should bow, of those in heaven, and of those on earth, and of those under the earth, [11] and that every tongue should confess that Jesus Christ is Lord, to the glory of God the Father.

John 19:17-30

[17] And He, bearing His cross, went out to a place called the Place of a Skull, which is called in Hebrew, Golgotha, [18] where they crucified Him, and two others with Him, one on either side, and Jesus in the center. [19] Now Pilate wrote a title and put it on the cross. And the writing was: JESUS OF NAZARETH, THE KING OF THE JEWS. [20] Then many of the Jews read this title, for the place where Jesus was crucified was near the city; and it was written in Hebrew, Greek, and Latin. [21] Therefore the chief priests of the Jews said to Pilate, "Do not write, 'The King of the Jews,' but, 'He said, "I am the King of the Jews."'" [22] Pilate answered, "What I have written, I have written." [23] Then the soldiers, when they had crucified Jesus, took His garments and made four parts, to each soldier a part, and also the tunic. Now the tunic was without seam, woven from the top in one piece. [24] They said therefore among themselves, "Let us not tear it, but cast lots for it, whose it shall be," that the Scripture might be fulfilled which says: "They divided My garments among them, And for My clothing they

cast lots." Therefore the soldiers did these things. ²⁵ Now there stood by the cross of Jesus His mother, and His mother's sister, Mary the wife of Clopas, and Mary Magdalene. ²⁶ When Jesus therefore saw His mother, and the disciple whom He loved standing by, He said to His mother, "Woman, behold your son!" ²⁷ Then He said to the disciple, "Behold your mother!" And from that hour that disciple took her to his own home. ²⁸ After this, Jesus, knowing that all things were now accomplished, that the Scripture might be fulfilled, said, "I thirst!" ²⁹ Now a vessel full of sour wine was sitting there; and they filled a sponge with sour wine, put it on hyssop, and put it to His mouth. ³⁰ So when Jesus had received the sour wine, He said, "It is finished!" And bowing His head, He gave up His spirit.

Mark 8:34

³⁴ When He had called the people to Himself, with His disciples also, He said to them, "Whoever desires to come after Me, let him deny himself, and take up his cross, and follow Me.

Mark 10:38

³⁸ But Jesus said to them, "You do not know what you ask. Are you able to drink the cup that I drink, and be baptized with the baptism that I am baptized with?"

Matthew 16:24

²⁴ Then Jesus said to His disciples, "If anyone desires to come after Me, let him deny himself, and take up his cross, and follow Me.

Luke 9:23

²³ Then He said to them all, "If anyone desires to come after Me, let him deny himself, and take up his cross daily, and follow Me.

Luke 14:27

²⁷ And whoever does not bear his cross and come after Me cannot be My disciple.

Galatians 2:20

²⁰ I have been crucified with Christ; it is no longer I who live, but Christ lives in me; and the life which I now live in the flesh I live by faith in the Son of God, who loved me and gave Himself for me.

Galatians 5:24

²⁴ And those who are Christ's have crucified the flesh with its passions and desires.

Galatians 6:14

¹⁴ But God forbid that I should boast except in the cross of our Lord Jesus Christ, by whom the world has been crucified to me, and I to the world.

Matthew 5:44

⁴⁴ But I say to you, love your enemies, bless those who curse you, do good to those who hate you, and pray for those who spitefully use you and persecute you,

1 John 3:2

² Beloved, now we are children of God; and it has not yet been revealed what we shall be, but we know that when He is revealed, we shall be like Him, for we shall see Him as He is.

1 Corinthians 15:51-53

⁵¹ Behold, I tell you a mystery: We shall not all sleep, but we shall all be changed-- ⁵² in a moment, in the twinkling of an eye, at the last trumpet. For the trumpet will sound, and the dead will be raised incorruptible, and we shall be changed. ⁵³ For this corruptible must put on incorruption, and this mortal must put on immortality.

Romans 14:10

¹⁰ But why do you judge your brother? Or why do you show contempt for your brother? For we shall all stand before the judgment seat of Christ.

1 Corinthians 5:8

⁸ Therefore let us keep the feast, not with old leaven, nor with the leaven of malice and wickedness, but with the unleavened bread of sincerity and truth.

James 1:12

¹² Blessed is the man who endures temptation; for when he has been approved, he will receive the crown of life which the Lord has promised to those who love Him.

Revelation 2:10

¹⁰ Do not fear any of those things which you are about to suffer. Indeed, the devil is about to throw some of you into prison, that you may be tested, and you will have tribulation ten days. Be faithful until death, and I will give you the crown of life.

Revelation 3:11

¹¹ Behold, I am coming quickly! Hold fast what you have, that no one may take your crown.

1 Peter 2:25

²⁵ For you were like sheep going astray, but have now returned to the Shepherd and Overseer of your souls.

John 10:11,14

¹¹ I am the good shepherd. The good shepherd gives His life for the sheep.

¹⁴ I am the good shepherd; and I know My sheep, and am known by My own.

Hebrews 13:20

²⁰ Now may the God of peace who brought up our Lord Jesus from the dead, that great Shepherd of the sheep, through the blood of the everlasting covenant,

Matthew 25:21,23

²¹ His lord said to him, 'Well done, good and faithful servant; you were faithful over a few things, I will make you ruler over many things. Enter into the joy of your lord.'

²³ His lord said to him, 'Well done, good and faithful servant; you have been faithful over a few things, I will make you ruler over many things. Enter into the joy of your lord.'

Revelation 22:3,5

³ And there shall be no more curse, but the throne of God and of the Lamb shall be in it, and His servants shall serve Him.

⁵ There shall be no night there: They need no lamp nor light of the sun, for the Lord God gives them light. And they shall reign forever and ever.

1 Corinthians 3:15

¹⁵ If anyone's work is burned, he will suffer loss; but he himself will be saved, yet so as through fire.

2 Peter 3:11-12

¹¹ Therefore, since all these things will be dissolved, what manner of persons ought you to be in holy conduct and godliness, ¹² looking for and hastening the coming of the day of God, because of which the heavens will be dissolved, being on fire, and the elements will melt with fervent heat?

Mark 13:22-27

²² For false christs and false prophets will rise and show signs and wonders to deceive, if possible, even the elect. ²³ But take heed; see, I have told you all things beforehand. ²⁴ "But in those days, after that tribulation, the sun will be darkened, and the moon will not give its light; ²⁵ the stars of heaven will fall, and the powers in the heavens will be shaken. ²⁶ Then they will see the Son of Man coming in the clouds with great power and glory. ²⁷ And then He will send His angels, and gather together His elect from the four winds, from the farthest part of earth to the farthest part of heaven.

Hebrews 12:2

² looking unto Jesus, the author and finisher of our faith, who for the joy that was set before Him endured the cross, despising the shame, and has sat down at the right hand of the throne of God.

Revelation 13:7,10,15

⁷ It was granted to him to make war with the saints and to overcome them. And authority was given him over every tribe, tongue, and nation.
¹⁰ He who leads into captivity shall go into captivity; he who kills with the sword must be killed with the sword. Here is the patience and the faith of the saints.
¹⁵ He was granted power to give breath to the image of the beast, that the image of the beast should both speak and cause as many as would not worship the image of the beast to be killed.

Revelation 7:9-17

⁹ After these things I looked, and behold, a great multitude which no one could number, of all nations, tribes, peoples, and tongues, standing before the throne and before the Lamb, clothed with white

robes, with palm branches in their hands, [10] and crying out with a loud voice, saying, "Salvation belongs to our God who sits on the throne, and to the Lamb!" [11] All the angels stood around the throne and the elders and the four living creatures, and fell on their faces before the throne and worshiped God, [12] saying: "Amen! Blessing and glory and wisdom, Thanksgiving and honor and power and might, Be to our God forever and ever. Amen." [13] Then one of the elders answered, saying to me, "Who are these arrayed in white robes, and where did they come from?" [14] And I said to him, "Sir, you know." So he said to me, "These are the ones who come out of the great tribulation, and washed their robes and made them white in the blood of the Lamb. [15] Therefore they are before the throne of God, and serve Him day and night in His temple. And He who sits on the throne will dwell among them. [16] They shall neither hunger anymore nor thirst anymore; the sun shall not strike them, nor any heat; [17] for the Lamb who is in the midst of the throne will shepherd them and lead them to living fountains of waters. And God will wipe away every tear from their eyes."

Jeremiah 30:7,11

[7] Alas! For that day is great, So that none is like it; And it is the time of Jacob's trouble, But he shall be saved out of it.

[11] For I am with you,' says the Lord, 'to save you; Though I make a full end of all nations where I have scattered you, Yet I will not make a complete end of you. But I will correct you in justice, And will not let you go altogether unpunished.'

Daniel 12:1

[1] "At that time Michael shall stand up, The great prince who stands watch over the sons of your people; And there shall be a time of trouble, Such as never was since there was a nation, Even to that time. And at that time your people shall be delivered, Every one who is found written in the book.

Matthew 24:15-28

[15] "Therefore when you see the 'abomination of desolation,' spoken of by Daniel the prophet, standing in the holy place" (whoever reads, let him understand), [16] then let those who are in Judea flee to the mountains. [17] Let him who is on the housetop not go down to take anything out of his house. [18] And let him who is in the field not go back to get his clothes. [19] But woe to those who are pregnant and to those who are

nursing babies in those days! [20] And pray that your flight may not be in winter or on the Sabbath. [21] For then there will be great tribulation, such as has not been since the beginning of the world until this time, no, nor ever shall be. [22] And unless those days were shortened, no flesh would be saved; but for the elect's sake those days will be shortened. [23] Then if anyone says to you, 'Look, here is the Christ!' or 'There!' do not believe it. [24] For false christs and false prophets will rise and show great signs and wonders to deceive, if possible, even the elect. [25] See, I have told you beforehand. [26] Therefore if they say to you, 'Look, He is in the desert!' do not go out; or 'Look, He is in the inner rooms!' do not believe it. [27] For as the lightning comes from the east and flashes to the west, so also will the coming of the Son of Man be. [28] For wherever the carcass is, there the eagles will be gathered together.

1 Thessalonians 4:17

[17] Then we who are alive and remain shall be caught up together with them in the clouds to meet the Lord in the air. And thus we shall always be with the Lord.

1 Thessalonians 5:1-2 (NIV)

[1] Now, brothers, about times and dates we do not need to write to you, [2] for you know very well that the day of the Lord will come like a thief in the night.

1 Thessalonians 5:9 (NIV)

[9] For God did not appoint us to suffer wrath but to receive salvation through our Lord Jesus Christ.

Matthew 24:22

[22] And unless those days were shortened, no flesh would be saved; but for the elect's sake those days will be shortened.

Joel 1:1-20

[1] The word of the Lord that came to Joel the son of Pethuel. [2] Hear this, you elders, And give ear, all you inhabitants of the land! Has anything like this happened in your days, Or even in the days of your fathers? [3] Tell your children about it, Let your children tell their children, And their children another generation. [4] What the chewing locust left, the swarming locust has eaten; What the swarming locust left, the crawling locust has eaten; And what the crawling locust left, the consuming locust has eaten. [5] Awake, you drunkards, and weep; And

wail, all you drinkers of wine, Because of the new wine, For it has been cut off from your mouth. [6] For a nation has come up against My land, Strong, and without number; His teeth are the teeth of a lion, And he has the fangs of a fierce lion. [7] He has laid waste My vine, And ruined My fig tree; He has stripped it bare and thrown it away; Its branches are made white. [8] Lament like a virgin girded with sackcloth For the husband of her youth. [9] The grain offering and the drink offering Have been cut off from the house of the Lord; The priests mourn, who minister to the Lord. [10] The field is wasted, The land mourns; For the grain is ruined, The new wine is dried up, The oil fails. [11] Be ashamed, you farmers, Wail, you vinedressers, For the wheat and the barley; Because the harvest of the field has perished. [12] The vine has dried up, And the fig tree has withered; The pomegranate tree, The palm tree also, And the apple tree-- All the trees of the field are withered; Surely joy has withered away from the sons of men. [13] Gird yourselves and lament, you priests; Wail, you who minister before the altar; Come, lie all night in sackcloth, You who minister to my God; For the grain offering and the drink offering Are withheld from the house of your God. [14] Consecrate a fast, Call a sacred assembly; Gather the elders And all the inhabitants of the land Into the house of the Lord your God, And cry out to the Lord. [15] Alas for the day! For the day of the Lord is at hand; It shall come as destruction from the Almighty. [16] Is not the food cut off before our eyes, Joy and gladness from the house of our God? [17] The seed shrivels under the clods, Storehouses are in shambles; Barns are broken down, For the grain has withered. [18] How the animals groan! The herds of cattle are restless, Because they have no pasture; Even the flocks of sheep suffer punishment. [19] O Lord, to You I cry out; For fire has devoured the open pastures, And a flame has burned all the trees of the field. [20] The beasts of the field also cry out to You, For the water brooks are dried up, And fire has devoured the open pastures.

Joel 2:1-17

[1] Blow the trumpet in Zion, And sound an alarm in My holy mountain! Let all the inhabitants of the land tremble; For the day of the Lord is coming, For it is at hand: [2] A day of darkness and gloominess, A day of clouds and thick darkness, Like the morning clouds spread over the mountains. A people come, great and strong, The like of whom has never been; Nor will there ever be any such after them, Even for many

successive generations. [3] A fire devours before them, And behind them a flame burns; The land is like the Garden of Eden before them, And behind them a desolate wilderness; Surely nothing shall escape them. [4] Their appearance is like the appearance of horses; And like swift steeds, so they run. [5] With a noise like chariots Over mountaintops they leap, Like the noise of a flaming fire that devours the stubble, Like a strong people set in battle array. [6] Before them the people writhe in pain; All faces are drained of color. [7] They run like mighty men, They climb the wall like men of war; Every one marches in formation, And they do not break ranks. [8] They do not push one another; Every one marches in his own column. Though they lunge between the weapons, They are not cut down. [9] They run to and fro in the city, They run on the wall; They climb into the houses, They enter at the windows like a thief. [10] The earth quakes before them, The heavens tremble; The sun and moon grow dark, And the stars diminish their brightness. [11] The Lord gives voice before His army, For His camp is very great; For strong is the One who executes His word. For the day of the Lord is great and very terrible; Who can endure it? [12] "Now, therefore," says the Lord, "Turn to Me with all your heart, With fasting, with weeping, and with mourning." [13] So rend your heart, and not your garments; Return to the Lord your God, For He is gracious and merciful, Slow to anger, and of great kindness; And He relents from doing harm. [14] Who knows if He will turn and relent, And leave a blessing behind Him-- A grain offering and a drink offering For the Lord your God? [15] Blow the trumpet in Zion, Consecrate a fast, Call a sacred assembly; [16] Gather the people, Sanctify the congregation, Assemble the elders, Gather the children and nursing babes; Let the bridegroom go out from his chamber, And the bride from her dressing room. [17] Let the priests, who minister to the Lord, Weep between the porch and the altar; Let them say, "Spare Your people, O Lord, And do not give Your heritage to reproach, That the nations should rule over them. Why should they say among the peoples, 'Where is their God?'"

Joel 3:14-16

[14] Multitudes, multitudes in the valley of decision! For the day of the Lord is near in the valley of decision. [15] The sun and moon will grow dark, And the stars will diminish their brightness. [16] The Lord also will roar from Zion, And utter His voice from Jerusalem; The heavens and earth will shake; But the Lord will be a shelter for His people, And the strength of the children of Israel.

Revelation 5:8

⁸ Now when He had taken the scroll, the four living creatures and the twenty-four elders fell down before the Lamb, each having a harp, and golden bowls full of incense, which are the prayers of the saints.

Daniel 7:7

⁷ After this I saw in the night visions, and behold, a fourth beast, dreadful and terrible, exceedingly strong. It had huge iron teeth; it was devouring, breaking in pieces, and trampling the residue with its feet. It was different from all the beasts that were before it, and it had ten horns.

Daniel 7:8

⁸ I was considering the horns, and there was another horn, a little one, coming up among them, before whom three of the first horns were plucked out by the roots. And there, in this horn, were eyes like the eyes of a man, and a mouth speaking pompous words.

Daniel 9:27

²⁷ Then he shall confirm a covenant with many for one week; But in the middle of the week He shall bring an end to sacrifice and offering. And on the wing of abominations shall be one who makes desolate, Even until the consummation, which is determined, Is poured out on the desolate."

Matthew 24:15

¹⁵ "Therefore when you see the 'abomination of desolation,' spoken of by Daniel the prophet,

Revelation 6:1-17

¹ Now I saw when the Lamb opened one of the seals; and I heard one of the four living creatures saying with a voice like thunder, "Come and see." ² And I looked, and behold, a white horse. He who sat on it had a bow; and a crown was given to him, and he went out conquering and to conquer. ³ When He opened the second seal, I heard the second living creature saying, "Come and see." ⁴ Another horse, fiery red, went out. And it was granted to the one who sat on it to take peace from the earth, and that people should kill one another; and there was given to him a great sword. ⁵ When He opened the third seal, I heard the third living creature say, "Come and see." So I looked, and behold, a black horse, and he who sat on it had a pair of scales in his hand. ⁶ And I

heard a voice in the midst of the four living creatures saying, "A quart of wheat for a denarius, and three quarts of barley for a denarius; and do not harm the oil and the wine." [7] When He opened the fourth seal, I heard the voice of the fourth living creature saying, "Come and see." [8] So I looked, and behold, a pale horse. And the name of him who sat on it was Death, and Hades followed with him. And power was given to them over a fourth of the earth, to kill with sword, with hunger, with death, and by the beasts of the earth. [9] When He opened the fifth seal, I saw under the altar the souls of those who had been slain for the word of God and for the testimony which they held. [10] And they cried with a loud voice, saying, "How long, O Lord, holy and true, until You judge and avenge our blood on those who dwell on the earth?" [11] Then a white robe was given to each of them; and it was said to them that they should rest a little while longer, until both the number of their fellow servants and their brethren, who would be killed as they were, was completed. [12] I looked when He opened the sixth seal, and behold, there was a great earthquake; and the sun became black as sackcloth of hair, and the moon became like blood. [13] And the stars of heaven fell to the earth, as a fig tree drops its late figs when it is shaken by a mighty wind. [14] Then the sky receded as a scroll when it is rolled up, and every mountain and island was moved out of its place. [15] And the kings of the earth, the great men, the rich men, the commanders, the mighty men, every slave and every free man, hid themselves in the caves and in the rocks of the mountains, [16] and said to the mountains and rocks, "Fall on us and hide us from the face of Him who sits on the throne and from the wrath of the Lamb! [17] For the great day of His wrath has come, and who is able to stand?"

Revelation 8:1-13

[1] When He opened the seventh seal, there was silence in heaven for about half an hour. [2] And I saw the seven angels who stand before God, and to them were given seven trumpets. [3] Then another angel, having a golden censer, came and stood at the altar. He was given much incense, that he should offer it with the prayers of all the saints upon the golden altar which was before the throne. [4] And the smoke of the incense, with the prayers of the saints, ascended before God from the angel's hand. [5] Then the angel took the censer, filled it with fire from the altar, and threw it to the earth. And there were noises, thunderings, lightnings, and an earthquake. [6] So the seven angels who had the seven

trumpets prepared themselves to sound. [7] The first angel sounded: And hail and fire followed, mingled with blood, and they were thrown to the earth. And a third of the trees were burned up, and all green grass was burned up. [8] Then the second angel sounded: And something like a great mountain burning with fire was thrown into the sea, and a third of the sea became blood. [9] And a third of the living creatures in the sea died, and a third of the ships were destroyed. [10] Then the third angel sounded: And a great star fell from heaven, burning like a torch, and it fell on a third of the rivers and on the springs of water. [11] The name of the star is Wormwood. A third of the waters became wormwood, and many men died from the water, because it was made bitter. [12] Then the fourth angel sounded: And a third of the sun was struck, a third of the moon, and a third of the stars, so that a third of them were darkened. A third of the day did not shine, and likewise the night. [13] And I looked, and I heard an angel flying through the midst of heaven, saying with a loud voice, "Woe, woe, woe to the inhabitants of the earth, because of the remaining blasts of the trumpet of the three angels who are about to sound!"

Revelation 9:1-21

[1] Then the fifth angel sounded: And I saw a star fallen from heaven to the earth. To him was given the key to the bottomless pit. [2] And he opened the bottomless pit, and smoke arose out of the pit like the smoke of a great furnace. So the sun and the air were darkened because of the smoke of the pit. [3] Then out of the smoke locusts came upon the earth. And to them was given power, as the scorpions of the earth have power. [4] They were commanded not to harm the grass of the earth, or any green thing, or any tree, but only those men who do not have the seal of God on their foreheads. [5] And they were not given authority to kill them, but to torment them for five months. Their torment was like the torment of a scorpion when it strikes a man. [6] In those days men will seek death and will not find it; they will desire to die, and death will flee from them. [7] The shape of the locusts was like horses prepared for battle. On their heads were crowns of something like gold, and their faces were like the faces of men. [8] They had hair like women's hair, and their teeth were like lions' teeth. [9] And they had breastplates like breastplates of iron, and the sound of their wings was like the sound of chariots with many horses running into battle. [10] They had tails like scorpions, and there were stings in their tails. Their power

was to hurt men five months. [11] And they had as king over them the angel of the bottomless pit, whose name in Hebrew is Abaddon, but in Greek he has the name Apollyon. [12] One woe is past. Behold, still two more woes are coming after these things. [13] Then the sixth angel sounded: And I heard a voice from the four horns of the golden altar which is before God, [14] saying to the sixth angel who had the trumpet, "Release the four angels who are bound at the great river Euphrates." [15] So the four angels, who had been prepared for the hour and day and month and year, were released to kill a third of mankind. [16] Now the number of the army of the horsemen was two hundred million; I heard the number of them. [17] And thus I saw the horses in the vision: those who sat on them had breastplates of fiery red, hyacinth blue, and sulfur yellow; and the heads of the horses were like the heads of lions; and out of their mouths came fire, smoke, and brimstone. [18] By these three plagues a third of mankind was killed--by the fire and the smoke and the brimstone which came out of their mouths. [19] For their power is in their mouth and in their tails; for their tails are like serpents, having heads; and with them they do harm. [20] But the rest of mankind, who were not killed by these plagues, did not repent of the works of their hands, that they should not worship demons, and idols of gold, silver, brass, stone, and wood, which can neither see nor hear nor walk. [21] And they did not repent of their murders or their sorceries or their sexual immorality or their thefts.

Revelation 11:15-19

[15] Then the seventh angel sounded: And there were loud voices in heaven, saying, "The kingdoms of this world have become the kingdoms of our Lord and of His Christ, and He shall reign forever and ever!" [16] And the twenty-four elders who sat before God on their thrones fell on their faces and worshiped God, [17] saying: "We give You thanks, O Lord God Almighty, The One who is and who was and who is to come, Because You have taken Your great power and reigned. [18] The nations were angry, and Your wrath has come, And the time of the dead, that they should be judged, And that You should reward Your servants the prophets and the saints, And those who fear Your name, small and great, And should destroy those who destroy the earth." [19] Then the temple of God was opened in heaven, and the ark of His covenant was seen in His temple. And there were lightnings, noises, thunderings, an earthquake, and great hail.

¹ Then I heard a loud voice from the temple saying to the seven angels, "Go and pour out the bowls of the wrath of God on the earth." ² So the first went and poured out his bowl upon the earth, and a foul and loathsome sore came upon the men who had the mark of the beast and those who worshiped his image. ³ Then the second angel poured out his bowl on the sea, and it became blood as of a dead man; and every living creature in the sea died. ⁴ Then the third angel poured out his bowl on the rivers and springs of water, and they became blood. ⁵ And I heard the angel of the waters saying: "You are righteous, O Lord, The One who is and who was and who is to be, Because You have judged these things. ⁶ For they have shed the blood of saints and prophets, And You have given them blood to drink. For it is their just due." ⁷ And I heard another from the altar saying, "Even so, Lord God Almighty, true and righteous are Your judgments." ⁸ Then the fourth angel poured out his bowl on the sun, and power was given to him to scorch men with fire. ⁹ And men were scorched with great heat, and they blasphemed the name of God who has power over these plagues; and they did not repent and give Him glory. ¹⁰ Then the fifth angel poured out his bowl on the throne of the beast, and his kingdom became full of darkness; and they gnawed their tongues because of the pain. ¹¹ They blasphemed the God of heaven because of their pains and their sores, and did not repent of their deeds. ¹² Then the sixth angel poured out his bowl on the great river Euphrates, and its water was dried up, so that the way of the kings from the east might be prepared. ¹³ And I saw three unclean spirits like frogs coming out of the mouth of the dragon, out of the mouth of the beast, and out of the mouth of the false prophet. ¹⁴ For they are spirits of demons, performing signs, which go out to the kings of the earth and of the whole world, to gather them to the battle of that great day of God Almighty. ¹⁵ "Behold, I am coming as a thief. Blessed is he who watches, and keeps his garments, lest he walk naked and they see his shame." ¹⁶ And they gathered them together to the place called in Hebrew, Armageddon. ¹⁷ Then the seventh angel poured out his bowl into the air, and a loud voice came out of the temple of heaven, from the throne, saying, "It is done!" ¹⁸ And there were noises and thunderings and lightnings; and there was a great earthquake, such a mighty and great earthquake as had not occurred since men were on the earth. ¹⁹ Now the great city was divided into three parts, and the cities of the nations fell. And great Babylon was remembered before

God, to give her the cup of the wine of the fierceness of His wrath. [20] Then every island fled away, and the mountains were not found. [21] And great hail from heaven fell upon men, each hailstone about the weight of a talent. Men blasphemed God because of the plague of the hail, since that plague was exceedingly great.

Matthew 24:22

[22] And unless those days were shortened, no flesh would be saved; but for the elect's sake those days will be shortened.

Revelation 6:7-8

[7] When He opened the fourth seal, I heard the voice of the fourth living creature saying, "Come and see." [8] So I looked, and behold, a pale horse. And the name of him who sat on it was Death, and Hades followed with him. And power was given to them over a fourth of the earth, to kill with sword, with hunger, with death, and by the beasts of the earth.

Revelation 9:15

[15] So the four angels, who had been prepared for the hour and day and month and year, were released to kill a third of mankind.

Zechariah 13:8-9

[8] And it shall come to pass in all the land," Says the Lord, "That two-thirds in it shall be cut off and die, But one-third shall be left in it: [9] I will bring the one-third through the fire, Will refine them as silver is refined, And test them as gold is tested. They will call on My name, And I will answer them. I will say, 'This is My people'; And each one will say, 'The Lord is my God.'"

Revelation 7:8

[8] of the tribe of Zebulun twelve thousand were sealed; of the tribe of Joseph twelve thousand were sealed; of the tribe of Benjamin twelve thousand were sealed.

Revelation 7:9-17

[9] After these things I looked, and behold, a great multitude which no one could number, of all nations, tribes, peoples, and tongues, standing before the throne and before the Lamb, clothed with white robes, with palm branches in their hands, [10] and crying out with a loud voice, saying, "Salvation belongs to our God who sits on the throne,

and to the Lamb!" [11] All the angels stood around the throne and the elders and the four living creatures, and fell on their faces before the throne and worshiped God, [12] saying: "Amen! Blessing and glory and wisdom, Thanksgiving and honor and power and might, Be to our God forever and ever. Amen." [13] Then one of the elders answered, saying to me, "Who are these arrayed in white robes, and where did they come from?" [14] And I said to him, "Sir, you know." So he said to me, "These are the ones who come out of the great tribulation, and washed their robes and made them white in the blood of the Lamb. [15] Therefore they are before the throne of God, and serve Him day and night in His temple. And He who sits on the throne will dwell among them. [16] They shall neither hunger anymore nor thirst anymore; the sun shall not strike them, nor any heat; [17] for the Lamb who is in the midst of the throne will shepherd them and lead them to living fountains of waters. And God will wipe away every tear from their eyes."

Zechariah 12:10-12

[10] "And I will pour on the house of David and on the inhabitants of Jerusalem the Spirit of grace and supplication; then they will look on Me whom they pierced. Yes, they will mourn for Him as one mourns for his only son, and grieve for Him as one grieves for a firstborn. [11] In that day there shall be a great mourning in Jerusalem, like the mourning at Hadad Rimmon in the plain of Megiddo. [12] And the land shall mourn, every family by itself: the family of the house of David by itself, and their wives by themselves; the family of the house of Nathan by itself, and their wives by themselves;

Romans 11:26

[26] And so all Israel will be saved, as it is written: "The Deliverer will come out of Zion, And He will turn away ungodliness from Jacob;

Galatians 3:16

[16] Now to Abraham and his Seed were the promises made. He does not say, "And to seeds," as of many, but as of one, "And to your Seed," who is Christ.

Revelation 20:12

[12] And I saw the dead, small and great, standing before God, and books were opened. And another book was opened, which is the Book of

Life. And the dead were judged according to their works, by the things which were written in the books.

Revelation 20:7-9

⁷ Now when the thousand years have expired, Satan will be released from his prison ⁸ and will go out to deceive the nations which are in the four corners of the earth, Gog and Magog, to gather them together to battle, whose number is as the sand of the sea. ⁹ They went up on the breadth of the earth and surrounded the camp of the saints and the beloved city. And fire came down from God out of heaven and devoured them.

Revelation 20:14

¹⁴ Then Death and Hades were cast into the lake of fire. This is the second death.

APPENDIX 1

Acts 2:1

¹ When the Day of Pentecost had fully come, they were all with one accord in one place.

Acts 2:4,11

⁴ And they were all filled with the Holy Spirit and began to speak with other tongues, as the Spirit gave them utterance.
¹¹ Cretans and Arabs--we hear them speaking in our own tongues the wonderful works of God."

Acts 2:42

⁴² And they continued steadfastly in the apostles' doctrine and fellowship, in the breaking of bread, and in prayers.

Matthew 28:19-20

¹⁹ Go therefore and make disciples of all the nations, baptizing them in the name of the Father and of the Son and of the Holy Spirit, ²⁰ teaching them to observe all things that I have commanded you; and lo, I am with you always, even to the end of the age." Amen.

Acts 17:11

[11] These were more fair-minded than those in Thessalonica, in that they received the word with all readiness, and searched the Scriptures daily to find out whether these things were so.

John 13:35

[35] By this all will know that you are My disciples, if you have love for one another."

Acts 2:43

[43] Then fear came upon every soul, and many wonders and signs were done through the apostles.

Acts 2:44

[44] Now all who believed were together, and had all things in common,

Acts 2:47

[47] praising God and having favor with all the people. And the Lord added to the church daily those who were being saved.

APPENDIX 2

Genesis 1:1,26 (NIV)

[1] In the beginning God created the heavens and the earth.
[26] Then God said, "Let us make man in our image, in our likeness, and let them rule over the fish of the sea and the birds of the air, over the livestock, over all the earth, and over all the creatures that move along the ground."

Exodus 3:14 (NIV)

[14] God said to Moses, "I AM who I AM. This is what you are to say to the Israelites: 'I AM has sent me to you.'"

Jeremiah 23:6 (NIV)

[6] In his days Judah will be saved, and Israel will live in safety. This is the name by which he will be called: The Lord Our Righteousness.

Exodus 31:13

[13] "Speak also to the children of Israel, saying: 'Surely My Sabbaths you shall keep, for it is a sign between Me and you throughout your

generations, that you may know that I am the Lord who sanctifies you.

Psalm 145:16
[16] You open Your hand And satisfy the desire of every living thing.

Genesis 22:14
[14] And Abraham called the name of the place, The-Lord-Will-Provide; as it is said to this day, "In the Mount of The Lord it shall be provided."

Daniel 4:34 (NIV)
[34] At the end of that time, I, Nebuchadnezzar, raised my eyes toward heaven, and my sanity was restored. Then I praised the Most High; I honored and glorified him who lives forever. His dominion is an eternal dominion; his kingdom endures from generation to generation.

Genesis 17:2 (NIV)
[2] I will confirm my covenant between me and you and will greatly increase your numbers.

Isaiah 6:8 (NIV)
[8] Then I heard the voice of the Lord saying, "Whom shall I send? And who will go for us" And I said, "Here am I. Send me!"

Judges 6:24 (NIV)
[24] So Gideon built and altar to the Lord there and called it The Lord is Peace. To this day it stands in Ophrah of the Abiezrites.

Ezekiel 48:35
[35] All the way around shall be eighteen thousand cubits; and the name of the city from that day shall be: THE LORD IS THERE."

1 Samuel 17:45 (NIV)
[45] David said to the Philistine, "You come against me with sword and spear and javelin, but I come against you in the name of the Lord Almighty, the God of the armies of Israel, whom you have defied."

Psalm 24:8
[8] Who is this King of glory? The Lord strong and mighty, The Lord mighty in battle.

Exodus 15:26

[26] and said, "If you diligently heed the voice of the Lord your God and do what is right in His sight, give ear to His commandments and keep all His statutes, I will put none of the diseases on you which I have brought on the Egyptians. For I am the Lord who heals you."

Exodus 17:10-15

[10] So Joshua did as Moses said to him, and fought with Amalek. And Moses, Aaron, and Hur went up to the top of the hill. [11] And so it was, when Moses held up his hand, that Israel prevailed; and when he let down his hand, Amalek prevailed. [12] But Moses' hands became heavy; so they took a stone and put it under him, and he sat on it. And Aaron and Hur supported his hands, one on one side, and the other on the other side; and his hands were steady until the going down of the sun. [13] So Joshua defeated Amalek and his people with the edge of the sword. [14] Then the Lord said to Moses, "Write this for a memorial in the book and recount it in the hearing of Joshua, that I will utterly blot out the remembrance of Amalek from under heaven." [15] And Moses built an altar and called its name, The-Lord-Is-My-Banner;

Psalm 23

[1] A Psalm of David. The Lord is my shepherd; I shall not want. [2] He makes me to lie down in green pastures; He leads me beside the still waters. [3] He restores my soul; He leads me in the paths of righteousness For His name's sake. [4] Yea, though I walk through the valley of the shadow of death, I will fear no evil; For You are with me; Your rod and Your staff, they comfort me. [5] You prepare a table before me in the presence of my enemies; You anoint my head with oil; My cup runs over. [6] Surely goodness and mercy shall follow me All the days of my life; And I will dwell in the house of the Lord Forever.

2 Samuel 5:20

[20] So David went to Baal Perazim, and David defeated them there; and he said, "The Lord has broken through my enemies before me, like a breakthrough of water." Therefore he called the name of that place Baal Perazim.

Genesis 21:33

[33] Then Abraham planted a tamarisk tree in Beersheba, and there called on the name of the Lord, the Everlasting God.

John 3:16

16 For God so loved the world that He gave His only begotten Son, that whoever believes in Him should not perish but have everlasting life.

Genesis 16:13

13 Then she called the name of the Lord who spoke to her, You-Are-the-God-Who-Sees; for she said, "Have I also here seen Him who sees me?"

Genesis 33:20

20 Then he erected an altar there and called it El Elohe Israel.

APPENDIX 3

2 Timothy 3:16

16 All Scripture *is* given by inspiration of God, and *is* profitable for doctrine, for reproof, for correction, for instruction in righteousness,

1 Peter 1:20-21

20 He indeed was foreordained before the foundation of the world, but was manifest in these last times for you 21 who through Him believe in God, who raised Him from the dead and gave Him glory, so that your faith and hope are in God.

John 5:26

26 For as the Father has life in Himself, so He has granted the Son to have life in Himself,

John 4:24

24 God is Spirit, and those who worship Him must worship in spirit and truth."

1 Timothy 6:16

16 who alone has immortality, dwelling in unapproachable light, whom no man has seen or can see, to whom be honor and everlasting power. Amen.

Hebrews 4:12

12 For the word of God is living and powerful, and sharper than any two-edged sword, piercing even to the division of soul and spirit, and of joints and marrow, and is a discerner of the thoughts and intents of the heart.

Acts 17:25

25 Nor is He worshiped with men's hands, as though He needed anything, since He gives to all life, breath, and all things.

Exodus 3:14

14 And God said to Moses, "I AM WHO I AM." And He said, "Thus you shall say to the children of Israel, 'I AM has sent me to you.'"

Psalm 48:14

14 For this is God, Our God forever and ever; He will be our guide Even to death.

Ezekiel 48:35

35 All the way around shall be eighteen thousand cubits; and the name of the city from that day shall be: THE LORD IS THERE."

Psalm 29:10

10 The Lord sat enthroned at the Flood, And the Lord sits as King forever.

Psalm 102:25-27

25 Of old You laid the foundation of the earth, And the heavens are the work of Your hands. 26 They will perish, but You will endure; Yes, they will all grow old like a garment; Like a cloak You will change them, And they will be changed. 27 But You are the same, And Your years will have no end.

James 1:17

17 Every good gift and every perfect gift is from above, and comes down from the Father of lights, with whom there is no variation or shadow of turning.

1 Samuel 15:29

29 And also the Strength of Israel will not lie nor relent. For He is not a man, that He should relent."

Numbers 23:19

19 "God is not a man, that He should lie, Nor a son of man, that He should repent. Has He said, and will He not do? Or has He spoken, and will He not make it good?

Psalm 33:11

[11] The counsel of the Lord stands forever, The plans of His heart to all generations.

Matthew 5:18

[18] For assuredly, I say to you, till heaven and earth pass away, one jot or one tittle will by no means pass from the law till all is fulfilled.

Matthew 24:35

[35] Heaven and earth will pass away, but My words will by no means pass away.

1 John 3:20

[20] For if our heart condemns us, God is greater than our heart, and knows all things.

Hebrews 4:13

[13] And there is no creature hidden from His sight, but all things are naked and open to the eyes of Him to whom we must give account.

Romans 16:27

[27] to God, alone wise, be glory through Jesus Christ forever. Amen.

Isaiah 6:3

[3] And one cried to another and said: "Holy, holy, holy is the Lord of hosts; The whole earth is full of His glory!"

Isaiah 40:25

[25] "To whom then will you liken Me, Or to whom shall I be equal?" says the Holy One.

Hebrews 1:13

[13] But to which of the angels has He ever said: "Sit at My right hand, Till I make Your enemies Your footstool"?

Jeremiah 33:6

[6] Behold, I will bring it health and healing; I will heal them and reveal to them the abundance of peace and truth.

Revelation 19:11

[11] Now I saw heaven opened, and behold, a white horse. And He who sat on him was called Faithful and True, and in righteousness He judges and makes war.

Hebrews 10:23

²³ Let us hold fast the confession of our hope without wavering, for He who promised is faithful.

Ephesians 4:30

And do not grieve the Holy Spirit of God, by whom you were sealed for the day of redemption.

Exodus 34:6-7

⁶ And the Lord passed before him and proclaimed, "The Lord, the Lord God, merciful and gracious, longsuffering, and abounding in goodness and truth, ⁷ keeping mercy for thousands, forgiving iniquity and transgression and sin, by no means clearing the guilty, visiting the iniquity of the fathers upon the children and the children's children to the third and the fourth generation."

Psalm 80:15

¹⁵ And the vineyard which Your right hand has planted, And the branch that You made strong for Yourself.

2 Peter 3:9

⁹ The Lord is not slack concerning His promise, as some count slackness, but is longsuffering toward us, not willing that any should perish but that all should come to repentance.

Nahum 1:3

³ The Lord is slow to anger and great in power, And will not at all acquit the wicked. The Lord has His way In the whirlwind and in the storm, And the clouds are the dust of His feet.

1 Corinthians 2:11

¹¹ For what man knows the things of a man except the spirit of the man which is in him? Even so no one knows the things of God except the Spirit of God.

Mark 14:36

³⁶ And He said, "Abba, Father, all things are possible for You. Take this cup away from Me; nevertheless, not what I will, but what You will."

Luke 1:37

³⁷ For with God nothing will be impossible."

Ephesians 1:11

¹¹ In Him also we have obtained an inheritance, being predestined according to the purpose of Him who works all things according to the counsel of His will,

Hebrews 10:23

²³ Let us hold fast the confession of our hope without wavering, for He who promised is faithful.

Revelation 19:11

¹¹ Now I saw heaven opened, and behold, a white horse. And He who sat on him was called Faithful and True, and in righteousness He judges and makes war.

1 Kings 8:50

⁵⁰ and forgive Your people who have sinned against You, and all their transgressions which they have transgressed against You; and grant them compassion before those who took them captive, that they may have compassion on them

1 John 1:9

⁹ If we confess our sins, He is faithful and just to forgive us our sins and to cleanse us from all unrighteousness.

1 Thessalonians 5:23-24

²³ Now may the God of peace Himself sanctify you completely; and may your whole spirit, soul, and body be preserved blameless at the coming of our Lord Jesus Christ. ²⁴ He who calls you is faithful, who also will do it.

2 Thessalonians 3:3

³ But the Lord is faithful, who will establish you and guard you from the evil one.

¹³ No temptation has overtaken you except such as is common to man; but God is faithful, who will not allow you to be tempted beyond what you are able, but with the temptation will also make the way of escape, that you may be able to bear it.

2 Timothy 2:13

¹³ If we are faithless, He remains faithful; He cannot deny Himself.

Isaiah 57:15

[15] For thus says the High and Lofty One Who inhabits eternity, whose name is Holy: "I dwell in the high and holy place, With him who has a contrite and humble spirit, To revive the spirit of the humble, And to revive the heart of the contrite ones.

Jeremiah 29:11

[11] For I know the thoughts that I think toward you, says the Lord, thoughts of peace and not of evil, to give you a future and a hope.

Ephesians 4:1-24

[1] I, therefore, the prisoner of the Lord, beseech you to walk worthy of the calling with which you were called, [2] with all lowliness and gentleness, with longsuffering, bearing with one another in love, [3] endeavoring to keep the unity of the Spirit in the bond of peace. [4] There is one body and one Spirit, just as you were called in one hope of your calling; [5] one Lord, one faith, one baptism; [6] one God and Father of all, who is above all, and through all, and in you all. [7] But to each one of us grace was given according to the measure of Christ's gift. [8] Therefore He says: "When He ascended on high, He led captivity captive, And gave gifts to men." [9] (Now this, "He ascended"--what does it mean but that He also first descended into the lower parts of the earth? [10] He who descended is also the One who ascended far above all the heavens, that He might fill all things.) [11] And He Himself gave some to be apostles, some prophets, some evangelists, and some pastors and teachers, [12] for the equipping of the saints for the work of ministry, for the edifying of the body of Christ, [13] till we all come to the unity of the faith and of the knowledge of the Son of God, to a perfect man, to the measure of the stature of the fullness of Christ; [14] that we should no longer be children, tossed to and fro and carried about with every wind of doctrine, by the trickery of men, in the cunning craftiness of deceitful plotting, [15] but, speaking the truth in love, may grow up in all things into Him who is the head--Christ-- [16] from whom the whole body, joined and knit together by what every joint supplies, according to the effective working by which every part does its share, causes growth of the body for the edifying of itself in love. [17] This I say, therefore, and testify in the Lord, that you should no longer walk as the rest of the Gentiles walk, in the futility of their mind, [18] having their understanding darkened, being alienated from the life of God, because of the ignorance that is in them, because of the blindness of

their heart; [19] who, being past feeling, have given themselves over to lewdness, to work all uncleanness with greediness. [20] But you have not so learned Christ, [21] if indeed you have heard Him and have been taught by Him, as the truth is in Jesus: [22] that you put off, concerning your former conduct, the old man which grows corrupt according to the deceitful lusts, [23] and be renewed in the spirit of your mind, [24] and that you put on the new man which was created according to God, in true righteousness and holiness.